COMPLETE GUIDE TO CAMPING AND WILDERNESS SURVIVAL

COMPLETE GUIDE TO CAMPING AND WILDERNESS SURVIVAL

by Vin T. Sparano

UNIVERSE

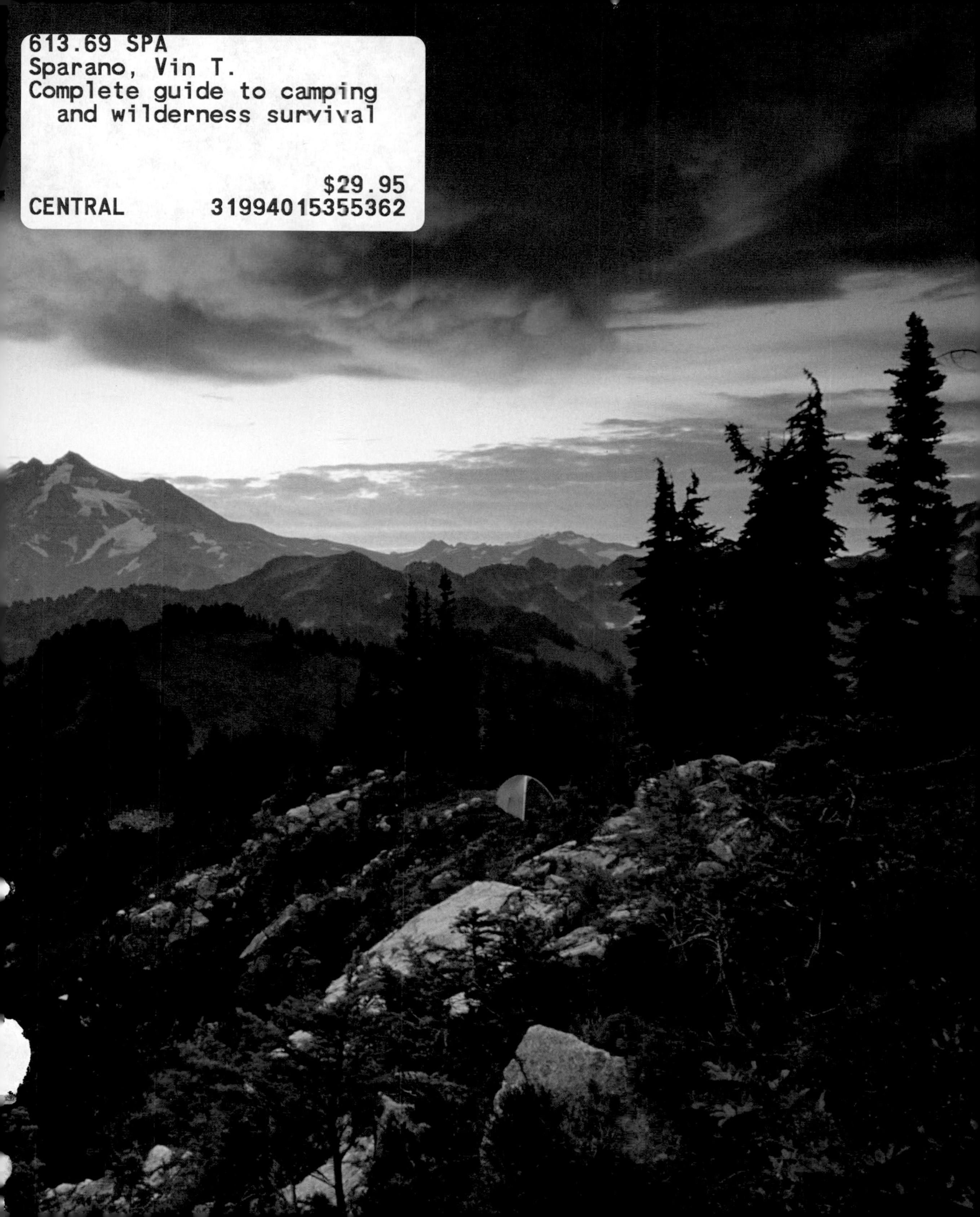

Published by Universe Publishing
A Division of Rizzoli International Publications, Inc.
300 Park Avenue South
New York, NY 10010
www.rizzoliusa.com

Project Editor: Candice Fehrman
Book Design: Lori S. Malkin
Text: Vin T. Sparano

2016 2017 2018 2019 / 10 9 8 7 6 5 4 3 2 1

Printed in China

ISBN-13: 978-0-7893-3119-9

Library of Congress Catalog Control Number: 2015952075

■ ■ ■

To my grandchildren:

Nicholas
Gina
Steven
Danielle
Allison
Connor
Jack
. . . and in loving memory of Joey

My greatest gift,
a wish that they all learn to
love life as I have

■ ■ ■

Contents

Preface

It is a great satisfying pleasure to know that I have been fortunate enough to learn, cherish, and cultivate my awareness and love of the outdoors. I can recall many dawns watching the sun lift itself over the horizon and listening to the sounds of awakening wildlife around me. The solitude and warmth of a campfire and a cup of coffee on the banks of a remote trout stream can only be called a miracle cure for the soul. I sometimes feel sorrow for those people who do not know enough to look skyward at the honking sound of a flight of geese. It is truly the sound of music to my ears.

With these thoughts in mind, my goal in these pages is to introduce campers, experienced and novice alike, to the many ways to enrich their adventures in our woods and waters. This book is not for those who visit a campground and never venture much farther than their car. As a hunter, fisherman, and camper, I frequently ventured off the trails to explore and hopefully find places where there were no other footprints.

If you are already a camper and sportsman, you are probably already aware of the value of being outdoors. But our learning process never ends. These pages will bring you up to date on equipment, ranging from fire starters to backpacks to recreational vehicles. I may also be able to entice you to try new adventures, such as the challenging concept of swamp camping.

We now live in an age of constant uncertainty and we sometimes think about the possibility that we may someday have to survive. Even with GPS and cell phones, campers and hikers get lost all the time. Most are usually found within 24 hours, but some are lost for several days or longer. If you're lost, what should you do? First, never fear the wilderness. If you are well equipped and knowledgeable about basic techniques, you will rarely get in trouble. Fear and panic are your worst enemies. Conquer them and you will always survive.

My special survival chapter in these pages will teach you the many ways you can master survival in the wilderness, ranging from trapping wildlife for food to building emergency shelters. While it is unlikely that you will have to resort to eating bugs and insects, I want to assure you that they belong on a survival menu. You will also discover a wide variety of edible wild plants that are not only delicious, but can also keep you alive.

A book of this scope requires the help of a host of good people. Special thanks goes to Candice Fehrman, my editor at Rizzoli/Universe. Candice was always there to keep me on track whenever I thought I'd never get through the thousands of photos and illustrations. I also want to thank Lori S. Malkin for designing a book that has so many mind-boggling elements that I sometimes wonder how she keeps everything in focus. Then there is Jim Muschett, my buddy and publisher at Rizzoli/Universe, who I want thank for his continuous support through the last three books I've produced for him.

There are many more people to thank for their help in creating this comprehensive guide to camping and survival. Special thanks to Karen Monger and Robert Gergulics for their excellent photos and information on wild edible plants. My friend Mac McKeever at L.L. Bean played a major role in providing photos and special campfire recipes from *The L.L. Bean Game and Fish Cookbook*. I also want to thank Katie Mitchell and Mary Mardis at Bass Pro and Joe Arterburn and Kellie Mowery at Cabela's for their help in supplying new gear photos.

Complete Guide to Camping and Wilderness Survival has been a massive effort with the goal of not only teaching you new camping skills but also moving beyond recreational camping into the area of wilderness survival. As I said, there is nothing to fear in the wilderness if you are prepared. This book will show you how to survive in our woods and waters.

—Vin T. Sparano
Editor Emeritus and Senior Field Editor
Outdoor Life

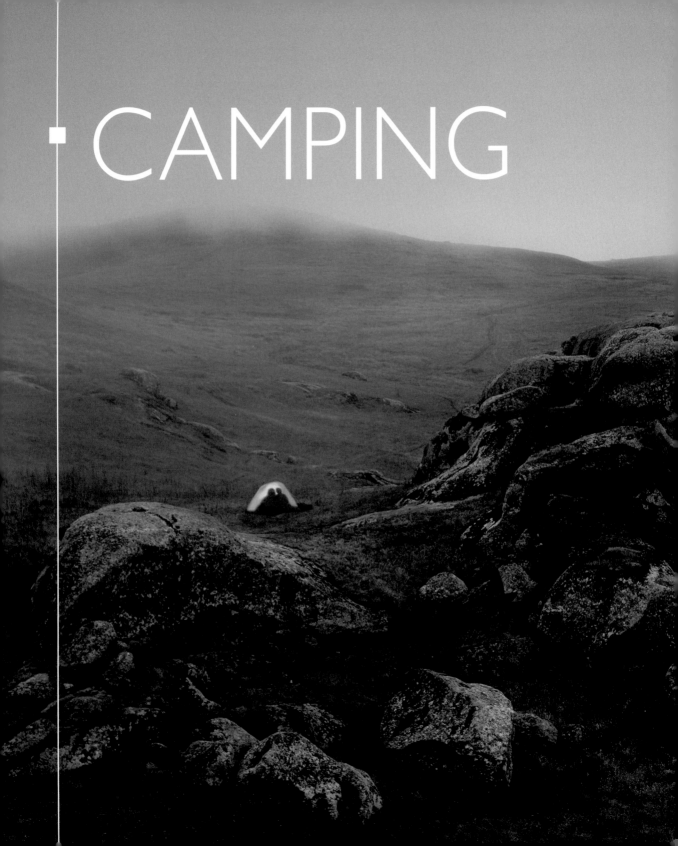

CAMPING

Section One
CAMPING

TENTS

Tents are manufactured in a variety of shapes and sizes, so whether you're just doing some backyard camping or heading for a couple of weeks in the mountains, there's probably a tent made for you and your family. Manufacturers frequently use different names to describe their tent models. The tent designs and names illustrated here are generally accepted to describe traditional tent designs and their features.

■ Wall Tents

Many campers, particularly those who have spent time in the Army, are familiar with the traditional wall tent. Its main advantages are that it has ample headspace, it can house a wood-burning stove in cold weather, and it readily sheds water off its inverted-V roof.

A psychological benefit of the wall tent is that it somewhat resembles a small house in design, but upon closer examination, you'll see it is not quite as comfortable as it looks, nor is it very stable in wind.

There usually are no floors or windows, nor netting at the flap doors. Moreover, the walls tend to be so low that the only walking space is directly below the ridgepole. The large end pole that stands in the center of the doorway is another nuisance.

A wall tent is inexpensive and to erect it you only need two upright poles, a ridgepole, guy ropes, and pegs. Ventilation is poor in rainy weather, and the tent offers little resistance to the wind. The door flaps leave myriad openings for insects and, if closed, make the tent's interior quite dark and warm. Automobile campers appreciate the heavy wall tent, as it can be pitched right next to their cars, but for those who wish to travel light, it is a poor choice.

The wall tent is generally available in sizes ranging from 6½ by 6½ feet to 16 by 20 feet, although larger sizes are available from custom tent makers. The wall tent in these bigger custom sizes is favored by many big-game outfitters and guides. These tents are fitted with wood-burning stoves and chimneys. On average wall tents, however, the side walls run from 2 to 4 feet in height, but 3 feet is standard. Heights at the center are usually 7 to 7½ feet, adequate for the average adult.

This type of tent with a 7-by-9-foot floor space will provide sufficient room for two campers with gear. A trio of campers will require at least a 9-by-12-foot wall tent for comfort.

■ Cottage or Cabin Tents

If you're planning a long stay in an area and need plenty of space, the cottage or cabin tent just might be the answer.

This style of tent features vertical sides that give you more space for your gear than tents with short side walls. The eaves are high and there are large windows with storm flaps. You've also got walking room to spare and sewn-in floors. Though the number of poles required to pitch it may approach 10, modern cottage tents generally employ light aluminum telescoping poles that are not difficult to handle. Guy lines are not required with most cottage or cabin tents, though the outside edges of the tent floor should be staked down. A large area of level ground is needed to put up the tent. An 8-by-10-foot tent can sleep four persons; a 9-by-12-foot tent can sleep five to six persons.

■ Umbrella Tents

The umbrella tent is best designed for the motorist who goes touring with his own shelter. A pyramid-shaped roof and straight sides distinguish this unit.

Wind resistance is exceptional and the vertical walls offer plenty of space for storing gear. The ample headroom lets you walk around without stooping, and, save for the door awning, there aren't any large, flat surfaces that will hold rain or catch snow. A big door and one or more windows in the sides give good ventilation on warm evenings.

A sewn-in, waterproof floor keeps out drafts, bugs, and surface moisture, while a 4- to 5-inch doorsill strip in some models wards off snakes and small animals. With assembly time ranging from four to five minutes, this is a fine tent to have when a storm is approaching.

One of the main faults of the umbrella tent, however, is its pole arrangement. If it has but one pole (rare nowadays), you will need a small umbrella frame to hold the cloth straight. The center pole takes up entirely too much room inside, and its only advantages are that you can reach up and slacken the umbrella to loosen the stakes and that useful shelves can be attached to the pole. Most current umbrella tents feature four aluminum poles, so if you're backpacking or canoeing, ignore this one.

Models come in interior- and exterior-pole styles. The former type can cause wear and capillary leaks due to metal rubbing against canvas. The latter is preferable, as there is no center pole. Thus, there is more room inside. The exterior-pole setup is somewhat heavier and more expensive, however.

Another drawback is weight—it weighs 30 to 65 pounds, depending on its size and method of pole support.

A couple can be accommodated by a 7-by-8-foot or an 8-by-8-foot model. Four persons would be better off in a 9½-by-9½-foot or 10-by-10-foot model. Don't get anything bigger, as it will be unwieldy to pitch. You're better off with two small umbrella tents if the crew is large.

Wedge Tents

Although the Boy Scouts and the US Army have taken a fancy to the wedge tent (also called the pup tent, A tent, Hudson Bay tent, or snow tent), it's not recommended if you're thinking of camping in any comfort. The wedge tent has no place to stand upright.

But there are several factors in this tent's favor: it's inexpensive, quite simple to erect, lightweight, sheds rain and snow rather well, and is quite stable (if properly pitched) on a windy day.

Heating this type of tent in cold weather is difficult, as a campfire inside is out of the question, and a small

heater can lead to asphyxiation if enough fresh air is not allowed in the tent.

A 5-by-7-foot tent of this style can sleep two persons. The weight with stakes and poles is approximately 6 pounds.

Pyramid Tents

For shedding rain and snow, the pyramid, or miner, tent is the best designed for the purpose. Also, when well pitched at the base and supported by an outside tripod of poles or a strong center pole, this tent can brave almost any windstorm.

A 7-by-7-foot tent of this style is adequate for sleeping and shelter, but buy the zipper-door type rather than the one with tie tapes, as there will be less chance of leakage at the door.

Keep the doors open on hot days and use a reflector fire when the weather is brisk; wood stoves are not suitable for these small tents. Another flaw is that they are somewhat cramped, and an alcohol, gas, or oil stove can make the air stuffy.

Baker Tents

Similar to the wall tent except for one wall that is raised to form a front awning, the baker tent is quite roomy and is exceptional as a campfire tent. Temperatures can be far below the freezing point, but this tent, provided it has a good fire in front of it, will keep you warm. Green logs or rocks can be stacked up behind the fire to reflect heat into the open tent.

Important: A waterproofing solution with fire-resistant chemicals should be used to treat the baker tent. Also, keep the fire at a reasonable level and the awning pitched high enough so that the two do not meet to create a hazard. As the roof is flat, a tight-woven fabric or a fine waterproofing is essential to help shed rain.

If you're looking for privacy, this tent is not for you. As the accompanying illustration shows, the front is wide open and, if the porch is dropped down, ventilation is minimal. In addition, in a driving rain the tent may have to be repositioned so as not to get the occupants wet.

Wind can be more harmful to a baker tent than it can to a wedge, pyramid, or wall tent. Therefore, face the tent away from prevailing winds and, if a storm is in the offing, anchor the tent with long stakes. The open baker tent offers poor protection from mosquitoes and other

TENT TYPES

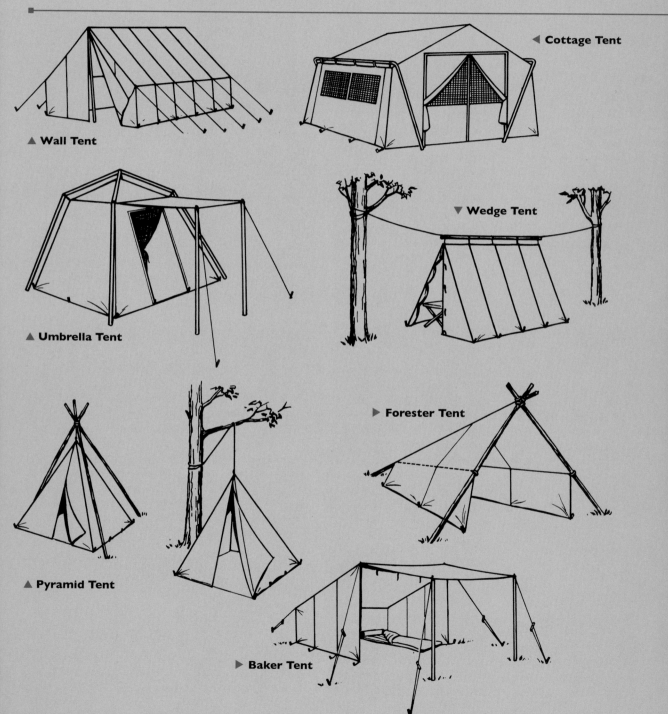

▲ Wall Tent

◀ Cottage Tent

▲ Umbrella Tent

▼ Wedge Tent

▶ Forester Tent

▲ Pyramid Tent

▶ Baker Tent

Canvas Lean-To Tarp

Pop Tent

Mountain Tent

Explorer Tent

Geodesic Tent

Tepee Tent

biting insects. Cheesecloth or netting placed over the entrance can be helpful, but bed nets for each individual are more convenient and effective.

A 6-by-8-foot baker tent will sleep two campers comfortably, and perhaps three with a tight fit. A baker larger than 8 by 10 feet will render your fire virtually useless.

■ Forester Tents

When there is a question of light weight and optimum warmth in cold weather, the forester tent is the best choice. The interior is designed so that the heat of a campfire will be well reflected throughout the entire unit. Pitching time is short, and the tent is stable if correctly pitched. It also sheds heavy rain and withstands high winds. The tent is small—typically 6 feet wide at the front and 8 feet deep. The shape of the interior is triangular, narrowing to a point at the back. Two campers will have sufficient sleeping room in this tent, but it is best for a lone camper who will have enough space for food and gear. During seasons when insects are a problem, individual bed nets are recommended for protection.

■ Lean-To Shelters

This shelter is not only the simplest one, but also the lightest and cheapest. It is merely a square sheet of fabric hemmed at the edges and provided with eyelets or loops through which supporting ropes are placed.

In the dry southwestern sections of the United States, outdoor enthusiasts have learned that a tent is rarely necessary from July through September; thus, the popularity of the lean-to.

An 8-by-10-foot shelter, preferably waterproofed, can be set up in a variety of ways: draped over a pole to resemble a pup tent, angled higher to create a baker-tent type of shelter roof plus an awning, raised as a flat roof, etc.

If the fabric is untreated, it could leak at once—and badly, too. Also, the fabric may wilt or burn if placed too close to a fire. Other disadvantages are deterioration from intense sunlight and the tendency of some material to tear.

■ Pop Tents

The canvas igloo or dome tent can be assembled in a short time. Commercial models are usually waterproof and mildew resistant, with an exterior rib setup to aid in pitching. One model, 7 feet in diameter, will sleep two adults. But if you're a trio, a 9-foot diameter would prove more satisfactory. Not all styles permit you to stand upright, so sweeping out the sewn-in floor could prove to be a problem.

There appears to be some controversy as to this unit's stability in high winds. Some experts say it can be set up in sand without stakes and remain sturdy; others assert that unless the individual or his gear is present inside, the pop tent may blow over.

Zippered storm flaps on some models will keep out wind and insects, and a window assists in cross ventilation. A few models also feature an awning.

■ Explorer Tents

The explorer tent has a number of advantages: it is lightweight, wind resistant, has adequate floor space, and, when checked thoroughly, is bug free.

This unit features a sewn-in floor as well as a large, netted front door.

In Canada and Alaska, mosquitoes can be a problem. For this reason, many outdoors enthusiasts turn to the explorer tent when they're northward bound. Once the netting sleeve has been tied shut—after shooing away any tiny stragglers—you're in for a comfortable evening. The steep walls are designed to readily shed rain and to provide additional storage space. A 7-by-7-foot explorer tent sleeps one or two campers and weighs a mere 10 to 12 pounds.

■ Mountain or Backpack Tents

In any weather except a very hot summer's day, the mountain tent (a form of backpacking tent) is a feasible proposition. But wintertime is the season when this tent really shows its stuff.

A stove—never an open wood fire—placed in the forepart of the tent will keep you warm in the coldest times. The vent at the peak of the tent must be opened before you light your stove, as the fumes can be lethal.

It is advisable with some models to take along one or two telescopic poles if the area you're camping in has no timber. This tent should be anchored to a point a minimum of 5 feet off the ground. Other styles, however, feature an exterior frame and a center pole or guy ropes that attach to pegs. The floor is sewn-in on most models. Front flaps are somewhat standard, and there is usually adequate screening to keep out insects.

Geodesic or Dome Tents

The geodesic simply means a domed framework of polygons in tension. There are no poles or structures inside the tent. The dome design is highly wind resistant and sheds rain and snow well. The tents are freestanding with minimal outside staking and pegging. Many of these new tents are made of breathable nylon taffeta with water-repellent, polyurethane-coated nylon floors. Setup is fast with the continuous shock-corded fiberglass frame-pole system.

A typical geodesic dome tent that measures 8 by 7 feet has about 43 square feet of usable space, will sleep two or three persons, and weighs 10 to 11 pounds.

Tepee Tents

If you're staying in one spot for a long while, the tepee is a good choice. Unfortunately, marketed models are not

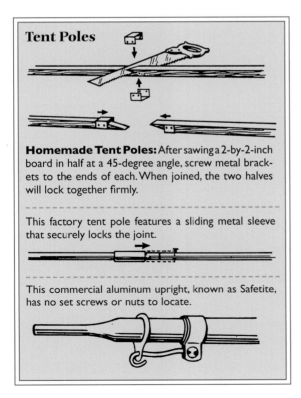

Tent Poles

Homemade Tent Poles: After sawing a 2-by-2-inch board in half at a 45-degree angle, screw metal brackets to the ends of each. When joined, the two halves will lock together firmly.

This factory tent pole features a sliding metal sleeve that securely locks the joint.

This commercial aluminum upright, known as Safetite, has no set screws or nuts to locate.

as well designed as the original Native American tepees. Some do feature smoke flaps, but they are smaller than those of the true tepee. The smoke leaves the tent at the point where the poles come together, rather than directly above the fire as in the early tepees. Tepees of old had an advantage: a weathertight seal would be created at the apex of the tent when the smoke flaps were closed. Contemporary tepees do not feature this.

The floor is oval shaped, and it is possible to stand upright within 3 feet of the front and 2 feet of the rear. As many as 15 people can be housed in an 18-by-21-foot tepee, but they would be rather uncomfortable. Wind resistance is high despite the extensive wall area. The tepee is primarily for permanence, so the heaviness of the total unit (300 pounds including cover, lining, poles, and pegs), plus the extensive time needed for its erection, rule it out if you're constantly on the move.

Tent Poles

Since most economy-minded campers are do-it-yourselfers, homemade tent poles are a good place to save money. Obtain a 2-by-2-inch board the same height as your tent. With a saw, cut the wood at a sharp angle into two equal pieces. Then, affix a metal bracket to the angled end of each piece. The two halves will lock together firmly when necessary.

One commercial model features a metal sleeve that slides to lock the joint. Another factory-made tent pole is the adjustable Safetite aluminum upright that has a metal clamp instead of set screws or nuts. If this pole is lost, you can substitute a wooden or steel pole in its place. Even a broomstick will work in an emergency. Both styles are available in several sizes to suit your tenting needs. For ultimate ease of use, look for tent poles that are shock corded together.

Tent Pegs

Just as tent poles can be homemade or purchased over the counter, the same goes for tent pegs, also known as tent stakes. The array available is large enough to satisfy any camper, as the following list of types indicates:

- Aluminum
- Plastic
- Steel
- Wood
- Metal spike
- Workshop wood
- Whittled branch
- Iron

The automobile camper can buy iron or aluminum tent pegs, as weight makes little difference. The

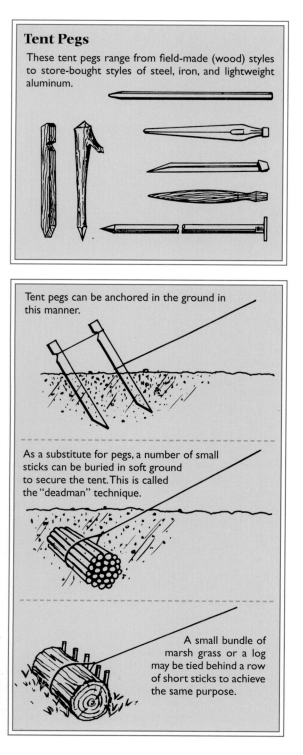

Tent Pegs

These tent pegs range from field-made (wood) styles to store-bought styles of steel, iron, and lightweight aluminum.

Tent pegs can be anchored in the ground in this manner.

As a substitute for pegs, a number of small sticks can be buried in soft ground to secure the tent. This is called the "deadman" technique.

A small bundle of marsh grass or a log may be tied behind a row of short sticks to achieve the same purpose.

backpacker, on the other hand, must keep pack weight in mind. Therefore, he may resort to cutting his own wooden stakes. The softer the ground, the deeper the stakes must be buried. As a substitute for tent stakes, you can bury a bundle of stiff marsh grass, brush, or sticks in sand or dirt. In winter, blocks of ice or frozen snow will also make for a more rigid tent when you're out of pegs.

■ Tent Fabrics

COTTON: You may have heard the terms "canvas," "duck," and "balloon silk" mentioned when you were looking for a cotton tent. All three are various forms of cotton used in the manufacture of tents. Canvas and duck are a bit heavier than balloon silk—a long-fibered, high-quality cotton. Until World War II, practically every tent was made of cotton. Today, nylon, Dacron, and other synthetic fibers, which have proven to be very lightweight, are replacing cotton in tent manufacturing.

Duck and canvas, if properly waterproofed, will shed water well, but are relatively heavy. The heavier the fabric, however, the stronger the tent. Conventional cotton tents are made in grades of 8, 10, and 12 ounces. The 8-ounce type is more fit for a hiking tent, while the 12-ounce type would be required for a wall tent and the like. Another advantage is that cotton "breathes" well. Thus, there's no stuffiness.

The disadvantages of a mediocre cotton tent are several: It weighs more than the synthetic tents, and it may leak water and tear readily. Also, this material can only be dry-cleaned, as machine washing would destroy it.

NYLON: This synthetic has two prime advantages for the camper—it is relatively lightweight and far less bulky to pack. Its disadvantages are that condensation forms in humid weather and, when the fabric is wet, the seams do not swell. This can lead to a clammy tent. Mountain tents and other styles valuable to the backpacker are often made of nylon.

Some nylon tents are waterproof, and some of the newer ones do breathe, as cotton does, but this material cannot be "breathable" and waterproof at the same time. Most of the nylon tents that breathe therefore come equipped with waterproof overhead flies (a cover suspended over the roof). Some nylon tents have cotton roofs—another solution to the same problem—and some are a blend of nylon and cotton.

DACRON: Like nylon, this synthetic is lightweight. It also stretches and shrinks much less than nylon and is more resistant to the effects of the sun. In addition, it can be either dry-cleaned or machine washed. Unfortunately, it tends to be bulky when rolled up, and also is somewhat water retentive.

POLYESTER: This tent fabric is spun polyester. It has nylon's strength, is lightweight, and breathes and repels water pretty much like cotton does. Like the other synthetics, polyester can be blended with cotton to achieve the desirable qualities of both fabrics.

Tents featuring blends of synthetic fibers and cotton are the most excellent of all for camping. They're highly water repellent, strong, lightweight, and porous enough to provide maximum comfort. Probably the best way to locate these models is to look for the ultrahigh price tags.

FLAME-RESISTANT TENTS: Regardless of fabric, more and more tents are now treated to be flame resistant—sometimes called fire retardant. It should be stressed that this treatment, though it is an excellent safety precaution, does not make the tents fireproof. A flame-resistant tent bears a label with wording that may vary slightly but with a clear message: "Warning: Keep all flame and heat sources away from this tent fabric. This tent is made with flame-resistant fabric . . . It is not fireproof. The fabric will burn if left in continuous contact with any flame source. The application of any foreign substance to the fabric may render the flame-resistant properties ineffective."

■ Pitching a Tent

A tent is not a house. It's not even a small cabin. Pitch your tent in the wrong place and you could be in for a cold, wet night. Once you have selected a level site free of rocks and vegetation that might damage the tent floor

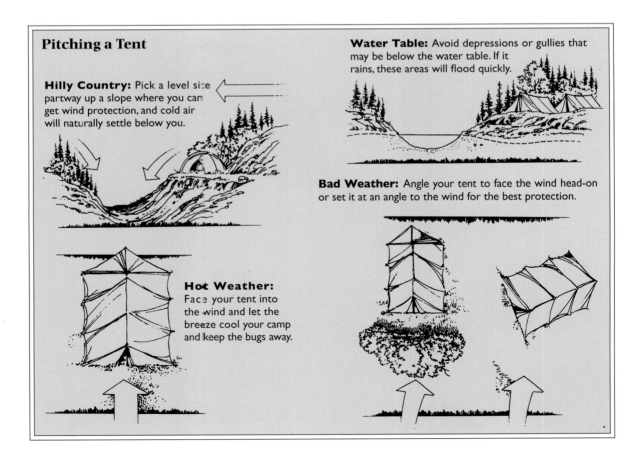

Pitching a Tent

Hilly Country: Pick a level site partway up a slope where you can get wind protection, and cold air will naturally settle below you.

Water Table: Avoid depressions or gullies that may be below the water table. If it rains, these areas will flood quickly.

Bad Weather: Angle your tent to face the wind head-on or set it at an angle to the wind for the best protection.

Hot Weather: Face your tent into the wind and let the breeze cool your camp and keep the bugs away.

or poke you in the back, you will have to deal with the two biggest campsite enemies: wind and water. In cold weather, you should find an area sheltered from the wind, but not at the bottom of a steep hill where you may get hit with frost-heaved rocks. If practical, pitch your tent facing east, so you can catch the morning sun.

It may be easier to drive a tent peg into soft ground, but that's also the type of terrain that holds moisture and dampness. Hard ground is better. Stay clear of dried riverbeds and gullies. In a sudden rainstorm, they can quickly fill with water.

In bad weather, look for a site in the lee of a fallen tree or huge boulder. Don't ditch (dig a rain trench around your tent) unless you own the land. Most tents

Tent Makes and Models

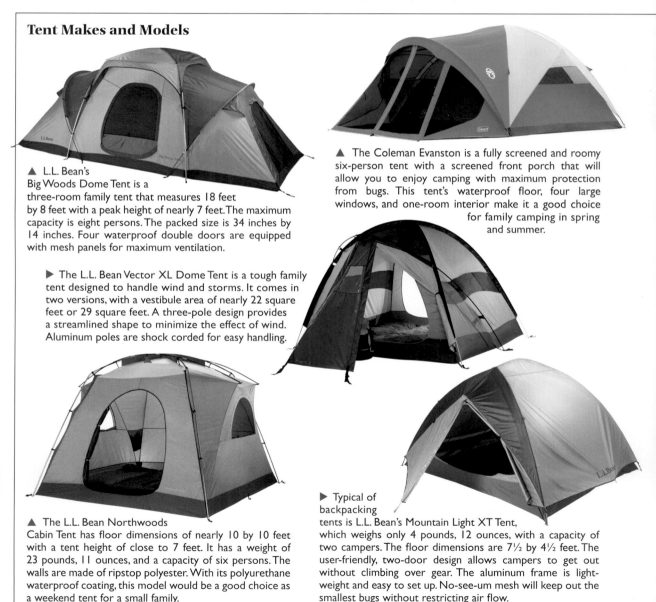

▲ L.L. Bean's
Big Woods Dome Tent is a
three-room family tent that measures 18 feet
by 8 feet with a peak height of nearly 7 feet. The maximum capacity is eight persons. The packed size is 34 inches by 14 inches. Four waterproof double doors are equipped with mesh panels for maximum ventilation.

▶ The L.L. Bean Vector XL Dome Tent is a tough family tent designed to handle wind and storms. It comes in two versions, with a vestibule area of nearly 22 square feet or 29 square feet. A three-pole design provides a streamlined shape to minimize the effect of wind. Aluminum poles are shock corded for easy handling.

▲ The Coleman Evanston is a fully screened and roomy six-person tent with a screened front porch that will allow you to enjoy camping with maximum protection from bugs. This tent's waterproof floor, four large windows, and one-room interior make it a good choice for family camping in spring and summer.

▲ The L.L. Bean Northwoods
Cabin Tent has floor dimensions of nearly 10 by 10 feet with a tent height of close to 7 feet. It has a weight of 23 pounds, 11 ounces, and a capacity of six persons. The walls are made of ripstop polyester. With its polyurethane waterproof coating, this model would be a good choice as a weekend tent for a small family.

▶ Typical of
backpacking
tents is L.L. Bean's Mountain Light XT Tent,
which weighs only 4 pounds, 12 ounces, with a capacity of two campers. The floor dimensions are 7½ by 4½ feet. The user-friendly, two-door design allows campers to get out without climbing over gear. The aluminum frame is lightweight and easy to set up. No-see-um mesh will keep out the smallest bugs without restricting air flow.

have sewn-in waterproof floors, so there is no need to destroy vegetation with a trench.

■ Care of Tents

Many tents have been in constant use for more than 20 years. Others have been inadvertently destroyed by campers in a matter of days. There is no reason why your tent, often the most expensive item of camping gear, cannot live a normal existence if you give it the proper care.

When you buy a tent, it is advisable to condition the canvas by pitching it for several days in the open air and spraying it lightly with your garden hose to get it used to moisture.

▼ The Coleman Jenny Lake is an eight-person fast-pitch cabin tent. Ideal for families, it even has a 2-by-2-foot closet for gear and clothes. The tent measures 13 feet by 9 feet by 6 feet, 8 inches. Designed for fast setup, the carrying weight of the Jenny Lake is 36 pounds.

▲ The L.L. Bean King Pine Tent is a six-person family tent designed to maximize interior space with easy setup. It features a screen room and a peak design that creates maximum headroom. The weight for the six-person model is 27 pounds. The King Pine is also available as a four-person tent.

▶ The Bass Pro eight-person Speed Frame Tent has a center height of nearly 7 feet. The steel pole frame and tent body come already attached for fast setup. It also has a screen porch and six windows. With a body of polyester, the tent weighs 28 pounds. It is a good roomy tent for a family.

▼ The Sportz Truck Tent is designed to make camping in the bed of your truck more comfortable. It weighs only 24 pounds and sleeps two persons. It features a sewn-in nylon floor and a 4-by-4-foot awning. Shock-corded and color-coded fiberglass poles make setup simple. Models vary with truck-bed lengths.

▲ Cabela's Ultimate Alaknak Tent is a hunting-camp design constructed of waterproof 250-denier polyester, which weighs a fraction of the amount of traditional canvas. All models are designed for stove heating with roof panel protection for a hot stovepipe. Models are available in three sizes: 12 by 12 feet, 12 by 20 feet, and 13 by 27 feet. The center height is nearly 10 feet. A floor liner is optional.

room; a kitchen with a sink, stove, and refrigerator; a dinette that converts to a bed; and space for storing groceries and clothing. The majority of these units also have an extended area over the cab to serve as sleeping quarters by night and storage space by day. The larger rigs may include a shower and toilet. Optionals include a radio, air conditioning, trailer hitch, step bumper, and auxiliary gas tank. One model even boasts an expanded rear door plus a ramp so that you can ride your ATV or snowmobile right up into the vehicle and tote it with you.

The camper—minus the truck—may weigh from 800 pounds to more than a ton. The length ranges from 6 to 15 feet or more.

The permanently mounted campers are often wider and longer than the other two styles because the bed of the truck is eliminated, and they're also superior in regard to self-containment. The chassis mounts vary between 10 and 18 feet and weigh from 1,500 to 2,700 pounds. The legal maximum width is 8 feet, and these beauties often have that expanse. Formerly, most units were 6 feet wide.

The chassis mounts are said to have better roadability and easier driving over lengthy hauls than the non-permanent campers, but campers as a whole have some advantages over the other RVs.

Since the vehicle is basically a truck—perhaps four-wheel drive—it can negotiate roads that a motor home or a travel trailer couldn't begin to navigate. The non-permanent pickup camper leaves the truck free for numerous other purposes.

If it's pouring outside, you can merely park the vehicle and proceed to prepare supper or simply relax. There are no problems with firewood or tent stakes.

Riding in the camper coach is permissible while on the road, so the cab needn't be overcrowded. An intercom can even be installed to aid communication between the rear and the cab.

Now for the disadvantages: Whenever you want to travel, you must take the entire camp with you. This necessitates securing gear and putting away all the utensils and dishes.

Highway driving can occasionally be frightening. A gusty headwind or strong crosswinds can turn the rig into a huge sail, making the driver's job a difficult one—power steering or no!

When the time comes to store this vehicle, you might be in for some trouble. Several suburban regions prohibit parking on driveways, necessitating the rental of space or the use of your garage. With the unit measuring from 8½ to 10 feet in height when it is high enough on the jacks to be loaded, or on the pickup itself, you'll probably find that the ceiling of your garage isn't quite high enough. Take this into account before buying.

■ Travel Trailers

The travel trailer is a permanent living area that features one or more rooms and is mounted on two or four wheels, depending on its weight and size. Travel trailers range in length from 12 to 35 feet, with the 22-footer apparently the most popular according to sales figures. The array of vehicles is extensive, and there is a comparably wide range of prices. The interiors are usually plywood, while the exteriors are aluminum. Foam insulation resides between the two, and the entire unit sits on a welded chassis of steel.

A 6-footer could stand up easily in the average trailer, as the overall distance from floor to roof is 7 to 8 feet. The unit is rarely less than 7 feet wide, and often closer to the maximum of 8 feet.

With the accent on compact and subcompact automobiles in recent years, the trailer industry has followed the trend and produced a large selection of mini travel trailers.

To be self-contained, a vehicle must be able to supply sewage disposal, water, and power. To do this, it must

Conventional travel trailers can range from 17 to 35 feet in length and can be a permanent living area with one or more rooms. The biggest advantage of a travel trailer over a pickup camper and motor home is that you can park it and use the car or truck without dragging the trailer wherever you go.

hold a minimum of 30 gallons of water, a holding tank for waste, and enough bottled gas to take care of the stove, heater, and refrigerator. The average travel trailer is conveniently self-contained, with a sleeping space, heater, toilet, and shower. When it comes to optionals, you can have air conditioning, television, stereo, and even a bathtub. With all of these comforts just behind the towing vehicle, it's easy to see why this RV is so popular.

The travel trailer also holds the upper hand over the pickup camper and the motor home in that you can park it and use the car or truck exclusively. With the other two options, you have to drag your kitchen sink along wherever you go.

But there is less of an area where you *can* go if you want to take the trailer. It won't negotiate the same roads that a pickup camper will, particularly if the latter is equipped with four-wheel drive. And also on the negative side, unless the trailer can be adjusted to a low silhouette to somewhat resemble a tent trailer, you may have some trouble driving it at first. Sway is a problem, often caused by poor distribution of weight over the axle of the trailer. To prevent it, try to place the bulk of the weight forward of the trailer's wheels. Also, decrease front-tire pressure prior to your trip. It can speed up tire wear, but it may save your life. Use an equalizer hitch to shift more weight to the car's front wheels if the trailer weighs more than a half ton. Power steering seems to be the culprit in many trailer accidents, as the inexperienced driver tends to oversteer once swaying begins.

As mentioned earlier in this section, you would be smart to have the correct options put on your vehicle during assembly. Such items as oversize radiators, extra blade fans, heavy-duty springs and shock absorbers, heavy-duty batteries and alternators, fade-resistant brake linings, etc., will cost you far more to put in after you've had the vehicle for a while.

Trailers can be used in winter, but you may want to store your own. If so, remember to do the following:

Drain the complete water system, septic holding tank, and the water heater. Also, drain traps or pour alcohol into them. Remove the tires to prevent deterioration. If you want to leave the tires on, jack up the trailer to relieve the tires of weight. Also take the hubcaps off, as they tend to rust quickly. When snow accumulates to more than a few inches on the trailer roof, clear it off—but not with a shovel. A broom will do.

■ Fifth-Wheel Trailers

Fifth-wheel trailers—often just called fifth-wheelers—are the newest type of RV. The fifth wheel is the hitch, a modification of the fifth-wheel hitch used on tractor-trailer rigs. It goes over the axle of a pickup truck and is bolted to the frame, not just to the floor of the truck bed. The trailer itself has a cutout so that it can hang over the pickup's bed by about 7 feet, reducing the combined length of towing vehicle and trailer. A 29-foot fifth-wheeler, for example, extends only about 22 feet from the rear of the truck when it's hitched.

This design has several purposes. Most obviously, it provides extra interior trailer space in proportion to the rig's overall length. The objective is spacious luxury. The type of hitch also reduces the trailer sway, helps protect against jackknifing, and makes for an extremely secure, safe coupling. In addition, hitching is easier. A big king-pin hangs down and couples to the hitch in the pickup bed. As you back the truck toward the kingpin, you can see it clearly, and this makes the connection easier than positioning a conventional coupler over a ball.

Fifth-wheelers come in a variety of lengths, from compact 18-footers to models as long as 35 feet. Most are in the 26- to 32-foot range. Some of the smaller ones can be towed by a half-ton pickup, but most need a three-quarter-ton or one-ton pickup truck.

Although the construction techniques are pretty much the same as for travel trailers, the insulation tends

Fifth-wheel trailers are designed to be hitch mounted to the bed of a pickup truck. Sizes can range from 26 to about 32 feet. The master bedroom is usually located in the overhang over the bed of the truck. Most fifth-wheel trailers require a three-quarter-ton or one-ton pickup truck.

to be better, the appliances bigger. Many fifth-wheelers are more like motor homes than travel trailers. The master bedroom, built into the overhang, may be big enough for a large double bed or twin beds. Some models have sliding glass patio doors and very spacious, open-looking interiors. And some have "tip-out" alcoves that crank out when parked at a campsite. Small couches or lounges fit to make the main floor less cluttered. Depending on size and interior features, fifth-wheelers sleep from four to eight persons. Like motor homes, they are, of course, expensive.

Motor Homes

The motor home is a self-contained home on wheels, and the driver sits near facilities for dining, cooking, sleeping, sanitation, water supply, and usually air conditioning.

One manufacturer's standard equipment includes wall-to-wall foam-padded nylon carpet, storage drawers, a four-burner stove with an automatic oven, a dinette that converts into a bed, tinted windows, two skylight roof vents, a fire extinguisher, a bedroom privacy curtain, four adjustable defroster vents, and many other worthwhile items. Optionals are quite numerous in many models. For the extra cost, you can include a home theater sound system, high-definition television, satellite system, trailer hitch, dash-mounted water-tank gauge, wraparound windshield curtains, headrests and armrests for driver and copilot, and many other conveniences to make for a safer and more enjoyable excursion in your motor home.

The rigs measure from 17 to 42 feet in length. The interior of most units is plywood with the outside constructed of molded fiberglass or aluminum. The counter and tabletops are made of material that can readily withstand any punishment.

Owing to the vehicle's enormous size and its overhang, you must travel on good roads. Parking also may be a problem, but this is not true in all cases. That same overhang, though, can come in very handy when you're launching a boat. And motor homes are excellent vehicles to tow such craft behind.

One drawback of the motor home is its shoebox shape, but some new models are being aerodynamically designed to cut down on the hazards of wind.

If you store your motor home during the winter, remove water from every pipe in the system and leave valves in the open position. Also make certain that water is drained from the toilet and toilet holding tank, and follow this up with a thorough cleansing and deodorizing. LP gas-tank valves should be closed securely, as well as

The motor home is literally a self-contained drivable home on wheels featuring facilities for dining, cooking, sleeping, sanitation, water supply, and air conditioning. Models can be up to 40 feet, but the most popular sizes are 20 to 24 feet. Parking, depending on size, can sometimes be a problem.

all windows and roof vents. The refrigerator should also be cleaned and emptied and the door left open. Take out all food from the vehicle, as well as such items as fishing tackle, which may leave undesirable odors. Give the vehicle a walk-through check on occasion, airing it out when possible. As tires are usually left fully inflated on the motor home, move the unit a couple of feet each week or so to avoid continuous stress on one section of the tire due to the total weight of the home being on it and the three to five other tires. Otherwise, jack up each wheel on occasion and slightly rotate it.

Van Conversions

Van conversions, also called van campers, have become extremely popular. One reason is that some models cost little more than a full-size station wagon. Another is that they're easier to handle and park than some of the bigger camping rigs, and they can be used for everyday purposes around home, like an ordinary van or station wagon. Thus, they combine the advantages of a super station wagon and "pocket" motor home. Many models provide not only sleeping bunks, but also a galley and even a shower and toilet, making them completely self-contained camping rigs.

The RV manufacturers convert all the standard van models—Chevrolet, Dodge, Ford, and GMC—using vans with both short and long wheelbases. Some RV companies stretch the width or length to provide jumbo interiors.

You can't stand up inside a standard van, so headroom is an important part of conversion. Most often, the roof is cut off and a raised fiberglass structure is substi-

This van camper from Classic Vans is a typical conversion van that offers most of the benefits of a motor home, but is easier to handle and park. Van campers can also be used as a second car for everyday chores. Interiors can include bunks, a galley, and even a shower and toilet.

tuted, resulting in more than 6 feet of interior height. However, the added frontal area can cause extra drag, and the increased height may make the vehicle slightly more susceptible to wind sway. Another approach is to increase headroom only in the galley area by building a dropped floor well. The disadvantage here is that you can only stand straight in that area—while preparing meals. Also, the floor well reduces ground clearance, which can be important on rough roads. A third way is to install an expandable top that lies almost flat (adding only about 4 inches to the van's height while driving) and can be popped up when parked to provide headroom.

A typical interior might have a dinette that can be turned into a double bunk, plus another double bunk over the driver's cockpit. The galley generally contains a sink, range, and refrigerator or cooler. Models with a lavatory contain a chemical toilet, wash basin, and shower.

■ Snowmobiles

The snowmobile is the only vehicle available for traveling in remote, snow-covered regions. It's steered by ski-type runners up front and is propelled by a continuously running belt or track below the vehicle that grips the surface of the snow and sends the sled flying over it.

Low-priced models are compacts with engines averaging 225 cubic centimeters, but the big ones are known in the snowmobiler's lingo as "class 5 modifieds." The latter is one of the largest on the market, featuring a 350-pound toboggan with an 85-horsepower, 800-cubic-centimeter engine. These machines hit 90 miles per hour and beyond with little effort.

The track on the typical snowmobile measures 15 inches in width and permits you to steer the vehicle by shifting your weight. Tracks, however, sometimes reach 30½ inches.

Snowmobiles can get into many areas where a car or an RV wouldn't stand a chance. Before the age of the snowmobile, conservation officers had to don their snowshoes. In times of accident or disaster in snowbound areas, help can get there quickly with a snowmobile to provide rapid medical assistance and transportation to a hospital. For the outdoors enthusiast, the snowmobile offers enjoyment. He can go hunting, ice fishing, racing, or skijoring (skiing behind a snowmobile) with the rig.

Unfortunately, some people chase deer and other game animals with their snowmobiles. This practice, of course, is against the law.

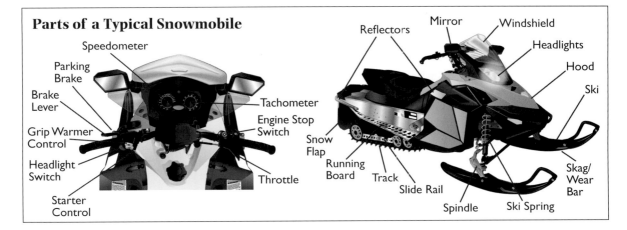

Parts of a Typical Snowmobile

Speedometer
Parking Brake
Brake Lever
Grip Warmer Control
Headlight Switch
Starter Control
Tachometer
Engine Stop Switch
Throttle

Reflectors
Mirror
Windshield
Headlights
Hood
Ski
Snow Flap
Running Board
Track
Slide Rail
Spindle
Ski Spring
Skag/ Wear Bar

Depending on snow conditions, here are the recommended riding positions for snowmobilers.

Kneeling

Posting

Sitting

Standing

size, and narrow cleats that often don't adhere to the ice and snow.

The heavier snowmobiles cannot negotiate all types of snow, but there are relatively new, lightweight models designed for better flotation on soft snow. Be careful with a heavier one, which may bog down. Also, be sure to wear appropriate clothing for safety and warmth. Insulated snowmobile suits are recommended, as are helmets, goggles, and face masks. Some of the snowmobiles themselves have built-in safety features, such as padded handlebars and breakaway windshields—excellent improvements.

In addition, the noise has been substantially reduced in recent years. Machines built since June 30, 1976, and certified by the Snowmobile Safety and Certification Committee of the International Snowmobile Manufacturers Association, emit no more than 73 decibels at 50 feet when traveling at 15 miles per hour, and similarly certified machines produced since February 1, 1975, emit no more than 78 decibels at 50 feet when traveling at full throttle. By comparison, snowmobiles built before 1969 produced 102 decibels.

Snowmobiling has become more than a mechanized means of traveling over snow; it has become a sport (and almost a way of life in some regions). Trail systems have been developed in forest lands to accommodate snowmobilers without interfering with skiers or other winter-sports enthusiasts. Regulations have been established by states—and in some cases by the snowmobilers themselves—to promote safety. Some trails have stop signs, yield signs, and even information kiosks at strategic locations. Perhaps the most important improvements have come from the snowmobiling clubs, which have promoted responsible snowmobiling—not only in terms of safety, but also in terms of concern for wild animals and forest vegetation. When carried on in such a responsible manner, the sport is harmless to wildlife.

Obviously, the snowmobile season is rather short. Therefore, correct storage of your vehicle is essential. Store it in a dry place, and block it off the ground to take the weight off the skis and track. Loosen the track tensioner. Drain the fuel tank and pour a quart of SAE 30 oil into the oil tank. Then, roll the machine from side to side so the fuel-tank walls are well lubricated. Drain the carburetor. Take out the spark plug and pour a tablespoon of SAE 30 through the spark-plug hole. Turn the engine over four times by pulling the starter rope. Then, replace the spark plug. Clean the outside of the engine and spread a thin film of oil over any of its exposed surfaces that could corrode.

Though a few snowmobiles on the market feature reverse transmission on an optional basis, most do not have standard reverse, making them somewhat dangerous. Accidents such as fatal or maiming collisions with automobiles, trains, pipes, fences, and the like also show the hazards of driving the vehicle. Other disadvantages include its heavy weight, its often low, cramped

■ All-Terrain Vehicles

The snowmobile's counterparts are the two- and four-wheel-drive all-terrain vehicles (ATVs)—tough, knobby-tired vehicles designed to take sportsmen nearly everywhere off-road. Used properly, an ATV can safely take you into remote areas to camp.

If you are a farmer, guide, or outfitter, an ATV can haul people and a trailer full of gear into a backcountry camp. It can also be used to rescue a lost camper or hiker.

ATVs are available in a variety of sizes with options ranging from front-load racks to rear cargo boxes and rifle scabbards. Most ATVs will carry loads up to 100 pounds on a front rack and up to 250 pounds on a rear-load carrier, and will tow 1,000 pounds or more. Many are two-wheel drives with a button to engage the four-wheel drive. An ATV can weigh from 400 to 800 pounds, depending on its power and utility. A typical sportsman's model will have a four-stroke, liquid-cooled

Built for several sportsmen traveling to remote grounds, the Kawasaki Mule 4010 can seat four people and their gear. The ATV can carry a payload from 400 pounds with four passengers to 800 pounds with two passengers. Selectable four-wheel drive to two-wheel drive gives the driver traction options.

The Kawasaki Brute Force 750 is typical of ATVs built for sportsmen who want to get into the backcountry. Powered by a liquid-cooled, four-stroke engine, the ATV has a 10-foot turning radius, weighs 695 pounds, and will carry up to 242 pounds on the front and rear racks.

500 engine, a DC outlet, disc brakes, and full steel skid plates to protect the bottom.

As with snowmobiles, ATVs sometimes suffer from a bad reputation because of the reckless antics of a few. ATVs, improperly used, can damage the environment by tearing up wet trails and by being ridden across streambeds and creeks. ATVs should also avoid livestock and wild game. Stressing game animals by driving too close can seriously sap their energy reserves when they may need it the most.

Ideally, ATV operators should not be under 18 years old. ATVs should be ridden only on designated roads and trails, and operators should wear helmets and hemmed and protective clothing. And, above all, operators should resist the urge to pioneer a new road or trail with an ATV.

The Ultimate Backcountry Camper

It is hard to imagine the backcountry limits you can put on some of the new all-terrain vehicles. The Kawasaki Brute Force, for example, can carry its driver and nearly 250 pounds on its racks and still tow a load of 1,250 pounds. For campers who want to explore the backcountry, an ATV makes sense. You can take enough gear for a remote extended camping trip that would normally be inaccessible to any other recreational vehicle. If you're a hunter, you can bring out most big-game animals. If you're a camping family that prefers wilderness campsites, there are ATVs that will carry up to four persons and 400 pounds of camping gear. The four-passenger ATVs will have some limits to off-road capabilities, but they can still get a group of campers and gear into remote areas. There are some restrictions on taking ATVs off road. Always check state and federal laws and stay on designated trails.

SWAMP CAMPING

Most campers avoid swamps and similar wetlands, but learning to travel and camp in this kind of wet terrain actually can open up new groundbreaking opportunities to explore, fish, and hunt that you've never experienced before. Deer, wild turkeys, feral hogs, and small game inhabit many swamplands, and angling in a swamp can reward you with remote waters for bass, catfish, and bream.

Years I ago I made my first camping trip in a swamp with Byron Almquist, a Louisiana canoe guide who specializes in swamp trips. Before we left Byron's store and headquarters, the Canoe and Trail Shop in New Orleans (www.canoeandtrail.com), we went over a checklist of equipment. Items of special note included a folding saw, fire starter, all-weather space blankets, a cook-fire grate, waterproof duffle bags or plastic trash bags for all gear, and triple the number of dry socks you'd normally take on a camping trip.

We did all our cooking on wood fires. Dry kindling may be found in the form of bark from some trees, and standing dead trees occasionally offer good firewood, but driftwood is often the only source of fuel. Swamp driftwood is damp, so fire starters are usually required. The grate, placed across two logs and over hot coals, makes a perfect stove.

Space blankets served two purposes. These emergency all-weather sheets are made of aluminized plastic and are feather light. A 56-by-84-inch sheet folds to about 8 by 6 inches. On a swamp trip they provide dry seats around the campfire and fine ground cloths for tents.

Because most swamp country must be traveled by canoe or kayak—backpacking would be an ordeal if not impossible—weight is not a critical factor. On our trip in the Pearl River Basin, carrying food was no problem. A cooler fit nicely into a canoe, and we took along ice and fresh food. Block ice, if conserved, will keep for three days or a little more in an insulated ice chest. Some newer coolers, such as Yeti and Xtreme Coleman, will hold ice for several days.

With our abundance of cargo space, Byron and I were able to carry a three-man nylon tent rather than a small backpacker's tent. It weighed less than 10 pounds and packed 8 by 15 inches. Sleeping on the damp ground is out of the question unless a ground

cloth and sleeping bag are between you and the swamp floor. Tents offer comfort and the convenience of storage space for equipment, but a hammock also makes a good bunk, especially if reasonably dry campsites will be scarce. Another option for off-the-ground camping is a tent cot. Several are available, but Kamp-Rite's Tent Cot will keep you 11 inches off the wet ground, with mesh doors and windows to keep insects out. This design is also used by the US military.

Mosquitoes and other insects can be a nuisance, so if you use a tent, make sure it has a securable net across the door and a sewn-in floor to keep insects out. If you sleep in a hammock, a mosquito-net drape will protect you from insects. Good insect repellent is a necessity. The only real danger from wildlife in swamp country, especially in the southern tier of the United States, is venomous snakes, specifically the Eastern cottonmouth. Cottonmouths have dark blotches on an olive body and broad, flat heads. During our trip in the Pearl River Basin, we saw only one cottonmouth. It swam by our canoes, totally disinterested in us. It's highly unlikely, but if someone is a victim of a snakebite, follow the recommended treatment in the first aid section of this book.

Eastern cottonmouths as well as Florida and western cottonmouths are frequently confused with nonvenomous water snakes. Cottonmouths have dark blotches on an olive body and broad, flat heads.

▼ The Kamp-Rite Tent Cot will keep you 11 inches off the ground. With a capacity of 300 pounds, the cot folds down to 33 by 30 by 6 inches. This design is used extensively by the US military. It is a good choice for off-the-ground camping or camping in swampy areas.

▲ The Bass Pro Eagles Nest Hammock is a single-person hammock for campers who may want to try swamp camping. This hammock will keep you dry, off the ground, and away from crawling insects. It weighs only 17 ounces and has a capacity of 400 pounds.

Sensible footwear is vital in swamp country. We frequently ran into shallow water where we had to climb out of our canoes and walk them. This meant mud and water up to our knees all day. Byron's solution was a nylon combat boot, which gives good support and washes off easily. I wore rubber skin-diver boots, which are supple and waterproof. Tennis shoes do not work well—I tried them. The first time you pull a foot out of deep mud, the shoe stays.

As you paddle through a swamp, downed trees will be your main obstacles, and they may be dealt with in two ways. If the log is large and on the water's surface, the man in the bow steps out onto the log and pulls the craft about halfway over it. The man in the stern then climbs to the bow, which seesaws the canoe over the log, and the man on the log can push it the rest of the way before getting in at the stern. If the downed tree is small and high enough above the water so that the canoe will pass beneath it, both passengers can step over the log as the craft floats under it. Small, finger-thick branches fall quickly to a folding saw.

Finding dry ground for a campsite requires some savvy. About mid-afternoon, Byron would begin looking at treetops in the distance. He explained that pine trees cannot survive heavy and constant concentra-

tions of water, so when you find pines in a swamp, you've located an area of high ground—and the best possible place to make camp.

Knowing the growth patterns of swamp trees will also keep you in the deeper channels. Cypress and tupelo grow in deep water, thriving where other trees cannot survive. As a result, cypress and tupelo trees line the deep channels much like buoy markers. Identification is not difficult. Both stand in water, and both have flared boles at their bases. The cypress has a shaggier bark and a more fluted base than the tupelo. If you cannot detect any current, which is the surest way to find the main channel, follow the cypress- and tupelo-lined route.

Get a GPS unit and carry topographic maps of the area you intend to camp in, and always carry a good compass—the swamp's thick canopy can block out sun and stars. Take your fully charged cell phone, but don't depend on it in deep swamp cover.

Traveling and camping at a leisurely pace, we averaged about three miles a day in the swamp. Allow time for retracing your paddle strokes if you get hemmed in. And before you leave home, file a float plan with a friend so that if you get lost, a rescue party will be able to locate you.

CAMP BEDDING

■ Sleeping Bag Insulation

The warmest and lightest insulation used in today's sleeping bags is down—the breast feathers of a goose or a duck. Besides being quite soft and warm, down holds the heat generated by the body. It does not, fortunately, hold body moisture. This throwing-off process is known as "breathing," and prevents the bag from becoming uncomfortably clammy.

"Loft"—the height of a sleeping bag when fully fluffed and unrolled—is a good indication of the bag's insulating ability. A couple of synthetic fillers, Polarguard and Hollofil, exhibit good loft and offer about two-thirds as much insulating efficiency as down per pound. Quallofil, a DuPont synthetic, has excellent loft, comes close to down in its insulating efficiency (and far surpasses down under wet conditions), and is almost as compactable as the finest goose feathers. There are 3-pound mummy-type sleeping bags with Quallofil insulation that have a temperature rating down to 5°F below zero. For certain purposes—canoe or boat camping,

wet-weather camping, or camping from spring through fall, when the temperature isn't extremely cold—the synthetics have several advantages over down.

For one thing, down becomes almost useless as an insulator when it gets wet, and it dries slowly. Polyester provides warmth even when wet, and it dries quickly. For another thing, down tends to shift around in a bag, making lumps and thin, cold spots unless extensive sewing "quilts" it in place. Polarguard is batting-like so it doesn't shift and needs little quilting. Hollofil needs almost as much quilting as down, while Quallofil seems to need a bit less. Finally, the synthetics cost less, primarily because the raw materials are cheaper than down.

Even some of the polyester-and-acrylic combination fillers provide some warmth when wet, assuming that outside temperatures aren't extremely cold. And, like down, the newer polyesters retain body heat while allowing body moisture to escape and evaporate. Some synthetic-filled bags are more compressible than down—in spite of their good loft when fluffed out—

Sleeping Bag Styles

A typical mummy bag for extreme cold is the Ascend Mummy Sleeping Bag rated for 40°F below zero. It has a double-layered quilt construction with four-chamber, hollow insulation, a polyester ripstop shell, and a poly-taffeta lining. The Ascend also has a chest baffle, hood, and a compression stuff sack. The weight is about 6 pounds.

The Bass Pro Rectangular Sleeping Bag, rated for zero degrees to 20°F below zero, is designed for big campers. The bag measures 40 inches by 94 inches. If you are looking for roomy comfort, a bag of this size would be a good choice. At weights of 8 or 9 pounds, depending on ratings, this bag is too heavy for backpacking.

The L.L. Bean Adventure 20/40 Sleeping Bag is designed for multiseason camping. Sleep with the 40-degree side up for warmer nights. If it cools off, flip it over to the 20-degree side. It's filled with Climashield synthetic insulation with overlapping baffles to eliminate cold spots. It is a good, versatile choice except in extremely cold temperatures.

and this can be another advantage when gear space is limited.

Other filler materials include wool, cotton (poplin), kapok, and Dacron. Except for Dacron, these insulators mat easily and aren't very resilient. Yet they may suffice in relatively thin, warm-weather bags, and such bags are relatively inexpensive.

The label or packaging of a good sleeping bag usually states the weight of the filler and the temperature range or minimum temperature at which the bag will keep you comfortable. Of course, with a bag that doesn't provide much insulation, you can wear extra sleeping clothes to add 20°F to 30°F effectiveness to the bag. But it pays to buy a bag of good quality—both for warmth and durability—and to compare weights and comfort ranges before deciding which one to buy. About 3 pounds of one synthetic filler, for example, may keep you comfortable when the temperature dips to 30°F, while you'll need only about 2 pounds of down at that temperature. Consider the kind of camping you'll be doing and the price you can afford—and then shop aggressively.

■ Styles

Sleeping bags come in two basic configurations—the rectangular bag and the mummy bag. A variation, designed for recreational vehicles, is called the station-wagon bag, but this is simply an oversize rectangular bag. The rectangular type is basically a three-season bag, but it is available in grades from summer weight to heavy winter weight. The mummy bag is intended primarily for cold weather and backpacking; it fits more closely and cinches tight around the head and shoulders, impeding exchange of inside and outside air.

Except for a few huge station-wagon bags, the rectangular style is usually offered in a choice of sizes. The youth size often measures about 26 inches by 66 inches. Most common is the adult or full size, which is 33 inches by 75 inches. The third size is king size, which usually measures 39 inches by 79 inches. Some companies also offer a tall size for people taller than 6 feet.

Two sleeping bags may be paired together by opening and completely unzipping both. One should be placed atop the other so that the bottoms of both zippers meet. Then, simply connect each zipper at the point where the two meet. Double bags when used by two persons tend to be warmer than they are when used individually.

A junior bag is a waste of money; get an adult bag for your youngster as, with proper care, it will last him for several years.

Rectangular bags in general are fine for car, canoe, and recreational-vehicle camping. But if you're backpacking, you'll probably have to put your faith in the mummy bag. You won't be making the wrong move, though.

As mentioned, weight is an important consideration to the backpacker, and the mummy bag is designed with this in mind. It is widest at the shoulders—usually 33 inches—and tapers to about 19 inches at the feet. This tapering makes the bag fit like a robe, and that means additional warmth. Some mummy bags can keep the sleeper comfortable at zero degrees and weigh only 3 or 4 pounds, half the weight of comparably warm rectangular bags. Mummy bags are usually filled with down and have nylon covers.

Another valuable item for the backpacker is the stuff bag, into which he actually stuffs his sleeping bag. This method of storage saves wear on the bag through compression fatigue and helps to fluff it up when you're extracting it for use. Stuff bags are usually waterproof.

■ Liners

Although a majority of sleeping bags on the market have an inner lining made of flannel, it is worthwhile to purchase an additional flannel or silk liner. If you can carry the extra weight, an extra liner helps to regulate warmth during the night. Should it be warm when you fall asleep, you can take out the lining completely or use it folded underneath as a mattress pad. If the temperature drops substantially later on, the liner can be readily shifted so that you sleep between the layers or under both of them. This separate liner will stop drafts where the sleeper's head protrudes and will provide further insulation near the areas of the zipper or snap fasteners, where cold air may enter.

By purchasing a variety of liners, you can adjust your sleeping bag for practically any weather. That's the reason why a four-season camper usually relies on liners. An advantage of the removable liner is that cleaning will be no problem, and the bag itself will remain unsoiled within. Tie tabs on your sleeping bag are good for quickly attaching or removing such liners.

Liners are also made of synthetics and fleece. One manufacturer claims that a 3-pound liner consisting of 2 pounds of polyester fibers will add approximately 20 degrees to the minimum comfort range.

■ Shells for Sleeping Bags

It is important that sleeping bags breathe, letting

body moisture escape. Otherwise, you wind up with a sauna effect.

Beware of any bag—especially a cheap one—advertised as waterproof. Such shells may be coated so they won't allow body vapors to pass through. On the other hand, some excellent waterproof shells, such as those made of a nylon and Gore-Tex laminate, do breathe while being impermeable to rain.

Economical station-wagon bags often have an inner shell of cotton flannel and an outer shell of heavy cotton. These bags are practical for warm-weather car camping or for use in a recreational vehicle. But since they are heavy, bulky, and highly moisture-absorbent in relation to the warmth they provide, they are not suitable for backpacking or canoe camping.

Better bags filled with down or polyester usually have inner and outer shells made of nylon in ripstop or taffeta weaves. Both fabrics breathe. They also feel good next to the skin, wear well, resist mildew and fading, and are unaffected by machine washing.

There are also bivouac covers, which serve as mini-tents but drape over you and your sleeping bag like a sock—complete with mosquito netting. These covers normally have an airtight and waterproof underside and a waterproof (though breathable) topside made of materials such as Gore-Tex. Larger bivouac covers can house a couple of sleepers and their gear. Though more restrictive than tents, these covers are lighter and get the nod from weight-conscious backpackers.

■ Zippers

Zippers on mummy bags typically run three-quarter length or full length down one side. A rectangular sleeping bag should be equipped with a heavy-duty zipper that runs completely down one side and across the bottom. This type of zipper permits you to open the bag completely for a thorough airing and lets you zip together two matching sleeping bags. Two bags zipped together will accommodate two adults or up to four youngsters.

For both mummy and rectangular bags, zippers should have slides at both ends that allow you to ventilate the head and foot ends independently. Both slides should have finger tabs inside and out.

Zippers themselves may be made of metal, nylon, or other synthetics. Metal tends to feel colder in cold weather, work harder in all weather, and frost up in winter. A sleeping-bag zipper should be large, whether it be of the conventional ladder design of most metal zippers or of the toothed-interlock or continuous-coil designs

used for synthetic zippers. Large zippers don't catch and abrade shell fabrics as readily as smaller, toothed zippers do—especially smaller metal-toothed zippers. Of all zippers, the continuous coil is easiest on fabric.

Most sleeping bags have a baffle panel—weather stripping made of insulated material to prevent air from traveling through the zipper. This strip lies along the inner surface of the zipper and, in better bags, may be from 1 to 1½ inches thick and from 3 to 4 inches wide. A cheaply made bag, needless to say, would have little or no weather stripping or a short (30- to 36-inch) zipper that may tend to drag when the bag is closed or opened.

■ Dry-Cleaned Bags

Proper airing of the sleeping bag is important, particularly when it has been dry-cleaned. An oft-told tale that bears repeating now deals with a teenager who slept in a bag that had only recently been dry-cleaned and then left for one and a half days in a car trunk. The boy's parents found him in a coma after the first night. Eleven days later, he was dead. The hospital reports said the cause of death was due to the inhaling of perchloroethylene fumes that had been trapped within the insulation. The solvents used in dry-cleaning may leave behind long-lasting lethal fumes. A thorough airing is a must.

■ Air Mattresses

An air mattress is not essential for sleeping in the outdoors, but it does add comfort. Most are made of nylon, which is lightweight enough for backpacking.

The chief drawback is that an air mattress can be used only at temperatures of about 45°F and higher unless you lay some insulation over the mattress. Otherwise, cold air in the mattress will convect body heat away.

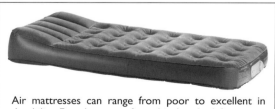

Air mattresses can range from poor to excellent in durability. For sheer comfort, this Aerobed features a built-in pillow and an internal pump powered by four D batteries. At the other end of the range, there are some models that have an I-beam or waffle design, which may not be as comfortable but are less expensive.

Another disadvantage is that air mattresses are subject to punctures as well as leakage from seams and valves, so a special patching kit should always accompany you on your travels.

Catalog listings of air mattresses often give both the deflated size and the inflated size. The latter is the one you should pay attention to, as that is what you will be sleeping on.

The average adult can be comfortably accommodated on a mattress measuring between 70 and 74 inches. A 6-footer would require the longest standard length—75 inches. A stout camper might need 32 inches of mattress across his back, but most people can fit comfortably on 28- to 30-inchers with adequate elbow room.

There are two designs of air mattress—the I-beam style and the tufted. The I-beam typically consists of five tubes that resemble steel construction beams when viewed from one end. The tufted design is waffle-like in appearance, and provides the sleeper with full support. It's more comfortable than the I-beam style, but is the more expensive of the two. When buying an air mattress, either I-beam or tufted, choose one with a metal valve, never the rubber or plastic type. The metal valves have screw tops.

If you sleep with a pillow, there's no need for you to do without one outdoors. Many air mattresses come with built-in air pillows, or else the pillows—either filled with down, synthetic fibers, or air—can be bought separately.

There are many air mattresses made solely of plastic or rubber. Avoid them. Although plastic or rubber air mattresses are lighter than the recommended fabric-rubber combinations, they are delicate and tear easily.

There are four ways to inflate an air mattress: a hand pump, a foot pump, a 12-volt or 120-volt pump, or your own lungs. You also have the option of choosing a self-inflating mattress. If yours doesn't inflate itself, using your own lung power isn't very difficult, but the resulting moist vapor can condense and freeze in cold weather. A hand pump adds weight to your gear. Lightweight plastic foot pumps are popular; although they are bulky, they provide dry air quickly.

When you inflate an air mattress, keep it out of the sun. Otherwise, the heat will cause the air to expand, possibly breaking the mattress. Also, never use a gas-station air-pressure pump to inflate a mattress.

To deflate an air mattress, unscrew the metal cap, leaving the valve completely open. Then, put a heavy object on the mattress to force air to escape more quickly. The last step is to slowly roll the mattress, beginning with the end opposite the valve, until all the air has been expelled.

When not in use, an air mattress should be blown up slightly and kept away from heat. Use it only for sleeping; it is not meant to be a surfboard. If the mattress does get wet, though, stand it up in an airy, shady place.

■ Foam Pads

Sleeping pads are of two basic types: hard, closed-cell foams and soft, open-cell foams. The hard pads contain sealed bubbles that resist compression. The soft pads contain bubbles and a network of passages that allow air to escape when compressed.

Hard-foam pads are sold in thicknesses ranging from ⅜ inch to 1 inch and provide almost as much insulating loft as the pad's thickness. Soft-foam or open-celled pads must be purchased four to five times as thick (usually 3½ inches) as hard foams to provide as much insulating loft when compressed under your body. Though more comfortable, soft-foam pads are bulkier to carry, and they absorb ground and body moisture, adding inconvenience and weight.

Both hard- and soft-foam pads can be purchased in various lengths and widths. To capitalize on the advantages of each type of pad, some manufacturers laminate them together. Here, the top layer is soft foam for comfort, and the bottom layer is hard foam for insulation and watertightness. Or you may see a soft-foam pad enclosed in a fabric cover. Better covers have a cotton upper surface so that body moisture won't be trapped on top and a lower surface of waterproof nylon.

Tough, young backpackers use hard foams almost exclusively. But age and desire for comfort usually lead even the toughest backpackers to combine the use of hard foam with either soft foam or an air mattress.

■ Canvas Cots

A cot can waste floor space if you have a sloping-wall tent. Also, it's quite a task to set up alone. Canvas cots also tend to let cold air circulate beneath them, but some 6-inch-high models come equipped with down or Dacron batting. This insulation isn't compressed by the camper's weight while he sleeps, so it remains at peak efficiency.

On the other hand, cots are comfortable, if weight and bulk are unimportant. If you decide on a canvas cot, get a model that is about 12 or 14 inches off the ground so it can double as a tent seat.

FOOTGEAR

■ Leather Boots

The sturdiest boots are those constructed totally of leather, the best all-around material for four-season wear. Leather boots permit the feet to "breathe," giving off moisture that would otherwise tend to make the camper's feet hot and uncomfortable and cause blisters. Some manufacturers have treated boots with waterproofing compounds, but leather so treated seals in body heat and moisture.

The proper height for a boot is about 8 inches. A higher boot may constrict your leg muscles as well as restrict free circulation. Also, high boots are hot and heavy in summertime. The boot should also be uninsulated, for reasons to be discussed shortly.

Avoid boots with leather soles and heels; they are not very water resistant. Leather soles wear quickly and slip on smooth rocks, pine needles, dry grass, and the like. Get boots with soles and heels of rubber or one of the tough synthetics. Rubber soles provide a good grip and are flexible, long lasting, and tough.

Many campers like boots with a platform or straight-bottom sole that has no heel. These soles are not recommended for mountain climbing. A heel permits you to hold back when you're descending a slope. Cleat-like treads (Vibram) are good if you hike on rocky trails.

Be certain that the tops of the boots are made of soft leather so that enough insulation is provided. The air space between the sock and the boot and the area around your foot should permit free, comfortable movement. In winter, a boot should keep cold air out and warm air in; that air space, if sufficient, will help achieve this dual purpose. The toe and heel should be hard to give your feet the protection they need.

Some styles of leather boots are insulated. If the temperature is below freezing and dry, such boots may be suitable for casual walking. But for all-around use, they are a poor choice. They become stuffy, heavy, and hot during strenuous activity, and when wet take a long time to dry. In cold weather, you are better off with plain leather boots and several pairs of socks of varied weights, which you can change if a pair becomes wet.

Before you try out your new boots on a hike, a thorough breaking in is in order. That's why shoe grease should be applied, but not to any particular excess.

Otherwise, your boots will become overly soft and all but worthless. Also, try short hikes at regular intervals with the new boots so that your feet will get accustomed to them. Bend your feet frequently to make each boot more pliable. Old-timers used to break in their boots by standing in a bucket of water until the boots were saturated, and then walking around in them until they were dry. Fortunately, this is no longer necessary.

Through proper care, you can add substantial life to your boots. When you're finished for the day and your boots are coated with mud, wash them off thoroughly. Then, fill them with wads of newspaper and place them in a warm, dry area (not above 100°F). When they're dry, rub some shoe grease into the leather to soften and waterproof it.

Another simple way to waterproof leather boots is to treat them with paraffin or a silicone-dressing spray. The method of waterproofing preferred by some outdoors enthusiasts is to use neatsfoot oil. (Keep the oil off rubber heels and soles, as it may prove harmful to them.) Prior to application, wash the leather with warm water and mild soap. The purpose of this measure is to open the leather's pores for better absorption of the oil. Be sure the leather is still wet when you rub on the oil. A handy applicator is an old toothbrush, as its bristles help get the oil deep into the seams.

For securing the boot to the foot, rawhide laces and eyelets have proved the best, with nylon strings running a close second. Some hikers prefer the quicker hooks, but they are not quite as reliable as laces. And if you get a cheap set of hooks, they'll break, rust, or bend in no time. Also, hooks often catch on twigs.

■ Rubber and Leather Boots

Though the all-leather boot is the best all-around boot for hiking, for wet weather many people prefer shoepacs. These boots have a leather top and a rubber bottom and are the perfect choice for hiking in rain, swamplands, and wet snow. The classic Bean Boot by L.L. Bean is a good example of a shoepac. The leather tops shed moisture well if they're properly oiled or greased and are flexible. As these tops aren't as airtight as they would be if they were of rubber composition, they provide good ankle support and a wide, roomy area for the foot. This air space lets you wear two pairs of socks—woolen over thermal—to withstand the cold down to zero degrees. The rubber bottoms of shoepacs perform the all-important function of keeping the feet dry.

As noted, shoepacs are designed for the wet-weather enthusiast. That's why the neatsfoot oil treatment described earlier should be used to waterproof the boots. But be careful not to harm the rubber bottoms when applying the oil.

Manufacturers have developed shoepacs up to 18 inches in height, but a model from 8 to 12 inches should prove adequate. The extra inches will just hinder the circulation in your leg, and will add extra lacing and unlacing time to your chores outdoors.

■ Rubber Boots (Uninsulated)

The camper who fishes on his outings often finds himself pushing boats off beaches, and sloshing in water in his small craft. The top choice in footgear for this person is the uninsulated rubber boot.

The optimum choice is a boot about 12 or 13 inches high with no more than three eyelets at the top. The remainder of the boot is totally enclosed, protecting the feet from water.

In extreme cold, two pairs of socks—heavy woolen ones over thermal or athletic-type socks—are warmer than a single pair of heavy socks, and keep your feet dry and comfortable for quite a while.

When you shop for footgear, take along two pairs of socks to ensure that you're getting the proper size. You're better off learning about a too-snug fit in the store than when your feet begin to hurt on a cold day outside.

■ Composition Boots

The best news in outdoor footgear is the constant improvement in boots that combine developments in modern technology, such as tough Cordura nylon and the waterproofing properties of Gore-Tex, a microporous membrane. The most popular boot of this type has a lug sole with a leather toe and heel. The rest of the boot, however, is made of light Cordura nylon. The entire boot is lined with Gore-Tex, which makes it virtually waterproof. The resulting boot is frequently half the weight of a full leather boot. It requires very little breaking in because the nylon sides mold more quickly to the foot than new leather. And the wearer can literally stand in water without getting wet.

For warm weather or early fall hiking, these boots are an excellent choice. If you expect to encounter colder temperatures, the same composition boots are also available insulated. Modern synthetic insulating materials such as Thinsulate and Insolite make them warmer per ounce of boot weight than any older type of insulation, yet they seem to "wick" away moisture. With proper socks, therefore, they don't tend to hold perspiration and make your feet uncomfortably clammy.

■ Rubber Boots (Insulated)

Insulated rubber boots are a good choice for ice fishing done in bone-chilling temperatures. These boots are much too heavy for conventional hiking, and even a lengthy walk will cause your feet to become clammy and sweaty.

Another disadvantage is that if you should snag the outside layer, water may seep into the insulated lining. The proper procedure at that point is to squeeze out the moisture toward the area of the punctures until it is completely outside. Then, prop open the tear with a twig or toothpick to let the insulation air out. Wait until all the moisture is removed before repairing the tear with a rubber-tube patch.

Many campers wear boot liners inside waterproof boots. These add to the warmth and reduce clamminess. Most liners have an outer layer of cotton tricot to act as a blotter and an inner layer of insulating, moisture-resistant acrylic fiber. For a comfortable fit with liners, you may need slightly larger boots than you'd otherwise wear. When buying new boots, therefore, it's best to try them on over the liners.

A final word on the insulated rubber boot: As mentioned, it can become clammy inside. By merely sprinkling talcum in the boot at night, you'll find that the clamminess will disappear, and your feet will slide in easier and not bunch up your socks uncomfortably.

■ Leather Boots (Insulated)

Though not quite as waterproof as the insulated rubber boot, the insulated leather boot has some virtues. It generally gives a more comfortable fit and provides better ankle support. You can't remove the insulation for cleaning and drying, and you can't adjust the boot to rising temperatures. Thus, the boots tend to become hot, stuffy, and heavy in warmer weather.

◄ The L.L. Bean Maine Hunting Shoe is a time-tested blend of soft and supple waterproof leather uppers with a chain-tread bottom. A steel shank in the arch provides good support in rocky terrain. This design comes in 10-, 12-, and 16-inch heights and both insulated and uninsulated models. For most situations, the 10-inch boot is the most practical. This design dates back to 1912.

▼ Typical of modern composition boots are the Rocky BearClaw 3D Boots, which have Thinsulate insulation and a Gore-Tex lining with a combination of full-grain leather and nylon uppers. Completely waterproof and breathable, BearClaws would be a good choice for multiseason camping. Many of these combination boots require little, if any, breaking in.

▶ Helix Waterfowl Waders are a good choice for surf fishermen. The breathable fabric allows heat-trapping layers, such as fleece pants, to be worn underneath. The boots are insulated with Thinsulate. Helix technology uses one continuous seam to wrap the wader leg in a spiral or helix pattern.

▲ Muck Woody Sport Boots are built for muddy, swampy conditions. With stretch-fit top bindings, four-way stretch nylon, and foam booties, these 15-inch boots will stay on in mud. Look for these or similar features when selecting a boot for swampy woods.

Most insulated leather boots are quite waterproof, but in wet weather over an extended period, some moisture will seep inside. To further waterproof your boots, try silicone-dressing sprays, paraffin, or the neatsfoot oil method described earlier.

■ Hipboots and Waders

Fishermen find themselves up to their knees—and often higher—in water. Hipboots or waders are an essential part of their equipment.

When the water is no more than knee-deep and a substantial amount of walking is required, hipboots will suffice. The uninsulated hipboot is best. It features the standard, heavy-rubber foot that is welded to a top of strong fabric—usually a laminated nylon-rubber-nylon sandwich—with a thin inner bond of waterproof rubber. Although some models are manufactured with uppers of rubber-coated fabric, the welded ones are recommended. Though the price is just a bit higher, they're more flexible and far lighter.

The winter steelheader or fall surf fisherman will find the insulated hipboot to be the best buy. The weather is usually bitter, and the core of insulation built into the shoe and ankle of the hipboot will keep him warm.

If you are a stream fisherman who wades on slick rocks, felt-soled hipboots are required. They provide sure-footed, quiet movement. The soles wear quickly, but can be replaced with special felt-sole kits available in sporting-goods stores. These kits also can be used to apply felt soles to rubber-soled boots.

Waders are simply hipboots with waterproof tops that extend to the waist, or even to the chest. Some have stocking feet of thin rubber or a rubberized fabric, over which wading shoes are worn. Others have boot feet with waterproof uppers. The boot-foot style is simpler to put on, carry, and store; it is also less apt to develop leaks.

■ Snowshoes

When snow depths reach a foot or more, conventional boots are rendered virtually ineffectual. At such times, snowshoes must be worn on outdoor treks. The purpose of the snowshoe is to distribute the weight of the body over a greater surface of snow than the shoe sole alone, thereby increasing support.

Snowshoes come in three basic styles—the Alaskan, the Michigan, and the bearpaw—plus several modifications of each of these styles.

The Alaskan is also known as the Yukon, pickerel, trial, or racing snowshoe. It's good for long-distance walking, even with a heavy load. Long and narrow, it has a conspicuous upward curl at the toe and a tail at the rear—a design suited to open country and powder snow with little timber or brush.

The "classic" style, the one that conforms to most pictures, is the Michigan, also known as the Maine or Algonquin snowshoe. It, too, has a tail, but tends to be wider and shorter than the Alaskan and with less front curl—usually 2 inches or under—making it suitable for brushy country.

The bearpaw has no tail and little (or occasionally no) front curl. Its shape is more or less oval, but the forepart is often slightly wider than the rear. Shorter than the other types, it's good for hilly, brushy terrain, especially where abrupt turns are common. This is believed to be the most ancient of all snowshoe designs.

Types of Snowshoes

Body Weight (pounds)	Michigan	Alaskan	Bearpaw
35 to 50	9 x 30"	——	——
50 to 60	10 x 36"	——	——
60 to 90	11 x 40"	——	——
100 to 125	12 x 42"	——	——
125 to 150	12 x 48"	10 x 48"	——
150 to 175	13 x 48"	10 x 56"	14 x 30"
175 to 200	14 x 48"	12 x 60"	13 x 33"
200 to 250	14 x 52"	——	14 x 36"

One modification, sometimes called the Green Mountain snowshoe, is narrower than the usual bearpaw and almost uniform in width. One advantage is that it's easy to learn to walk on and is very maneuverable. Another is that it's compact. Green Mountain snowshoes and more or less similar models are popular with snowmobilers and, indeed, are sometimes called snowmobile snowshoes.

Another variation, known simply as a modified bearpaw, has a short tail, which helps to prevent twisting. Still another, usually called the cross-country snowshoe, is a narrow, slightly elongated bearpaw (like the Green Mountain) with a tail that helps prevent twisting, but isn't long enough to snag. Good for relatively even but somewhat brushy terrain, it's essentially a cross between the bearpaw and the Alaskan.

Traditionally, snowshoes are composed of frames made of ash—a tough and flexible wood—and rawhide

Snowshoes

Left: For relatively open country with just traces of brush or timber, the Alaskan snowshoe will suffice. **Middle:** In areas of heavy brush, use the Michigan snowshoe. **Right:** When you need to make frequent turns, such as on hills or mountains, your best bet is to strap on a pair of bearpaws.

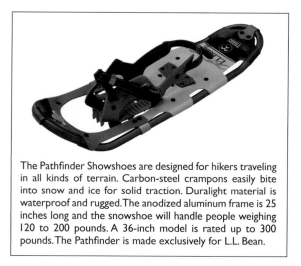

The Pathfinder Showshoes are designed for hikers traveling in all kinds of terrain. Carbon-steel crampons easily bite into snow and ice for solid traction. Duralight material is waterproof and rugged. The anodized aluminum frame is 25 inches long and the snowshoe will handle people weighing 120 to 200 pounds. A 36-inch model is rated up to 300 pounds. The Pathfinder is made exclusively for L.L. Bean.

webbing. The webbing must remain taut to perform properly, and freezing weather does the trick. Thus, keep snowshoes far from the campfire and warm cabins. Moisture can dangerously stretch the webbing. Using spar varnish or polyurethane, you can give your webbing a protective, waterproof coat. Additional wrappings of rawhide near the snowshoe's toe can add to its life. As crusted snow usually affects the toe area first, this precaution should prove useful. The size of the snowshoe depends on the weight of the snowshoer. The chart on the previous page will help you determine the correct size for your boot.

Between seasons, remove and replace all broken, weak, or frayed webbing. Clean the entire snowshoe rapidly with soap and water to prevent any unnecessary stretch. Dry the pair a minimum of 36 hours if some or all of the rawhide has been replaced.

In recent years, several new materials for snowshoe frames have come into use, as have two new kinds of webbing. In addition to fine-grain ash, frames are now made of aluminum, magnesium, or synthetics. Frames of metal or plastic are durable, won't warp, and require no maintenance. On the other hand, wood has more aesthetic appeal, won't usually crack in extreme cold, and doesn't readily cake with heavy snow.

Instead of naked or varnished rawhide webbing, leading snowshoe makers now offer rawhide coated with polyurethane, which has superior moisture resistance. Most modern of all is nylon-coated neoprene lacing, which is very strong, doesn't stretch or absorb water, doesn't attract gnawing animals, and needs no seasonal varnishing or any other maintenance. With use, however, it does become abraded and hairy looking, so a great many snowshoers prefer the tradition of rawhide combined with the protection of polyurethane.

As you may suspect, a device is needed to hold the snowshoe to your boot. The harness is a leather or leather-and-nylon strap arrangement that permits the toe to tilt downward and the heel to rise.

CAMP CLOTHING

■ Warm Weather

UNDERWEAR: The underclothing you wear at home or at work will suffice, although cotton boxer-type shorts, which cling less to your skin, are more comfortable than the jockey style. Two pairs of shorts and two T-shirts will last for a hike of less than a week, one set for wearing and one for washing. Drying in the sun ordinarily takes about two hours.

Though underwear can go for two days without a wash, the same does not go for your socks. A daily change and washing are necessary for health and comfort. Cotton wash-and-wear socks are recommended; wool may be too warm and scratchy. Light wool sweat socks with low boots are fine only in mountainous areas. In coastal regions that are flat and sandy, you may not need socks but simply sneakers. Prior to a day's hike, cut down on perspiration with a healthy sprinkle of foot powder or baby powder in your boots.

Waffle-weave underwear is intended for cooler temperatures, but the top part worn under a thin cotton shirt will keep you warm in an early morning chill.

OUTERWEAR: Khaki (cotton) pants are appropriately light and durable. Look for cuffless models that are an inch or so shorter than your regular pants, because cuffs tend to catch mud, water, stones, and twigs. Denim pants are also sturdy, but should be loose fitting for the active camper.

Allow extra room between your crotch and the top of your trousers for bending and taking lengthy steps. Roomy pockets are important, but don't overfill them. Make sure the seams have been reinforced for longer wear.

Shorts are acceptable in hot areas, but they don't guard against underbrush and sunburn. A short-sleeved cotton shirt during the day is fine, but be careful of too much sun on your forearms. At night, when mosquitoes and other insects appear, you will need a long-sleeved cotton shirt. Shirttails that fall well below the waist are advisable. Have a sweater or sweatshirt on hand for the evenings.

As mentioned in the Camp Bedding section, waterfowl down is the prime insulating material, but synthetics, such as Thinsulate, are acceptable and less expensive. A lightweight, quilted, insulated jacket that uses a good synthetic will keep the early morning fisherman comfortably warm and dry all summer.

HEADGEAR: A cotton baseball cap screens your head from the sun. Though the bill in the front shields your face from rain, you may need the additional protection of a light nylon, hooded jacket to cover your neck in a downpour.

■ Cool Weather

UNDERWEAR: On cool days, when the temperature hovers around 40°F, leave on the warm-weather shorts and T-shirt, but add a one- or two-piece suit of cotton underwear with full sleeves and legs. Thermal-weave or waffle-weave underwear supplies greater warmth and more ventilation than the flat design. The weaving pattern consists of protrusions and hollow pockets close to the skin that trap body heat.

Two-layer underwear—often labeled Duofold—is another reliable insulated model. The smooth cotton layer facing the skin absorbs perspiration and passes it through the insulating air space to the outer layer of cotton, nylon, and wool. Moisture evaporates from the outer layer.

Wool socks are unparalleled for warmth. Make sure they extend a couple of inches over your boot tops. To prevent blisters on your feet, wear a thin pair of cotton socks underneath. The combination keeps your feet comfortable and free of moisture.

OUTERWEAR: A good choice for cool weather are the heavy-duty work khakis simply called "work clothes" by most stores. As with summer outdoor pants, cuffless styles are best. Wear the inseam a few inches shorter than usual and look for reinforced seams. The cut of the pants should be full rather than ivy-league trim to facilitate climbing, bending, and the like. An extra inch between the crotch and belt is also helpful.

If you prefer wool pants, get a lightweight pair. Twill fabric, which frequently consists of 65 percent Dacron polyester and 35 percent cotton, is a sturdy and less expensive alternative.

Loose-fitting trousers are important. A size larger at the waist may not be flattering, but with a heavy shirt, thicker undergarments, and a sweater to tuck in, it is a wise idea. A belt or suspenders are fine, and deep pockets on the trousers are also convenient.

Fall is a good time for lightweight wool or flannel shirts. These too should allow freedom of movement. Wool is warmer, and with a waffle-weave turtleneck worn underneath, you're ready for real cold. The shirttail should extend several inches below the waist so it doesn't slip out while you're moving. The buttons should be big so they are easy to handle with cold fingers.

A quilted, insulated jacket ensures warmth if the insulating agent is down or a good-quality synthetic. The quilting prevents the insulation from bunching up. Excess moisture is absorbed and expelled through the insulation and fabric. Slip the jacket on whenever a shirt alone won't be enough. The jacket should have pockets and a strong, trustworthy zipper.

Down jackets are matchless for warmth and insulation, but prices are high. In cool weather, synthetics such as Thinsulate, Polarguard, and Thermoloft are quite adequate. When available, choose garments with Gore's Windstopper fabric, which stops cold wind from penetrating, yet remains breathable.

HEADGEAR: A billed cap of wool, cotton, or leather is the first choice. The beret and the tam-o-shanter are underrated as hats in the United States, but either one supplies a large amount of heat to your head and body. Both styles can be pulled down to protect your ears, and each is compact, inexpensive, and long lasting.

A watch cap—the type worn by merchant seamen—or a ski hat is acceptable. If it isn't too cool, they can be worn with the cuff doubled up, and in harsh cold, both can be pulled down to cover the neck, ears, and forehead.

■ Cold Weather

When temperatures drop to zero degrees and below, your life may depend on the clothing you wear.

UNDERWEAR: The T-shirt and boxer shorts you wore in summer and fall should be the first clothes you put on. Follow with a full set of waffle-weave, quilted, or polypropylene underwear. The waffle-weave design traps body heat and permits moisture to escape at the neck, a more rapid exit point than the underwear itself. The quilted underwear gives warmth by stopping the circulation of air inside your clothing. Polypropylene is a synthetic fiber with the softness of cotton and the wicking ability to pull moisture away from the body for evaporation.

A properly fitted sock is snug enough not to bunch around the toe or heel, but is not so tight it causes discomfort.

Top-grade wool socks provide superior warmth and durability through many hard months and washings. Avoid colored wool, which may cause an allergic reaction, infect a blister, or discolor other clothing you may have thrown in your laundry pail.

Wool socks reinforced with a strong synthetic such as Dacron or nylon last longer and are less expensive in the long run, but lose some advantage in ventilation, softness, and warmth. Socks made totally of nylon, Dacron, Orlon, or another synthetic are also not on par with wool when it comes to softness and getting rid of moisture. Cotton socks are comfortable only until they're soaked with water or perspiration.

The wisest choice, however, is a pair of good-quality, wool socks worn over a pair of cotton socks. Whatever the height of your boots, select socks that are 3 inches higher. Lap the extra material over the boot.

OUTERWEAR: Cuffless wool pants and a lightweight wool shirt—with large buttons for ease of handling—furnish ample warmth when worn over the proper underwear. The advantage of wool to the camper who also hunts is that it is noiseless. Wool also does a fine job of shedding and repelling water. Similar fabrics include Polartec and fleece.

Take along a quilted jacket insulated with down or one of the better synthetics. The camper who feels too restricted in a quilted jacket might choose a less cumbersome vest insulated with down or a good synthetic. A vest with a good zipper front, a button-down collar, and a flap pocket on either side is a treasure; more so

when it is low enough in the rear to cover the kidneys. In extreme cold, the topmost outer garment can also be an oversize wool hunting shirt or jacket.

Heavy wool or leather gloves worn over a pair of cotton work gloves protect the hands. Although mittens may keep you somewhat warmer, they inhibit your ability to grasp utensils and the like, so gloves are a better choice.

HEADGEAR: A wool cap with earflaps along with a wool or cotton scarf is suitable. In a windy area, this combo is perfect. Place the scarf around the neck or over your head under the cap. Hoods tend to restrict head movement and muffle sounds coming from the sides and back, but a scarf can be quickly loosened when necessary.

The watch cap and ski hat tend to hamper peripheral vision. They are acceptable substitutes for the wool cap, however, because they pull down completely to protect almost everything from the top of the head to the neck, revealing only the eyes, nose, and mouth.

■ Raingear

There are two styles of raingear: the rainsuit and the poncho. The rainsuit is a waterproof jacket and pants combo, while the poncho is a square of waterproof fabric with a hole for the head. The poncho does little to restrict the arms, but flares enough to protect the legs—when you are standing—and let in cooling air.

For sitting in a boat most of the day, take a rainsuit. It keeps your entire body dry whether you are standing or sitting. It should have drawstring pants and a hooded zipper jacket with elastic or snap-fastener wrists. These features will also keep out wind.

Though somewhat expensive, Nylon shell fabric with waterproof Gore-Tex is a good buy in rainsuits. It's durable, waterproof, lightweight, and doesn't stiffen as much in cold weather as the popular and less expensive rubberized cotton suits. The inexpensive vinyl or plastic suits are worthless because they rip. Easily split seams, snagged material, and stiffness in cold weather are further drawbacks.

The backpacker, however, may find the poncho preferable to the rainsuit because of its lighter weight. A poncho with a rear flap will protect the pack as well. Don't buy a cheap poncho. A good one slips on easily and doubles as a ground tarp, makeshift lean-to, or tent. Most serious outdoors enthusiasts own both a rainsuit and poncho.

No discussion of raingear would be complete without a special look at Gore-Tex, a form-fitting stretch material that keeps the wearer from getting wet. What is Gore-Tex? The key to the unique, waterproof, windproof, breathable performance characteristics of Gore-Tex fabric lies in the patented microporous membrane that is laminated to outer shell fabrics. The Gore-Tex membrane is composed of 100 percent expanded polytetrafluoroethylene. This is the same resin that composes DuPont's Teflon. The Gore-Tex membrane contains 9 billion pores per square inch, each 20,000 times smaller than a water drop, but 700 times larger than a water vapor molecule. The membrane, therefore, effectively blocks wind and wet weather but lets perspiration vapor pass through.

In two-layer Gore-Tex fabric, the Gore-Tex membrane is laminated to one side of an outer shell fabric. In three-layer Gore-Tex fabric (for heavier uses), the membrane is sandwiched between a shell fabric and a tricot knit fabric. Because the Gore-Tex membrane is permanently bonded to fabrics, it does not peel off or degrade after washing like most "waterproof" coatings or treatments. It is also not subject to contamination by body oils.

Today, outdoors enthusiasts will find Gore-Tex fabric in everything from rainwear, cycling gear, and dress outerwear to accessories such as waterproof boots, gloves, socks, and hats.

CAMP LIGHTING

■ Gasoline Lanterns

For all-around use, the gasoline lantern is the most practical camp light. The fuel employed is white or unleaded gasoline (readily available throughout the United States) or kerosene, and it is fed from a pressure tank to relatively fragile mantles made of ash. A vapor given off by the gasoline collects in one or two mantles and is ignited with a match. Should the lantern flare at this point, check for a generator leak. A wise move is to bring along a spare generator—they also tend to clog—and one or two extra mantles. They do add weight to the total unit, but you'll be in the dark without them should something go wrong.

Pumping a built-in tank device before lighting and at intervals during the burning should inspire adequate candlepower. If the pressure drops and the light seems to dim or pulsate at times, bring the pump into play to correct the pressure.

The typical gasoline lantern is constructed of stainless steel and brass with a porcelain reflector (also called a deflector) to provide ventilation and help direct the light in a wide circle or in one particular spot. A globe of clear Pyrex glass encircling the lit mantles is durable enough to withstand heat. The capacity of the fuel tank is normally 2 pints, enough for 10 to 12 hours of intense light. Before bedtime, turn off the fuel valve. The minute amount of vapor remaining in the mantles will give you enough light to get into your sleeping bag. The gasoline lantern is unaffected by wind, rain, and cold. It is a valuable piece of camp equipment, but its weight—often close to 10 pounds when you add in fuel—rules it out for the backpacker.

■ Propane Lanterns

If your camping is usually confined to summer weekends, the propane-gas lantern is for you. There is no generator to clog and replace or liquid fuel to spill and perhaps taint your food. Working off lightweight propane gas that is sold in a 16.4-ounce (usually disposable) cylinder, this lantern can give you anything from a soft glow to a bright beam. Large-capacity propane tanks are also sold.

As with gasoline lanterns, one or more mantles are used to catch the gas vapors, but no pumping and

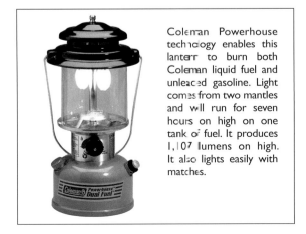

Coleman Powerhouse technology enables this lantern to burn both Coleman liquid fuel and unleaded gasoline. Light comes from two mantles and will run for seven hours on high on one tank of fuel. It produces 1,107 lumens on high. It also lights easily with matches.

priming are required. Porcelain reflectors are also featured to place the light where you want it. One propane cylinder can last from eight to 12 hours, depending on how intense a light you require.

Since you never know how much gas remains in the cylinder, it is a necessity to take along a pair of cylinders, as well as extra mantles.

Weight is a problem with propane lanterns and backpackers should avoid them. But if you are traveling by automobile, propane lanterns are suitable, provided the weather isn't too cold. Otherwise, the pressure in the tank drops and you're lucky if you even get a dim glow.

■ Battery-Powered Lights

Flashlights are available in all stores stocking camp gear, but get the right kind. There are three- and four-cell models that throw a lot of light, but a two-cell flashlight is adequate, especially if it's a super-bright, long-lasting LED flashlight. Also, anything larger than two cells means surplus weight. Choose a model with an angled

Coleman technology has produced the Coleman CPX 6 Classic LED Lantern, which will put out 200 lumens for up to 25 hours. It will run on four D batteries or an optional CPX 6 rechargeable power cartridge. It will hang in any position, including sideways. It is a good choice when safety is a factor.

head so that it can be hung on your belt or stood on end, leaving both hands free.

Besides being durable and water resistant, the flashlight should have a shiny or bright finish—perhaps with a luminous stripe painted on it—so it can be located easily. A hang-up ring is also helpful, and a slightly recessed glass lens is close to shatterproof because of the protective lip. Some of the new LED flashlights are ultrabright, with bulbs that last up to 100,000 hours, and some never need replacing. LED lights are brighter, with more than 500 lumens of bright beam.

Dry-cell batteries aren't too efficient when the weather turns cold; they'll throw a rather dim light. Your best bet is to warm them in your hands or place them under your sleeping bag at night.

When carrying your flashlight in your pack, tape the switch in the off position or reverse one of the batteries in the tube. This will prevent you from accidentally turning on the flashlight. Also, keep in mind that batteries last longer when they are burned for only short periods of time.

If you prefer a battery-powered lantern to a flashlight, you can get up to 50 hours of intense light if the weather is mild. These lanterns work on 6-volt batteries and generally weigh about 5 pounds. If weight is not important, get the widebeam rather than the searchlight model.

■ Candles

Primitive is the word for the candle as a light source, but it's 100 percent reliable and multipurpose. It can be used

Camp Heaters

Called catalytic heaters because they use a catalyst—usually platinum—that burns the fuel (gasoline, propane, etc.), these heaters do not produce any flame, odor, or carbon monoxide. The catalytic heater provides an effective heat that can be regulated according to your needs. The heat output is measured in BTUs—British Thermal Units. Because of its safety, the catalytic heater is well ahead of other types on the market.

The Mr. Heater Base Camp Buddy puts out 3,800 BTUs and will heat up to 100 square feet. The unit runs on a 16.4-ounce propane cylinder and has a safety shut-off. It is certified for indoor and outdoor use, and it is especially effective for campsites.

to boil a pot of water, start a fire, or mend a leaky spot in your tent.

No matter what kind of camper you are—backpacker through RVer—a few handy candles are a worthwhile investment. It must be stressed that the proper kind is the stearic-acid plumber's candle, made of animal fat. Paraffin candles that you may have at home for decorative purposes or for maneuvering when a fuse blows are useless in camp. Paraffin will melt in a warm pack.

Never leave your tent unattended with a burning candle inside, even if it is in a candle lantern—as it should be.

And a final note of caution on the use of candles: Some modern waterproofing mixtures have proven to be flammable. If you are a backpacker and recently have waterproofed your small tent with a commercial product, carefully check the ingredients. Should any one of them be flammable, do **not** use a candle in your tent.

CAMP TOOLS

■ Hatchets

Way back when trees were plentiful, many campers wielded a full-length ax, relegating the smaller hatchet to novice woodchoppers. Nowadays, when wood is an all-too-precious resource, the hatchet has become the most common woodcutting tool at the campsite.

Invest extra money in a premium-quality hatchet. The one-piece styles are the best, with all-steel construction from the head to the bottom of the handle. A cheap hatchet, which may have loose headwork, might injure a nearby camper or shatter after several sessions of chopping. As perspiration can make a handle slippery, get a hatchet with a handle of rubber, wood, or leather lamination, which will provide a secure grip.

Should you prefer a hatchet with a wood handle, make sure the handle is chemically bonded to the head. This process ensures that it will rarely, if ever, come loose. Some choppers prefer wood handles because there isn't as much cushioning in them. Though the resultant shocks may be uncomfortable, they signify that you are chopping ineffectively. When the shocks cease, you will know you are handling your hatchet correctly.

Some hatchets feature neither the one-piece construction nor the bonded head. These models frequently use a wedge to secure the head to the handle. As this is far from safe, check this type of hatchet frequently during chopping.

Hatchets—also known as belt axes—come in a number of sizes and weights. The right choice obviously depends on your own needs. For all-around use, however, a hatchet with a 1-pound head and handle about a foot long is an excellent choice. Slightly larger ones are preferred by some campers, and manufacturers have recently offered much smaller ones as well. The light,

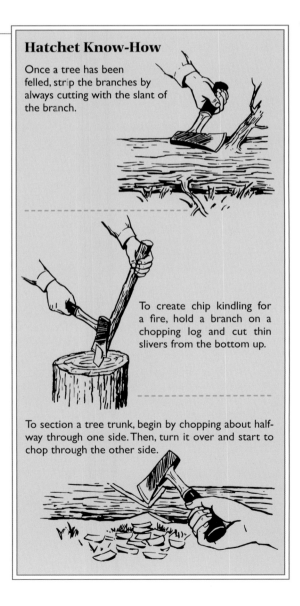

Hatchet Know-How

Once a tree has been felled, strip the branches by always cutting with the slant of the branch.

To create chip kindling for a fire, hold a branch on a chopping log and cut thin slivers from the bottom up.

To section a tree trunk, begin by chopping about half-way through one side. Then, turn it over and start to chop through the other side.

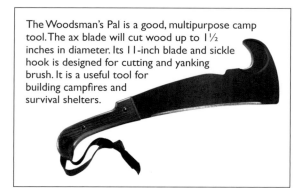

The Woodsman's Pal is a good, multipurpose camp tool. The ax blade will cut wood up to 1½ inches in diameter. Its 11-inch blade and sickle hook is designed for cutting and yanking brush. It is a useful tool for building campfires and survival shelters.

very short-handled models, sometimes called backpacker's axes or hunter's axes, are fine for chopping kindling or the wood for a small campfire, and they can also be used to fashion wooden tent stakes (but then, so can a knife). They're useless for heavier work, though adequate for their intended purpose.

Despite its smaller size when compared to the ax, the hatchet is an important tool that needs special care. Never throw a hatchet. Besides ruining the bit and other important parts, you may injure someone. Only use a hatchet to hammer metal stakes or nails if it is a half-hatchet, which features a regular hatchet blade at one end of the head and a tempered hammer head on the other end. A conventional hatchet used for such purposes soon becomes worthless.

A durable leather sheath with a sturdy leather buffer strip or rivets facing the cutting edge should be used to carry the hatchet. If you don't have a sheath handy, drive the blade into a stump or log so it is not dangerously exposed. (Avoid the double-bitted hatchet on the market featuring blades at both ends of the head. It is dangerous except in the hands of a skilled chopper.)

To cut a piece of wood, use the contact method. Place the edge of the hatchet on the stick. Lift the two and then bring them down together hard on the chopping block. To split the wood, place the hatchet edge in a crack. Again, lift the two and bring the hatchet and stick down hard on the log or stump. Once contact has been made, slightly twist the hatchet hand to separate the pieces.

On a cold day, heat the hatchet slightly before putting it to work so it won't become brittle and crack.

To pass a hatchet to another person, hold it vertically, head down, with the blade facing away from the two of you. Give the receiver more than enough room to grasp the top of the hatchet handle. When you are carrying it in camp, hold the hatchet firmly by its head, keeping the cutting edge away from you.

If not inside your pack while hiking, the hatchet should be strapped to the outside and sheathed. When the hike is a short one, sheath the hatchet and carry it on your belt on your right hip. Never strap it near the groin or kidney area. Another useful tool in camp is the Woodman's Pal, a unique combination tool with an 11-inch carbon-steel blade that will cut branches up to 1½ inches with a single stroke.

■ Axes

Some chopping chores call for an ax. A camping trip, in this case, is usually for a week or more, and the work might include felling a tree or cutting firewood.

Among the many types of axes available, there are four common ones—the Hudson Bay single-bit, the Michigan single-bit, the Kentucky single-bit, and the Michigan double-bit.

Experienced choppers agree that a head that provides maximum steel-to-wood contact is best. This means the squarish Michigan-style head is preferred to the Hudson Bay or tomahawk-type head, which has little steel-to-wood contact in proportion to the size of the bit. The tomahawk head has a lot of eye appeal and was popular with French Canadian trappers when weight was a big factor, but it's a poor design when compared to a Michigan head.

If you're selecting an ax for a permanent camp, your best bet is a full-size cabin ax, which usually has a 36-inch handle and a 3½- to 4-pound head. Stick with the Michigan head, which is the best design for nearly all situations. Avoid double-bit axes unless you're an experienced woodcutter. The dangers of using a double-bit ax far outweigh the advantages.

Fancy burl may be desirable in a shotgun stock, but not in an ax handle. You can, however, learn how to pick the best handle in your sports shop. Nearly all wood ax handles, incidentally, are made from hickory. First, eliminate handles with obvious flaws, such as knots in the wood. Next, narrow your selection down to handles that have straight grains running the entire length. Then, look at the cross-sectioned area of the handle butt. Make a quick count of the number of grains running across the butt and apply this rule: the fewer the grains, the stronger the handle. And grain should run roughly parallel to the long axis of the oval cross section. Avoid axes with painted wood handles. There's no telling how many flaws lie hidden under a coat of paint.

Handles are varnished for two reasons: eye appeal or protection from moisture during shipping and storage. Bare wood, however, affords a better grip. Your ax will be more comfortable to use if you remove the varnish from the handle.

Apply bright-yellow, red, or bright-blue paint to the ax head once you buy it. The paint will help you locate the ax in weeds or brush if it is lost. The paint also assists in bonding the handle and head together. Last, if the paint cracks over the eye, it is a clear danger signal that the handle is loosening inside and may come off at any time.

The handle of an ax, no matter what the size, should be made of seasoned hardwood with a grain that is both fine and straight. The handle itself should also be straight. Check to see that the "hang" of the ax is proper. Hang is determined by holding the ax in front of you and sighting down as if it were a rifle. If the center of the handle is in line with the cutting edge of the blade, the hang is correct.

Inspect the point where the handle fits the eye of the steel head, unless you have a one-piece model. If even the slightest gap shows there, look for another ax. An imperfect fit means the handle may work loose soon after continued chopping or pounding.

Several manufacturers use a chemical bond to anchor the ax handle to the head. This holds more

Ax Care and Safety Tips

Here are some final bits of advice to remember when using an ax:

1 • Always wear gloves when using and sharpening your ax.

2 • Never carry an ax over your shoulder. Hold it close to the ax head, blade pointed downward and at your side. If you trip, hold it or throw it away from you.

3 • Between cutting sessions, bury the blade of your ax in a log or lay it under a log so that no one can blunder into the blade.

4 • Use a wood chopping block. Never cut on rock and other hard surfaces.

5 • Never use the butt end of the ax head to drive anything heavier than a tent peg. Using it as a wedge or to drive wedges will weaken and perhaps crack the eye.

6 • A split handle is best removed by sawing it off below the head and driving the rest of it out of the top with a steel bar. You can also burn it out if you bury the blade in wet earth to protect the heat-tempered edge.

7 • Logs will split more easily if you aim for the cracks in the top of the log you're about to split. They indicate weak sections. Avoid the knots; split around them.

Types of Axes

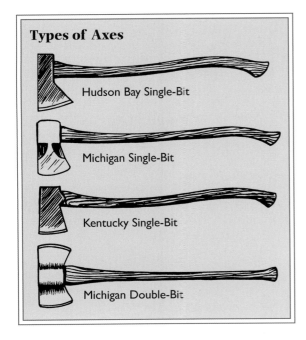

Hudson Bay Single-Bit

Michigan Single-Bit

Kentucky Single-Bit

Michigan Double-Bit

securely than the wedges—either wood or steel—that conveniently attach the two parts. Wedges, however, are efficient.

If you want to avoid wood handles, pick one of the all-steel one-piece axes. With some cheap models, you'll experience a shock to the hands when chopping, but one manufacturer solved the problem with a nylon-vinyl grip.

There are a few important safety factors to keep in mind when you chop wood. First, check your ax for a loose head or a damaged handle. If the head continually comes loose, replace the handle. If you're on a trip, you can temporarily solve the problem by soaking the head in a bucket of water. The wood will swell and tighten against the head.

Before you start cutting, hold your ax at arm's length and turn a complete circle. Then, move the ax

How to Sharpen a Double-Bit Ax

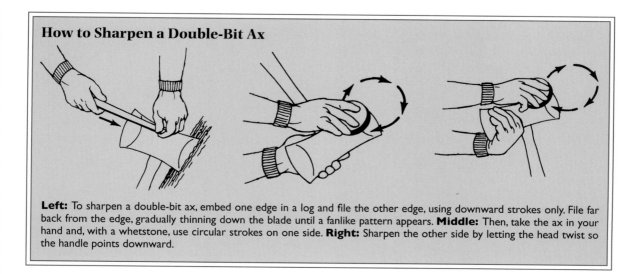

Left: To sharpen a double-bit ax, embed one edge in a log and file the other edge, using downward strokes only. File far back from the edge, gradually thinning down the blade until a fanlike pattern appears. **Middle:** Then, take the ax in your hand and, with a whetstone, use circular strokes on one side. **Right:** Sharpen the other side by letting the head twist so the handle points downward.

slowly overhead in an arc. Clear away any limbs or brush that will be in your way and could deflect your ax during a swing. Also, no one should be within 30 feet of the person with the ax. Check the cutting edge. A dull ax is a dangerous tool. A sharp ax will dig into wood, but a dull blade can bounce off and strike your leg.

Sharpening an ax is a two-stage job. You'll need a file, such as a Nicholson Black Diamond, and a round whetstone. (If there's any paint on the metal where you'll be filing, first remove it with sandpaper. Otherwise, the paint will clog the file and the whetstone.)

Anchor the ax blade securely. If you're in the field, where there is no vise, drive a wood peg into the ground and brace the single-bit head against it. A double-bit can be driven into a log to hold it in position. When sharpening, wear gloves to protect your hands.

Start with the file, pushing it from toe to heel (top to bottom) of the blade, about 1 inch back from the edge. The purpose of this step is to cut some of the metal away from the blade so that the taper is uniform. Nearly all new axes have a blade that is too thick. When a good taper is achieved, a fine edge can be easily put on the bit with a round whetstone.

Don't tackle the entire job with only a whetstone. A whetstone is fine for honing a knife, but it is not designed to cut enough metal from an ax head. The whetstone is only used for honing the bit after the blade has been taken down with a file. Don't use the file directly on the cutting edge; that's a job for the whetstone.

Perhaps the most common woodcutting job for the average camper is trimming limbs off downed trees and then chopping the limbs into firewood. Trimming limbs is safe and easy if you follow this advice.

First, always trim toward the top of the tree, which will point the limbs away from your body. Keep the trunk between you and the limbs you're trimming. For example, stand on one side of the log and trim the far side first, then change position. There's almost no chance of hitting your legs if there's a tree trunk between you and the blade.

If this is not possible and you have to stand on the same side as the ax, stand slightly forward of the limb you're trimming and swing the ax so that the blade strikes the limb behind your legs.

To cut a limb into campfire lengths, hold it firmly against a stump or log and chop it away from you at

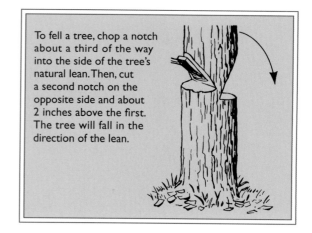

To fell a tree, chop a notch about a third of the way into the side of the tree's natural lean. Then, cut a second notch on the opposite side and about 2 inches above the first. The tree will fall in the direction of the lean.

Camp Saws

Basic camp tools should include a hand saw. These handy camp saws are available at any well-equipped outdoors stores. These saws will handle most jobs, from gathering firewood to building a tree stand to quartering an elk.

about a 45-degree angle. Using a three-quarter-length ax, you should have no trouble cutting limbs up to 1 inch in diameter with a single blow.

■ Camp Saws

To cut wood neatly into particular sizes, the saw is the proper tool. An ax or a hatchet wastes a lot of wood, can't be too exact, and stands the chance of causing injury with flying chips or the blades themselves. Saws are precise, much faster than either ax or hatchet, and a camper can get the knack of using them with just a couple of minutes of instruction.

Lighter saws are suitable for camping, as the heavier models are impractical to carry along. There are three saws used by backpackers and other campers who must limit the bulk and weight of their packs: the bow saw, the folding saw, and the cable saw.

The collapsible bow-type saw, also known as the Swede saw, features a thin, narrow blade of flexible steel. This blade is held taut by a tubelike, jointed metal frame, which can be taken apart and slipped into a case up to 1½ feet long. Several models are designed to carry spare blades.

A blade from 20 to 24 inches in length handles wood from 8 to 10 inches in thickness. Larger-diameter logs, however, require the use of a 30- or 36-inch blade.

Bow-saw frames come in U shapes and L shapes, but the former is recommended. The L-shaped models, though more compact, diminish the amount of blade that may be applied on the wood.

The folding saw is even more compact than most bow saws and will still do the same job. The safest camp saws will either fold or have a case, protecting the camper from exposed teeth. The cable saw is the most compact of all, but it requires two hands and is sometimes difficult to use.

■ Knives

Selecting a quality knife, never an easy task, is no longer quite so difficult. Even though a growing emphasis on knives in recent years has resulted in many fine models on the market, you can narrow down the selection by following a few simple rules.

First, there is no need for a knife with a blade longer than 5 inches. I've found that a straight blade or a slight drop-point design works best for most field chores. Remember that knives frequently are used more for camp jobs than for dressing and skinning game.

Second, on a sheath knife, check the tang (the blade extension around which the handle is attached) and make sure it extends well up into or through the handle. This is the strongest design.

Grip the knife in your hand. Does the handle extend ¼ inch or so beyond each side of your hand? If so, it fits your hand properly. If not, it doesn't fit properly and will probably be uncomfortable to use for extended periods.

Selection of blade steel is another consideration. Stainless steel is very hard and will not sharpen easily with just a few quick strokes, but it is easy to maintain because it won't rust. Carbon steel, on the other hand, is easier to sharpen and will take an edge faster, but it generally requires more care than stainless does.

The choice of sheath-type or folding knife is pretty much a matter of personal preference. Many sportsmen prefer a folding knife. The reason is simple. A Buck Folding Hunter, for example, has a 3¾-inch blade, but it's still only 4⅞ inches long when carried folded on a belt or in a pocket. For big jobs at camp or home, though, most sportsmen like a sheath knife, also with a 4- or 5-inch blade.

What about sharpening a knife? A dull knife is both annoying and dangerous, especially in the woods where you may be rushing a chore. It's a good idea to carry a sharpening steel and a pocket-size whetstone to touch up the blade when it begins to dull. Many steels have two sharpening surfaces: a grooved side to put a uniform cutting edge on the blade and a smooth surface

for final honing. These steels are not designed to take an appreciable amount of metal from the edge, so on knives that are quite dull, a stone must be used. For this job, you should carry a double-sided whetstone to get the edge back on your knife if it's badly dulled on bone or wood. Use a whetstone with a coarse 100 grit on one side and a medium-fine 240 grit on the other. Usually about 10 strokes per side on the medium-fine grit and 10 on the steel will sharpen a knife well enough for most jobs.

A dirty stone will make sharpening a tough job. If a stone is glazed smooth with dirt, wash and scrub it with kerosene or a detergent, then let it dry out thoroughly. Whetstones should never be used dry, however. If you're using the stone in the field, wet it with snow, spit on it, or even put carcass fat on it. The idea is to float steel filings above the surface of the stone so that the stone's pores are not clogged. Some manufacturers produce stones that are already oil filled, but for stones that do not have

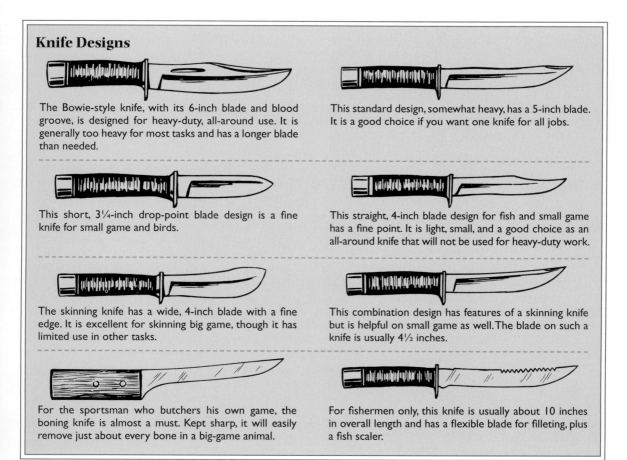

Knife Designs

The Bowie-style knife, with its 6-inch blade and blood groove, is designed for heavy-duty, all-around use. It is generally too heavy for most tasks and has a longer blade than needed.

This standard design, somewhat heavy, has a 5-inch blade. It is a good choice if you want one knife for all jobs.

This short, 3¼-inch drop-point blade design is a fine knife for small game and birds.

This straight, 4-inch blade design for fish and small game has a fine point. It is light, small, and a good choice as an all-around knife that will not be used for heavy-duty work.

The skinning knife has a wide, 4-inch blade with a fine edge. It is excellent for skinning big game, though it has limited use in other tasks.

This combination design has features of a skinning knife but is helpful on small game as well. The blade on such a knife is usually 4½ inches.

For the sportsman who butchers his own game, the boning knife is almost a must. Kept sharp, it will easily remove just about every bone in a big-game animal.

For fishermen only, this knife is usually about 10 inches in overall length and has a flexible blade for filleting, plus a fish scaler.

Typical Knives

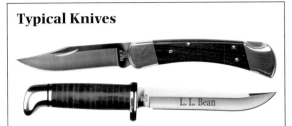

The Buck Folding Hunter and Pathfinder knives are traditional and successful designs that continue to handle nearly all chores for generations of campers and sportsmen. The Buck knife has a 4-inch stainless-steel clip blade. The Pathfinder has a leather handle and a 5-inch blade.

A tough, high-tech, multi-purpose knife is the Gerber Bear Grylls, which will do double duty as a camp tool and a survival knife. It's available with a serrated blade or a fine edge. The high-carbon steel blade measures 4.8 inches. The survival model comes with an emergency whistle, diamond sharpener, fire starter, and nylon sheath.

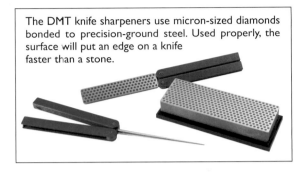

The DMT knife sharpeners use micron-sized diamonds bonded to precision-ground steel. Used properly, the surface will put an edge on a knife faster than a stone.

this feature, it's important to use a generous amount of honing oil and to bear down hard as you move the edge of the blade across the stone. The oil, in addition to floating the steel filings, allows the blade to move smoothly. Your stone will stay cleaner longer if you wash your knife completely before you sharpen it.

Keep in mind that any field sharpening steels or small whetstones are designed to put a quick edge on a knife. They will get you out of a tight spot, but don't expect them to put a lasting edge on your knife. For that final edge, you'll have to use better, mounted stones such as a Washita for sharpening and perhaps a Hard Arkansas for final honing.

Folding Knife Blade Designs

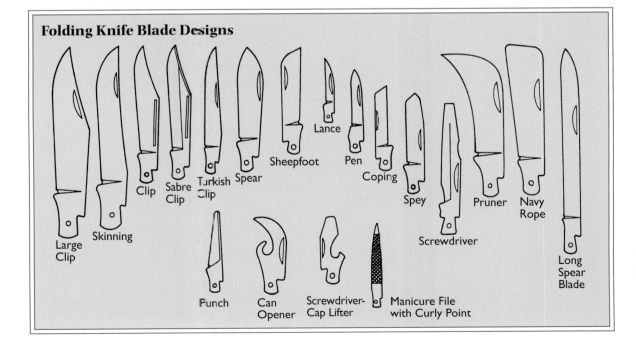

Large Clip, Skinning, Clip, Sabre Clip, Turkish Clip, Spear, Sheepfoot, Lance, Pen, Coping, Spey, Screwdriver, Pruner, Navy Rope, Long Spear Blade, Punch, Can Opener, Screwdriver-Cap Lifter, Manicure File with Curly Point

The accompanying sidebar shows how to sharpen a knife correctly. Once you have cleaned both the knife and the stone, oil the stone generously and spread the oil over the entire surface of it. A hard, steady pressure will be necessary as you begin to draw the edge of the knife across the stone, starting at the heel of the blade and ending each stroke by lifting the handle to sharpen the point. Alternate sides of the blade until you have made 10 to 15 strokes on each side. A fine, hard honing stone will give a keen edge if you draw the knife as if you were taking a thin slice off the top of the stone. A key factor in putting a good edge on any knife is maintaining

a constant angle, usually 15 degrees, between the back of the blade and the stone. You can keep the angle constant for 30 or 40 strokes and then ruin all this work by changing the angle for the last six strokes. If this is your problem, pick up a device that will maintain this critical angle. Most devices are nothing more than a combination clamp and guide bar. Fit this onto your blade, hold the guide bar flat against the stone, and you can be sure of a constant angle.

The last step is stropping the knife against a piece of leather or cardboard. This is the only step in which you draw the edge backward with each stroke, instead

How to Sharpen a Knife

Step 1 • A good stone will last a lifetime with some care. Never use it dry. Oil the stone generously, spreading the oil over the entire surface of the stone. After the job is done, apply more oil and wipe the stone clean. Oil floats steel particles above the stone, so that they do not clog it.

Step 2 • Grip the knife as shown, maintaining an angle of 15 degrees between the back of the blade and the stone. Applying hard, steady pressure, draw the knife across the stone, beginning at the knife heel. Draw the knife across the stone as if you were taking a slice off the top of the stone.

Step 3 • As you come to the edge of the stone, lift the handle and sharpen the point. Repeat these strokes 10 to 15 times on each side of the blade. Do not alternate strokes. Sharpen one side, then the other. A very dull knife may need more than 15 strokes.

Step 4 • You can check the sharpness by drawing the blade across your fingernail. A well-sharpened blade will bite in and not slide across your fingernail.

Camp Shelf

If you are a camper or backpacker who prefers to travel light, you should learn how to make camp life easier. One way is to use small tree limbs to make simple furniture. If you need a table, shelf, or washbasin stand, you can make one easily by learning how to lash limbs together. Start by lashing two limbs on both sides of the tree. Next, following the numbered sequence, weave and lash the limbs together. Any rope will do, but nylon parachute cord works best. You are not building a raft, so the limbs do not have to be absolutely rigid or close together. Spacing can vary, depending on what will be placed on the shelf. Leverage, much like that of a climbing tree stand, will hold your shelf in place. A good working height for a shelf is 34 inches from the ground, and it should extend out about 15 inches from the tree.

34 in.

Fishing Pliers

For many years, the only tool on a fisherman's belt was a small pair of pliers with spring-loaded handles and a wire cutter on the side of the jaws. To make mine slip-proof, I put pieces of surgical tubing over the handles. The pliers measured only 4½ inches long, probably too short when dislodging big hooks from big fish with sharp teeth. I used mine mostly to pull knots tight, cut monofilament and wire, and rig baits. These pliers worked fine for one or two seasons, but then the cutters got dull and the spring-loaded handles always had to be oiled regularly to keep them working freely.

A lot has happened over the years! Today, fishermen now have a choice of dozens of fishing tools to hang on their belts, ranging from pliers made from titanium and aircraft aluminum to plastic. The new multipurpose pliers will also do a variety of jobs. Most models will crimp, cut braid and wire, and are totally corrosion proof. And those long-nose models will keep your fingers safely away from sharp teeth and hooks.

The price tags on some of these pliers are a real enigma. They range from $12 to more than $300. Are the inexpensive models good? Can fishermen justify dropping hundreds of dollars on a pair of pliers? Are they worth the money? Is it easier to buy $12 pliers and throw them away at the end of the season? Those expensive titanium pliers may well outlive you. These are tough questions to answer. Let your fishing budget be your guide.

Offshore Angler 7½-inch aluminum pliers have double-coated carbon steel jaws and tungsten replaceable cutters that cut tough fishing lines, including braid.

of moving it forward as you did on the whetstone. Stropping lays down any roughness and "sets" the edge. You can check the sharpness by carefully pulling the edge toward you across your thumbnail. A well-sharpened knife will grab and stop. If it slips, it needs more strokes on the stone.

After getting a final edge on your knife, don't jam it back into its sheath unless you're going back in the field. Leather sheaths collect and hold moisture, which will rust a knife. The best way to store a knife is to oil it lightly, wrap it in waxed paper, and store it where no one will accidentally blunder against the edge or point.

BACKPACKS

Throughout this section on camping, there have been references to the backpacker, the camper who takes to the open air with all he needs on his back.

A typical rucksack, which sometimes comes with a small frame, can carry gear and food for a full day. When packing a rucksack, keep heavy gear next to your lower back to minimize sagging.

The combined weight of the pack and frame should be about 5 pounds. When backpacking in flat country or rolling terrain, keep the weight in your backpack high, so that the center of gravity is on or above your shoulders (see Pack A). When packing a load in rocky or steep country, load your pack low so that the center of gravity is at the middle of your back (see Pack B).

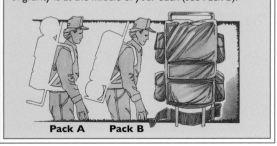

Pack A   Pack B

◀ L.L. Bean's Rucksack is typical of this Continental design. With a 2,000-cubic-inch capacity, the rucksack will hold enough gear for a full day of hiking and camping and possibly an overnight spike camp.

▶ The L.L. Bean Daypack will store all the gear you need for a day in the field. The fleece-lined pockets will protect optics and GPS units. The capacity of the pack is 1,500 cubic inches. It is a good choice for hikers and fishermen.

The backpacker is a keen weight watcher. He keeps in mind at all times that he should have with him the barest of essentials, and not one ounce more.

There are five basic pack designs. The type the individual camper needs depends upon the load he expects to carry as well as the distance he must carry it. The five designs are: daypack, rucksack, backpack and frame, packbasket, and hip or waist pack.

■ Daypack

The daypack, known to most campers as the knapsack, is pretty much what its name indicates—a pack that is useful on a daytime outing. It is little more than a rectangular canvas or nylon pack with shoulder straps that may or may not have side pockets, but never a metal frame.

When filling the daypack, place soft items—a poncho or a sweater—against the part of the pack that will press against your back. Also, don't load this pack too heavily, as the total weight of the full pack will pull down uncomfortably on your shoulders and against your back.

For pack material, nylon is recommended for the adult camper, as it is lightweight and waterproof. However, for youthful campers, who may carelessly toss their packs

▶ The RedHead Hybrid Pack is actually a two-in-one pack. The lower detachable section is a waist pack that can be used for hands-free hiking and hunting. When attached to the large compartment, the total pack has a capacity of 2,625 cubic inches. It is a good combination pack for all field activities.

◀ Cabela's Alaskan Outfitter Pack and Frame is a good choice for the serious camper and hiker who intends to spend several days in the field. The main compartment has a 5,300-cubic-inch capacity, and there are several outside pockets. The pack can be removed and the frame used to pack bulky gear, such as a small outboard motor. The pack and frame weigh about 12 pounds.

▶ The RedHead Enduroflex Field Frame can handle most heavy, bulky gear that can't be comfortably carried in a conventional pack. Small outboard motors, camp stoves, and even a tent can be lashed to this frame. A padded waist belt and suspended back allows air to flow between the frame and the carrier.

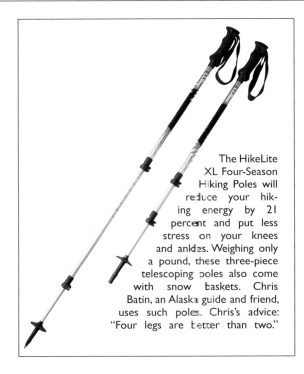

The HikeLite XL Four-Season Hiking Poles will reduce your hiking energy by 21 percent and put less stress on your knees and ankles. Weighing only a pound, these three-piece telescoping poles also come with snow baskets. Chris Batin, an Alaska guide and friend, uses such poles. Chris's advice: "Four legs are better than two."

around, a canvas daypack can take more punishment and is less expensive. Some daypacks have waist straps as well as shoulder straps to take some weight off the shoulders.

■ Rucksack

The rucksack seems to fall midway between the daypack and the larger packs for carrying big loads on long outings. The backpacker who uses the rucksack is usually out for a full day and must cook a couple of meals in the field.

Unlike the daypack, the rucksack features one or two outside pockets as well as an inside or outside metal frame. This frame prevents the pack from sagging, and puts less tension on the back. These features make it preferable to the daypack in numerous ways. Some rucksacks, however, do not have metal frames.

A sleeping bag is too bulky to put inside a rucksack, but it can be rolled short and lashed to the top or rolled long into a horseshoe shape and lashed to the top and sides. This pack is ill suited for backpacking canned goods, steel traps, and other hardware that can bite into your back. The rucksack should have web or leather shoulder straps that are a minimum of 2 inches wide and thick enough so as not to curl into narrow bands from a heavy pack. These bands can cut mercilessly into your shoulders.

Strong buckles, snaps, and rings of bronze, brass, or rustproof steel are essential. Beware of an overabundance of tricky snaps, zippers, and buckles. They add to the cost, and usually just bring trouble.

Although such synthetics as nylon and Dacron are being used widely for rucksacks, a good choice is heavy canvas. The extra weight will seem inconspicuous, considering the padding to your back that canvas provides. Incidentally, a canvas pack is also simpler to waterproof and keep waterproofed than one made of synthetic fibers.

■ External and Internal Framed Backpacks

For the serious backpacker whose trips last from one to two weeks, the backpack and frame is the best choice. In the 1980s, most backpacks of this type consisted of an external frame constructed of a light metal alloy and a backpack with both shoulder straps and back supports. The frame is attached to the backpack.

Of all the frames, those made of magnesium are the best. They are lightweight and sturdy, but they are expensive. A practical choice is a frame of an aluminum alloy. It will have shoulder and waist straps, and on some

▶ L.L. Bean's White Mountain Pack is a new design that is more streamlined and user-friendly. The shoulder straps are adjustable up to 3 inches. It is also available in a women's model with a custom sternum strap. It is made from double ripstop nylon.

◀ A new concept in backpacks is the L.L. Bean Day Trekker 25, which features a Boa-closure system that stabilizes the load with the turn of a knob. The pack is designed to carry a full day's load of gear for hikers and campers. The pack weighs only 2 pounds.

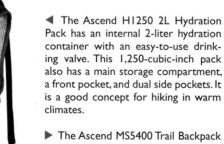

◀ The Ascend H1250 2L Hydration Pack has an internal 2-liter hydration container with an easy-to-use drinking valve. This 1,250-cubic-inch pack also has a main storage compartment, a front pocket, and dual side pockets. It is a good concept for hiking in warm climates.

▶ The Ascend MS5400 Trail Backpack is a big-capacity pack for large backpacking loads. This model has a capacity of 5,400 cubic inches and measures 32 by 14 by 10½ inches. It has a built-in load adjustment and support system. It is a good choice for long weekend camping trips.

Leave No Trace Seven Principles

The seven principles of Leave No Trace might seem unimportant until you consider the combined effects of millions of outdoor visitors. One poorly located campsite or campfire may have little significance, but thousands of such instances seriously degrade the outdoor experience for all. Leaving no trace is everyone's responsibility.

1. Plan Ahead and Prepare

- Know the regulations and special concerns for the area you'll visit.
- Prepare for extreme weather, hazards, and emergencies.
- Schedule your trip to avoid times of high use.
- Visit in small groups when possible. Consider splitting larger groups into smaller groups.
- Repackage food to minimize waste.
- Use a map and compass to eliminate the use of marking paint, rock cairns, or flagging.

2. Travel and Camp on Durable Surfaces

- Durable surfaces include established trails and campsites, rock, gravel, dry grasses, or snow.
- Protect riparian areas by camping at least 200 feet from lakes and streams.
- Good campsites are found, not made. Altering a site is not necessary.
- In popular areas:
  - Concentrate use on existing trails and campsites.
  - Walk single file in the middle of the trail, even when wet or muddy.
  - Keep campsites small. Focus activity in areas where vegetation is absent.
- In pristine areas:
  - Disperse use to prevent the creation of campsites and trails.
  - Avoid places where impacts are just beginning.

3. Dispose of Waste Properly

- Pack it in, pack it out. Inspect your campsite and rest areas for trash or spilled foods. Pack out all trash, leftover food, and litter.
- Deposit solid human waste in catholes dug 6 to 8 inches deep, at least 200 feet from water, camp, and trails. Cover and disguise the cathole when finished.
- Pack out toilet paper and hygiene products.
- To wash yourself or your dishes, carry water 200 feet away from streams or lakes and use small amounts of biodegradable soap. Scatter strained dishwater.

4. Leave What You Find

- Preserve the past: examine but do not touch cultural or historic structures and artifacts.
- Leave rocks, plants, and other natural objects as you find them.
- Avoid introducing or transporting nonnative species.
- Do not build structures or furniture or dig trenches.

5. Minimize Campfire Impacts

- Campfires can cause lasting impacts to the backcountry. Use a lightweight stove for cooking and enjoy a candle lantern for light.
- Where fires are permitted, use established fire rings, fire pans, or mound fires.
- Keep fires small. Only use sticks from the ground that can be broken by hand.
- Burn all wood and coals to ash, put out campfires completely, and then scatter the cool ashes.

6. Respect Wildlife

- Observe wildlife from a distance. Do not follow or approach them.
- Never feed animals. Feeding wildlife damages their health, alters natural behaviors, and exposes them to predators and other dangers.
- Protect wildlife and your food by storing rations and trash securely.
- Control pets at all times, or leave them at home.
- Avoid wildlife during sensitive times: mating, nesting, raising young, or winter.

7. Be Considerate of Other Visitors

- Respect other visitors and protect the quality of their experience.
- Be courteous. Yield to other users on the trail.
- Step to the downhill side of the trail when encountering pack stock.
- Take breaks and camp away from trails and other visitors.
- Let nature's sounds prevail. Avoid loud voices and noises.

models nylon mesh to keep the load away from the back. This mesh allows air to circulate between pack and back.

Since you need room for all of your equipment, a good backpack has five or six outside pockets for smaller, oft-used items. Inside the pack itself are two large compartments for larger items. Below the pack, on the frame, there is room to strap on a sleeping bag. Gear that won't fit inside the pack can be safely lashed to the frame.

External-framed backpacks are still in wide use today and offer some definite advantages. Remember that the backpack and frame can be removed from one another, permitting the packer to lash such bulky objects as an outboard motor to the frame for easy transportation.

In the 1990s, backpacks with internal frames, usually aluminum stays, were developed. Internal-framed backpacks are designed to conform more closely to the body. One manufacturer, REI, went one step further and developed a hybrid it calls perimeter-frame packs. It routes a small-diameter aluminum tube around the periphery of the pack and the design gives the pack the load capacity of an external design. There is a wide range of backpack designs available today, and choice pretty much becomes a matter of personal preference.

There are certain things to look for in choosing a framed backpack. The best choice for lightness is a waterproof nylon backpack, as it will keep the rain off your gear. Look for a top flap on the pack that is long enough to cover the top of the bag when it is full; heavy-duty, corrosion-proof zippers on the exterior side and back pockets that won't jam and will keep out dirt and

The RedHead Dry Creek Waist Pack is ideal for the day hiker who wants to carry only essential gear and still keep both arms free. The pack weighs about 1 pound, has a capacity of 850 cubic inches, and has side and front pockets.

rain; seams and pockets that can withstand rugged use; and shoulder and waist straps that are at least 2 inches wide so they won't curl up and cut you. Also, shoulder straps and harnesses for back support should be adjustable to allow for tightening and taking up slack as the load is increased or decreased.

Don't buy a pack just because it fulfills these requirements, though. Try on various models. Internal and external framed packs should permit the load to be carried vertically with its center of gravity close to your back. In this manner, the weight will be transferred to the legs, the most powerful part of the human body.

The backpack should weigh approximately 2 pounds, the pack frame 3 to 4 pounds. That means the frame and pack together should weigh close to 5 pounds.

The total amount of gear and food carried depends on the individual. An average man can camp on his own for three days, using a good pack and frame, with carefully selected equipment and freeze-dried food weighing a total of 30 pounds. That same man can stay in the bush for up to two weeks if he carries a pack with 40 pounds of sustenance.

■ Pack Basket

The pack basket is an old-time favorite that seems to retain limited popularity because of tradition rather than utility.

Made of thin strips of wood from willow or ash logs, the pack basket is light and rigid. The construction protects the contents from breakage and the packer's back from rough or sharp objects inside. Canoeists favor it for packing odd-size canned goods and gear. Nevertheless, the basket is not recommended for general backpacking.

The Allagash Pack Basket is typical of this classic design. A pack basket is one of the safest means of carrying breakable goods. This model is made of handwoven maple. It has adjustable straps, and is a good choice for carrying odd-shaped objects.

■ Hip or Fanny Pack

This pack provides an ideal alternative for the person who doesn't like to carry a pack by means of shoulder straps. As the name implies, the pack rests on the hips and lower back, and easily carries whatever small gear a sportsman or camper might bring along on a one-day trip.

■ How to Pack a Backpack

How you load your pack is critical. A 50-pound pack may seem manageable when you start out, but it will wear you down quickly after a mile or so. Learn to trim your load. Get rid of those food boxes and cans. Repack everything in leakproof, sealable plastic bags. When you shop, look for dehydrated or freeze-dried foods.

How much weight you can carry depends on your size, strength, and appetite. There is a limit to how much a person can comfortably carry over a certain period of time. With carefully selected gear and food, an average man can camp for about three days with a backpack that will weigh 30 pounds. Here are some safe limits for maximum backpack weights:

Men: 35–40 pounds
Women: 20–30 pounds
Children: 15 pounds

Stray from these weight limits and you'll find backpacking a chore rather than a pleasure. Take a few backpack trips and you will soon discover how little you actually need to camp in the woods.

CAMPFIRES

To start a campfire, clear a site—always on rock or dirt—by removing all ground debris for at least 3 feet on all sides. This prevents any combustible material such as rubbish and underground roots from igniting and causing a possible forest fire. When using the top of a ledge for your fire, beware of small cracks through which hot coals might tumble into flammable material.

A good fire for cooking, lighting, or heat starts with tinder, thin sticks of kindling, and medium-size sticks of firewood. Stack them loosely or in pyramid fashion in that order. Then stand on the upwind side and light the tinder from there. This directs the flame upward and into the mass of tinder. Lighting from the downwind side leaves you little opportunity to direct the flame.

Once the tinder is well ignited, blow on it or fan the fire gently with your hat. The tinder will light the slim sticks, which in turn will set the medium-size sticks ablaze. Tinder, which forms the bottom layer of the fire, is any small-size fuel that ignites readily. Any scrap of dry paper will do, especially waxed paper and the like.

There are also wood sources of tinder. Birch bark that is stripped and wadded loosely and dry cedar bark both perform well. Sagebrush bark, dead evergreen twigs still on the tree with brown needles intact, and dry, dead grass or weeds that are crushed into a ball are also effective. Pitch is a primary burning agent that is found in the decayed trunks and upturned roots

of woods such as spruce, pine, and fir. It also works efficiently as tinder when sliced up with the wood still attached. To tell if a wood contains pitch, alert yourself to the resinous odor and weighty heft of the wood. Even heavy rains don't change the quality of pitch slabs as excellent tinder.

If you are handy with a knife and adept at whittling, you can make fuzz sticks (also known as fire sticks). Shave lengthy splinters from almost any dry, soft stick, leaving as many splinters attached as possible. When you have what resembles a tiny pine tree, thrust it upright into the ground and place some tinder around it. Set a match to the lower slivers, and you have a fine fire starter.

You can squirt a little kerosene, stove gasoline, or lighter fluid on the kindling as an alternative to gathering tinder. Be sure, however, to use these liquid fuels prior to striking your match to prevent an explosion. Kindling, which consists of thin, dry sticks, is ordinarily placed loosely in a tepee shape above the tinder or crisscrossed on top of it.

The basic firewood is not added until both tinder and kindling are in place. This wood is necessarily heavier than the kindling, usually longer, and from 3 to 4 inches, or possibly even 6 inches, in thickness. Small logs or thick branches are prime sources of this firewood, which catches from the combustible material beneath to provide a strong and stable fire.

Firewood Characteristics

Species	Heat Value	Ease of Splitting	Ease of Starting	Sparks
Alder	Medium/Low	Easy	Fair	Moderate
Apple	Medium/High	Difficult	Difficult	Few
Ash	High	Easy/Moderate	Fair/Difficult	Few
Aspen	Low	Easy	Easy	Few
Beech	High	Difficult	Moderate	Few
Birch	Medium	Moderate	Easy	Moderate
Cedar	Medium/Low	Easy	Easy	Many
Cherry	Medium	Easy	Difficult	Few
Cottonwood	Low	Easy	Easy	Moderate
Cypress	Low	Easy	Easy	Few
Dogwood	High	Difficult	Easy	Few
Douglas Fir	Medium	Easy	Easy	Moderate
Elm	Medium	Difficult	Moderate	Few
Fir, Grand Noble	Medium/Low	Easy	Easy	Moderate
Gum	Medium	Difficult	Moderate	Few
Hemlock	Medium/Low	Easy	Easy	Many
Hickory	Medium/High	Difficult	Difficult	Few
Juniper	Medium	Difficult	Fair	Many
Larch	Medium/High	Easy/Moderate	Easy	Many
Locust	Very High	Very Difficult	Difficult	Very Few
Madrone	High	Difficult	Difficult	Very Few
Maple, Hard	High	Easy	Difficult	Few
Maple, Soft	Medium	Easy	Fair	Few
Oak	Very High	Moderate	Difficult	Few
Pecan	High	Easy	Difficult	Few
Pine, Lodgepole	Low	Easy	Easy	Moderate
Pine, Ponderosa, White, Yellow	Medium/Low	Easy	Easy	Moderate
Pinyon	Medium	Easy	Easy	Few
Redwood	Low	Easy	Easy	Few
Spruce	Low	Easy/Moderate	Easy	Moderate
Sycamore	Medium	Difficult	Moderate	Few
Walnut	Medium/High	Easy/Moderate	Fair	Few
Willow	Low	Easy	Fair	Moderate

Woods vary in burning qualities. They catch fire primarily in relation to their dryness, cut size, and resin content. They give heat and good cooking coals primarily in relation to their density—the denser the wood, the more mass available for combustion.

Any dry (seasoned) wood will be good kindling if cut to finger thickness. Wood of conifers tends to catch fire more easily than that of deciduous trees because their high amounts of resin ignite at lower temperatures than the gases generated from wood fibers alone. But conifers tend to be smokier, and their resin pockets cause more popping and sparks.

If you are forced to burn unseasoned wood, as in a survival predicament, ash is one of the best because of its low moisture content "on the stump." For cooking, if very dry, the densest deciduous woods are best. These include oak, hickory, locust, beech, birch, ash, and hawthorn. Yet in parts of western states, you may find that conifers are the only woods available. In northwestern Canada and Alaska, birch and alder are about the only abundant, dense deciduous woods.

Oak and hickory rate as good wood, but remember that these hardwoods will quickly take the edge off an ax or saw—something you may want to keep in mind

Begin the fire in the center of the corridor, and wait until you see that the surrounding rocks are hot and the trench is lined with a bed of coals. Using a piece of dry firewood, push the blazing wood to one end of the trench. The remainder stays at the other end for cooking. When the cooking coals seem to be losing their vigor, move some of the other coals to the cooking area.

Some campers prefer two keyhole fires rather than one, particularly for large groups of campers, so there is always a substantial amount of hot coals to work with.

if you're on an extended trip. And if sparks and smoke bother you, avoid pine and spruce, tamarack, basswood, and chestnut.

■ Hunter's Fire

Among the many possible arrangements of the basic campfire, the hunter's fire is a simple, dual-purpose one that provides hot coals for cooking along with heat and light.

Start your fire as described earlier and wait for a bed of hot coals to form. At that point, place two green logs on either side of the fire to resemble a corridor. If this is done before the coals form, the fire will eventually eat right into the logs. Rocks can also be used to form a corridor. The camper out for a brief time or on a string of one-night stands on a pack trail or canoe route benefits most from this type of fire.

If the fire dies down, place a support under the ends of the logs to let more air in through the sides.

■ Keyhole Fire

Like the hunter's fire, the keyhole fire supplies heat and light, and a place for cooking chores. Also for short-term use, this campfire consists of flat, small rocks arranged in a keyhole shape. It features a corridor 3 to 6 feet long and 1 foot wide and a circle adjacent to the rectangle.

■ Trench Fire

When stoves and wood are nowhere to be found, and the pots you are using have no bails, set up a trench fire.

Dig a trench as deep as you need, parallel to the direction of the prevailing wind. Leave the upwind end open to provide an effective draft. If the trench is very narrow, its sides may support the pots. Otherwise, you may need to use green sticks to hold up your cooking gear.

Camp Tips

- Campfire wood can be split more easily if you aim for the cracks in the top end grain of a dry log. Cracks indicate weak sections in the grain. Most of the time the cracks will also automatically detour the split around knots in the log.

- If you prefer open fire cooking, pack a small steel grid that you can prop on rocks or across logs. You'll have a flat surface for steaks or a skillet. If you carry these grids in a plastic bag, you won't even have to clean them until you get home.

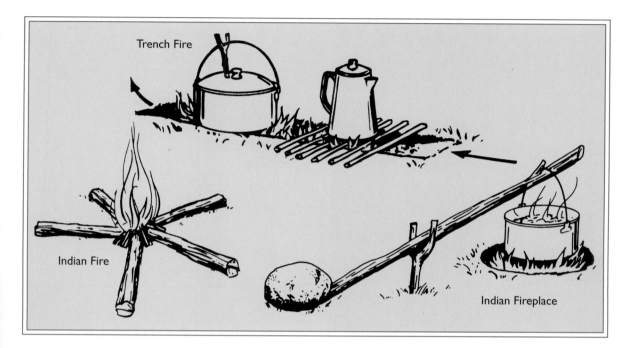

■ Indian Fire

When wood fuel is at a premium and it is necessary to conserve what you have, try the Indian fire. Note that five thick logs radiate outward from the center. Tinder should be placed at this midpoint. As the logs burn, push them gradually into the middle.

■ Indian Fireplace

If you have to contend with strong winds, the Indian fireplace is appropriate. Dig a hole that is a bit larger than your kettle and build a small fire at the bottom. Using a fork-shaped stick to support a straight stick with one end secured in the ground, hang the kettle over the hole. If you have enough fuel, set the pot in the hole itself, but be sure there is adequate space at the bottom for air to circulate.

The lower end of the stick for hanging the kettle doesn't have to be buried or driven into the ground if a heavy enough rock or log is handy. Just lay this weight on the end of the stick or wedge the stick under it securely.

■ Reflector Fire

The reflector fire provides heat to a tent or an oven. A small raft of 1-inch-thick logs, rocks or sod, or alumi-

num foil will direct heat to the desired spot. A conventional fire built in front of the reflector safely warms up a baker tent or practically any other type of tent.

Reflector Fire

Swedish Fire Lay

The reflector oven using this fire lets you bake biscuits and such.

The reflector fire requires flames to project enough heat to a selected spot. Coals alone unfortunately radiate in all directions, making cooking more difficult.

Dingle Stick

One of the simplest and most practical campfires uses the dingle stick, a device that holds a pot securely over a fire. The accompanying illustrations show two arrangements of the dingle stick. Be sure to choose a durable stick for either one.

Swedish Fire Lay

An efficient fire for heating a single kettle, pot, coffeepot, or frying pan is the Swedish fire lay. It's especially convenient in confined spaces. Its foundation is a small fire with the sticks arranged in a star shape, like the basic Indian fire. Around this foundation, three split chunks of log, each about a foot long, are stood on end. Tilt the split logs in at the top, propping them against one another to form a pyramid. The heat travels up the logs

to the top, and eventually they'll begin to burn. But even before they do, the top will be hot, and it serves as a base for the cooking utensil.

Rain or Snow

Starting a fire in driving rain or snow is usually possible, and often easy. On rain-soaked ground, you can construct a foundation for the fire using slabs of bark, rocks, or broken limbs. On snow, build the foundation from thick pieces of green or punky and wet downfall. Avoid building fires beneath trees capped with snow, as the rising heat will melt the snow and possibly extinguish your fire.

The optimum wood under these conditions comes from standing dead trees. Most of the wood chopped from their insides will be dry enough to burn. Birch bark, pitch-saturated evergreen, and white ash are excellent choices, even when moist.

When you have gathered tinder, kindling, and firewood, look for a natural overhang—a rock ledge, for example. If none is available, improvise with a flat rock, a slab of bark, or a log propped up at an angle. A poncho, a canvas tarp, or a tent awning is even better.

Prepare the firewood and search out a dry area to strike a match on. Your match case will probably be dry, and zippers and buttons on the inside of clothing will work in a pinch. Try scraping the match against your thumbnail, or even on the edge of your teeth as a last resort. Then, shield the initial fire until the heavy firewood is securely aflame. At that point, the fire stands little chance of being put out by the elements.

Make certain to carefully douse any fire you build with bucketful after bucketful of water when you are finished with it. Don't stop until every piece of wood and all coals are drenched. Then, stir the coals until all sparks and steam are gone. A healthy mound of wet mineral soil guarantees that the fire is completely and safely extinguished.

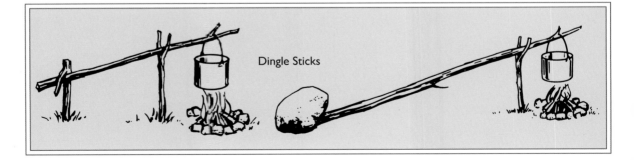

Dingle Sticks

ROPES AND KNOTS

Ropes for camp use are made of either natural or synthetic materials. The natural fibers come in hemp, available in such types as manila and sisal, and in cotton strands of everyday cotton fiber that has been specially treated.

Synthetic fibers such as Dacron, nylon, and polypropylene often prove to be from 50 to 100 percent stronger than hemp or cotton rope of equal diameter. These waterproof synthetics do not swell or kink when they are wet. They are likewise unaffected by such hemp maladies as fungus, mildew, and dry rot.

A disadvantage of synthetics is the price. Cotton rope typically costs one-tenth the amount of most synthetic rope of the same diameter. Hemp costs are usually one-third the amount of synthetics. And knots made with synthetic rope do not hold as well as those made with hemp or cotton. In the case of nylon rope, the stretch range may be up to 20 percent of the total length.

The accompanying chart shows the approximate breaking strengths in pounds of dead weight of the various types of ropes. The safe working load for a brand-new rope is one-quarter the breaking strength. If the rope has been through average use, figure one-sixth of the breaking strength. Dropping the load or jerking the rope doubles the strain, and knots and splices diminish its strength, sometimes drastically.

To care for a hemp rope, remember that moisture causes damage. Keep this rope as dry as possible, whether you are storing it or using it. By hanging hemp or cotton rope in a dry, high, cool place, you protect it from harmful rodents. The sweat-salt traces left on a rope by human hands attract mice and rats with their ever-sharp teeth.

Synthetics need little protection from water, but they can be substantially weakened by acids, oils, and intense heat.

▪ WHIPPING

The purpose of whipping, using several turns of a strong thread, is to prevent the end of a rope from unraveling. Hold the thread taut during the wrapping turns. The section of the thread where the arrow points is given a half dozen turns once the pull-through loop has been formed. The loop should be pulled snug and the end trimmed. If the rope is synthetic, melt it with a cigarette lighter for a tighter seal. Hemp and cotton also seal more securely if dipped in a quick-setting glue.

▪ CLOVE HITCH

This is the most effective and quick way to tie a boat line to a mooring post. It can be tied in the middle or end of a rope, but it is apt to slip if tied at the end. To prevent slipping, make a half hitch in the end to the standing part.

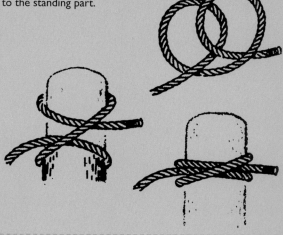

Approximate Breaking Strength of Ropes (pounds)

Diameter (inches)	Sisal	Manila	Polypropylene	Dacron	Nylon
¼	480	600	1,050	1,600	1,800
⅜	1,080	1,350	2,200	3,300	4,000
½	2,120	2,650	3,800	5,500	7,100
¾	4,320	5,400	8,100	11,000	14,200
1	7,200	9,000	14,000	18,500	24,600

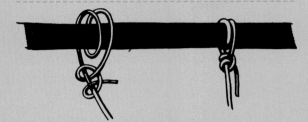

TURNS WITH HALF HITCHES

To make a simple knot for tying a rope end to a pole or ring, make two turns around the object, followed by a pair of half hitches. For additional strength, use more of each.

GUY-LINE HITCH

The guy-line hitch tightens tent and other guy ropes that need adjustment. Begin with two basic overhand knots, with the rope running through the top one. The bottom overhand knot will slide up or down to give or take slack on the guy line or tent rope. You needn't worry about tearing the tent fabric with this hitch.

TIMBER HITCH

This knot is very useful for hoisting spars, boards, or logs. It is also handy for making a towline fast to a wet spar or timber. It holds without slipping and does not jam.

HORSE HITCH

An infallible knot for tying a horse or boat line to a tree, pole, or ring is the horse hitch. The running end of the rope passed through a broad loop at the completion of the hitch will make it more secure.

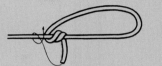

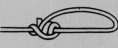

TAUT-LINE HITCH

Primarily for tightening tent ropes, the taut-line hitch is actually a running loop that holds under strain.

Form a loop around the anchor. Then, with the running end, make a pair of small turns around the standing part, spiraling it in the direction of the inside of the loop. A half hitch tied around the standing part, outside of the big loop, completes the loop knot.

SQUARE KNOT

Also known as the reef knot, the square knot attaches two ends of the same rope, or joins two similar-size ropes or lines. The chances of this knot slipping are nil.

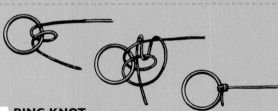

RING KNOT

This knot works best when tied to a ring, such as a swivel end or a metal loop in a lure. If you are using slick monofilament fishing line, do not trim the loose end too closely or it may slip.

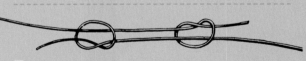

WATER KNOT

Any fisherman should be familiar with the water knot. Adequate for joining fishing lines, leaders, ropes, or small cords, the water knot begins with an overhand knot made loosely in the end of either line. Put the running end of the other line through it and secure it using an overhand knot around the first line's standing part. Next, pull both overhand knots together. Half hitches on either side will tighten the knot. Trim the water knot carefully to prevent it from catching in your rod guides.

■ FIGURE-EIGHT KNOT

Tie the figure-eight knot just like the overhand knot, but give the loop a half twist before the running end is passed through. Also an end knot, the figure eight is slightly less compact than the overhand but significantly stronger.

■ SLIP KNOT

The slip knot is simple and won't untie very quickly. A half hitch or two around the standing part of the rope or line will further bind this knot.

■ REEF KNOT

Probably the most useful and popular of all knots, this is also known as the square knot. Used to join two ropes or lines of the same size, it holds firmly and is easily untied.

■ TYING LINE TO A CLEAT

This is the correct method for tying line to a cleat. The half hitch that completes the fastening is taken with the free part of the line. The line can then be freed without taking up slack in the standing part.

■ TO PREVENT TWISTED ROPE FROM UNRAVELING WHEN CUT

For nylon, polyester, and polypropylene, tape the rope around the circumference as shown. Cut in the middle, leaving tape intact on either side. When cutting these synthetic fibers with a pocketknife or scissors, fuse the cut ends by match flame to prevent untwisting. Tape is unnecessary if a "hot knife" is used. Heat will melt and fuse the cut ends.

■ FISHERMAN'S BEND

An important knot because of its strength and simplicity, it is used for making the end of a rope fast to a ring, spar, or anchor, or for a line to a bucket. It is more secure when the end is tied as shown.

■ SHEET BEND

Used aboard a boat for joining small or medium-sized ropes, this knot is sometimes used for attaching the end of a rope to an eye splice.

■ CARRICK BEND

The carrick bend will join ropes to tow or support hefty loads. It doesn't jam and can be easily untied.

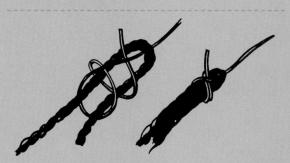

■ DOUBLE-SHEET BEND

When you are linking up a pair of ropes of varied diameters, try the double-sheet bend. Make the simple loop in the thicker of the two ropes, using the thinner one for the turns. The double-sheet bend is preferable to the single style because it is safer and takes perhaps a second longer to finish up.

BOWLINE

The bowline is often used for temporary anchor knots. It never jams or slips if properly tied.

DOUBLE BOWLINE

Make an overhand loop with the end held toward you, exactly as in the ordinary bowline. The difference is that you pass the end through the loop twice—making two lower loops, A and B. The end is then passed behind the standing part and down through the first loop again as in the ordinary bowline. Pull tight. Used as a seat sling, the outside loop B goes under the person's arms, and the inside loop A forms the seat.

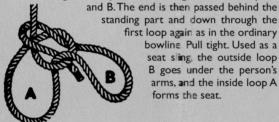

BOWLINE ON A BIGHT

The bowline mentioned earlier has a variation called bowline on a bight, which is especially useful for climbing.

Make an overhand loop and place the bight through it. Pull the bight downward to the end of the big loop formed by the running end. Then, separate the bight, putting the big loop through it. Slide the running-end bight upward so it goes around the standing part. Pull it tight, and the knot is ready.

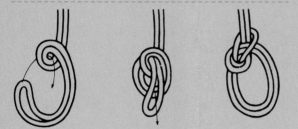

BUTTERFLY LOOP

When three persons are climbing, the person in the middle should be held with a fixed or butterfly loop. This loop also makes an excellent harness for dragging weighty loads.

Make a bight as big as you want the loop to be. Twist it one complete turn, forming a loose figure eight. Fold this double loop over the standing part to produce a pair of intertwined loops. Pass the tip of the original bight through the two loops where the overlapping takes place. Pull on the bight to tighten.

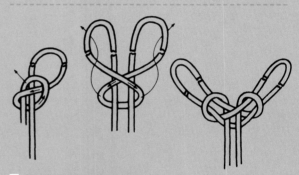

SPANISH BOWLINE

Different from the bowline on a bight in that its two loops are separated, the Spanish bowline is another variation. It functions as an improvised seat and backrest.

A slip knot about twice the size of either of the completed loops is the first step. Give the loop a half twist so the standing part crosses in the rear. Keep the running end of the slip knot tight against the standing part where they form parallel lines. At the same time, hold the turn at the back of the knot, and immediately slide the bight next to the running end outward. Stop when it forms a loop equal in size to the original slip knot.

The resulting X pattern should now be slid up the loops until both are rather small. Reach through the pair from the back, taking the bight below the X and pulling it through. You will now have both loops and an X pattern between the two.

Fishing Knots

All knots reduce—to a greater or lesser degree, depending on the particular knot—the breaking strength of the line. Loose or poorly tied knots reduce line strength even more. For that reason, and to avoid wasting valuable fishing time, it is best to practice tying the knots at home. In most cases, it's better to practice with cord or rope; the heavier material makes it easier to follow the tying procedures.

It is important to form and tighten knots correctly. They should be tightened slowly and steadily for the best results. In most knots requiring the tyer to make turns around the standing part of the line, at least five such turns should be made. Now let's take a look at the range of fishing knots. Included are tying instructions, as well as the uses for which each knot is suited.

■ BLOOD KNOT

This knot is used to connect two lines of relatively similar diameter. It is especially popular for joining sections of monofilament in making tapered fly leaders.

I • Wrap one strand around the other at least four times, and run the end into the fork thus formed.

2 • Make the same number of turns in the opposite direction with the second strand, and run its end through the opening in the middle of the knot, in the direction opposite that of the first strand.

3 • Hold the two ends so they do not slip (some anglers use their teeth). Pull the standing part of both strands in opposite directions, tightening the knot.

4 • Tighten securely, clip off the ends, and the knot is complete. If you want to tie on a dropper fly, leave one of these ends about 6 to 8 inches long.

■ DOUBLE SURGEON'S KNOT

This knot is used to join two strands of greatly unequal diameter.

I • Place the two lines parallel, with the ends pointing in opposite directions. Using the two lines as a single strand, make a simple overhand knot, pulling the two strands all the way through the loop, and then make another overhand knot.

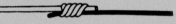

2 • Holding both strands at each end, pull the knot tight, and clip off the ends.

■ IMPROVED CLINCH KNOT

This knot is used to tie flies, bass bugs, lures, and bait hooks to line or leader. This knot reduces line strength only slightly.

I • Run the end of the line through the eye of the lure, fly, or hook, and then make at least five turns around the standing part of the line. Run the end through the opening between the eye and the beginning of the twists, and then run it through the large loop formed by the previous step.

2 • Pull slowly on the standing part of the line, being careful that the end doesn't slip back through the large loop and that the knot snugs up against the eye. Clip off the end.

SHOCKER KNOT

This knot is used to join two lines of unequal diameter.

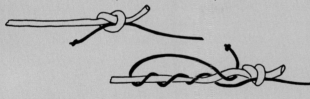

TRILENE KNOT

Used in joining line to swivels, snaps, hooks, and artificial lures, the Trilene knot is a strong, all-purpose knot that resists slippage and premature failures. It's easy to tie and retains 85 to 90 percent of the original line strength. The double wrap of monofilament line through the eyelet provides a protective cushion for added safety.

1 • Run the end of the line through the eye of the hook or lure and double back through the eye a second time.

2 • Loop around the standing part of the line five or six times.

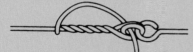

3 • Thread the tag end back between the eye and the coils as shown.

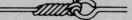

4 • Pull up tight and trim the tag end.

MULTIPLE CLINCH KNOT

This knot is used to join line and leader, especially in baitcasting. This knot slides through rod guides with a minimum of friction.

A loop is tied in the end of the line. Then, the leader is run into the loop, around the entire loop four times, and then back through the middle of the four wraps.

PALOMAR KNOT

This is a quick, easy knot to use when tying your line directly to a hook.

1 • Pass the line or leader through the eye of the hook and back again to form a 3- to 5-inch loop.

2 • Hold the line and hook at the eye. With the other hand, bring the loop up and under the double line and tie an overhand knot, but do not tighten.

3 • Hold the overhand knot. With the other hand, bring the loop over the hook.

4 • Pull the line to draw the knot to the top of the eye. Pull both the tag end and running end to tighten. Clip tag end off about ⅛ inch from the knot.

PERFECTION LOOP KNOT

This knot is used to make a loop in the end of line or leader.

1 • Make one turn around the line and hold the crossing point with your thumb and forefinger.

2 • Make a second turn around the crossing point, and bring the end around and between loops A and B.

3 • Run loop B through loop A.

4 • Pull upward on loop B.

5 • Tighten the knot.

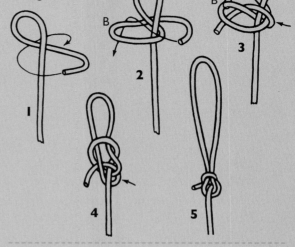

■ DOUBLE SURGEON'S LOOP

This is a quick, easy way to tie a loop in the end of a leader. It is often used as part of a leader system because it is relatively strong.

1 • Double the tag end of the line. Make a single overhand knot in the double line.

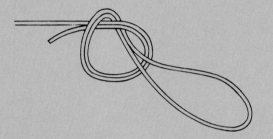

2 • Hold the tag end and standing part of the line in your left hand and bring the loop around and insert through the overhand knot again.

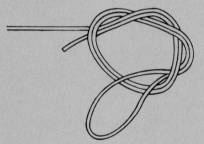

3 • Hold the loop in your right hand. Hold the tag end and standing line in your left hand. Moisten the knot (don't use saliva) and pull to tighten.

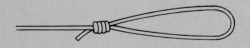

4 • Trim off the tag end.

■ OFFSHORE SWIVEL KNOT

This knot is used to attach your line to a swivel.

1 • Slip a loop of double-line leader through the eye of the swivel. Rotate the loop a half turn to put a single twist between the loop and swivel eye.

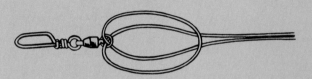

2 • Pass the loop with the twist over the swivel. Hold the loop end, together with both strands of double-line leader, with one hand. Let the swivel slide to the other end of the double loops now formed.

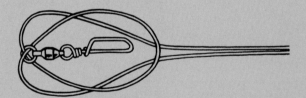

3 • Still holding the loop and lines, use your other hand to rotate the swivel through the center of both loops. Repeat at least five times.

4 • Continue holding the strands of double-line leader tightly, but release the end of the loop. As you pull on the swivel, loops of line will begin to gather.

5 • To draw the knot tight, grip the swivel with pliers and push the loops toward the eye with your fingers, still keeping the strands of leader pulled tight.

■ NAIL KNOT

This is the best knot for joining the end of a fly line with the butt end of a fly leader. The knot is smooth, streamlined, and will run freely through the guides of the fly rod. Caution: This knot is designed for use with modern synthetic fly lines; do not use it with an old silk fly line for the knot will cut the line.

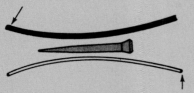

1 • Place the end of the fly line and the butt end of the leader—pointing in opposite directions—along the length of a tapered nail. Allow sufficient overlap.

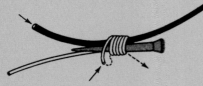

2 • Wrap the leader five or six times around itself, the nail, and the fly line, keeping the windings up against one another. Run the butt end of the leader back along the nail, inside the wraps.

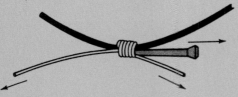

3 • Pull both ends of the leader tight, and then remove the nail and tighten again by pulling on both ends of the leader.

4 • Pull on both line and leader to test the knot, and clip off the ends, completing the knot.

■ END LOOP

This knot is used to form a loop in the end of a line.

1 • Double the end of the line for about 6 or 8 inches.

2 • Wrap the double line around itself at least six times.

3 • Take the end of the doubled line and pass it through the first loop as shown.

4 • Now, tighten the knot by pulling on the loop and the tag end at the same time.

■ DROPPER LOOP KNOT

This knot is frequently used to put a loop in the middle of a strand of monofilament.

1 • Make a loop in the line and wrap one end overhand several times around the other part of the line. Pinch a small loop in the middle and thrust it between the turns as shown by the simulated, imaginary needle.

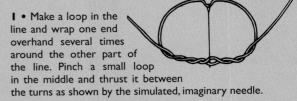

2 • Place your finger through the loop to keep it from pulling out again, and pull on both ends of the line.

3 • The knot will draw up as shown below.

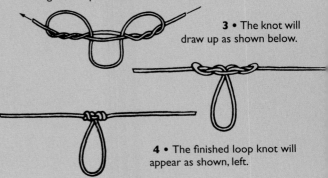

4 • The finished loop knot will appear as shown, left.

BIMINI TWIST

This knot is used to create a loop or double line without appreciably weakening the breaking strength of the line. It is especially popular in bluewater fishing for large saltwater fish. Learning this knot requires practice.

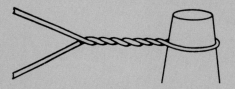

1 • Double the end of the line to form a loop, leaving yourself plenty of line to work with. Run the loop around a fixed object, such as a cleat or the butt end of a rod, or have a partner hold the loop and keep it open. Make 20 twists in the line, keeping the turns tight and the line taut.

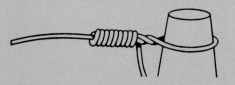

2 • Keeping the twists tight, wrap the end of the line back over the twists until you reach the V of the loop, making the wraps tight and snug up against one another.

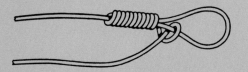

3 • Make a half hitch around one side of the loop and pull it tight.

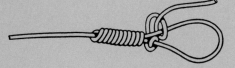

4 • Then, make a half hitch around the other side of the loop, and pull this one tight, too.

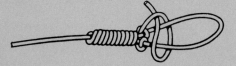

5 • Now, make a half hitch around the base of the loop, tighten it, clip off excess line at the end, and the bimini twist is complete.

HAYWIRE TWIST

This knot is used to tie wire to the hook, lure, or swivel, or make a loop in the end of the wire.

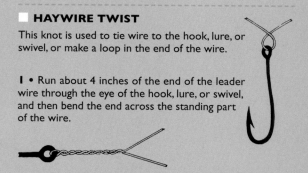

1 • Run about 4 inches of the end of the leader wire through the eye of the hook, lure, or swivel, and then bend the end across the standing part of the wire.

2 • Holding the two parts of the wire at their crossing points, bend the wire around itself, using hard, even, twisting motions. Both wire parts should be twisted equally.

3 • Then, using the end of the wire, make about 10 tight wraps around the standing part of the wire.

4 • Break off or clip the end of the wire close to the last wrap so that there is no sharp end, and the job is complete.

DOUBLE NAIL KNOT

This knot is used to join leader sections of the same or slightly different diameters. This is especially useful in saltwater fly fishing and in making heavy salmon leaders.

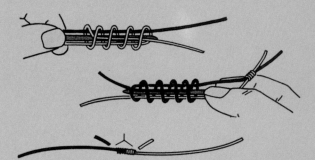

The tying procedure involves making two nail knots, one around each of the two leader sections. As each knot is formed, it is tightened only enough to prevent it from unraveling. When both are formed, each leader is pulled slowly so that the knots tighten together securely.

■ SPIDER HITCH

This knot serves the same function as the bimini twist, but many anglers prefer the spider hitch because it's easier and faster to tie—especially with cold hands—and requires no partner to help, nor any fixed object to keep the loop open. Plus, it's equally strong.

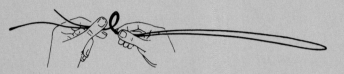

1 • Make a long loop in the line. Hold the ends between your thumb and forefinger, with the first joint of the thumb extending beyond your finger. Then, use your other hand to twist a smaller reverse loop in the doubled line.

2 • Slide your fingers up the line to grasp the small reverse loop together with the long loop. Most of the small loop should extend beyond your thumb tip.

3 • Wind the doubled line from right to left around both your thumb and the small loop, taking five turns. Then, pass the remainder of the doubled line (large loop) through the small loop.

4 • Pull the large loop to make the five turns unwind off the thumb, using a fast, steady pull—not a quick jerk.

5 • Pull the turns around the base of the loop tight and then trim off the tag end.

■ WORLD'S FAIR KNOT

This is an easy-to-tie terminal tackle knot for connecting line to a swivel or lure.

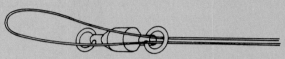

1 • Double a 6-inch length of line and pass the loop through the eye.

2 • Bring the loop back next to the doubled line and grasp the double line through the loop.

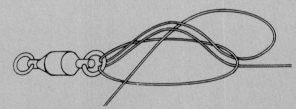

3 • Put the tag end through the new loop formed by the double line.

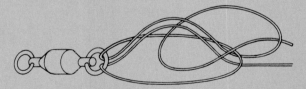

4 • Bring the tag end back through the new loop created by step 3.

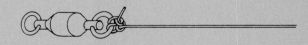

5 • Pull the tag end snug, and slide the knot up tight. Clip the tag end.

BOATING
FOR CAMPERS

Section Two
BOATING
FOR CAMPERS

• CAMPING BOATS • CANOES AND KAYAKS •
• BOATING SAFETY • FORECASTING WEATHER •

BOATS FOR CAMPING

Boat camping is a natural way to extend your enjoyment of life in the outdoors. Instead of having to backtrack to your starting point toward the end of the day, just when things are going well, you can put ashore at the first suitable site if you are prepared for camping. If your boat is big enough, you can anchor and camp aboard. Still another version of boat camping is to trailer or cartop a boat to your base camp and extend your range from there by means of the boat.

For those whose primary pleasure is camping, a boat gets you away from crowded, metropolis-like campgrounds. Going camping by boat gives you a private preserve in the outdoors, brings you closer to unspoiled nature, and increases your alternatives for camping locations tenfold.

■ Camping with Small Boats

When you camp with a canoe, kayak, cartopper, inflatable, johnboat, or other really small boat, you can pack your supplies and tent or sleeping bags in the boat, travel through the wilderness on water, and then make your camp ashore. This style suits many lake chains and small rivers. With careful packing, there is room for your supplies, gear, and two adults, or a couple and a small child in this size boat.

When you plan your trip, make a list based on roughing it, with the minimum amount of equipment, only one change of clothing, backpack-style tents, concentrated and freeze-dried foods, and a streamlined fishing outfit. There is a distinct pleasure in traveling light, and as the experience progresses, you'll be glad to have discovered a simple way to camp. Portages will be light, and if you get a dunking, the damage will not be irreparable.

A canoe for camping should be from 16 to 18 feet long. If you are going to camp on a lake, use a canoe with a keel. This will help you hold your course easily in a wind. With canoe ends slightly rockered, you can adjust course fairly easily even with a heavy load. For canoe camping on a river, avoid a canoe with much of a keel and stick to the camping length. Loaded with gear, a canoe with a keel will catch rocks and snags too often for comfort. The camping length, as opposed to shorter white-water canoes, will keep handling easy. There is a lot in favor of using a small motor on a canoe for camping. In that case, choose a canoe with full rather than fine ends so the motor will not cause the ends to dig in.

Kayaks also make excellent boats for camping. Select a touring or expedition model with a sit-in cockpit. This design will allow you to store gear where it will be safe and dry. A 14-foot kayak might be adequate, but a 16- or 17-footer will give you more space for gear.

A cartop boat will increase your load capacity, and using an outboard will extend your range considerably compared to paddling or drifting. Don't forget that you

Open boats are good equipment carriers for extended float trips. Some can even be rigged to carry a couple of kayaks for exploring backwaters.

The Sun Tracker Fishin' Barge 20 DLX, a 20-foot pontoon boat, is a good choice for overnight fishing and camping on big lakes and bays. With an economical 40-horsepower four-stroke outboard, this pontoon boat can easily hold anglers and camping gear.

will have to carry enough gas to make it between refueling points. Determine gas-pump locations in advance, and make sure you can get to them from the water's edge. Cartop fishing boats are ideal for light camping.

Inflatable boats are excellent for drift camping on a large river. Four passengers can camp with a 16-foot inflatable. An inflatable of this size can carry big loads, and the relatively wide beam makes it easy to load and stay aboard for long hours without getting cramped. At night you can use an inflatable as a lean-to over your sleeping bags and avoid carrying a large tent.

A full-size johnboat of 16 feet or so is too big and heavy to cartop, but it's a good candidate for trailering or loading in the back of a truck with your gear already packed in the boat. The johnboat design is excellent for boat camping, as it can carry great loads for its size. Depending on the number of campers, you may prefer a smaller johnboat that can be cartopped. It's always easier to drive with your boat on top of your car than trailering it behind the vehicle.

Another option for on-water camping is a pontoon boat, which can be beached or anchored near shorelines. For a bigger group, a pontoon boat makes sense. Depending on the size, a tent can even be pitched on the deck and, with safety precautions, food can be cooked on a grill.

■ Family Runabouts

When a family with a new runabout gets over its novelty and has learned to water ski, going camping with the boat is an interesting next step. This is an imaginative and ambitious way to use the family's recreational resources.

Since runabouts have more beam and weight capacity than a fishing boat or canoe of the same length, you are not quite so limited in the amount of

gear and supplies aboard. Often there is enough space to do simple cooking and bed down. Runabouts from 16 to 19 feet suit camping best. You can use the runabout to go greater distances at faster speeds with its greater horsepower capacity. If the boat is not big enough to eat and sleep aboard, use its range to reach choice campsites with more variety.

A family boat of 18 or 19 feet is generally big enough for four passengers, if they are good organizers. Boats of this size have several advantages. You can travel on large, open waters such as the Great Lakes, large river estuaries, and the Inland Waterway, moving in close along shore on bad-weather days or to camp for the night, and also pass through fairly shallow places when necessary. Many families enjoy camping vacations in the Florida Keys aboard large runabouts. These boats are a size that can be trailered at fair highway speeds, so reaching a distant vacation area is not a big problem.

Many makers offer camper tops as options for family runabouts. These vary considerably in quality of materials, workmanship, and design. Shop with your eyes open when buying a runabout if you think you will use it for camping. A good camper top is made of high-grade nylon with double seams, double zippers, tough plastic windows, and nylon-mesh screening. Designs that have at least one large area with stand-up height are the most useful. A tight closure all around is usually achieved with a plastic rubber channel that presses together, and strong grommets and double-reinforced eyelets anchor the camper top to the boat. If you cannot get a camper top to suit you with the boat you want to buy, shop around for a good tent maker who will make the top to your specifications.

Optional camper built-ins are a good investment if they are efficiently designed and well made. Choose your gear and boat options carefully, such as a fold-up alcohol stove or a portable propane stove that stows out of the way in a side storage space under the gunwales. Deluxe double lounge seats with comfortable padding and vinyl covering are made to fold down to make a bed for one person. Removable seats can be lifted out to make more space on deck for sleeping bags.

Houseboats and Cruisers

Whether this should be called camping depends on your own point of view and how you go about it. If you want to camp, you'll do so, and some families are inveterate campers even in a 50-foot houseboat with automatic laundry and an electric stove. The lure of building a campfire ashore, and tenting along the way, is very attractive when you have a boat with shallow draft that can be beached. With a small houseboat or pontoon boat, camping is still a natural extension of what you can do with such a boat. Planning is more relaxed because you can keep more aboard. People who like camping in a travel trailer or motor home will find houseboats to their taste.

Houseboats and small cruisers are used extensively on big rivers, along the shores of the Great Lakes, and on other open waters where you can keep in touch with the shore and duck in if the weather blows up. These hulls usually have fairly shallow drafts, so you have many options in where you go.

One pleasure with a houseboat or small cruiser is to nose up to a riverbank or anchor near shore, and then have a barbecue ashore, follow deer tracks, explore islands, or walk the beaches. You can tow a small dinghy or stow it on the cabin roof for fishing and going ashore. Some houseboats and cruisers carry a bicycle to run into towns along the way for groceries, laundry, and mail.

Canoes and Kayaks

A camper who has never used a canoe or kayak to reach backwater havens is missing a rare wilderness experience. These silent boats can take you deep into remote areas that are hardly ever reached by most people.

Most canoes in the 16- to 17-foot range will work fine. Aluminum canoes are noisy, but they are also tough. Some space-age canoes made of Kevlar or Royalex ABS material are so tough that they can take as much abuse as aluminum.

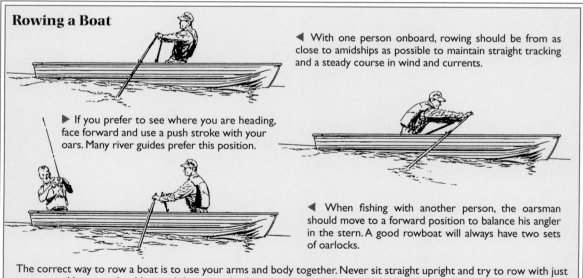

Rowing a Boat

◀ With one person onboard, rowing should be from as close to amidships as possible to maintain straight tracking and a steady course in wind and currents.

▶ If you prefer to see where you are heading, face forward and use a push stroke with your oars. Many river guides prefer this position.

◀ When fishing with another person, the oarsman should move to a forward position to balance his angler in the stern. A good rowboat will always have two sets of oarlocks.

The correct way to row a boat is to use your arms and body together. Never sit straight upright and try to row with just your arms. Use your shoulders and the strength of your trunk. Long, strong strokes with oars are more efficient and less tiring than short strokes. With a little practice, you will be able to maintain a course by pulling a little harder on one oar than the other. You can pivot or turn a boat by pulling on one oar and pushing on the other. A pull on the right oar and a push on the left oar will turn the bow clockwise. Reverse the strokes to turn the bow counterclockwise. You can slow down and stop a boat by dropping both oar blades in the water and holding them stationary. When rowing with outboard power, tilt the engine up and keep the weight forward to reduce transom drag.

Canoes and Kayaks

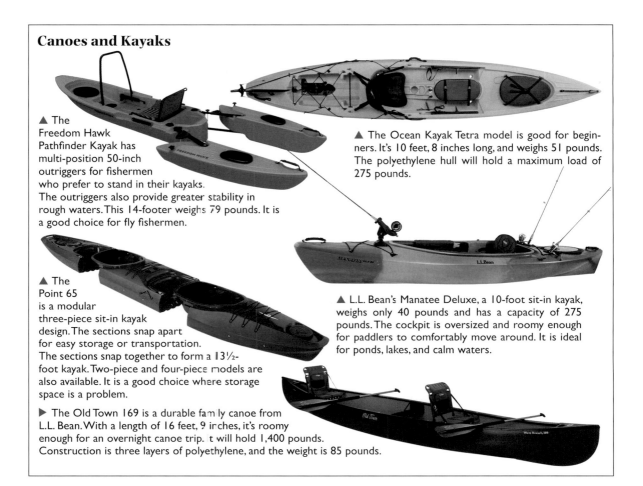

▲ The Freedom Hawk Pathfinder Kayak has multi-position 50-inch outriggers for fishermen who prefer to stand in their kayaks. The outriggers also provide greater stability in rough waters. This 14-footer weighs 79 pounds. It is a good choice for fly fishermen.

▲ The Ocean Kayak Tetra model is good for beginners. It's 10 feet, 8 inches long, and weighs 51 pounds. The polyethylene hull will hold a maximum load of 275 pounds.

▲ The Point 65 is a modular three-piece sit-in kayak design. The sections snap apart for easy storage or transportation. The sections snap together to form a 13½-foot kayak. Two-piece and four-piece models are also available. It is a good choice where storage space is a problem.

▲ L.L. Bean's Manatee Deluxe, a 10-foot sit-in kayak, weighs only 40 pounds and has a capacity of 275 pounds. The cockpit is oversized and roomy enough for paddlers to comfortably move around. It is ideal for ponds, lakes, and calm waters.

▶ The Old Town 169 is a durable family canoe from L.L. Bean. With a length of 16 feet, 9 inches, it's roomy enough for an overnight canoe trip. t will hold 1,400 pounds. Construction is three layers of polyethylene, and the weight is 85 pounds.

For most canoe camping, pick out a 17-footer. It will weigh 60 to 80 pounds and hold roughly 1,000 pounds of gear and people. Don't plan on putting more than two passengers in a canoe this size.

If you're new to canoeing, pick a model with a keel, which will make it easier to paddle in a straight line for long distances. White-water models that have no keel (or a very shallow keel) are designed for fast maneuverability and not suitable for cruising. A good cruising canoe should have a beam of at least 36 inches and a center depth of 12 to 14 inches. The beam should be carried well into the bow and stern so it can carry the maximum amount of gear and food.

Wood canoe paddles may look pretty, but you're better off with tough resilient fiberglass paddles. If you insist on wood, always carry a spare. For both the bow and stern paddler, pick a paddle that reaches between your chin and eyes.

The kayak is a direct descendant of the seagoing kayaks of the Eskimos of the Far North. The basic kayak is a slender, closed-decked craft with a body-fitting cockpit and a waterproof skirt that seals the hatch around the paddler, who feels that he is "wearing the boat."

A two-bladed paddle propels the boat, and a small rudder at the stern assists in steering, making the kayak track straight, or holding the craft in position. The kayak is light, fast, and easy to handle in nearly all types of water.

Various models are designed for touring, fishing, white-water, and sea kayaking. White-water kayaks are nearly always single-cockpit crafts designed for high maneuverability and minimal effort in paddling upriver or downriver. White-water models are usually 13 to 15

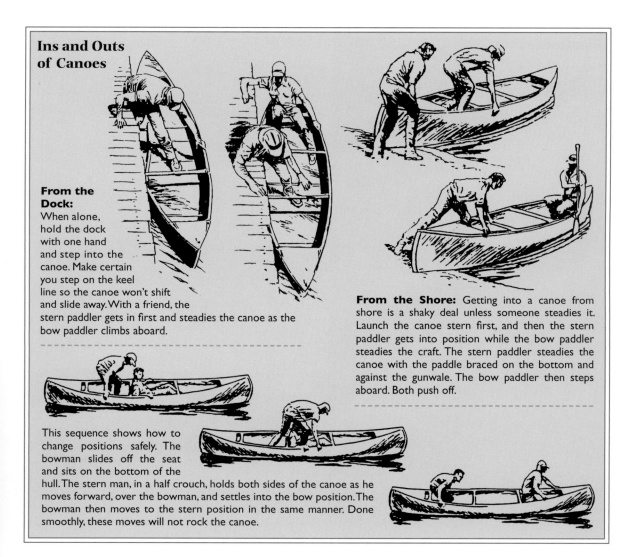

Ins and Outs of Canoes

From the Dock:
When alone, hold the dock with one hand and step into the canoe. Make certain you step on the keel line so the canoe won't shift and slide away. With a friend, the stern paddler gets in first and steadies the canoe as the bow paddler climbs aboard.

From the Shore: Getting into a canoe from shore is a shaky deal unless someone steadies it. Launch the canoe stern first, and then the stern paddler gets into position while the bow paddler steadies the craft. The stern paddler steadies the canoe with the paddle braced on the bottom and against the gunwale. The bow paddler then steps aboard. Both push off.

This sequence shows how to change positions safely. The bowman slides off the seat and sits on the bottom of the hull. The stern man, in a half crouch, holds both sides of the canoe as he moves forward, over the bowman, and settles into the bow position. The bowman then moves to the stern position in the same manner. Done smoothly, these moves will not rock the canoe.

feet long with beams of 23 inches or so. Skilled paddlers can run white water forward, backward, or even broadside in a kayak.

Touring kayaks, sometimes called expedition kayaks, are designed to carry one or two paddlers and range from 16 to 18 feet. Sea kayaks are bigger crafts with exceptional load capacities—as much as 900 pounds—and range from 18 to 22 feet in length with 30-inch beams. Some sea kayaks can accommodate three paddlers, and several manufacturers build collapsible and inflatable kayaks for ease of storage for traveling kayakers. Some inflatables feature multi-chambered bodies and aluminum-frame reinforcements. One touring

model for two paddlers measures 12 feet with a beam of 34 inches. It weighs only 37 pounds and has a capacity of 350 pounds. It will store into a package that measures 35 by 19 by 7 inches.

Almost any kayak can also be used for fishing, but beginning around 2010, kayaks designed specifically for fishing literally stormed the outdoor market. Today, kayaks are used to fish all waters, from farm ponds to offshore waters for billfish. Kayaks can now take anglers into remote backwaters of fresh and salt water that were previously inaccessible.

There are at least a dozen kayak manufacturers producing models suitable for fishermen. First, a fisherman

Unswamping a Canoe

▼ **Step 1** • The man overboard holds on to your canoe and steadies it as you roll the swamped canoe and simultaneously lift one end onto your gunwale.

▼ **Step 2** • Work the canoe so it's entirely out of the water, resting upside down across the gunwales of your canoe. Allow the water to drain out.

▼ **Step 3** • Making certain the canoe is balanced across your gunwales, roll it over slowly. The swamping victim should still be in the water, steadying your canoe.

▶ **Step 4** • Slide the empty canoe back into the water. Now it's ready to go. Steady the craft against your canoe, allowing the person in the water to pull himself aboard.

must decide whether he wants a sit-in or a sit-on model. Sit-in kayaks have a cockpit in which you sit, which is the traditional kayak design. Sit-on models have no cockpit, but are molded with exposed seat arrangements on top of the kayak—a design most fishermen seem to prefer. The sit-in models may be drier and warmer in some waters and allow you to keep more gear covered and dry, but the sit-on kayaks are easier to get on and off—an important factor for fishermen who also like to wade.

There are additional advantages to sit-on models. Some newcomers to kayaking harbor a fear of capsizing and getting trapped upside down underwater. If you capsize with a sit-on kayak, you simply roll the kayak over and climb back on. Sit-on kayaks are also more comfortable if you are big with long legs. Most sit-on models have watertight hatches, which make them a good choice for divers and photographers. Sit-on kayaks also tend to be more stable than the traditional sit-in models.

Good fishing kayaks should measure 12 to 14 feet with a beam of about 30 inches and weigh 60 to 80 pounds. Stability in a fishing kayak is a key factor. Those long, slender kayaks may be faster, but short,

beamier models will be more stable and a better choice for fishing. For extra stability, some models offer removable outriggers.

INS AND OUTS OF CANOES: The cardinal rule for using canoes is don't stand! Standing is one of the most common causes of people falling out of, or capsizing, canoes. Rule No. 2 is never swim away from your canoe if you get dumped. Most canoes have enough flotation to keep afloat until help arrives. Never be afraid of your canoe. I did some testing several years ago and I was amazed at how difficult it was to intentionally tip a canoe over from a sitting position. Getting in and out of a canoe, however, can be tricky unless you follow some basic procedures (see illustrations on opposite page).

UNSWAMPING A CANOE: As mentioned, the most important rule in canoeing is don't stand! Standing is the most common cause of people falling out of canoes, but the rule is often violated by sportsmen who are casting, fighting fish, or hauling an anchor. Equally important if your canoe swamps is to never leave it to try to swim toward shore. Most modern canoes will keep you afloat, even when full of water. In fact, you can sometimes paddle a swamped canoe to shore with only your hands.

If another canoe swamps, you can use your canoe as a rescue craft to get the swamped canoe back into service without having to beach it (see box on previous page).

Paddleboards

Sportsmen who are interested in kayaks and canoes are also likely to be interested in paddleboarding, a water sport dating back to 1926 when some boards were made of redwood. The big comeback of paddleboarding started around 1996, and this water sport is still growing. Paddleboarders can lie down or kneel on a paddleboard, but standing has become the new norm. Manufacturers recommend paddleboards roughly 10 to 12 feet long with a fixed rudder and a weight capacity of about 250 pounds. The boards, which look like surfboards, are usually constructed of a polyethylene outer shell over a watertight polyurethane inner core. Paddles should be 8 to 10 inches taller than the paddler. Some paddles have an angle built in for better efficiency.

The Pelican Surge Stand-Up Paddleboard is 10 feet, 4 inches long, and weighs 33 pounds. It's made of a polyethylene outer shell over a polyurethane inner core. The EVA deck is skidproof. A removable fiberglass fin helps tracking.

Paddleboards are designed for use in calm water or light surf conditions. As a beginner, you should start out by kneeling on paddleboards first. When you feel comfortable with the balance and stability, place your hands on the sides of the paddleboard and try to stand up, placing your feet where your knees were. Falling is part of the learning process. If you fall, aim for the side of the board and fall into the water. Never fall on the board, which could cause injury.

SAFE BOATING

If you're already a boater, or a camper who wants to combine camping with boating, you'll have to learn some boating basics. Unfortunately, boaters don't have a clean record when it comes to accidents afloat. This has little to do with the prerequisites of fishing, but much to do with neglecting to control the boat and guard personal safety aboard. A sportsman who has not schooled himself in basic boating safety and safe habits will forget about them in an emergency. Here's your chance to start right.

Basic Tool Kit

Every boat must be equipped to get home on its own. The exact selection of tools, spare parts, and supplies necessary must be suited to your boat and motor and to problems you are most likely to encounter. Here are the items that should be in a basic tool kit:

- Ordinary pliers
- Vise-grip pliers
- Diagonal-cutting pliers
- Long-nose electrician's pliers
- Screwdrivers
- Spark-plug wrench to fit
- Combination open-end and box wrenches in sizes ⅜ to ¾ inch
- Sharp knife

Spare Parts

Keep these spare parts on hand:

- Spark plugs of correct specifications
- Distributor cap, rotor, condenser, and point set
- Fuel pump and filter
- Oil filter
- Water-pump impeller
- V-belts to match each size used
- Spare fuel lines, cocks, and fittings
- Gaskets and hoses

- Bailing-pump diaphragm
- Fuses and bulbs to double for each used

■ All-Purpose Kit

For an all-purpose kit, include the following:

- 50-foot chalk line
- Nails, screws, bolts and nuts, and washers
- Hose clamps
- Electrical tape
- Insulated wire
- Cotter pins
- Elastic plastic bandage material and duct tape
- Machine oil

■ Safe-Boating Procedures

First, it is important to know your boat. Get familiar with its equipment and discover its limitations. If it's a livery rental, check it over completely before you push off.

Make a habit of checking off safety equipment aboard. First, locate the safety items required by law. Then, compare your optional equipment with the Coast Guard's list of recommended equipment. Count the life preservers, and make sure that each passenger has one that will keep him afloat in the water.

Carry a proper chart, GPS, compass, VHF, and a fully charged cell phone. Put camping and other gear where they are secure and won't clutter walkways and footing.

Check the fuel supply, and the condition of the tank and feed line. Make sure the spark is strong and regular. Take along at least 1½ times as much fuel as you estimate you will need. If you run into heavy waves, your boat will take more fuel to go the same distance.

Gasoline vapors are explosive and will settle in the low areas of a boat. During fueling, keep doors, hatches, ports, and chests closed, stoves and pilot lights off, electrical circuits off, and absolutely no smoking! Keep the fill nozzle in firm contact with the fill neck to prevent static spark. Don't spill, for you'll have to dry it up before starting the engine. Do not use gasoline appliances aboard—they're lethal risks. Use alcohol and other less volatile fuels.

After fueling, ventilate thoroughly before pressing the starter. One minute is the minimum safe ventilation time. Big boats should be ventilated longer, with effective blowers operating and all ports opened. Keep your fuel lines in perfect condition and the boat's bilges clean.

Outboard Motor Troubleshooting Checklist

Follow these steps to check the condition of your outboard motor:

- Check gas supply and tank pressure; squeeze the bulb several times.
- Check to be sure the propeller is not wrapped in weeds, line, or net. If line is wrapped around the prop, try to slow reverse to loosen it. Then, cut off pieces until you can pull the rest free.
- Look for loose wires and clamps at battery terminals.
- Remove ignition wire from any spark plug and crank the motor. A spark should jump from the wire end to the engine head; if there is no spark, check back to the ignition switch.
- If you have a hot spark, look into the fuel feed, pull the gas feed line off from the side of the outboard, and blow through the line until you hear bubbles in the tank.
- Clean the carburetor bowl and fuel filter.

Electrical equipment, switches, and wiring are some prime sources of boat fires and explosions. Keep batteries clean and ventilated.

Do not overload your boat. Make sure you have safely adequate freeboard before casting off. Look ahead to water conditions and weather changes you may encounter.

Keep an alert lookout. If you have a boat longer than 20 feet, name your mate and agree that he'll keep lookout any time you can't. You have more to watch out for than other boats and shallow water. Watch for obstructions such as rocks and floating logs.

Swimmers are hard to see in the water. Running through swimmers or a swimming area is the most sensitive violation a boat can make. If in doubt, give beaches and rafts a wide swing.

Your wake is potent. You can swamp small craft such as canoes or rowboats, damage shorelines and shore property, disturb sleepers, and ruin fish and wildlife sport for hours by running fast through small passages and shallows. You are always responsible for any damage caused by your wake.

Quartering a Following Sea

Quartering may be the only solution to crossing a following sea. Your speed, however, must be faster than the waves running at your stern. You'll have to make corrections with each wave you meet. As you cross the crest, wave action tries to turn a quartering boat broadside by pushing its stern into the trough between it and the next wave crest. You must power your boat into the direction of the trough to properly point your bow toward the next crest. (Note the direction of the outboard and prop in the illustration.) Never allow wave action to push your boat parallel to the trough.

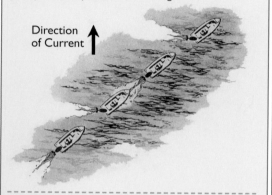

Direction of Current

Mouth of River or Inlet

Wherever a current enters a body of water—this is true for river mouths as well as ocean inlets—you can expect to find relatively calm water at the edge of the intruding flow. Usually this calm transition zone is marked by surface wave action. When running any inlet, always ride the back of the wave in front of you. Never power over its crest, or drift far enough back to be picked up by the crest of the following wave.

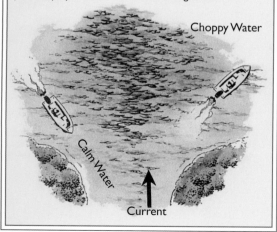

Choppy Water

Calm Water

Current

Learn the Coast Guard navigation rules and obey them at all times. Copies are available to download free on the Coast Guard website. Most collisions are caused by one-time violations.

Make sure at least one other person aboard knows how to operate the boat and motor in case you are disabled or fall overboard. Know a plan of action you will take in emergencies such as a man overboard, bad leak, motor that won't run, collision, bad storm, or troublesome passenger.

Storm signals and danger signs are often informal. Learn to read the weather, and keep alert to what passing boats are trying to tell you.

Wear your life preserver and make all your passengers, especially children, wear life preservers at all times. In a capsizing, remember that you are safer if you stay with the boat, where you can be seen. It will also help you stay afloat until help arrives.

Under Coast Guard legislation, it is illegal for anyone to build, sell, or use a craft that does not conform to safety regulations. Check with your dealer, and check yourself to make sure your boat measures up.

■ Small Boat, Big Water

The best way to stay out of trouble on open water is to learn how to read the wind and weather. The National Oceanic and Atmospheric Administration (NOAA) issues marine weather forecasts every hour with details of winds and seas. If you have a VHF-FM radio, NOAA weather radio broadcasts weather and warnings continuously on these frequencies: 162.400 MHz, 162.425 MHz, 162.450 MHz, 162.475 MHz, 162.500 MHz, 162.525 MHz, and 162.550 MHz. Matching the wind forecast with the accompanying chart will give you a good idea of the seas you can expect to encounter.

But such forecasts are regional, and local conditions can be radically different—thunderstorms, for instance. You can determine the distance in miles of an approaching thunderstorm by counting in seconds the interval between seeing a lightning flash and hearing its accompanying thunder, and then dividing by five. For example, if it takes 10 seconds to hear the thunder, the storm is 2 miles away.

But that knowledge won't help much if you don't have time to get to safety. Odds are you're going to get caught on the water eventually. Knowing how to handle difficult seas in a small boat is insurance all sportsmen should have.

Wind/Sea Relationships

	Velocity (knots)	Conditions
Calm Conditions	0–3	Sea like a mirror
	4–6	Ripples, less than 1 foot
	7–10	Smooth wavelets, 1 to 2 feet
	11–16	Small waves, 2 to 4 feet
Small Craft Warning	17–21	Moderate waves, 4 to 8 feet, whitecaps
	22–27	Large waves, 8 to 13 feet, spray
	28–33	High waves, 13 to 20 feet, heaped seas, foam from breaking waves
Gale Warning	34–40	High waves, 13 to 20 feet, foam blown in well-marked streaks
	41–47	Seas rolling, reduced visibility from spray, waves 13 to 20 feet
Storm Warning	48–55	White seas, very high waves, 20 to 30 feet, overhanging crests
	56–63	Exceptionally high waves, 30 to 45 feet
Hurricane Warning	More than 63	Air filled with foam, sea white, waves over 45 feet

Storm Warning Signals

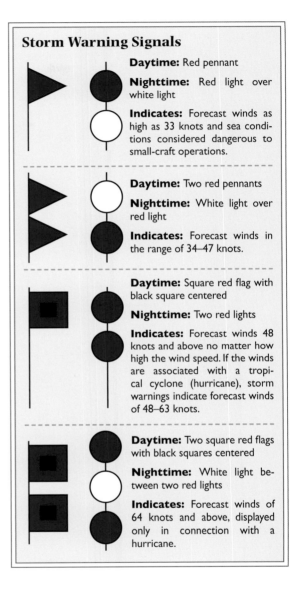

Daytime: Red pennant

Nighttime: Red light over white light

Indicates: Forecast winds as high as 33 knots and sea conditions considered dangerous to small-craft operations.

Daytime: Two red pennants

Nighttime: White light over red light

Indicates: Forecast winds in the range of 34–47 knots.

Daytime: Square red flag with black square centered

Nighttime: Two red lights

Indicates: Forecast winds 48 knots and above no matter how high the wind speed. If the winds are associated with a tropical cyclone (hurricane), storm warnings indicate forecast winds of 48–63 knots.

Daytime: Two square red flags with black squares centered

Nighttime: White light between two red lights

Indicates: Forecast winds of 64 knots and above, displayed only in connection with a hurricane.

■ Coast Guard–Approved Equipment

For safe boating under most conditions, you are required by federal law to carry Coast Guard–approved equipment aboard your craft. Coast Guard–approved equipment simply means that it has been approved by the Commandant of the U.S. Coast Guard and has been determined to be in compliance with U.S. Coast Guard specifications and regulations relating to materials, construction, and performance.

Here are the Coast Guard recommendations for the most essential lifesaving equipment you must have onboard under federal law.

FIRE EXTINGUISHERS: Each approved fire extinguisher is classified by a letter and a Roman numeral according to the type of fire it is designed to extinguish and its size. The letter indicates the type of fire:

A: Fires of ordinary combustible materials

B: Gasoline, oil, and grease fires

C: Electrical fires

Fire extinguishers must be carried on **all** motorboats that meet one or more of the following conditions:

Buoys

Buoys are traffic signals that guide boaters safely along waterways. They can also identify dangerous areas, as well as give directions and information. The colors and numbers on buoys mean the same thing regardless of what kind of buoy on which they appear.

Red colors, red lights, and even numbers • These indicate the right side of the channel as a boater enters from the open sea or heads upstream. Numbers usually increase consecutively as you return from the open sea or head upstream.

Green colors, green lights, and odd numbers • These indicate the left side of the channel as a boater enters from the open sea and heads upstream. Numbers will usually increase consecutively as you return from the open sea or head upstream.

Red and green horizontal stripes • These are placed at the junction of two channels to indicate the preferred (primary) channel when a channel splits. If green is on top,

the preferred channel is to the right. If red is on top, the preferred channel is to the left. The light color matches the top stripe. These are also sometimes referred to as junction buoys.

Nun buoys • These cone-shaped buoys are always marked with red markings and even numbers. They mark the right side of the channel as a boater enters from the open sea or heads upstream.

Can buoys • These cylindrical-shaped buoys are always marked with green markings and odd numbers. They mark the left side of the channel as a boater enters from the open sea or heads upstream.

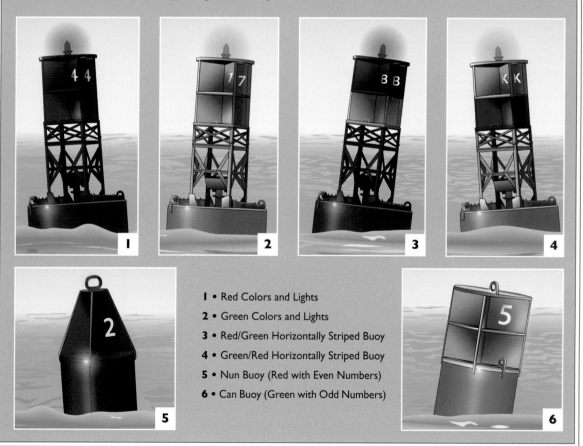

1 • Red Colors and Lights

2 • Green Colors and Lights

3 • Red/Green Horizontally Striped Buoy

4 • Green/Red Horizontally Striped Buoy

5 • Nun Buoy (Red with Even Numbers)

6 • Can Buoy (Green with Odd Numbers)

Fire Extinguishers

Extinguishers approved for motorboats are hand portable, of either B-I or B-II classification or their UL equivalents, and have the following characteristics:

Coast Guard Classes	UL Listing	Foam (gallons)	CO$_2$ (pounds)	Dry Chemical (pounds)	Halon (pounds)
B-I	5B	1¼	4	2	2½
B-II	—	2½	15	10	10
—	10B	—	10	2½	5

- Inboard engines
- Closed compartments under thwarts and seats where portable fuel tanks may be stored
- Double bottoms not sealed to the hull or not completely filled with flotation material
- Closed living spaces
- Closed stowage compartments in which combustible or flammable materials are stored
- Permanently installed fuel tanks

There is no gallon capacity to determine if a fuel tank is portable. However, if the fuel tank is secured so it cannot be moved in case of a fire or other emergency, or if the weight of the fuel tank is such that people onboard cannot move it in case of a fire or other emergency, then the Coast Guard considers the tank permanently installed.

Dry chemical fire extinguishers without gauges or indicating devices must be inspected every six months. If the gross weight of a carbon dioxide (CO$_2$) fire extinguisher is reduced by more than 10 percent of the net weight, the extinguisher is not acceptable and must be recharged. Check extinguishers regularly to be sure that the gauges are free and nozzles clear.

Fire-extinguisher requirements are classified by the size of the vessel:

1. Boats less than 26 feet in length with **no** fixed fire-extinguishing system installed in machinery spaces must have at least one approved Type B-I hand-portable fire extinguisher. When an approved fixed fire-extinguishing system is installed in machinery spaces, no Type B-I extinguisher is required. If the construction of the boat does not permit the entrap-

ment of explosive or flammable gases or vapors, no fire extinguisher is required.

2. Boats 26 feet to less than 40 feet in length must have at least two approved Type B-I or at least one Type B-II hand-portable fire extinguishers. When an approved fixed fire-extinguishing system is installed, only one Type B-I extinguisher is required.

3. Boats 40 feet to not more than 65 feet in length must have at least three approved Type B-I or at least one Type B-I and one Type B-II hand-portable fire extinguisher. When an approved fixed fire-extinguishing system is installed, one fewer Type B-I or one Type B-II extinguisher is required.

Note: Coast Guard–approved extinguishers carry the following label: Marine Type USCG Approved, Size —, Type —, 162.208/, etc. UL-listed extinguishers not displaying this marking are also acceptable, provided they are of the above sizes and types and carry a minimum UL rating of 5-B:C.

PERSONAL FLOTATION DEVICES (PFDs): All boats must be equipped with U.S. Coast Guard–approved life jackets called personal flotation devices, or PFDs. The quantity and type depends on the length of the boat and the number of people onboard or being towed. Each PFD must be in good condition, the proper size for the intended wearer, and, very important, must be readily accessible.

■ Type I: Offshore Life Jacket

These PFDs provide the most buoyancy. They are effective for all waters, especially open, rough, or remote waters where rescue may be delayed. They are designed to turn most unconscious wearers to a face-up position.

■ Type II: Near-Shore Vest

These vests are intended for calm, inland waters or where there is a good chance of quick rescue. This type will turn some unconscious wearers to a face-up position, but will not turn as many people to a face-up position as a Type I.

■ Type III: Flotation Aid

These vests are good for calm, inland waters, or where there is a good chance of quick rescue. They are designed so wearers can place themselves in a face-up position. The wearer may have to tilt his head back to avoid turning facedown in the water. It is generally the most comfortable type for continuous wear.

Personal Flotation Devices

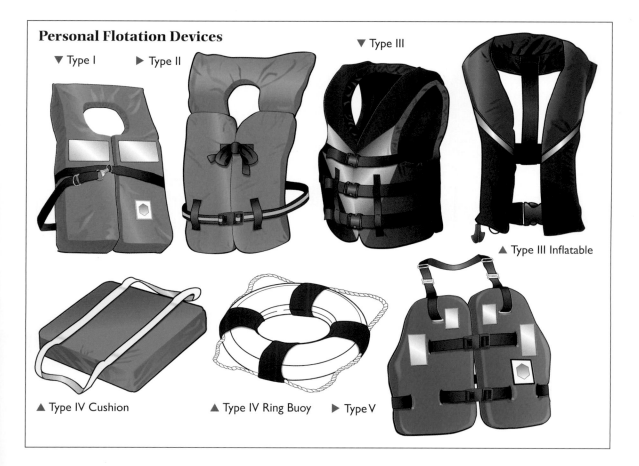

▼ Type I   ▶ Type II   ▼ Type III

▲ Type III Inflatable

▲ Type IV Cushion   ▲ Type IV Ring Buoy   ▶ Type V

■ **Type IV: Throwable Device**

These cushions or ring buoys are intended for calm, inland waters where help is always present. They are not designed to be worn, but to be thrown to a person in the water and held by the victim until they are rescued.

■ **Type V: Special-Use Device**

These PFDs are intended for specific activities and may be carried instead of another PFD only if used according to the label. Some Type V devices provide significant hypothermia protection. Type V PFDs must be used in accordance with their labels to be acceptable.

Note: U.S. Coast Guard–approved inflatable life jackets are authorized for use by people over 16 years of age. They must have a full cylinder and all status indicators on the inflator must be green or the device does not meet the legal requirements. Inflatable life jackets are more comfortable, which encourages regular wear.

VISUAL DISTRESS SIGNALS: All recreational boats, when used on coastal waters, the Great Lakes, territorial seas, and those waters connected directly to the Great Lakes and territorial seas, up to a point where a body of water is less than 2 miles wide, must be equipped with visual distress signals. Boats owned in the United States operating on the high seas must also be equipped with visual distress signals. The following are exempted from the requirements for day signals and only need to carry night signals:

■ Recreational boats less than 16 feet in length

■ Boats participating in organized events, such as races, regattas, or marine parades

■ Open sailboats less than 26 feet in length not equipped with propulsion machinery

■ Manually propelled boats

Pyrotechnic visual distress signals must be Coast Guard approved, in serviceable condition, and stowed to be readily accessible. They are marked with a date showing the serviceable life, and this date must not have passed.

Coast Guard–approved pyrotechnic visual distress signals and associated devices include:

- Pyrotechnic red flares, handheld or aerial
- Pyrotechnic orange smoke, handled or floating
- Launchers for aerial red meteors or parachute flares

Non-pyrotechnic visual distress signaling devices must carry the manufacturer's certification that they meet Coast Guard requirements. They must be in serviceable condition and stowed to be readily accessible. This group includes:

- Orange distress flags
- Electric distress flags

No single signaling device is ideal under all conditions and for all purposes. Consideration should therefore be given to carrying several types. For example, an aerial flare can be seen over a long distance on a clear night, but for closer work, a handheld flare may be more useful.

HANDLING AND STORAGE OF PYROTECHNIC DEVICES:

Pyrotechnic devices should be stored in a cool, dry location and must be readily accessible in case of an emergency. Care should be taken to prevent puncturing or otherwise damaging their coverings. A watertight container, such as a surplus ammunition box painted red or orange and prominently marked "distress signals," is recommended.

If young children are frequently aboard your boat, careful selection and proper stowage of visual distress signals becomes especially important. If you elect to carry pyrotechnic devices, select devices that are in tough packaging and that would be difficult to ignite accidentally.

Coast Guard–approved pyrotechnic devices carry an expiration date. This date cannot exceed 42 months from the date of manufacture and at such time the device can no longer be counted toward the minimum requirements.

A wide variety of signaling devices, both pyrotechnic and nonpyrotechnic, can be carried to meet the requirements of the regulation.

Boats less than 16 feet long operating in coastal waters, and certain other exempted boats listed in the previous section, need only carry signaling devices when operating at night. All other recreational boats must carry both night and day signaling devices.

Sound-Signaling Devices for Vessels Less than 20 Meters (65.6 Feet) in Length

1 • Vessels 12 meters (39.4 feet) or more in length, but less than 20 meters (65.6 feet), must carry on-board a power whistle or power horn and a bell.

2 • Vessels less than 12 meters (39.4 feet) need not carry a whistle, horn, or bell. However, the navigation rules require signals to be made under certain circumstances, and you should carry some means for making an efficient signal when necessary.

The following is an example of the variety and combinations of devices that can be carried in order to meet the requirements:

- Three handheld red flares (day and night)
- One electric distress light (night)
- One handheld red flare and two parachute flares (day and night)
- One handheld orange smoke signal, two floating orange smoke signals, and one electric distress light (day and night)

All distress-signaling devices have both advantages and disadvantages. The most popular, because of cost, are probably the smaller pyrotechnic devices. Pyrotechnics make excellent distress signals, universally recognized as such, but they have the drawback that they can be used only once. Additionally, there is the potential for both injury and property damage if pyrotechnics are not properly handled. Pyrotechnic devices have a very hot flame and the ash and slag can cause burns and ignite materials that burn easily. Projected devices, such as pistol-launched and handheld parachute flares and meteors, have many of the same characteristics of a firearm and must be handled with the same caution and respect.

Under the Inland Navigational Rules, a high-intensity white light flashing at regular intervals from 50 to 70 times per minute is considered a distress signal. Therefore, a strobe light used in inland waters should only be used as a distress signal.

The handheld and the floating orange smoke signaling devices are good day signals, especially on clear days. Both signals are most effective with light to moderate winds because higher winds tend to keep the smoke close to the water and disperse it, which makes it hard to see.

The distress flag must be at least 3 by 3 feet with a black square and ball on an orange background. It is accepted as a day signal only and is especially effective in bright sunlight. The flag is most distinctive when waved on something such as a paddle or boat hook or flown from a mast.

The electric distress light is accepted for night use only and must automatically flash the international SOS distress signal (• • • − − − • • •). Flashed four to six times each minute, this is an unmistakable distress signal, well known to most boaters. The device can be checked anytime for serviceability if shielded from view.

Red handheld flares can be used by day, but are most effective at night or in restricted visibility, such as fog or haze. When selecting such flares, look for the Coast Guard approval number and date of manufacture. Make sure that the device does not carry the marking, "Not approved for use on recreational boats."

◼ Navigation Lights

REQUIRED ON BOATS BETWEEN SUNSET AND SUN-RISE: Recreational boats operating at night are required to display navigation lights between sunset and sunrise. Although most recreational boats in the United States operate in waters governed by the Inland Navigational Rules, changes to the rules have made the general lighting requirements for both the Inland and International rules basically the same. The differences between them are primarily in the options available.

1. A power-driven vessel less than 20 meters (65.6 feet) in length shall exhibit navigation lights as shown in Figure 1. If the vessel is less than 12 meters (39.4 feet) in length, it may show the lights as shown in either Figure 1 or Figure 2.

2. On a vessel less than 12 meters (39.4 feet) in length, the masthead light must be 1 meter (3.3 feet) higher than the sidelights. If the vessel is 12 meters or more in length but less than 20 meters (65.6 feet), the masthead light must not be less than 2.5 meters (8.2 feet) above the gunwale.

3. A power-driven vessel less than 50 meters in length may also, but is not obligated to, carry a second masthead light abaft of and higher than the forward one.

4. A power-driven vessel less than 7 meters (23 feet) in length and whose maximum speed cannot exceed 7

Range and Arc of Visibility of Lights
For Vessels Less than 20 Meters (65.6 Feet) in Length

Light	Visible Range in Miles		Arc in Degrees
	Less than 12 Meters	12 Meters or More	
Masthead light	2	3	225
All-around light	2	2	360
Side lights	1	2	112.5
Stern light	2	2	135

knots may, in international waters **only**, in lieu of the lights prescribed above, exhibit an all-around white light, and shall, if practicable, also exhibit sidelights.

SAILING VESSELS AND VESSELS UNDER OARS:

1. A sailing vessel less than 20 meters (65.6 feet) in length shall exhibit navigation lights as shown in either Figure 3 or Figure 4. The lights may be combined in a single lantern carried at the top of the mast as shown in Figure 5.

2. A sailing vessel less than 7 meters (23 feet) in length shall, if practicable, exhibit those lights prescribed for sailing vessels less than 20 meters in length, but if it does not, it shall have ready at hand an electric torch or lighted lantern showing a white light that shall be exhibited in sufficient time to prevent collision (see Figure 6).

3. A vessel under oars may display those lights prescribed for sailing vessels, but if it does not, it shall

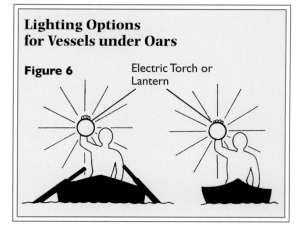

Lighting Options for Vessels under Oars

Figure 6　　Electric Torch or Lantern

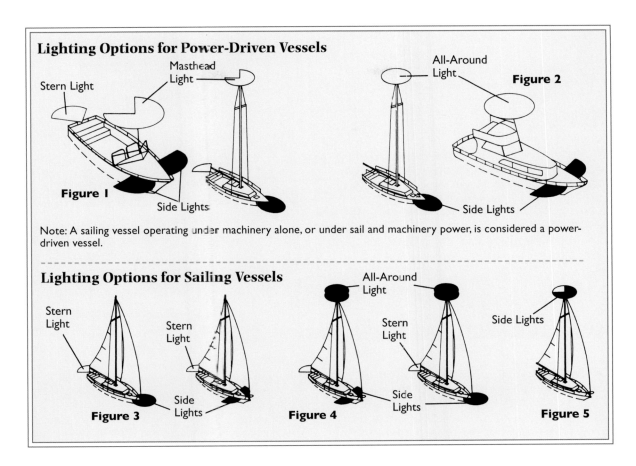

Lighting Options for Power-Driven Vessels

Stern Light · Masthead Light · Figure 1 · Side Lights

All-Around Light · Figure 2 · Side Lights

Note: A sailing vessel operating under machinery alone, or under sail and machinery power, is considered a power-driven vessel.

Lighting Options for Sailing Vessels

Stern Light · Side Lights · Figure 3

All-Around Light · Stern Light · Side Lights · Figure 4

Side Lights · Figure 5

have ready at hand an electric torch or lighted lantern showing a white light that shall be exhibited in sufficient time to prevent collision (see Figure 6).

LIGHTS USED WHEN ANCHORED: Power-driven vessels and sailing vessels at anchor must display anchor lights. However, vessels less than 7 meters (23 feet) in length are not required to display anchor lights unless anchored in or near a narrow channel, fairway, or anchorage, or where other vessels normally navigate.

An anchor light for a vessel less than 20 meters (65.6 feet) in length is an all-around white light visible for 2 miles exhibited where it can best be seen. A vessel less than 20 meters in length in inland waters, when at anchor in a special anchorage area designated by the Secretary of Transportation, does not require an anchor light.

DAY SHAPES: A vessel proceeding under sail when also being propelled by machinery shall exhibit forward,

where it can best be seen, a conical shape, apex downward (see Figure 7), except that for Inland Rules, a vessel less than 12 meters in length is not required to exhibit the day shape (see Figure 8).

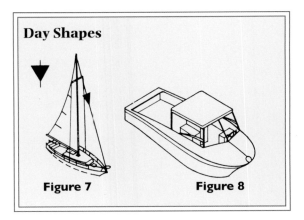

Day Shapes

Figure 7 · Figure 8

■ Loading Your Boat

There are several things to remember when loading a boat: distribute the load evenly, keep the load low, don't overload, don't stand up in a small boat, and consult the U.S. Coast Guard maximum capacity plate. On boats with no capacity plate, use the accompanying formula to determine the maximum number of people your boat can safely carry in calm weather.

The length of your vessel is measured in a straight line from the foremost part of the vessel to the aftermost part of the vessel, parallel to the centerline, exclusive of sheer. Bowsprits, bumpkins, rudders, outboard motors, brackets, and similar fittings are not included in the measurement.

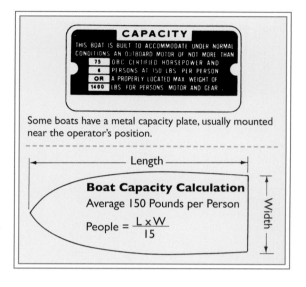

Some boats have a metal capacity plate, usually mounted near the operator's position.

Boat Capacity Calculation
Average 150 Pounds per Person

$$\text{People} = \frac{L \times W}{15}$$

HANDLING WIND, WEATHER, AND WATER

If you're a camper who wants to try boating, you better learn to have a healthy respect for both fresh and salt water. I recall a terrible boating tragedy years ago that could have been avoided. Eight men in a 28-foot pleasure craft got caught in 20-foot seas and 70-mile-per-hour winds about 30 miles off the East Coast of the United States. In a miraculous Coast Guard rescue, seven men were saved, but one man was never found.

The wife of a survivor told reporters, "I don't understand why the captain took the boat out. The captain didn't want to go. He said it was too windy."

I'll venture a guess why the captain took the boat out. It was probably a long-planned fishing trip, no one wanted to be disappointed, and the weather didn't look bad at the dock.

I remember that day and I also remember a weather forecast that would have kept me at the dock. I don't care how many friends showed up to go fishing, I would have treated them to breakfast at a local diner and sent them home. They would be disappointed, but alive. The open water is no place to prove that you have more guts than brains.

Never forget that if you own and run a boat, you are also the captain, and you are totally responsible for the safety of your passengers. If someone gets hurt on your boat, you have to take the blame. I get scared when I see a boat pass me with young children sitting

on the bow with their feet hanging over the side. One bumpy wake and a child could easily be killed by the prop. I get angry when I see a boater pulling a water skier in a channel with heavy boat traffic. I wonder what is going through the minds of small-boat operators who disappear in ground swells as they head offshore when a small-craft advisory flag is flying in plain view. I say a prayer when I see a family overload a boat and head out for a day of fishing with 2 inches of freeboard.

High winds and rough water can turn a pleasant day into a life-threatening nightmare. The best way to stay out of trouble is to learn how to read the weather, wind, and water. And it's equally important to know when to cancel a trip and stay home. This advice is even more important to fishermen who tend to use smaller boats and go out in marginal weather.

Rule No. 1: Check the weather. The National Weather Service issues marine forecasts every six hours with details of winds, seas, weather, and visibility. Heavy static on your AM radio may also indicate nearby storms. The National Weather Service also posts visible warnings at prominent locations along the shore, including Coast Guard stations, lighthouses, yacht clubs, and marinas.

One of the problems with weather forecasts is that they are not always right. Sometimes you may have to make judgment calls on your own. Learn to read simple weather signs. Watch for dark, threatening clouds, which nearly always indicate a thunderstorm or squall. Any steady increase in wind or sea is another sign of bad weather.

If you're on the water, don't wait too long to make a decision. Calm winds and water can turn into a gusty electrical storm in as little as 30 minutes. If you've taken all precautions and you still get caught in a storm, pinpoint your location or note your GPS location on a chart before heavy rain reduces your visibility. Watch for other boats, secure hatches, lower antennas and outriggers, stow all loose gear, and, most important, make sure everyone is wearing a life jacket.

Once the storm hits, try to take the first and heaviest gusts of wind on the bow of the boat. Approach waves at a 45-degree angle to keep the propeller underwater and reduce pounding. If there is lightning, unplug the radio and electrical equipment. Stay away from metal objects and order your passengers to stay low. If you don't lose power, you should be able to ride out almost any storm.

■ How to Forecast Weather

There are dozens of signs that will give you a hint of approaching weather patterns and a whole bunch of weather axioms that will prove true most of the time. Learning how to read some basic signs is fun and it can keep you out of trouble in the outdoors, but it's still important to remember that no weather forecasting system is 100 percent accurate.

There probably isn't a boatman alive who hasn't heard the axiom, "Red sky at night, sailor's delight. Red sky in the morning, sailors take warning." The red sky in the morning may well mean rain that day because there's enough moisture in the air to redden the sky at sunrise. Because of atmospheric conditions, that prediction may come true in the northern United States but it won't work in tropical climates where red sunrises are common.

I've also heard the axiom, "A ring around the moon means rain." If you only look for a ring around the moon, you will get rain about 50 percent of the time. You can get better odds, however, if you're more observant. If you notice a falling barometer along with that ring around the moon, you can be sure of rain within 24 hours about 80 percent of the time.

There are other weather signs to help you in the outdoors. Birds, for example, perch on wires, rooftops, and trees more often before storms because low-pressure air is less dense, making it a lot harder to fly. Waterfowl

hunters also know that ducks and geese fly a lot higher in good weather than in bad. One reason, other than visibility, is that low pressure affects their ears.

Pay attention to most clouds. Generally, the high clouds will not rain on you, no matter how threatening they look. It's those low clouds that will pound you with rain. You can also forecast impending rain by observing smoke from any smokestack. If the smoke rises, you will get fair weather. If the smoke, however, is driven downward by low pressure, rain is on the way.

If you're in the woods and you sense that smells and scents are stronger around you, there's a good chance that you will get rain. Odors held captive by high pressure escape as the barometer drops, which nearly always means bad weather.

In coastal areas, rain is more likely at low tide than at high tide. A falling tide reduces atmospheric pressure. In the country, check the trees. Leaves show their backs or undersides before a rain. Vegetation grows to prevailing winds and a change in wind direction, which also means a change in weather, turns them over.

Listen to the sounds of boats, gunshots, distant voices, and so on. If the sounds are loud and hollow, you could get rain. A lowering cloud ceiling acts like a sounding board and will bounce noise back to you.

If weather starts to turn bad, note the direction of lightning. If it's in the west or northwest, the storm will probably reach you. Storms to the south or east, however, will usually go past.

When you leave your campsite in the morning, look at the grass. A heavy dew on grass at night and in early morning is a sign of fair weather. Dew forms at those times only when the air is dry and the skies are clear.

Are all of these weather signs true all of the time? Not on your life! But they work most of the time, which is about all you can say for any weather forecast.

■ Lightning and Your Boat

No other kind of foul weather will make a person feel as helpless as lightning. And there's good reason to be scared. Lightning is deadly, but there are certain precautions to take to minimize the risk of being struck.

Lightning is a discharge of static electricity from a charged cloud to earth or from one cloud to another. The electric charge is created when a cumulus cloud is formed in an updraft of warm, moist air. This combination results in a huge buildup of static electricity in a big cumulonimbus cloud. The top part of the cloud holds a positive charge and the bottom part holds a negative charge from the friction of the updraft. When a thunder-cloud passes overhead, the negative charge induces the earth to take on a positive charge, usually at the highest points, such as tall buildings, poles, or even humans. These charges in clouds and ground are normally kept apart by air, which acts as an insulator. When the static charge becomes strong enough, however, it overcomes the resistance of the air, and lightning occurs.

When a lightning bolt with a current of more than 100,000 amps passes through the atmosphere, the air is heated and expanded, creating a strong vacuum. It's this rapid expansion and collapse of air that creates the loud shock wave known as "thunder."

Thunder can also tell you how far you are from lightning. Count the seconds between lightning and thunder, and then divide by five. The answer is the distance between you and the lightning in miles. If there's a five-second lapse between lightning and thunder, for example, the lightning is a mile or so away.

If you're in a boat on a lake or offshore, lay fishing rods down and head for cover. If you're in a cabin boat and can't reach land ahead of the storm, stay in the cabin and close all the hatches. If you're running the boat, stay as low as possible at the controls. Lower all fishing rods, antennas, and outriggers. Don't hold any gear connected with the grounding system, and don't hold lifelines or rigging. Avoid acting as a bridge between conductive objects. Never touch outriggers, radio antennas, or electrical appliances until the storm has passed. Keep the boat's bow in the wind as much as possible and head for shore. Passengers should wear life jackets and stay in the cabin or as low as possible in the boat.

■ Get Ready for Hurricanes

Don't wait for a 12-hour warning to start preparing your boat for a hurricane. Do it now! You may need more time than you think to work out a plan of action that will secure and protect your boat in a storm. Now is the time to think about extra lines and special storm gear.

Even the best plan of action, however, cannot guarantee that your boat will survive a hurricane. Some hurricanes prove so violent that boats and people are helpless in their path. Fortunately, not all hurricanes are killers and there are some precautions you can take to keep storm damage to a minimum.

Most boaters believe their real threat of damage comes from winds and waves. This isn't so. Most boat damage comes from storm surge, which means high water. In fact, storm surge accounts for nine out of 10 hurricane-related deaths.

The safest place for your boat is out of the water. If you have a trailer, load your boat on it and take it home. If the boat and trailer fit in your garage, park it there and leave your car outside. Your boat is lighter than your car and can get blown off your trailer in hurricane winds. If you must leave your boat and trailer outside, put it where it will get the best protection from the wind, trees, and electrical lines. Let some air out of the trailer tires, block the wheels, and make sure the boat is strapped securely to the trailer.

You have two options when you leave your boat on a trailer. First, if it's a heavy boat, take out the drain plug to allow rainwater to drain quickly out of the hull. If your boat is light, however, and you are concerned that it may blow off the trailer, leave the drain plug in and fill the hull with water from a garden hose to add more weight. Don't put in too much water or you will damage the hull. Remember that rain will add more water and weight.

Don't trust a storage rack, even if your marina says it's a safe place. There may be other lighter boats that could be blown off their cradle and into your boat. Tell your marina to take your boat out of the rack and block it securely in a safe area. Your marina may balk at this, but be insistent.

If you are forced to leave your boat in the water, make sure it is tied securely, which means double lines. Most boats require five lines: two bow lines, two stem lines, and one spring line. If a hurricane is approaching, you will need 10 lines. It's also wise to go up one size larger than your normal dock lines. Line your boat with as many rubber fenders as you can find to protect the craft from the dock. Always give your lines chafe protection where they will come in contact with the boat or cleats. Neoprene hose is best, but canvas wrapped in place with duct tape will do in a pinch.

If your slip is a small one, look around for a bigger one that's empty and ask your marina if you can use it. The more distance you put between your boat and the pilings and bulkhead, the safer it will be.

Mooring and anchoring in a protected harbor that is not crowded is a safe way to ride out a hurricane, but only if the mooring is a permanent installation and you back it up with two additional storm anchors.

When you leave your boat, take all loose gear and electronics with you and use duct tape to seal all hatches, windows, vents, and doors. When you feel your boat is ready for a hurricane, the next step is an important one:

go home! When hurricane-force winds hit your boat at 100 miles per hour, there will be nothing you can do.

You can now track a hurricane by phone, which may give you enough warning to secure your boat. When a hurricane is headed your way, you can get official hurricane advisories issued by the National Oceanic and Atmospheric Administration (NOAA) or the Weather Channel.

■ Man Overboard!

If you're a camper, you're probably also a fisherman, and most fishermen will have their boats in the water before warm summer temperatures arrive. They will push the season and launch for trout, flounder, and other species that will start biting in early spring. One truth that is hard to accept is the fact that many fishermen are not dedicated boatmen. Fishermen are usually interested more in fishing than boating . . . and this means a potential danger to themselves and their passengers.

One distinct danger is falling overboard into cold water. Even if you are a good swimmer, the effects of cold water may be more than your body can handle. Cold water can rob your body of heat very quickly. When your body temperature drops, hypothermia becomes a very real threat to life.

Don't be misled into believing that water has to be 35 degrees to be dangerous to someone falling overboard. Cold water is anything below 70 degrees. When the water temperature drops to as low as 35 degrees, survival is usually based on the physical condition of the victim.

Panic and shock are the first and most dangerous hazards to a fisherman falling overboard. Cold water can shock the body and sometimes induce cardiac arrest. Remember how your breath is taken away when you dive into a pool? The same reaction happens when you fall headfirst into cold water. Your first gasp for air will fill your lungs with water. You may also become disoriented for a minute or two before you realize what is happening to you.

If at all possible, get back into your boat as quickly as possible. Your life may depend on it. Unless you have a big boat, this may not be as difficult as it sounds. The majority of fatal boating accidents involve small boats with outboard motors. Most small boats, even if capsized, can be righted and reentered.

Small boats are legally bound to have enough flotation to support all occupants. If you can right the boat,

Float Plan

File a float plan. Tell someone where you are going and when you plan to return. Tell them what your boat looks like and other information that will make identifying it easier should the need arise. Print a copy of the float plan from the Coast Guard website (www.uscgboating.org/safety/float_planning.aspx), fill it out and leave it with a reliable person who can be depended upon to notify the Coast Guard, or another rescue organization, should you not return as scheduled. Do not, however, file float plans with the Coast Guard.

A PDF version of this form can be downloaded from the U.S. Coast Guard website.

climb back into it and bail out the water. If you can't right the boat, climb onto the hull and hang on. It's critical that you get out of the cold water.

If the boat slips away and you can't reach it, there are certain precautions to take in the water until help arrives. Unless there is no chance for a rescue, do not try swimming. It will drain body heat and, if you're like most people, you will not be able to swim very far in cold water.

Your best bet is to remain still and get into a protective position to conserve heat and wait for a rescue. This means protecting your body's major heat-loss areas, such as your head, neck, armpits, chest, and groin. If there is more than one person in the water, huddle together to preserve body heat.

Treatment of cold-water victims varies. The first signs of hypothermia are intense shivering, loss of coordination, mental confusion, blue skin, weak pulse, irregular heartbeat, and enlarged pupils. If the victim is cold and only shivering, dry clothes and blankets may be all that is necessary.

If the victim is semiconscious, move him to a warm place and into dry clothes. Make him lie flat with his head slightly lower than his body, which will make more blood flow to the brain. You can also warm the victim with warm towels to the head, neck, chest, and groin.

Of course, it's always easier to avoid problems by taking a few simple precautions. First, wear a life jacket at all times, especially during cool weather. Whenever possible, wear several layers of wool for insulation. Wool, even when wet, will retain body heat.

If you suddenly find yourself in the water, make sure your life jacket is snug. Keep clothing buttoned up. The water trapped in your clothes will be warmed by your body heat and keep you warm.

■ Why Boats Sink

The mere thought of a boat sinking out from under its skipper and his passengers will send chills down the back of the toughest boater. Will he calmly handle the situation or will he go to pieces and panic? Why did it happen? What did he do wrong?

According to statistics, boaters should worry more about sinking at the dock than out on the water. Statistics show that three out of four recreational boat sinkings happen right at the dock. Fortunately, most dockside sinkings can be prevented.

First, never depend completely on an automatic float switch to turn on your bilge pump when water

gets into your hull. Bilge pumps and switches, because of their location, get dirty and will sometimes jam in the off position and not turn on your pump at all or get stuck in the on position and kill your battery. Both cases are bad news and could sink an unattended boat. Check your bilge pump and switches before every trip. In fact, automatic float switches should be replaced every other year. These switches are inexpensive and easy to wire to a bilge pump.

Learn how to tie your boat correctly at the dock, especially in tidal water. If your boat swings or drifts too freely at the dock, it could get stuck under the dock and get pushed under the water when the tide rises. This kind of sinking happens all too often.

Make it a point of learning every through-hull underwater fitting on your boat. Draw the locations of the fittings on a piece of paper and check them every time the boat is out of the water. Look inside the hull. Do all the fittings have seacocks? Do they all work? Do you close them when you leave the boat unattended? Do you keep them well lubricated? It's the kind of maintenance and attention that will keep your boat afloat.

Remember that your boat can take on water from above the waterline as well as from below. Check all deck fittings, fastenings, and hatches. Not all boat manufacturers use a good sealant on fastenings and some of them leak. Hose down your cabin and decks, and then look for leaks inside and in the hull. If you see a leak, fix it. You can sink from rainwater just as easily as from a leak below the surface.

Water from washings at the dock can sometimes get trapped in the hull. To get this water out, try this trick. When your bow lifts up, just before you get on a plane, manually switch on your bilge. If you have to, keep the bow high until all the bilge water rushes to the pump and gets pumped out.

Continually check all hoses and clamps. Clamps are cheap. If they look rusty, replace them. In fact, you should keep an assortment of different size clamps in your toolbox. Pay special attention to hoses that have sharp bends. If any look stressed or kinked, replace them. Replacing a hose when your boat is on a trailer is easy. It's a panic problem, however, if it happens 5 miles from shore. It's also a good idea to double clamp all hoses.

If you're shopping for a boat, look for designs with self-bailing cockpits. This means the deck is above the waterline. Any water coming into the boat will drain out the transom scuppers and not stay in the boat or hull. This is a comforting thought in a heavy sea. Most of the tough breed of small fishing boats built for offshore fishing have this feature. Many small, less expensive ski boats, however, do not have self-bailing cockpits. Stay away from them.

Make sure your transom drains, transom wells, and scuppers are clean and not clogged with dirt. Water must be allowed to drain out. The best time to check these drains and flush them out is when you're washing your boat with a hose and good water pressure.

Maintenance of through-hull fittings, seacocks, hoses, bilge pumps, and switches is easy. Make a checklist and do it often. This is especially important if you leave your boat unattended for long periods of time.

If you leave your boat in the water, you should also get a mooring cover that protects your boat from bow to stern. This kind of full cover will give you peace of mind the next time it storms and your boat is 50 miles away at the marina where it may not get any attention.

■ Why Boats Blow Up

A day on the water can be an exhilarating experience, but when things go wrong with your boat, it can also be a frightening experience. The thought of a fire or explosion on a boat is even more terrifying. If you're far from land, there is no safe place to run.

Fires and explosions can only come from faulty fuel systems or human error. Fortunately, both are avoidable if you take certain precautions. First, let's start with the deck. Is your gas cap clearly labeled "gasoline"? As far-fetched as it sounds, there are cases on record where a clueless gas attendant has pumped gasoline into a rod holder or into a water tank.

All boats must have an overside drain or tank vent for your fuel tank. Make sure that excess fuel or fumes at the gas dock will not find their way into your boat or bilge. Make sure your vent has a mesh screen in place, which could keep fumes from igniting in the fuel line.

If your fill hose is worn or frayed, replace it. But make certain you buy the right hose. It should be stamped "USCG Type A2," which is fire resistant. Your filler cap should also be grounded with an electrical wire from the fill opening to the tank, so that any static electricity from the dock hose will flow to the ground without causing a spark.

It's critical that you run your blower to clear your bilge of gas fumes before starting your engine. Check the blower hose and make sure it's not crushed, broken, or twisted. After you've run your blower, sniff the bilge with your nose, which is probably the best fuel detector of all. If you have any doubts, don't start your engine. This is especially true at the fuel dock, where most explosions and fires occur.

If you're buying a new or used boat, check the fuel tanks. Any tank over 7 gallons should have a label with the manufacturer's name, date of manufacture, capacity, and material. It should also say, "This tank has been tested under 33 CFR 183.580." If you can't find this label, avoid the boat or have the tank replaced.

Even if you have all the right fittings and parts, you can still get into trouble if you are careless. Explosions are most likely to occur at the fuel dock, when a leak in the fill or vent system may not be discovered until the tank is topped off.

When you refuel, take certain precautions. First, close all hatches and turn off the battery switch and stove. Fill the tank yourself, if you can, and never fill it to the very top. If you do, and the gas expands, you could get spillage in your boat and bilge. After refueling, run the blower for a full five minutes or longer, and then sniff the bilge with your nose before starting the engine.

If you use outboard-motor tanks, take them out of the boat and do your refueling on the dock. This is the safest procedure. Unfortunately, most inboard and stern-drive boats don't have this option.

Let's suppose, for example, that you don't notice a fuel leak until it is too late and you're out on the water with a bilge full of gas. Do you know what to do? Here's the best and only procedure. Do not start the engine or use any electrical equipment other than your VHF radio or cell phone—and this should be only after you turn off all other electrical circuits. Next, turn off your battery switch and have all your passengers put on life jackets and stay on deck. Finally, call the Coast Guard and describe your problem and situation. They will instruct you on the next step.

If you find gas has leaked into your boat at the dock, order all guests off the boat. Turn off the battery switch and shore power. Notify the marina manager and call the fire department.

Don't wreck your day or endanger your guests because you don't know how to handle a gas emergency. Most of these procedures are simple common sense.

CAMPFIRE COOKING

Section Three
CAMPFIRE COOKING

• CAMP STOVES • CAMP COOK KITS •
• CAMP FOODS AND MENUS • RECIPES •

CAMP STOVES

An open wood fire in a public campground is becoming a rare sight. For too long, careless campers haphazardly cut down trees for fuel and left their fires unattended, causing costly forest fires that destroyed thousands of acres of woodland every year. As a result, most campgrounds today prohibit open fires. Even if they didn't, the lack of available wood would be a prohibition in itself. Thus, the modern camper has been compelled to carry a stove on his camping trips, and in some ways has improved his lot. Certainly people who like to cook are more at home with a stove than a wood fire. A stove does away with blackened cooking utensils, hot sparks, and eye-watering smoke.

■ Wood Stoves

The sheepherder's stove is the best known of this type, but due to their weight and awkwardness, wood stoves in general are fading from the camping scene. The sheepherder's stove is constructed of sheet metal and often features a small oven for baking, as well as several sections of piping to carry smoke outside the tent. A fireproof collar around the pipe where it passes through the tent is a necessity. Some models fold flat and have telescoping piping. Nevertheless, the wood stove is impractical for the average camper, particularly because modern tents are not equipped to handle stove-pipes. The exceptions are the newer stoves designed to burn small pieces of wood while also recharging your electronic devices.

■ Gasoline Stoves

With white, unleaded gasoline a readily available commodity these days, the gasoline stove has become the leader among camp stoves. It's fine for year-round use, as bitter-cold weather has little or no effect on gasoline.

The typical gasoline stove with just one burner weighs 2½ pounds and has a tank capacity of 2 pints of fuel, which should keep it burning approximately 3½ hours. For large families, there are two- and three-burner gasoline models that weigh up to 25 pounds.

The two-burner stove is the best choice for general camping. For large families on a short outing, one two-burner and one single-burner stove are better than one bulky three-burner stove. But for cabin or long-term camping, choose the three-burner model. A backpacker can get along with just one burner. Some backpacker models tip the scales at a mere 20 ounces and can fit in a large coat pocket. Campers and hikers who just want a quick pot of coffee or hot soup during the day appreciate the lightweight one-burner stoves.

The Bass Pro BioLite Camp Stove is a good cooking source for backpackers. This wood-burning stove will allow you to cook a meal while charging your electronic gadgets. It burns twigs and sticks and has a built-in fan for a more efficient fire. It measures only 8 inches high.

The BioLite Base Camp Grill allows you to cook for a group while charging your small electronics with a built in five-watt USB charger. It is designed to burn firewood and small branches. The grill measures 13 inches in diameter.

■ Propane Stoves

Highly popular among warm-weather campers is the stove that runs on propane gas, also known as LP, or liquefied petroleum. In winter, propane stoves do not work well because the cold tends to reduce the temperature of gas, thereby diminishing volatility and ultimately the vital heat output.

A 5-pound, single-burner stove is typical, with a usually disposable 14.1- or 16.4-ounce cylinder of gas. A double-burner stove weighs about 12 pounds and often uses a separate cylinder for each burner. For extended stays in camp, many manufacturers make large-capacity, refillable tanks of propane that can be carried aboard a plane or packhorse.

As with gasoline stoves, a two-burner stove is recommended for general camping, and one single-burner and one double-burner model for larger families. The advantages of propane gas over white gasoline

Propane Stoves

A Bass Pro single-burner propane stove turns any standard 16.4-ounce propane cylinder into a stand-up camp stove that will produce 16,000 BTUs of power. It is designed with a 7½-inch grid and four folding feet for extra stability.

Two stainless-steel burners produce 25,000 BTUs of propane heat on the Bass Pro Outfitter Stove. It uses any standard 16.4-ounce propane cylinder. It features a high-altitude regulator, electronic ignition, and a heavy-duty steel frame built to handle heavy pots. The stove measures about 24 inches by 13 inches and is about 6 inches high.

The Camp Chef Outdoorsman Stove is designed for people who plan to camp for more than a couple of days. Two burners produce 90,000 BTUs from a 20-pound propane tank for up to 15 hours of cooking time. The stove weighs 41 pounds and stands 31 inches high. It is a good choice for a deer camp or tailgating.

are the ease with which it lights and its carrying convenience. Also, no pumping, priming, or pouring are necessary because the sealed containers of propane readily attach to the stove.

On the other hand, propane is not as easily available throughout the country as gasoline. Before leaving home, take into account the length of your trip, whether or not you are carrying an ample supply of propane gas, and the proximity of stores stocking propane along your route. Another problem with propane is that you're never quite sure if you are running low. Thus, it's a good idea to have two cylinders.

Getting down to economics, studies have shown that the average camp meal costs a few cents to cook with gasoline, but approaches 50 cents when propane is used. With the advantages that propane stoves have in summer, many campers care little about the added expense. Another featherweight gas used in contemporary stoves is butane, also a liquefied petroleum.

■ Canned Heat

Known commercially as Sterno, this is a solid, non-melting fuel that's odorless, safe, and burns clearly and steadily until totally consumed. You can extinguish it as many times as you like by simply replacing the pry-off top. The touch of a match will quickly re-light it. Sterno is sold in several sizes. The 7-ounce can, for example, will burn for 1½ hours. A pint of water can be brought to a boil with Sterno in just 15 minutes, but canned heat is not intended for much else. Stoves designed specifically for cans of Sterno can be

purchased, ranging from inexpensive stamped-metal racks to two-burner models.

■ Reflector Oven

This device is used for baking bread, rolls, pies, muffins, cake, fish, and meat at your campsite. It is a simple, collapsible, lightweight (about 3 pounds) contraption made of sheet aluminum that reflects the heat of a stove or campfire onto the food. A stainless-steel shelf provides more even heating, but an aluminum shelf will suffice. A good shelf can handle up to 10 pounds of food.

■ Dutch Oven

If you could take only one pot on a camping trip, it would have to be a Dutch oven. Why? Because it does everything! In addition to helping create great one-pot dinners that require very little attention, it can also be used to bake, grill, and stir-fry. Introduced to the Americans by Dutch traders, it was improved by Paul Revere, who added a flat top with a turned-up edge (to hold coals) and three stubby legs (to sit over coals). It was the most important cooking pot for pioneers as they moved westward, and today it's an essential piece of gear for sportsmen, outfitters, camp cooks, and anyone else who enjoys preparing meals outdoors. In fact, there's only one drawback to a good Dutch oven. It's heavy. An 8-quart pot may weigh nearly 20 pounds—it's obviously not for backpackers.

When buying a Dutch oven, avoid aluminum, steel, and glass-lined versions since they don't distribute heat evenly and can cause your food to scorch. Instead, look for a cast-iron pot, which retains heat and distributes it equally throughout. And stick to the traditional oven, with the flanged lid and legs.

All cast-iron Dutch ovens must be seasoned before being used for the first time. Wash the pot thoroughly with a mild dishwashing detergent to remove the wax coating used for protection in shipping. Rinse with hot water and dry with a paper towel. Grease the inside of the pot and the lid with pure vegetable shortening (do not use margarine or butter), and then place in a 250 to 300°F oven for 15 minutes. Remove the pot, carefully drain off any excess oil, and return to the oven for another hour. Allow the pot to cool at room temperature. Your Dutch oven is now ready for use.

Your first step in cooking with it is to get some hot coals. You can get them in the traditional way from a campfire (a keyhole campfire is best) or you can cheat

This Lodge Logic 5-Quart Dutch Oven is preseasoned by an electrostatic spray system that applies just the right amount of vegetable oil, which deeply penetrates the pores of the cast iron. Dutch ovens are popular with camp cooks because they do everything and excel at one-pot meals that require little attention.

Dutch-Oven Cooking

Controlling the temperature of your Dutch oven when cooking in camp or the outdoors takes a bit of trial and error to master. There are quite a few variables involved, including ambient temperature, altitude, humidity, and wind, as well as the fuel you use. The aspiring outdoor chef will find it to be as much of an art as a science. Fortunately, you will get the hang of it pretty quickly once you learn a couple of basic concepts. The information provided below should provide you with a pretty solid understanding of what you need to know to get started.

For the beginner, it is easy to start with two basic rules of thumb: the "Rule of Three" and "Double Up." Both are used with charcoal briquettes as the heat source and both provide the same result temperature-wise. The rule you use depends upon what type of cooking you are doing.

The Rule of Three

For baking, you want to have more heat coming from above. In order to get to 325°F for 30 to 40 minutes, take the diameter of your oven and add three to determine the number of coals to place on top of your oven. Subtract three to determine the number of coals to place beneath your oven. Place your coals in an evenly spaced checkerboard pattern to obtain even heat.

Tip: For stew, chili, etc., you will want more heat coming from the bottom, so just reverse the Rule of Three (oven diameter minus three on top, plus three underneath for 325°F).

Double Up

For roasting, you want to have even heat coming from both top and bottom. To get to 325°F for 30 to 40 minutes, use a number of coals that is double the diameter of your Dutch oven. Place an equal number of coals in an evenly spaced checkerboard pattern on top of and beneath your oven to obtain even heat.

Frying

When frying foods in your Dutch oven, you will obviously want to have all of the heat coming from the bottom. This also applies when using the lid of your oven as a griddle. To do this, support the upside-down lid of your oven with a couple of bricks or flat stones. Place your coals under the lid and you'll have a griddle that is ideal for making pancakes or fried eggs.

A Note on Charcoal

For temperatures other than 325°F, you will obviously need to add or subtract briquettes. Typically, you should add two charcoal briquettes for every 25 degrees of temperature needed. Also, these methods are based upon the use of regular charcoal briquettes. Do not use Match Light charcoal for Dutch-oven cooking. Match Light briquettes are soaked with lighter fluid, which causes them to burn hotter and faster than conventional charcoal.

Dutch-Oven Venison Recipe

Taken from *Backcountry Cooking* by J. Wayne Fears

Serves 12

Salt and pepper to taste	*Hot water*
Meat tenderizer	*Dry onion soup mix*
6-pound venison roast	*Worcestershire sauce*
	Cold water

Put salt, pepper, and meat tenderizer on the venison roast. Make a thick paste with the hot water and dry onion soup mix, and coat the entire roast. Sprinkle Worcestershire sauce over the roast. Add a cup of cold water to the Dutch oven, place the roast in the oven, and cover. Place in hot coals, adding coals to the lid, for approximately 4 to 5 hours.

by using charcoal briquettes. In fact, many Dutch-oven recipes now specify the number of briquettes you'll need for the lid and beneath the pot.

With a Dutch oven, you can cook either above ground or below ground. It may take some practice, but you can prepare a venison stew in a Dutch oven in the morning, bury it in hot coals, and it will be ready for dinner when you return to camp in the evening. You can also use your Dutch oven to bake a batch of biscuits or an apple pie.

■ Box Oven

Coleman manufactures a collapsible oven—the box oven—which has about the same capacity as a typical Dutch oven and can be used with a gasoline stove for baking pies, biscuits, etc.

This oven may be used on wood fires after some modifications have been made, provided it is always placed over the coals, never over the flame. Otherwise, your food will become smoked.

CAMP COOK KITS

For a party of four campers willing to accept the fact that filet mignon will not be on the menu, the most practical cook kit—in automobile, tent, or trailer camping—is a nesting set in which the pots, pans, plates, and cups fit inside one another. A typical aluminum cook kit for four campers should include:

- one 8-quart kettle
- one 4-quart stew pot
- one 2-quart stew pot
- two frying pans with handles
- one spouted pot
- four plates
- four plastic cups

Extra plates and cups can be purchased for a group of more than four. Cups should be plastic rather than aluminum, since aluminum gets too hot to hold or drink from. Aluminum also lets liquids cool too quickly.

If you don't mind some additional weight, there are commercial kits made of stainless steel. Much more durable than aluminum and simpler to clean, stainless steel is also more expensive. Make sure that the plates, frying pans, and cups are not too thin, as they too will become too hot or cold to handle.

Teflon keeps food from sticking and makes cleaning easier. Teflon-coated utensils require special tools to protect the thin coating from scratching, but if the added weight and bulk are no problem, these are excellent items.

In addition to knife, fork, and spoon sets for each camper, the cook needs a tool kit and it should include:

- one carving knife
- one paring knife
- one potato peeler
- one long fork
- one spoon
- one ladle
- one turner
- one bottle/can opener

The backpacker, who must limit his supplies to a minimum, may be inclined toward a more compact unit, which should include:

- one 1-quart pot
- one 5½-inch frying pan
- one 1-pint bowl
- one 1-cup mug

Examine any mess kit before buying it. It is best to discover a missing utensil in the store. Avoid gadgets advertised to simplify camp meals—from folding toasters to corn poppers to immersion heaters—until you are certain you need them. Begin with the basics and experiment.

To make cleaning easier, use all-purpose paper (toilet paper, for example) to wipe excess food out of your plate immediately after eating. Beware of slipshod

Coleman's Camp Oven is made of aluminized steel and can be used on any camp stove to trap heat for baking and warming. It features a thermostat to control heat and folds flat for easy packing.

The Coleman Pack-Away Camp Kitchen makes setting up a campsite easy. The stove sits conveniently on a side stand. The design holds everything you need to prepare meals for several days. It is made of powder-coated steel and folds compactly for packing and storage.

washing, which can produce gastric upsets such as dysentery the next meal around.

A pair of lightweight cotton gloves may save the cook from getting burned, cut, or grimy. And while soap, towels, dishrags, and scouring pads (plastic, steel wool, or copper wire) add ounces to your gear, they also speed up the cleaning and drying process.

Aluminum foil, though not recommended as a cook kit in itself, proves quite useful as a supplementary item. As a pot liner, foil keeps food from gumming up the pot. Wrapped around the bottom of the pot, it stops blackening from the fire. The same result can also be achieved by rubbing the pot's exterior with a bar of soap.

Paper plates and cups save time in cleaning up, but the choice is up to you.

The travel kitchen or chuckbox is recommended if you're camping in a motorized vehicle. Available assembled or in kits, these kitchens have five or six compartments to separately store items such as utensil kits, cleanup kits, nonperishable foods, and the like. Because of weight and bulk, the kitchen is inappropriate for horsepacking, canoeing (with portages), and backpacking trips. Many campers make woodbox arrangements with their own modifications after several years of camping.

Canteens come in various styles—round, oval, and a flask-shaped model that clips to the belt. All can be filled with practically any liquid and, if you care to, you can freeze the entire contents. Aluminum models are more rugged than plastic ones. Some feature a chained screw cap and most have a shoulder strap. Canvas covers ward off dirt and dents.

The main concern in purchasing a canteen is proper size. Many tenderfoot campers make the mistake of hauling along a canteen with a 4-quart capacity. That's a gallon, and awfully heavy to carry. For most daylong outings, a 1-quart model is sufficient. For weekends, a 2-quart canteen is advisable, particularly if potable water is a rarity in the area you are in. Water-purification tablets are inexpensive and valuable if you're not sure how drinkable the water is.

CAMP FOODS AND MENUS

To plan nutritious camp menus, consider these four basic questions:

1. How many meals of each type (breakfast, lunch, etc.) will there be?
2. Where will the meals be prepared (in a blind, on a mountainside, etc.)?
3. How will the supplies be transported (backpack, RV, packhorse, etc.)?

4. How many people are in the group and what kind of appetites do they have?

Apply the answers to the three main groups of food—carbohydrates, proteins, and fats—and determine the necessary amount of calories.

Calories supply energy. How many calories you need depends on your weight, your rate of metabolism, and how much work you are doing. Everyday camping chores use up about 3,000 calories per day, while backpacking requires 4,000 calories for the same period. Cold weather and a steep climb may call for as many as 5,000 calories. When your intake of calories is less than your output, fat already stored by your body will be burned off. To prevent weight loss, it is necessary to consume a sufficient amount of calories daily.

The protein requirement depends primarily on body weight. A man weighing 130 pounds needs 60 grams of protein per day, while a 175-pound man needs 80 grams. Protein is essential because it builds and repairs body tissues. Good sources are cheese, meat, milk, eggs, and fish.

A wide variety of dehydrated or freeze-dried foods is available through sporting-goods stores, camp-equipment dealers, and even supermarkets. Both processes take as much water out of the food as possible to permit lightweight packing and simple preparation.

Straight dehydration is an air-drying process wherein heat dries the food but leaves it flexible. Once the food is cooked, the water returns. Freeze drying, on the other hand, removes water by quick-freezing and placing the food in a vacuum chamber. The pressure drops in the chamber and heat is added. The ice then sublimates slowly, meaning it goes directly from solid to gaseous form with no intermediate liquid state. The resultant food is the same size, slightly paler, and far lighter. Soaking the food from 10 to 30 minutes brings on the flavor. Besides being odor-free, the freeze-drying process leads to finer taste and quality than standard dehydration.

The outdoor cook should stress simplicity, but

Nutrition Information for Freeze-Dried Foods

Several companies produce complete lines of freeze-dried food for campers, hikers, survivalists, or anyone interested in these lightweight packaged foods. Here, courtesy of Mountain House, is a nutritional chart of its line of entrées. The data here is a typical example of the nutritional values of foods from other companies as well.

Product				Calories		Fat/Grams		Milligrams
Product Name	Pkg. Net Wt. (ounces)	Servings per Pkg.	Serving Size	Total	From Fat	Total	Saturated	Cholesterol
Beef Stew	4.30	2.5	1 cup	150	40	4.5	1	20
Beef Stroganoff with Noodles	4.80	2.5	1 cup	250	100	11	4	40
Beef Teriyaki with Rice	5.75	2.5	1 cup	260	25	2.5	0.5	10
Chicken à la King with Noodles	6.35	3	1 cup	260	80	9	2.5	50
Chicken Breasts with Rib Meat and Mashed Potatoes	3.70	2	½ pkg.	210	30	3	1.5	55
Chicken Teriyaki with Rice	5.01	2.5	1 cup	230	20	2	0.5	20
Chili Mac with Beef	4.80	2.5	1 cup	240	60	7	2.5	30
Lasagna with Meat Sauce	4.80	2.5	1 cup	240	70	8	3.5	25
Long Grain and Wild Rice Pilaf	5.08	2.5	1 cup	220	35	4	2	10
Macaroni and Cheese	6.81	3	1 cup	310	130	15	7	35
Mexican Style Rice and Chicken	5.40	3	1 cup	220	45	5	2	20
Noodles and Chicken	4.73	2.5	1 cup	220	45	4.5	0.5	40
Pasta Primavera	4.80	2.5	1 cup	170	30	3.5	2	10
Potatoes and Cheese with Broccoli	4.37	2.5	1 cup	200	40	4.5	2.5	15
Rice and Chicken	6.38	3	1 cup	270	80	10	1.5	10
Seafood Chowder	4.44	2.5	1 cup	230	90	10	6	60
Spaghetti with Meat Sauce	4.51	2.5	1 cup	230	45	5	2	20
Sweet and Sour Pork with Rice	6.10	2.5	1 cup	280	45	5	1.5	40
Turkey Tetrazzini	4.27	2.5	1 cup	230	70	8	1.5	30

variety is possible. Have cereal with dried fruit one day and pancakes with syrup the next. Lunches can go from cheese to sausage to peanut butter. Suppers can be more elaborate if you'd like, and precooked items are worthwhile in that respect. By adding water to certain foods, the camp chef can prepare delicious chicken or beef stew. And water is always available if you are near a stream or lake.

Consider prepackaging such foods as sugar, salt, bacon, and flour. There's no need to lug along much more than a quarter of the contents. Premeasure this food, and then pack and label it, specifying for which meal and which day it is intended.

Remember to include supplementary or trail foods. They are not a part of any set meal, but they may increase flavor (condiments, for example), add flexibility to the menu, or give rapid-fire energy. Supplementary foods should be high in protein. Trail foods can substitute as lunch or emergency food when cooking a full meal is impractical. Often high in calories, fat, and carbohydrates, foods such as raisins, nuts, chocolate, bacon, candy bars, and hard candy provide instant energy and keep the saliva flowing in your mouth so it doesn't become uncomfortably dry.

Keep in mind that fresh food is fine the first day out, but thereafter stick to foods that will not spoil quickly, if at all, on what might be a humid trail.

■ Camper's Grub Box

The campsite chef, whether at a cabin back in the bush or in a tent camp in some wild country, should compile a grub box. Your mode of transportation determines to some extent what you can take to a campsite. If you're going into a permanent camp or cabin by truck, grub logistics are simple; you can usually take all you will need to produce breakfast, lunch, and dinner.

If you're a backpacker, however, your food lists will change drastically. Freeze-dried foods will be your best bet if you're carrying your grub box on your back (see Camp Foods and Menus on page 107). You can trim weight by buying canned and boxed foods and repacking them in leakproof, labeled plastic bags. You can premeasure contents and carry only what you will need. If you're backpacking, you will also need more energy. Everyday camping chores will burn about 3,000 calories a day, but a backpacker will burn 4,000 calories during the same time period.

The average camper, who may travel to a campsite by truck or ATV, has no such limitations. He can put together a grub box with enough basic ingredients to turn out healthy and acceptable camp meals. You can add or subtract to suit your particular camp cooking requirements, but the following is a list of cooking ingredients and seasonings that should be in a basic grub box:

Grams				
Sodium	Carbs	Dietary Fiber	Sugars	Protein
620	16	2	2	12
820	29	1	3	10
760	48	2	13	11
750	29	2	2	16
800	21	2	2	24
700	41	2	13	10
650	31	3	3	12
330	28	3	7	14
660	44	2	3	6
640	31	1	1	14
620	32	6	3	13
870	34	1	2	9
330	28	1	4	6
370	31	5	7	9
740	41	1	1	7
840	23	1	7	13
560	32	3	5	12
950	47	1	16	12
700	22	1	5	14

- Garlic powder
- Onions
- Celery salt
- Green peppers
- Potatoes
- Dried mushrooms
- Flour
- Sugar
- Butter
- Rice
- Coffee
- Tea
- Dried beans
- Ketchup
- Mustard
- Vinegar
- Pancake flour
- Cornmeal
- Jams and jellies
- Cooking oil

Sample Grub List

On our annual fishing trips to Canada, my fishing buddy Fred Bekiarian has always assumed the responsibility of doing all the food shopping and cooking. Over the years, Fred has learned what he will need in camp to produce excellent dinners for his discriminating buddies. I rank Fred as a master camp chef, and his grub list is based on many trips to remote Ontario and Quebec lakes where supplies were sometimes nonexistent. His list includes supplies to feed three fishermen for a total of 12 meals over four days: dinner on Thursday; breakfast, lunch, and dinner on Friday, Saturday, and Sunday; and breakfast and lunch on Monday. Study Fred's list below and use it to create your own shopping list for your next trip.

■ INGREDIENTS

- 2 cans corn
- 2 cans string beans
- 1 box mashed potatoes
- 2 packages gravy
- Flavored breadcrumbs
- Flavored rice
- Pesto sauce
- 1 pound cavatelli
- Cookies (optional)
- 2 cases water
- Soda or iced tea
- Olive oil (optional)

- Cento vinegar (optional)
- Pickles
- Hot peppers
- Ketchup
- Mustard
- Mayo
- 1½ pounds ham
- ½ pound salami
- 1 pound turkey
- Broccoli florets
- Baking potatoes
- 6 heads romaine lettuce
- Garlic

- 3 large onions
- 18 to 20 chicken legs
- 3 steaks
- 3 chicken breasts
- 6 large hamburgers
- 4 dozen eggs
- 3 packages frozen sausage
- Coffee
- Half and half
- ½ gallon milk
- 1 large tub butter
- 1 pound bacon
- Biscuits
- ½ gallon orange juice
- Hamburger rolls
- 6 loaves bread
  (rye, Irish soda, or white)
- 2 pounds cheese slices, wrapped

■ OTHER SUPPLIES

- Garbage bags
- Freezer bags
- Lunch bags
- Aluminum foil
- Plastic wrap
- Paper plates
- Paper cups
- Plastic utensils
- Liquid and bar soap
- Toilet paper
- Paper towels

The traditional shore lunch of fried fish, especially if it's walleye fillets, frequently becomes the highlight of any fishing or camping trip. Don't forget the potatoes, beans, and onions.

How much food to take on the trip depends on the number of campers. For example, if lunches are taken for a camping trip, each person will probably consume four slices of bread a day for lunch. On a three-day trip with four campers, that comes to 12 slices per person or 48 slices for the trip. There are about 18 slices in a loaf of bread. Pancakes? Figure four cups of flour each time you make a batch for four campers. Eggs? Four campers eating two eggs a day will mean you have to carry two dozen eggs. Bacon? Figure three slices of bacon per camper per day or roughly two pounds of bacon. An average one-pound package of bacon has 18 slices.

This is roughly the formula you would use to determine quantities for your grub box, and it applies to nearly all foods from steaks to fish fillets to pork chops. You can also supplement your menu with the game and fish you catch, but don't count on it.

■ The Campsite Cooler

One of the most important pieces of camping equipment is your cooler. Without a good cooler, your perishable

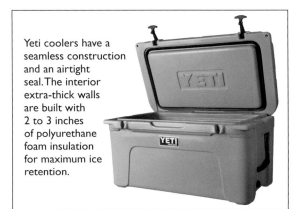

Yeti coolers have a seamless construction and an airtight seal. The interior extra-thick walls are built with 2 to 3 inches of polyurethane foam insulation for maximum ice retention.

foods will likely spoil or melt within 24 hours. Some of the new coolers available today will keep food fresh for several days. The Coleman Xtreme coolers, for example, will keep ice for six days in temperatures up to 90 degrees. The tough Yeti coolers will also keep ice for several days.

There are also ways to ensure that your ice will stay frozen as long as possible. You should prepare your cooler by putting several bags of ice in it the night before to chill the interior. If you have access to a walk-in freezer, you can also store your cooler in the freezer the night before your camping trip. When you put ice in a cooler, break the bags open and spread the ice to cool the interior sides of the cooler.

At your campsite, never put your cooler in the sun. Find a shady location and try not to open the cooler too often. I've gone a step further and placed a wet burlap sack over the cover. When the ice starts to melt, leave the ice water in the bottom of the cooler. It will continue to chill the interior of the cooler and keep canned and bottled liquids cold. The only exception is to make sure your food is not in direct contact with the water so it doesn't become soaked.

If you're a fisherman, take an extra cooler on your boat. Under no circumstances should you toss fish in the bottom of the boat, let them lie there in the sun, and gather them up at the end of the day. Place your fish on a bed of crushed ice in a cooler and they will stay fresh. When saltwater fishing, I've added salt water to the ice to make an ice slush and then I drop my fish in it. It will keep the fish fresh and firm.

■ Animal-Proof Your Camp

If you're a hiker, fisherman, or camper, there is always the chance that you will encounter bears or other wild animals. How you behave may determine the outcome.

Most advice on bears focuses on grizzlies, but the information can just as easily be applied to black bears and other wild animals. Most animals will avoid you, but there will always be the one that will break the rules.

If you're at a designated campsite, take all garbage with you. Don't leave it in a trash barrel to attract animals.

If you're a hunter, animal carcasses or parts of carcasses should be stored at least 100 yards from any campsite or trail. In bear country, never sleep within 100 yards of any animal carcass.

If you encounter a grizzly, your behavior can affect the situation. The Wyoming Fish and Game Department advises that you should first try to slowly leave the area. Keep calm, avoid direct eye contact, back up slowly, and speak in a soft monotone. Never run and do not try to climb a tree unless you are sure that you have time and ability to climb at least 10 feet before the bear reaches you. Grizzlies can run faster than you can.

If a grizzly charges, stand your ground. Bears will often mock charge or run past you. If you're unarmed and a bear overpowers you, assume a cannonball position, covering your head and neck with your hands and arms. Stay in this position until you are sure that the bear is gone.

Getting it Right

In bear country, make sure that all food, beverages, and scented toiletries are stored out of reach of bears at night or when your camp is unattended during the day. Hang your food 10 feet off the ground and 4 feet from any vertical post, or store it inside a bear-resistant container, such as a car, pickup cab, or hard-sided container. Coolers, pop-up campers, and tents are **not** bear-resistant containers.

RECICES

I have many memories of remote camping and fishing trips, but what I most often picture in my mind's eye is sitting around an open fire at the day's end watching a venison tenderloin or a brace of red-fleshed brook trout cooking in a skillet or grilling over a bed of coals. I can't imagine any trip without such a campfire experience. Years ago, I was lucky enough to get a copy of *The L.L. Bean Game and Fish Cookbook*. It is an excellent collection of recipes, and my friends at L.L. Bean have given me permission to share some of those recipes especially selected for campfire cooking. All of the recipes in this chapter can be made in camp although some may require a little forethought so you can pack the appropriate ingredients. Try them on your next camping trip.

Big Game

■ Buck and Bourbon

Serves 6

5 tablespoons flour
1 teaspoon salt
¼ teaspoon pepper
2 to 2½ pounds venison, cut into 1½-inch cubes
2½ tablespoons oil or lard
2 medium onions, diced
½ cup chopped green pepper
2 cloves garlic, diced
1 cup tomato sauce, canned or homemade
½ teaspoon thyme or crushed rosemary (or both)
3 ounces bourbon
½ cup water with beef bouillon cube

Combine the flour, salt, and pepper. Shake or roll the venison cubes in this mixture to coat. In a skillet (with a lid for later use), add the oil or lard and then brown the meat cubes over low to medium fire. Don't crowd the meat pieces. Remove as they are ready, and then set aside. Saute the onions, green pepper, and garlic in the same skillet until soft. Add the browned meat cubes and remaining ingredients, cover, and simmer slowly for about 1½ hours. Check for liquid two or three times. If the meat cubes were well floured, the stew will be properly thickened when finished.

Cooking over an open fire is great, but washing charred pots can be a tough job. Try wrapping the outside of your pots with aluminum foil. When you're finished cooking, simply peel off the foil. It's quicker and easier than scouring the pots. If you don't want to carry foil, rub the bottom of the pot with a bar of soap. Most of the dirt will come off easily.

■ Caribou Broth and Vegetables

Serves 4 to 6

3 quarts water
2 to 3 pounds shank meat (or any stew meat)
1 shank bone sawed in pieces (at home, use beef marrow bone)
2 beef bouillon cubes
3 carrots, cut up in chunks
1 onion, sliced
3 potatoes, diced
2 ribs celery with leaves
1 (29-ounce) can tomatoes
Salt and pepper to taste
½ cup chopped parsley
½ teaspoon thyme (optional)
2 bay leaves (optional)
¼ teaspoon savory (optional)

If you are in camp, put on a stewing kettle as soon as you have a fire up, and put in the water, meat, bone, and bouillon cubes. Bring to a boil, and set back to simmer for a couple of hours. Before you go to bed, set the kettle with its lid askew where it will cool. The next morning, remove and discard the "pan" of congealed fat. That night, rally your camp mates to prepare the vegetables. While they are peeling, scraping, and dicing the carrots, onion, potatoes, and celery, put the kettle of broth and meat on the wood range or sheet-iron stove and bring to a boil. Add the diced vegetables, canned tomatoes, salt, pepper, and herbs and simmer covered for 20 to 30 minutes, depending on how large the carrot and potato chunks have been cut.

The Best Venison

Baffin Island in the Northwest Territories can be downright mean to hunters. It's cold, windy, and wet. Campfires are a luxury on Baffin. There are no trees, and the only vegetation is lichen and moss. The shoreline is a maze of ankle-twisting rocks. But the caribou hunting more than made up for the aches and pains in my body.

I had taken a nice caribou with a perfectly symmetrical rack and a big shovel that nearly touched the bull's nose. I was hunting with Jim Zumbo, an old friend and *Outdoor Life*'s former hunting editor. When we finally got back to our tent camp at dusk, we were wet, cold, and hungry. I was ready for dinner. The cook tent, however, had a shocking surprise for us. Our cook was boiling several foil packets of frozen ravioli! I realize that we were on Baffin Island, not a very user-friendly place, but Jim and I knew we could do better than soggy ravioli.

We visited the caribou I had killed earlier that day and Jim took the tenderloins from the bull. We doused them with lots of pepper and fried them in butter until the meat was medium rare. Sliced into medallion-size pieces, the meat was by far the best meal of the trip. Jim and I wondered how many hunters overlook the tenderloins even though they are easy to prepare in camp. In a survival situation, it's also one of the quickest meals you can get from a deer you've had to kill for food.

It's true that venison should be allowed to cure for at least a week before eating, but this is not true of the tenderloins, which can be eaten soon after a deer, caribou, or elk is brought into camp. Prepared properly, the tenderloins can be turned into delicious dinners.

The tenderloins are two small strips of meat, measuring about 1 to 2 inches in diameter and about 12 to 15 inches long. Obviously, the bigger the animal, the bigger the tenderloins. They are located on both sides of the backbone inside the upper chest cavity. The tenderloins can only be removed from inside the chest cavity. Don't confuse the tenderloins with the backstraps, which are cut away from both sides of the backbone from outside the carcass. Backstraps, incidentally, produce your venison filet mignon. But even the backstraps cannot compare with the tenderloins, the most tender part of a deer.

As soon as you field dress that deer, cut out the tenderloins. Do it before the air has a chance to toughen the meat's surface. Use a small knife to separate the tenderloins from the cavity. Once the initial cut is made, you may be able to pull the tenderloins free. But do it carefully because the meat is so tender it may tear.

Cooking the tenderloins back in camp is easy. Because the meat is tender and tasty, a simple recipe that will not alter the flavor is best. In a deer camp, where you want to keep cooking time down to a minimum, cut the tenderloins into medallions about ½ inch thick and coat them with salt, pepper, and a touch of garlic powder. Then, sauté the pieces in a hot skillet greased with butter until the meat is rare and pink inside.

Venison Liver

Venison liver is usually the main course in a deer camp. When you take the liver out of your deer during the field-dressing operation, wipe it clean and put it in a plastic bag. Back in camp, soak it in a pan of water with a cup of salt. Keep changing the water until the liver is thoroughly purged of blood, and then pat dry.

Preparing liver is easy. All you need is about a pound of bacon, four or five onions, flour, and butter. First, fry the bacon in a skillet. In a second skillet, sauté the sliced onions in butter until they are soft and transparent. When both the bacon and onions are done, set them aside. Now, flour the liver, which you've already cut into slices ½ inch thick, and fry them in the skillet with the bacon drippings. Take care not to overcook the liver. Serve the bacon and onions over the liver. A bottle of very dry cabernet sauvignon will further enhance the meal. Eating venison liver is a matter of taste. Some people will love it and others will never touch it.

A word of caution: when you field dress a deer and remove the liver, it should be dark red and uniform in color. If you see white spots or flukes in the liver, these are parasites and you should probably discard the liver. There are various opinions about the edibility of a liver with suspicious spots, but unless you are in a dire survival situation, I recommend you discard a spotty liver.

Venison Heart

It's unfortunate that many hunters routinely discard the heart from a deer or elk. Venison heart can be tough, but when handled and prepared properly, it is truly a specialty dish. I've eaten deer and elk hearts several times on hunts with Jim Zumbo. A deer heart is not big and will generally feed two people. An elk heart, however, is about the size of a pineapple and enough for several people. For preparation, I defer to Jim, an expert on wild-game cookery. The following recipe is from his book *Amazing Venison Recipes*.

Venison Heart Like You've Never Had It Before

Serves 6

1 venison heart
Cooking oil
⅔ cup uncooked rice
⅓ cup chopped celery
¼ cup chopped green pepper
2 ounces canned mushrooms, sliced
10¾ ounces condensed cream of mushroom soup
2 tablespoons dry onion soup mix
¼ teaspoon garlic salt
¼ teaspoon parsley flakes

Rinse the heart and remove the outer membrane. Cut the heart open and cube the tender fleshy parts, discarding gristle, venous hard parts, and any fat. Brown the cubes in cooking oil. Add water and simmer for 45 minutes. Add the uncooked rice, celery, and green pepper. Bring to a boil. Reduce heat, cover, and simmer until the rice is tender (about 20 minutes). Drain the mushrooms and then stir into the heart mixture along with the mushroom soup, dry onion soup mix, garlic salt, and parsley flakes. Simmer for 10 minutes more.

■ Joe Murray's Venison or Moose Steak

Serves 6 to 8

4 to 5 onions
3 green peppers
18 to 20 mushrooms
¼ pound butter
2 bay leaves
3 to 4 pounds venison or moose steaks, 1½ to 2 inches thick
Salt and pepper
4 garlic cloves, smashed

Dice the onions, green peppers, and mushrooms. Take a cast-iron frying pan and fry them up in the butter with the bay leaves. Then, take the steak and rub salt, pepper, and smashed garlic cloves into the meat on both sides. Fry the meat with the onions and peppers. Do not overcook the meat, as this will make it tough.

■ Vension Liver à la Mario

Serves 6

2½ pounds venison liver, sliced ½ inch thick
½ cup flour
Salt and pepper
6 tablespoons butter
2 tablespoons lemon juice

The famous game restaurateur Mario prepared venison liver this way: Dip the liver in flour, salt, and pepper, and then sauté it over a fairly high heat in the hot butter, turning it once. Mario liked it rare, so cook about 4 minutes on each side. Stir in the lemon juice, loosening the browned particles in the process, and then pour the lemon butter over the liver.

Make Jerky in Your Kitchen

When frontiersmen headed west and mountain men ran traplines in the Rockies, these adventurers had a common problem: no refrigerators or freezers. The only way they could preserve meat was to dry it. We don't have those problems today, but sportsmen still enjoy making and eating dried meat. We prefer to call it jerky. It's a great trail food and it's easy to make in your kitchen before you head out on a camping trip.

If you don't get a deer this season and your hunting buddy won't share his venison, all is not lost. You can still make jerky from domestic beef. Jerky is nothing more than raw meat with all the moisture removed. Just make sure the meat is very lean. You must also trim away all fat, sinew, and gristle. Too much fat in jerky can cause rancid meat. For the record, fatty meat, such as bear and wild boar, does not make very good jerky. Round steak from a deer, elk, moose, caribou, or antelope makes the best game jerky.

You can use the sun to dry meat, but it's safer and more convenient to use your kitchen oven or a fruit dehydrator. Always remember that you are drying the meat and not cooking it.

First, cut the meat (venison, if you're lucky) with the grain into strips about 6 inches long, 1 inch wide, and ¼ inch thick. Next, coat the meat with salt and pepper, then brush heavily with Liquid Smoke, which you can find in any supermarket. Let the meat marinate overnight in your refrigerator.

The next day, drain the meat on paper towels and place the strips in your oven. It's best to run a toothpick through the end of a strip and hang it from your oven rack. Put a tray under the meat to catch the drippings. Most ovens will have room for about two dozen strips.

Now, set your oven to 130°F or its lowest setting. Use a meat thermometer to make sure the oven stays at 130°F. Drying time may vary slightly, but most of the time it takes about 10 to 12 hours. It's important to leave the oven door slightly open to allow moisture to escape.

If it has dried properly, the meat will be dark with no moisture in its center. You should be able to bend the strips of meat without breaking them. You can store the meat in any moisture-proof container. A jar with a tight lid will do, but I prefer ziplock plastic bags. You can eat jerky anytime. Just bite off a piece and start chewing. The saliva from your mouth will reconstitute the dried meat into tasty food.

There is no need to limit yourself to beef and venison. You can just as easily make turkey or pheasant jerky. Because you will need strips, the meat must come from the breasts of these birds. Cut the strips 2 or 3 inches long with the grain of the meat running lengthwise. Season the breast meat the same way as venison or domestic beef. The drying process, however, may take less time. Depending on the thickness of the cuts, 4 to 6 hours in your oven, set on the lowest temperature, should do it.

There are all kinds of variations to making jerky. If you don't like the taste of Liquid Smoke, marinate the meat in equal parts of soy sauce and Worcestershire sauce and ¼ teaspoon of garlic powder. If you like it hot, substitute cayenne pepper for the garlic powder. You can also rub the meat with a sugar cure before drying, and then coat the meat with steak sauce after drying. Making jerky is easy so don't be afraid to experiment with various seasonings. If you don't know where to start, you can always find prepared blends in most sporting-goods stores.

Food Dehydrators

You can invest in a food dehydrator to make your own jerky—as well as dry fruit for making trail mix. Most dehydrators operate at temperatures from 90 to 160°F. The low temperature prevents food from cooking while evaporating water. The RedHead 8-Tray Food Dehydrator has 1,200 square inches of drying space powered by a 620-watt heating element. The unit measures only 13 by 13 by 18 inches.

■ Moose Stew
Serves 6

3 ½ pounds stew meat, cubed (can use the
   eyes of venison chops)
Salt and pepper
½ teaspoon powdered thyme, divided
3 to 4 tablespoons flour
2 to 3 tablespoons lard, oil, or bacon fat
1 large onion, diced
½ green pepper, diced
3 carrots, sliced
2 celery tops with leaves
½ teaspoon marjoram
2 to 3 big shakes of Worcestershire sauce
2 cups red wine, or enough to cover
1 clove garlic, smashed
2 teaspoons beef bouillon powder (or 2 cubes)

Sprinkle meat cubes with salt, pepper, and half of the thyme, and then coat heavily with flour. In a Dutch oven, melt the fat and sauté the meat cubes in several batches so the pieces are not crowded, removing those that are nice and brown to make way for more. When all the meat is browned, sauté the onion, green pepper, carrots, and celery in the same pan, adding more fat if necessary, until the onions are barely translucent. Return the meat to the pan, add the rest of the ingredients, cover, and simmer for about 1½ hours. Add water as the liquid absorbs the flour from the meat cubes. You may have to do this several times.

Small Game

■ Chicken-Fried Rabbit with Cream Gravy
Serves 4

2 cottontail rabbits, cut into serving-size
   pieces
6 tablespoons flour, divided
Salt and freshly ground pepper
5 tablespoons lard, for starters
¾ cup milk
½ cup heavy cream

Shake the rabbit pieces in a paper bag with 4 tablespoons flour, salt, and pepper. Pick a heavy skillet (with a lid) that, when crowded, will just hold the rabbit pieces. Melt the lard in it until hot, then turn the heat to medium, crowd in the rabbit pieces, and for the next 10 to 12 minutes stand over the skillet, turning and adjusting the pieces until all sides are golden brown. As you brown the pieces, their floured surfaces may absorb enough fat to require more lard; add as needed. Now, turn the heat to low, cover the skillet, and simmer for 12 minutes or so. Turn the pieces, if need be, during this process. Turn the heat to medium or medium high, remove the lid, and, turning the pieces when needed, evaporate the moisture for another 10 minutes or so. Remove the rabbit to a hot platter, pour off all but 3 tablespoons or so of the fat, stir 2 tablespoons flour into the fat and dredgings, and cook over low heat for 2 minutes or so. Off the heat, stir in the milk, and then cook on low heat until it starts to thicken. Stir in the cream and continue to heat, but do not boil.

■ Brunswick Stew
Serves 4

1 squirrel, cut into 6 or 7 pieces
Flour
Salt and pepper
3 tablespoons butter
8 cups boiling water
1 teaspoon thyme
1 cup fresh corn
1 cup lima beans
3 potatoes, quartered
¼ teaspoon cayenne
2 onions, sliced
2 cups canned tomatoes with juice

Roll the squirrel pieces in flour, salt, and pepper. Brown the pieces in butter. Add the squirrel and all other ingredients except the tomatoes to the boiling water, cover, and simmer for 1½ to 2 hours. Add the tomatoes and continue to simmer another hour.

Cooking A Cottontail

Let's start with the basic premise that if a rabbit is to taste good it must be field dressed with the same promptness and care as a deer. A deer must be field dressed on the spot with all internal organs removed. The same care should be taken with cottontails to ensure good game flavor. When your cottontail is ready for the pot, the one recipe that will do justice to any rabbit is Hasenpfeffer, an old-time German dish. Here's how to prepare it.

---

1 rabbit, cut into serving pieces
¼ teaspoon pepper
1 teaspoon salt
1 sliced onion
3 garlic cloves
2 bay leaves
8 ounces vinegar
8 ounces water
¼ cup butter or margarine
1 cup sweet or sour cream

First, marinate the rabbit pieces in the measured ingredients of pepper, salt, onion, garlic cloves, bay leaves, vinegar, and water. Use an earthenware crock, placed in a refrigerator for 48 hours, turning the pieces occasionally. Remove the pieces and brown them in butter, adding a little marinade from time to time. Allow the meat to simmer for about one hour or until tender. Remove the pieces and add the cream to make gravy. Pour the gravy generously over the rabbit into a serving dish. If you wish to experiment a bit, substitute wine for the equal parts of water and vinegar. Another variation is making the marinade with equal parts of water and beer or ale. Hasenpfeffer is usually served with potato pancakes or potato dumplings. Though the recipe is traditionally a rabbit dish, it works equally well with venison or any other game.

■ Jan Herbert's Maine-Style Rabbit Stew
Serves 6

1 to 2 rabbits
8 carrots
2 large onions, cut up
6 ribs celery and leaves, cut up
6 to 8 boiled potatoes, cut up
1 tablespoon salt
Pepper to taste
Flour

Dress and wash the rabbit. Put it in a kettle with lightly salted water to cover, and cook until just tender. Remove the rabbit, take the meat from the bones, and put the meat back in the cooking water. Add the carrots, onions, and celery. When the other vegetables are tender, add the potatoes. Season with salt and pepper. Thicken the stock with a thick paste of flour and water.

Game Birds and Waterfowl

■ Doves Delaware Sautéed with Bacon Cream Sauce
Serves 2 to 3

12 slices bacon
Salt and pepper
6 to 8 doves
3 egg yolks
1½ cups heavy cream
1 teaspoon sweet Hungarian paprika

In a skillet large enough to accommodate the doves, sauté the bacon until just crisp. Remove and drain on paper towels. Salt and pepper the birds. Sauté the birds over medium heat in the bacon fat, making sure you do it on all sides. This should take 10 to 15 minutes. Take out the doves and keep them warm. Pour off all but 3 tablespoons of the hot fat. Beat the egg yolks with the cream, add the 3 tablespoons of fat, and then put the mixture back in the skillet and cook over low heat just to thicken, stirring constantly and making sure the mixture does not boil. Stir in the paprika and serve the sauce in a gravy boat. Garnish the doves with the crisp bacon.

■ Grilled Doves

Serves 2

¼ cup oil
2 cloves garlic or shallots, minced
1 teaspoon dried rosemary, crumbled
Salt and pepper
6 doves, split down the back and flattened

Mix the oil, garlic or shallots, rosemary, and salt and pepper, and brush the mixture over both sides of the birds. Grill for 7 to 8 minutes on each side, basting several times with the oil mixture.

■ Grouse or Chukars with Garlic

Serves 2

4 grouse or chukars
3 chicken livers or 2 chicken livers and
   the grouse liver
2 tablespoons butter, divided
¼ cup bacon fat
25 cloves garlic, skins removed*
2 sprigs parsley, minced
½ cup white wine
½ cup tomato sauce or puree
Juice of 1 lemon

In a small Dutch oven, sauté the grouse or chukars and the livers slowly in 1 tablespoon of butter and the bacon fat until nicely browned. Add the garlic and parsley and continue sautéing gently for 3 minutes or so. Remove the livers and set aside. Add the wine and tomato sauce to the Dutch oven. Cover and simmer gently for 1 hour and 15 minutes or until grouse or chukars are tender. Add more white wine if liquid cooks down. Remove the birds to a hot platter and strain the sauce through a fine sieve, using a spoon to squash through the garlic pulp. Smash the cooked livers into a paste and add to the sauce, along with the juice of the lemon. Reheat. You can, if you wish, warm the birds again in the sauce as it is reheating. Just before serving, stir 1 tablespoon of butter into the hot sauce until melted.

* An easy way to remove the skins is to drop the cloves first into boiling water for a minute.

■ Viola Hamilton's Pan-Fried Quail (or Doves)

Serves 5 to 6

10 to 12 quail (or doves)
Salt and pepper
1 pound bacon

Wash the cleaned birds and season with salt and pepper. Place the bacon in a large skillet or frying pan over medium heat, separating the slices with a long-handled fork as cooking begins; brown the bacon until done and crispy. Remove the bacon from the pan, but keep it in a warm place. Put the birds in the bacon grease and cook 4 to 5 minutes, turning continuously to cook evenly and prevent burning. Remove from the pan, drain on paper towels, and serve immediately with warm bacon.

■ Woodcock Kennebunk

Serves 4

4 woodcock, with giblets
6 to 8 slices of bacon
3 tablespoons mushroom ketchup, divided
Salt and pepper
1 medium onion, finely diced
6 tablespoons butter
¾ cup port wine (or dry marsala)
Anchovy paste (a couple of 1-inch squeezes)
Beach plum or currant jelly (optional)

Loosen the woodcock skin near the neck, work it loose from the breast with your fingers, insert a bacon strip on each side, and pull skin back in place. Moisten birds inside and out with half of the mushroom ketchup. Salt and pepper the bird inside and out and stuff each with giblets and its share of the diced onion. In a small saucepan, melt the butter and then add the wine, remaining mushroom ketchup, and anchovy paste, and cook to just bubbling. Use this to baste. If you wish to serve some of the sauce separately, you can increase the quantity by adding a tablespoon or two of either of the jellies to the sauce; stir and heat. Spit and broil the birds for about 15 minutes, depending on the size of the bird, basting often.

■ Roast Teal
Serves 2 to 4

Salt and pepper
4 teal
2 tangerines, peeled, halved, and stuck in
*   several places with a fork*
8 strips bacon
½ cup port wine
1 tablespoon lemon juice
1 cup beach plum jelly (or plain plum or
*   red currant)*
½ tablespoon flour
2 tablespoons water

Salt and pepper the birds inside and out and place half of a well-punctured tangerine in each bird. Truss the bird to bind down the two slices of bacon that you wrap around each teal. Place in a Dutch oven. In a small skillet, heat the wine and lemon juice, then stir in and dissolve the jelly. Ladle it over the birds and roast in a 400°F Dutch oven for 18 to 25 minutes, depending on how rare you like your duck. Remove the little ducks to a platter and make the sauce by first skimming off the bacon fat, then stirring in over a simmering flame the ½ tablespoon of flour stirred into 2 tablespoons of water. Simmer until the sauce is somewhat thickened, pour over the birds, and serve.

Fish

■ Trout Sautéed in Butter
Serves 4

Salt and pepper
4 fresh trout, dressed but with heads and tails
*   left on*
A few tablespoons flour
6 tablespoons unsalted butter (1 teaspoon
*   cooking oil will work in a pinch)*
Parsley sprigs, for garnish
Lemon wedges, for garnish

Salt, pepper, and coat the trout by rolling them in the flour. Melt the butter in a big iron skillet. When the butter is hot (over medium heat) but has not yet shown color, lay in the trout and turn the fire to low. A steady, low heat will do two things: cook the trout slowly and at the same time brown the trout. You must police this process continuously, and it will take about 15 to 20 minutes, depending somewhat on the size of the trout. A pliable spatula and a spoon or fork are the best utensils. Just as soon as the flour coating has set on the down side, loosen each trout occasionally, shaking the skillet gently to keep the slowly browning trout free. Add a bit of oil or butter if necessary. After 10 minutes of slow browning, turn each trout carefully using two utensils and repeat the above process. When you serve the trout, pour a bit of butter over each and garnish with a sprig of parsley and a wedge of lemon.

■ Trout and Vegetables in Foil
Serves 4

4 (10-inch) trout
Juice of ½ lemon
Salt and pepper
½ teaspoon thyme (or ¼ teaspoon thyme,
*   ¼ teaspoon tarragon)*
2 carrots
2 small onions
3 ribs celery
4 tablespoons butter

Clean the trout, leaving on the heads and tails, and sprinkle inside and out with lemon juice, salt, pepper, and herbs. Dice the vegetables, mix, and strain. Sauté the vegetables in butter until they are soft, and then stuff each fish before wrapping it loosely in foil. Place in a Dutch oven at 450°F for 15 to 20 minutes.

L.L. Bean's Brook Trout

Mr. Bean's personal recipe for brook trout shows that he knew the secret of slow cookery for fish: Cut the heads off, clean, and wipe dry. Fry out a liberal amount of pork fat. Roll in flour with a little salt added. Drop in frying pan when fat comes to a boil. Turn often to avoid burning. Fry slowly until every trout is crisp and well browned. Place on hot platter on clean paper to absorb the fat. Have a cut lemon on the table for those who want it. Pork fat is much better than bacon fat or butter, and flour is much better than meal. ■

The Tastiest Fish

I live on the New Jersey shore, where the striped bass is king. But I don't like eating stripers because they are one of the blandest fish I've ever eaten. Unless you cover a striper fillet with some fancy sauce or dressing, it will have nearly zero taste. You don't agree? Maybe you have different taste buds. I love to catch stripers; I just don't like to eat them. In the Northeast, I'll swap a striper any day for a fluke or sea bass.

I'm also convinced that where you eat your fish makes a difference. A fried grouper sandwich in the Florida Keys will always taste better than the same sandwich in New York. So, with that geographic disclaimer, just what is the tastiest fish? Let's get started by listing what I believe are the top 10 tastiest fish in salt water. Some of these species can't be found in all parts of the country, but I'm still going to try to rate the species regardless of where they are found.

1 • Hogfish — This species is sometimes called the captain's fish because some charter captains will take it home for dinner.

2 • Yellowtail Snapper —There are more than 100 species of snappers all over the world, but the yellowtail gets the highest rating, followed by the red snapper, mutton snapper, and then mangrove snapper. Admittedly, all snappers taste great.

3 • Summer Flounder (Fluke) — My Northeast favorite, the summer flounder is great breaded and fried golden brown with a touch of lemon juice.

4 • Grouper — Like the snapper, there are many species of groupers and they all taste good. The 5- to 15-pounders are preferred for the dinner table. Stay away from the heavyweight groupers. Fish biologists claim these older fish may have consumed too many smaller fish that feed on toxin-producing algae. There is always the risk of ciguatera poisoning. Ciguatera toxin is harmless to fish, but poisonous to people.

5 • Salmon (Wild) — Only wild salmon get a top rating. Farm-raised salmon are sometimes tasteless.

6 • Tripletail — Maybe because they hide under crab pots and are hard to catch, tripletail are excellent eating. Or maybe it's because they look so much like freshwater black crappies, which are superb eating.

7 • Dolphin (Mahimahi) — Encrusted with coconut, fried, and flambéed with Grand Marnier, you would be hard put to find a better fish dinner than dolphin.

8 • Yellowfin and Bluefin Tuna — The best way to eat tuna is sushi, or coated with black pepper, seared 10 seconds on each side, and served with lots of wasabi.

9 • Cobia — Beer-battered and deep-fried chunks are delicious, but cobia is also a favorite on the grill. Look for cobia feeding under huge rays in clear water.

10 • Mako Shark — I actually prefer mako to swordfish, and it's a lot cheaper, too.

Runners-up are cod, wahoo, striped bass, halibut, snook, and weakfish. Of this group, cod and wahoo are the best. Wahoo may look a bit like a king mackerel, but that's where the similarity ends. Wahoo meat is white and tastes great.

Here are a few fish that will never make my list of tasty fish: amberjack, king mackerel (unless smoked), grunts, bluefish (unless they are small 2- to 4-pounders), bonito, pickerel, or pike.

For freshwater fishermen, I have a short list and I can only come up with five species that I rate high for the table. Here they are in order of taste:

1 • Walleye	**4 • Trout**
2 • Black Crappie	**5 • Yellow Perch**
3 • Catfish	

I suspect that at least half of the fishermen who read this will not agree with my choices. I will also admit that fish preparation may be a critical factor, but I will still stick to my guns. These species are my top choices.

■ Grilled Rainbow Trout
Serves 2

2 rainbow trout, whole, gutted
Olive oil
Butter
Salt and pepper
Sage or parsley (optional)
Lemon wedges

Coat the entire bodies of the rainbow trout with olive oil. Put several pats of butter inside the cavities, and then season with salt and pepper. Additional spices can also be used, such as sage or parsley. With a grill set at 350°F, a whole trout, depending on size, should take about 10 to 12 minutes on each side to cook. When the meat is firm and flakes easily, the trout is done. Serve with lemon wedges. Brook and brown trout can also be substituted.

■ Broiled Salmon (or Lake Trout) Steaks with Shallots and Tarragon
Serves 4

⅓ cup olive oil
2 tablespoons lemon juice
2 tablespoons finely chopped shallots or scallions
½ teaspoon dried tarragon, crumbled to powder
Salt and pepper
4 salmon steaks, about 1½ inches thick
4 tablespoons butter, melted
Black olives, for garnish
Parsley, for garnish
Lemon wedges, for garnish

Combine the oil, lemon juice, shallots or scallions, tarragon, salt, and pepper, and beat or shake to uniformity as you would French dressing. Coat each side of the steaks with the dressing, lay the steaks on a greased grill over a tray, pour the remainder of the dressing over the steaks, and roast about 4 inches under the heat for 7 to 8 minutes for each side. Baste often with the melted butter during the roasting process. (If fillets are used, cook for a shorter time, depending on thickness of the fillets.) If you can recover it, retrieve some of the hot basted liquid and pour over each steak. Garnish with black olives, parsley, and lemon wedges.

■ Fried Walker Lake Trout
Serves 6

1 lake trout or char, or several grayling
½ teaspoon salt
¼ teaspoon pepper or lemon pepper
Cornmeal (enough for dredging)
Shortening (enough for frying)
2 tablespoons butter
1 cup sour cream
½ teaspoon lemon juice

Clean and wash the fish and cut into serving-size pieces, leaving the skin on. Salt and pepper and coat thoroughly with cornmeal. In a frying pan, bring ¼ to ½ inch of shortening to high heat, add the fish, and fry for approximately 4 minutes. Turn and cook for 3 minutes more. Fish should be nicely browned. Put cooked fish on a hot serving platter. Pour off the fat from the pan and replace with the butter, add the sour cream, and stir with a spoon to loosen any dredgings. Cook for several minutes, but do not boil. Remove from the heat, add lemon juice, stir, and pour over the trout.

■ Fast and Easy Walleye Shore Lunch
Serves 2 to 4

2 to 4 walleye fillets, skinned
Flour
Vegetable oil
Salt and pepper
4 potatoes, sliced
2 onions, sliced
Lemon wedges

Coat the fillets completely with flour and fry in vegetable oil until the fillets are golden brown. Season with salt and pepper to taste. In another skillet, fry the sliced potatoes and onions. Serve together with the fillets and lemon wedges. Note: If you can't catch walleye, use panfish, perch, or bass.

The Wonderful Shore Lunch . . . or Is It?

There are two schools of thought about traditional shore lunches. Are they wonderful wilderness eating experiences? Or the worst mess of greasy food you can ever imagine? I've had both.

Many years ago, I was fishing a lake in Canada with several friends in June. We decided to have a classic shore lunch, but we couldn't catch walleyes, which are the most common fare for a shore lunch. We had to settle for a skinny 3-foot pike, a species that is normally released because most fishermen can't stand eating it. Yeah, I know. You have some secret formula to blow up the bones in oil and make pike delicious. Sorry, I'll pass.

We picked a brushy spot to beach our boats, clean the pike, and start a fire. We lasted about three minutes. Hordes of black flies descended on us and the pike. It got so bad that we raced for the boats and the safety of a breeze out on the lake. We left the pike . . . bones and all. I didn't try a shore lunch again for many years.

I've learned a lot since that bad experience and my shore lunches get better and better. On a trip to Alaska, I smoked a silver salmon fresh from the ocean. My guide used a small smoker with pine boughs. We ate it for lunch with lemon juice, tomatoes, and onion slices. Shore lunches can't get much better than that.

A silver salmon shore lunch may be out of reach for most of us, but my grandson Joey and I also had a shore lunch in Canada that any fisherman can duplicate wherever the law will allow an open fire or camp stove on a shoreline. We were fishing on Lake Mistassini in Quebec. Our guide Stanley, an Ojibway, did all the cooking.

We caught plenty of walleyes, almost one on every cast. When it was time for lunch, Stanley found a small, sandy shoreline. Joey gathered enough wood and started a small fire. Stanley used two frying pans. From our boat, he took a can of beans and two small bags of potatoes and onions, which he cut into bite-size pieces. He rolled the walleye fillets in flour and fried them in one pan with the onions and potatoes. The beans went in the other pan. All the frying was done in vegetable oil. The only seasonings Stanley carried were flour, salt and pepper, and a lemon.

Watching Stanley cook a shore lunch over an open fire was a lesson in culinary simplicity. Cleanup was equally as simple. He wiped the frying pans clean with moss and stashed them in two plastic bags. It proved to be one of the finest shore lunches I have ever enjoyed.

You can make shore lunches as simple or as complicated as you wish. This is not like tailgating at a football game, and you don't need fresh walleye fillets or a silver salmon. A shore lunch will taste just as good with bass, yellow perch, or bluegill. If you don't like beans, try something else. Truth is, a shore lunch with good friends will always taste good, even if it doesn't.

Stanley, left, an Ojibway guide, and my grandson, Joey Andelora, cook a walleye shore lunch in Quebec.

■ Pan-Fried or Sautéed Yellow Perch
Serves 2 to 3

6 small yellow perch, 7 to 9 inches long
Salt and pepper
Cornmeal (or combine with flour)
4 tablespoons bacon fat, lard, or butter
*   and oil*
4 tablespoons butter
1 lemon (optional)

Dress, scale, and wash the fish, pat dry, salt and pepper, and then dredge the fish in the cornmeal or cornmeal-and-flour combination. Heat the fat until it is hot enough to cook at once, but not burning, sputtering hot. Lay in the fish, turn heat down to a barely medium flame, and begin to brown the fish. At the same time, begin the process of loosening the fish from the pan bottom with a thin metal spatula. Taking 8 to 10 minutes on each side (turn heat to low if it seems to "fry" too fast), brown the fish slowly until crisp. Do not overcook. Sometimes it is a bit tricky to brown without overcooking. When the flesh is opaque, the fish is done; one hopes it's all browned by then. Add 4 tablespoons butter to the skillet after removing the fish and, if you like, squeeze in the juice of a lemon. Stir the fat and juices to loosen the dredgings, and pour over the browned fish.

■ White Perch in Beer
Serves 4

6 tablespoons flour
2 tablespoons yellow cornmeal
½ teaspoon dill weed or tarragon
1 teaspoon salt
1 tablespoon paprika
1 can beer
4 white perch, scaled and sprinkled inside
*   and out with lemon juice*
4 tablespoons lard or cooking oil

Mix the flour, cornmeal, dill weed or tarragon, salt, and paprika in a bowl, and then add the beer and beat until smooth. Dip the fish in the beer batter one at a time. Heat the lard or oil in an iron skillet and sauté the fish for 8 to 9 minutes on each side.

■ Smallmouth à la Spednik, Sautéed Bass Meunière
Serves 2

2 (1½-pound) bass, dressed, heads and tails
*   removed, and skinned*
⅓ cup yellow cornmeal
⅓ cup flour
Salt and pepper
5 tablespoons butter (or 3 tablespoons butter
*   and 2 tablespoons oil)*
Parsley, for garnish
1 tablespoon vinegar

Dredge the bass in a mix of cornmeal, flour, salt, and pepper, and sauté slowly in the melted butter over medium heat until well browned. Turn carefully with a spatula and brown the other side. When the flesh has turned opaque, remove to a warm platter and garnish with parsley. Stir vinegar into the fat and dredgings. Heat and pour over the fish.

■ Quick and Easy Fried Panfish or Crappie
Serves 2

2 (½-pound) panfish or crappie fillets
Salt, for sprinkling
Lemon-pepper seasoning, for sprinkling
1 to 2 cups dry pancake mix
Fat or oil, for frying
Tartar sauce

Wash and dry the fish. Dip the fish into clean, cool water, and then sprinkle lightly with salt and lemon-pepper seasoning. Coat the fish lightly with pancake mix. In a frying pan, fry in deep fat or 1½ inches of hot oil at 350°F for 4 to 5 minutes on each side. (Fish is done when browned on both sides and it flakes easily when tested with a fork. Be careful not to overcook.) Remove fish from the pan and drain on a paper towel. Serve with tartar sauce. If desired, fish may also be panfried over medium to low heat in just enough fat or oil to keep it from sticking until done as described above.

Fish Fillet Knives

Hold a knife in your hand. Do you like the way it looks and feels? If you do, you can probably do any cutting job with it, including filleting everything from a walleye to a 500-pound bluefin tuna. If you don't like the way a knife fits in your hand, you will never learn to use it effectively and it can literally be dangerous to use.

It's important to separate fish knives from hunting knives. I cherish my hunting knives and some of them may become family heirlooms. A hunting knife that may be used once a year to field dress a buck can cost hundreds of dollars. Fish knives are different. They rarely cost more than $15 to $35. Fillet knives are also work tools and designed for hard use and abuse from the elements, especially salt water. I have even used sandpaper to remove rust from a knife left too long on a boat. It's not that difficult to put a good edge back on a fillet knife, even if it has a stainless-steel blade.

Choosing a blade steel is actually a simple choice. I prefer stainless steel for fish knives. Carbon steel may be easy to sharpen but, unfortunately, it will rust and require more care than stainless steel. If you prefer a knife that's easy to sharpen but tougher to maintain, then buy a fillet knife with a carbon-steel blade. It's easy to put a razor edge on carbon steel with a whetstone. A good whetstone will last a lifetime with some care. Never use it dry. After you sharpen your knife, apply more oil to it and wipe it clean. Oil floats steel particles above the surface, so they do not clog the stone. Use a Washita stone, preferably mounted and clamped to your work surface so it does not move. It is very important that you maintain a 45-degree angle between the back of the blade and the stone as you draw the blade across the stone, as if you were taking a slice off the top.

On the other hand, if you want a fish knife that is nearly maintenance free, buy a knife with a stainless-steel blade. You can put a sharp edge on stainless steel with a whetstone, but if you're worried about maintaining that all-important 45-degree angle on the edge, an electric knife sharpener or a sharpening kit will ensure the correct angle and make the job easier.

The blade on a fillet knife should always have a slightly upturned tip. This design keeps the blade tip from accidentally tearing skin or flesh during filleting. If you can find one, buy a fillet knife with a serrated tip, which will make that initial cut into the fish skin easy. Blade length can vary, depending on the species of fish you usually fillet. A 4-inch blade makes an excellent trout knife, but a 7- to 10-inch blade is better for bigger fish and saltwater species.

Avoid fish knives with smooth, slick handles. Fish slime will make them dangerous to use. Fish knives should have rough, nonslip rubber or plastic handles. Many fillet knives on the market today have checkered polypropylene handles that are sanitary and easy to keep clean.

Most fishermen tend to be careless with fish knives because they are inexpensive and will invariably be lost long before they wear out. But that's not reason enough to let a knife get rusty and dull. All knives should be kept sharp, clean, and coated with oil when not in use. Never store a knife in a sheath, especially a leather sheath, which will spot and corrode a blade from the acid in the leather. Remember, if a knife looks good and feels good in your hand, you probably picked the right knife.

This Dexter-Russell 8-inch fillet knife is a good size for nearly all fish species. The handle is slip-resistant polypropylene. Travel with the knife in a sheath, but never store it long-term in a sheath. Keep knives sharp, oiled, and stored with the blade wrapped in wax paper.

■ Codfish Maine Style
Serves 4 to 6

1½ cups cooked, flaked codfish
2 hard-cooked eggs
¼ teaspoon paprika
Celery salt, for sprinkling
Salt
Pork fat
Diced pork scraps (bacon fat and bacon bits
    may be substituted)
2 cups cooked rice
Parsley, for garnish

Combine flaked fish, chopped egg whites, paprika, and celery salt. Add salt to taste. Heat this mixture in melted fat with the pork scraps, tossing frequently in the pan to prevent burning. Pile hot cooked rice on a platter, toss the seasoned hot fish over the rice, and garnish with egg yolks and parsley.

■ Weakfish à la Pepper
Serves 4

1½ pounds weakfish or seatrout fillets
1 teaspoon garlic salt
½ teaspoon lemon-pepper seasoning
½ teaspoon instant chicken broth
½ cup boiling water
2 tablespoons vegetable oil
¼ cup tomato sauce
1 teaspoon capers
½ medium green pepper, cut into rings
½ medium red pepper, cut into rings

Cut the fish into 4-inch pieces and sprinkle with garlic salt and lemon-pepper seasoning. Dissolve instant chicken broth in boiling water. Cook the fish in vegetable oil in a 12-inch nonstick frying pan over moderate heat for 5 minutes, turning often. Add the tomato sauce and capers to the frying pan. Reduce heat; cover and simmer for 10 minutes. Top with the pepper rings and cook 5 minutes longer or until the fish flakes easily when tested with a fork and the peppers are tender.

■ Hearty Fisherman Stew
Serves 6

2 pounds white, lean fillets
1½ cups sliced celery
½ cup chopped onion
1 clove garlic, minced
¼ cup butter
1 (28-ounce) can tomatoes, undrained
1 (8-ounce) can tomato sauce
2 teaspoons salt
½ teaspoon paprika
½ teaspoon chili powder
¼ teaspoon pepper
2 cups boiling water
1 (7-ounce) package spaghetti, uncooked
¼ cup grated or shredded Parmesan cheese

Skin the fillets and cut into 1-inch pieces. In a 5-quart Dutch oven, cook the celery, onion, and garlic in butter until tender. Add the tomatoes, tomato sauce, salt, paprika, chili powder, and pepper. Bring to a simmer. Cover and cook slowly for 15 to 20 minutes. Add the boiling water and uncooked spaghetti; stir and cover. Cook slowly about 10 minutes or until the spaghetti is almost tender. Add the fish; cover. Cook slowly about 10 minutes more or until the fish flakes easily when tested with a fork. Serve hot with Parmesan cheese sprinkled on top.

■ Fried Catfish
Serves 6

6 (½- to 1-pound) catfish fillets, skinned
2 teaspoons salt
¼ teaspoon black pepper
2 eggs, beaten
2 tablespoons milk
2 cups cornmeal
Oil, for frying

Sprinkle both sides of the catfish fillets with salt and pepper. In a shallow dish, mix the eggs and milk. Add the cornmeal to another shallow dish. Dip the fillets in the egg mixture and then roll in the cornmeal. Place the fillets in a frying pan with ⅛ inch of hot oil and fry to a golden brown on both sides. Drain on paper towels and serve.

◼ Sautéed Grayling
Serves 4

6 (10- to 13-inch) grayling, heads and tails
    removed
½ cup yellow cornmeal
6 to 8 tablespoons butter
Parsley, for garnish
2 tablespoons very finely diced onion
½ teaspoon tarragon
¼ teaspoon chervil
4 tablespoons lemon juice
Salt and pepper

After dredging the fish in the cornmeal, sauté them in butter in a big skillet until done, about 20 minutes total over a slow fire. Remove the fish to a warm platter garnished with parsley. Add the onion, tarragon, and chervil to the dredgings and butter (add more butter if necessary), and cook quickly until the onion is soft. Stir in the lemon juice, loosening the dredgings as you do so, season to taste, and pour butter and lemon sauce over the fish.

◼ Pan-Fried Tuna
Serves 4

1½ pounds tuna fillets
4 tablespoons olive oil, divided
2 cloves garlic, crushed
¼ stick butter
3 tablespoons fresh chopped herbs
    (such as winter savory, rosemary, or thyme)
Parsley or lemon balm, for garnish

Slice the fillets very thinly (about ⅛ inch thick). In a bowl, add 2 tablespoons of olive oil to the garlic and then coat the fillets with it. Heat the remaining olive oil and the butter in a large frying pan and toss in the fresh herbs, sautéing lightly for 1 minute. Turn up the heat, add the fillets, and fry for about 3 minutes, turning them gently from time to time. Serve with the pan juices and garnish with parsley or lemon balm.

◼ Mako Shark Marinated and Grilled on Skewers
Serves 4

2 cloves garlic
½ teaspoon salt
2-pound mako shark (or swordfish), cut in
    1-inch cubes
Juice of 2 limes
⅓ cup olive oil
Freshly ground pepper
2 dozen bay leaves

Smash the garlic cloves and peel. Then, chop fine and mash with the salt to make a paste. Rub this mixture over the pieces of fish. Place in a bowl and pour the lime juice and oil over, then grind a liberal amount of pepper on top. Toss and let marinate for 1 hour. Thread chunks of fish alternately with bay leaves onto four skewers. Grill over a fire close to the heat for 8 to 10 minutes, turning once and brushing with the marinade.

Other Campfire Recipes

◼ Change-of-Pace Camp Ham Dish Supper
Serves 2

A big slice of ham, ½ inch thick
2 tablespoons bacon grease
¾ cup coffee
3 heaping tablespoons sour cream
1 heaping teaspoon prepared mustard
½ teaspoon sugar, preferably brown

Fry the ham on both sides in the hot bacon grease until it is well browned. It's OK if it sticks a bit, for you want the brown dredgings. Remove ham to a hot pie plate. Stir in the coffee, being certain that you loosen all of the dredgings. Let it simmer. Just before you serve the ham, stir in and blend the sour cream, mustard, and sugar. Let it heat, but do not boil. Serve in a mug or tin cup doubling as a gravy boat.

■ Quick Camp Baked Beans
Serves 3 to 4

6 frankfurters in 1-inch slices (or a tin of Spam or
    even corned beef)
1 tablespoon butter
1 onion, finely chopped
4 slices bacon, diced
1 (28-ounce) can baked beans
2 teaspoons prepared mustard
1 tablespoon brown sugar (or substitute 1 table-
    spoon blackstrap molasses)
¼ cup ketchup

In a Dutch oven, sauté the frankfurter slices in butter. When they are half brown, add and sauté the onion and bacon until just softened. Pour in the beans, stir the remainder of the ingredients in thoroughly, and cook for 30 minutes. This will give you time for a drink.

■ "Bread" Bannock or Scone
Serves 8 to 10

4 cups flour
4 teaspoons baking powder
½ teaspoon salt
4 tablespoons butter or lard
½ cup evaporated milk
1 cup water

Mix the dry ingredients together in a bowl. Then cut the butter or lard into the mix (use your fingers to crumble the mix until it is pebbly). Make a hole in the center and pour the liquid in all at once. Mix it. Gather around the edges of the bowl with a fork until it all comes together magically into one lump of dough. Knead it five or six times quickly and turn out onto a floured board (or the oilcloth top of the camp table). Shape and pat into a circle (be sure it is at least ½ inch thick) and bake in a lightly greased, medium-hot skillet or griddle about 10 minutes on each side. (With a bit of practice, you can learn to flip it over.) If it's scones you want, cut the circle into wedges and cook with the wedges (or farls) put back into the skillet to make a circle, their sides just barely touching. When baking scones, you might wish to make two smaller circles and use two skillets.

■ Corn Pone
Serves 6

1½ cups yellow cornmeal
¼ to ½ cup white flour
2 teaspoons baking powder
1 teaspoon salt
1 cup milk
1 egg, beaten
3 tablespoons melted bacon fat

Mix the dry ingredients. Add the milk and beaten egg and stir to make the mix uniform. Stir in the bacon fat. Heat a lightly greased griddle or skillet and drop the batter onto the surface, spreading it out with a kitchen spoon. When one side is brown, turn and brown the other side. Both sides should brown in 2½ to 3 minutes.

■ Camp Coffee
Makes 8 cups

8 cups cold water (one cup is a standard-size
    coffee mug)
9 slightly rounded tablespoons coffee
1 eggshell

Put the cold water and coffee in the pot with two halves of an eggshell. Bring the mixture to a boil and then immediately set it off the fire to steep a bit (but not get cold). Pour in ⅛ cup cold water to settle the grounds. Don't boil the coffee and don't start camp coffee in warm water. Take the water right out of that first morning bucket from the spring or lake.

■ L.L. Bean's Camp Potatoes
Serves 4

¼ pound salt pork
4 medium onions
8 medium potatoes
Salt and freshly ground pepper

Fry the salt pork in a frying pan until crisp. Remove the pork. Dice the onions and fry until soft. Dice the potatoes, add the onions, and cook in a covered pan until done. Remove the cover and brown. Add the cooked salt pork after chopping very fine. Do not stir. Turn when brown on the bottom. Salt and pepper to taste.

Frijoles (Fried Beans)
Serves 8 to 10

1 pound Mexican beans (or pinto or red kidney
beans)
1½ quarts water
½ cup rendered salt pork fat, lard, or bacon fat
Salt and pepper

Wash and pick the beans, then put them in a pot with the water and cook at a low simmer for 2 hours or so. Test them for doneness, bearing in mind that you want them tender, but not mushy. When they are done, heat the fat in a big, heavy skillet and begin frying by putting in a few beans. Then, mashing half of them with the back of a wooden spoon, and adding a bit of the bean liquid each time, continue frying until you have used up all the beans and the liquid they were boiled in and have them at the desired consistency. If they seem too watery when you mash half of each added batch of beans and water, smash a third of the beans. Salt and pepper to taste.

Cornmeal Mush
Serves 4

1 cup yellow cornmeal
1 cup cold water
1 teaspoon salt
4 cups boiling water, divided

Stir together the cornmeal, cold water, and salt until thoroughly wet and smooth. Pour the boiling water over the cornmeal in top of a double boiler, stir, and set over 2 additional cups of boiling water. If you are cooking on a camp stove, push pan over area of less heat and cook for 3 minutes, stirring constantly. As it begins to thicken (don't let it stick), be careful, for when those thick bubbles explode they can burn the hell out of you. Cover, set the top of the double boiler over the bottom, and cook over water for 15 minutes (or longer if you have the time). The mush can now be served as a hot cereal.

Mock Maple Syrup
Makes about 1½ cups

⅔ cup light brown sugar
⅓ cup white sugar
½ cup water
2 tablespoons butter

Put sugars into a saucepan, add water, and stir to dissolve. Heat to a boil and let it bubble slowly for 3 minutes. Stir and melt in the butter. If you follow the instructions, this syrup will keep for some time without crystallizing, but it's better to make it up batch by batch each time you serve pancakes or French toast. If you make it at home, stir in a tablespoon of white corn syrup, which will inhibit crystallization for certain. If you do make up a batch to keep on hand in camp, don't stir in the butter until you heat the syrup again before serving.

Bacon and French Toast Breakfast
Serves 3

Bacon
3 eggs
1 cup milk
¼ teaspoon salt
2 teaspoons sugar
½ teaspoon vanilla extract (optional)
6 slices bread
1½ cups syrup (see above)

Fry the bacon and reserve the fat. In a bowl, beat the eggs, then beat in the milk, salt, sugar, and vanilla extract, and pour into a shallow dish or pie pan. Dip both sides of bread slices in the batter (don't soak it to a mush) and brown in the bacon fat until done. Serve with syrup.

WILDERNESS SURVIVAL

Section Four

WILDERNESS SURVIVAL

Survival is the art of making efficient use of any available resource that can help sustain an individual. If a person is able to think clearly and objectively about an emergency situation—because he has prepared for it—he is far more likely to survive than someone who panics and is unable to take full advantage of the resources that may be at hand.

To survive, five basic needs—sustenance, medical care, fire, shelter, and rescue—must be met. Few survival situations are identical, and not all of the needs must be met in every case. However, when thinking about and planning for survival, it is important to prepare for emergencies in which *all* of these needs must be met.

PLANNING AHEAD

It is ironic that many survival situations often strike the ill prepared. The day hiker, who is wearing nothing but shorts and a T-shirt, invariably is the one caught in an unexpected late-spring snowstorm. Likewise, boats never seem to sink when there are enough life jackets to go around.

Planning and preparing for emergencies is more than carrying a survival knife into the woods with a compass on the end and three matches inside. Preparation requires investing time to be physically and mentally fit, and thoughtful planning and intelligent selection of resources that will be available when you need them.

Mental preparation starts with the belief that it can happen to you. Nobody buckles their seat belt with the intention of getting into an accident. Likewise, it is foolhardy to head into the woods without enough gear to

This survival knife is typical of many models available today. The back of the blade has sawlike serrations for cutting wood and rope. The pouch on the sheath holds essential survival items, including fire starters, flint, compass, and fish hooks and line.

help you get through a day when Mother Nature throws you a curveball.

The will to survive is influenced by skill, faith, and courage. The more practice, the more skill. The more skill, the greater the faith. The greater the faith, the more confident you are, and the more enjoyable your outdoor experience can be.

PREPARING A SURVIVAL KIT

Preparation is the key. Far more is involved than simply buying a prepackaged survival kit. It is unlikely that any single kit will meet your specific needs. As

a reminder, sustenance, medical care, fire, shelter, and rescue are the major categories of needs a survivor may have. Equally important, however, is thinking about these needs in the context of the environment that you will be in. A midsummer hike in the Grand Canyon requires different gear than a December snowshoe trip in the Rockies. As an example, carrying water to meet a sustenance need in the desert may make more sense than carrying water-purification tablets, a logical choice when hiking in an area where water is plentiful. The need for water does not change, but how an individual prepares to meet that need does.

Select the items for your survival kit based on their versatility, multifunctionality, and practicality. While improvising is not one of the five basic needs for survival, it is an important process in bringing all of these needs together. For example, surgical tubing, selected as a tourniquet for a first-aid kit, can be used for collecting water from an improvised solar still, drinking water from your water-collection containers, or making a slingshot.

■ Daypack or Hiker Survival Kit

The following items are recommended for a complete, quality daypack or hiker survival kit. These items have been selected for their versatility for all survival-related emergencies. No kit, however, can be entirely right for every situation. These items form the basic foundation on which you should build after taking into account your activity and the environment. While the list may seem long, consider that many of these items are small and light, and a number of the items (such as knives and saws) are tools you will want to take with you anyway for everyday use. The daypack survival kit includes:

- Fully charged cell phone
- GPS (global positioning system)
- 1-gallon water bag or container (collapsible or folded)
- Water-purification tablets
- 3,600-calorie, nonperishable food ration (Datrex, MRE, etc.)
- Hard candy
- Container for boiling water
- Large, fixed-blade knife
- Pocket knife with locking blade
- Flint and steel fire starter
- Fire-lighting tinder
- Windproof and waterproof matches (strike-anywhere versions are best)
- Waterproof match case
- Lighter
- Flashlight with spare batteries
- Three 12-hour, high-intensity Cyalume snap lights

- Signal mirror
- Whistle
- Compass
- Compact strobe light
- First-aid kit (should include prescription medicines and large compresses, and should be adequate for the environment)
- Saw
- Multiperson emergency tube shelter
- Survival bag
- Mylar space blanket sleeping bag
- Space blanket
- Wool gloves
- Wool hat
- Dry socks
- Emergency poncho or rain jacket
- Cord or rope
- Compact sewing kit
- Multitool (Leatherman, etc.)
- Sharpening stone
- Carry/storage bag (sealed for pilfer resistance)

Optional items:
- Fishing kit
- Snare wire
- Surgical tubing

■ Vehicle Survival Kit

The following items are recommended for a complete, quality vehicle survival kit. While items like jumper cables, tire chains, and road flares are not normally considered part of a vehicle survival kit, but rather safety items, far too many survival situations have started along the side of the road because they were not present. Be ready to improvise! For example, if your car overheats because of a ruptured hose, wait for the car to cool and fix the rupture with duct tape. This may not be the perfect fix, but it can get you to the next town or nearest phone.

Remember also that your vehicle is poorly insulated and that as soon as you lose your power to run the heater or air conditioner, the car will become an icebox or an oven. If you are using part of the car as shade, shelter, or a wind block, don't forget to keep your fire well away from the vehicle. Getting outside the vehicle can greatly improve your survivability, but do not leave your vehicle or fail to cannibalize all of the resources it may offer. The thought of cannibalizing your car can be disheartening when you think about its cost, but any vehicle can be replaced, so don't fret too long. The mirrors make great signals; the hubcaps can boil water; the tires can make a dark black, smoky signal fire; and the insulation in the seats can insulate you outside as well. A good vehicle survival kit includes:

- Cell phone (a good recommendation for any traveler)
- GPS
- Spare tire
- Flashlight
- Jack
- Gas can
- Spool of 20-gauge wire
- Tire chains
- Flat tire repair kit
- Ground tarp
- Jumper cables
- Tool kit
- Tow rope
- Road flares (red Cyalume 12-hour snap lights also work well)
- Shovel
- Duct tape
- 1 gallon of water
- Blanket
- Saw
- Emergency poncho or rain jacket
- Wool gloves
- Wool hat
- Multitool (Leatherman, etc.)
- Cord or rope
- Large emergency tube shelter or tarp
- Mylar emergency space blanket
- Sleeping bags (during certain weather conditions)
- Water-storage container
- Water-purification tablets
- Six red, 12-hour Cyalume lights
- Six yellow, 12-hour, high-intensity Cyalume lights
- 3,600-calorie, nonperishable ration (Datrex, MRE, etc.)
- Signal mirror
- Whistle
- Compact strobe light
- First-aid kit (should include prescription medicines, trauma dressings, and other large bandages)
- Surgical tubing
- Large, fixed-blade survival knife
- Pocket knife with locking blade
- Flint and steel fire starter
- Fire-lighting tinder
- Windproof and waterproof matches (strike-anywhere versions are best)
- Waterproof match case
- Lighter
- Compact sewing kit
- Holding container (sealed for pilfer resistance)

Survival Tools

It's almost impossible to build a shelter, cut firewood, or skin a rabbit without some basic survival tools. A pocket chain saw may be difficult to use at first, but it will make quick work of gathering firewood. A fixed saw may be bulkier, but easier to use. The Redhead Paracord knife has the additional feature of a wrapped parachute cord that can be removed and used for a survival task. The Redhead 15-inch machete will cut wood up to 1½ inches thick and is a valuable tool for building campfires and shelters.

■ Survival Guns

Most sportsmen firmly believe that carrying a firearm or at least having one accessible in a wilderness setting is a comforting idea and I absolutely agree. We all hope we never end up in a survival situation in the woods, but many sportsmen still like to think about what kind of firearm makes the most sense if you're a fisherman, camper, backpacker, or just a hiker.

First, decide why you want to carry a firearm. Is it for food or protection against dangerous wildlife? If you're a hunter and concerned about bears, for example, any big-game rifle you may be carrying in North America will usually suffice. There is a maze of calibers out there, but generally anything over .30 caliber will keep you safe in bear country. I've owned rifles from .243 Winchester to .458 Winchester Magnum, but I've taken more big game with my .30-06 than any other rifle in my cabinet.

If you're not a hunter and you prefer the convenience of carrying a handgun when hiking or camping in bear country, I'd recommend a .44 Magnum or .357 Magnum handgun. There are even heavier handgun calibers, but they are not practical for most hikers and campers. The .44 Magnum will give you a more comfortable edge over the .357 Magnum, but with either caliber you'd better be a good shot. The added advantage of the .357 Magnum is that the gun can also handle less-expensive .38 Special ammunition for target practice.

If you don't mind the extra weight and length of a long gun, a short-barreled 12 gauge with slugs will also

Camp and Survival Guns

The Harrington & Richardson Survivor is a single shot that will handle .45 Colt or .410 Bore. This model has a polymer stock with a buttstock storage compartment. As its name implies, the Survivor would be hard to beat as a survivor or camp tool.

The Savage Model 42 is a single-shot break action with two barrels, a .22 Long Rifle or .22 WMR in the top barrel and .410 Bore in the bottom barrel. A longtime favorite combination, the Model 42 is an ideal extra camp gun.

The Ruger Bearcat is a single-action revolver chambered for .22 Long Rifle. The Bearcat, weighing 24 ounces, is the lightest revolver made by Ruger and should be of special interest to campers, hikers, and fishermen who feel the need to have a kit gun in their pack.

If you choose a handgun, make sure you handle it correctly. This is the two-hand hold you should learn well, since it's foolish to use the less-steady one-hand hold when shooting at live game.

give you peace of mind when hiking in grizzly country. Of course, if you are intentionally hunting grizzlies, you should choose some of the bigger centerfire magnums.

But what if you live in a state where applying for a handgun-carrying permit may be difficult and you're still concerned about walking your dog in bear country? If this is the case, your choice is limited. I would look for the lightest short-barreled 12-gauge shotgun I could find and carry a half-dozen slugs in my pocket. Stoeger, for example, offers a 12- or 20-gauge double-barreled shotgun called the Coach Gun. A 20 gauge will

A .22-caliber rimfire makes the perfect plinking caliber, which will also bring down small animals in a survival situation. This Ruger Single-Six has the added option of changing cylinders for .22 Magnum cartridges.

also work if you prefer something trimmer and lighter. If you're a licensed hunter, you probably already own a 12- or 20-gauge shotgun.

But what is the best survival firearm if you're not a hunter and you may be forced to live off the land? That's not a likely situation, but let's look at the options. If you want to kill a rabbit or squirrel for dinner, there is certainly no need for a magnum handgun. A small .22-caliber handgun would be OK for a sitting rabbit, but trying to shoot a flushed grouse for dinner with a handgun may leave you hungry. There are better choices.

Many years ago, I bought a Savage Model 24 over/under. The top barrel is chambered for .22 Long Rifle and the bottom barrel for 20-gauge loads. I still have that old Savage and will never sell it. At one time, the Air Force ordered 15,000 of these guns as survival rifles for pilots. That old Model 24 has changed over the years, though. The new Model 42 is now a single-shot break action with two barrels, a .22 Long Rifle or .22 Winchester Magnum in the top barrel and a .410 Bore in the bottom barrel. The stock is made of black polymer. It's a great survival gun and a nice one to have around camp.

My second choice for a survival gun would be the Harrington & Richardson Survivor, which is a single shot that will handle .45 Colt or .410 shotshells. This model also has a storage compartment in the buttstock. This gun will work whether your game is sitting or flying. This would also be hard to beat as a survival or camp gun.

Admittedly, you may never find yourself in a survival situation where you have to hunt for food or protect yourself against wildlife, but it sure is fun buying the gun that you believe will do the trick and keep you safe in the woods.

How to Make Spoon Lures

If you find yourself stranded or lost near any body of water, there's a good chance you may find fish, and nearly all species are edible. You can make a very effective fishing lure from any kind of metal or plastic spoon. Most spoons will have a natural fish-catching wobble. Jig the spoon in deep holes or undercut banks and you may well catch dinner. Here's how to make a spoon lure:

Step 1 • Use any size spoon. A teaspoon will work for trout, bass, and walleyes. A tablespoon makes a good muskie or saltwater lure.

Step 2 • With plastic spoons, cut off the handle at the base with heavy metal snippers. You will have to use a hacksaw to cut the handle off a metal spoon.

Step 3 • File or sand the burrs off, and drill two holes in the end of the spoon.

Step 4 • Attach a snap swivel to the front end of the spoon and a treble or single hook with a split ring to the other end.

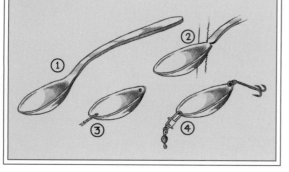

SUSTENANCE: WATER

Sustenance is the need for food and water, which supplies your energy, increases your metabolism, regulates your temperature, and allows your mind to work rationally. Most healthy adults can miss a few meals without significant distress. However, even the healthiest adults can go no longer than a few days without water before they become delirious and lose vital body functions. While ready-to-eat, low-water rations make excellent additions to many survival kits, far too much emphasis is placed on food and not nearly enough on water, water storage, and water purification.

■ Making Potable Water

Rainwater collected in clean containers or in plants is generally safe for drinking. However, you must purify water from lakes, ponds, swamps, springs, or streams, especially those near human habitation. When at all possible, you must disinfect all water by using iodine or chlorine or by boiling. You can purify water by:

- Using water-purification tablets.

- Pouring five drops of 2 percent tincture of iodine in a canteen full of clean water, and 10 drops in a canteen of cloudy or cold water. (Let the canteen stand for 30 minutes before drinking.)

- Boiling water for one minute at sea level, adding one minute for each additional 1,000 feet above sea level, or boiling for 10 minutes no matter where you are.

- Using a commercial water-purification device.

POTABLE DRINKING-WATER SYSTEM DEVICES: Having to purify water is a bother. The only reason to carry any drinking-water purifier at all is to protect your health against microbiological and chemical contaminants. Water-related health threats can occur any time you are in contact with water: drinking water directly, using water as a food or beverage ingredient, using water for washing or brushing your teeth, or using water to clean cookware.

Primary exposure to drinking-water contaminants occurs at the following times:

- When collecting raw water for purification. To avoid this threat, use a separate container for your raw water supply whenever possible. Be selective when possible.

Choose a source least likely to be badly polluted.

- During purification. Be careful to prevent dirty water from dripping or flowing into purified water.

- When storing your purifier either at meal sites or campsites or in your carry pack.

- Especially when handling the purifier during storage, back washing, brushing, scraping, or other maintenance functions.

Remember, the primary microorganisms of concern in most wilderness recreation areas are tough, hardy cystic parasites that resist heat and cold (even freezing temperatures), drought, chlorine, iodine, and just about everything else. And while bacteria are relatively fragile and have very short life cycles, often less than a day, cysts can exist for months. All microorganisms of chief concern are invisibly small and cannot be seen, smelled, or detected in any quick and easy manner. Accordingly, you must rely on knowledge of your area and on common sense.

It is widely known today that *Giardia* or *Cryptosporidium* have been found in water supplies essentially in every country in the world. Therefore, you should always protect against parasitic cysts and insist on 100 percent reduction. Where one cyst can infect, a 99.9 percent reduction may not be good enough, especially when there is no known treatment for some cysts.

There have been essentially no waterborne typhoid, cholera, or Hepatitis A epidemics in the United States for the last 50 years, so the likelihood of their occurrence from a U.S. wilderness water source is very low.

The LifeStraw Personal Water Filter is a light 2-ounce filter that allows you to drink directly from lakes and rivers. The filtration system exceeds EPA standards for water filtration. The LifeStraw can filter up to 264 gallons of water. It measures 1 by 8½ inches. This is a great addition to any camper's or hiker's pack.

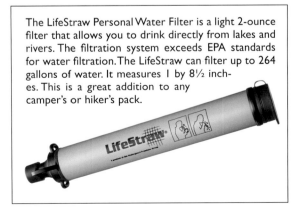

Pesticides, herbicides, and other chemicals can be present anywhere downwind or downstream from major agricultural and industrial areas even hundreds of miles away. These contaminants concentrate in streams, rivers, and lakes.

Asbestos fibers can be found in very high numbers of more than a million fibers per liter in most western and some eastern wilderness waters. Even though trace amounts of these chemicals won't make you ill today, no one wants to drink asbestos fibers if they can easily be avoided.

Micron ratings must be absolute to be meaningful, and precise measurements are essentially impossible to make. Micron ratings pertain only to the physical removal or straining of particles, so absolute micron ratings are only one means of evaluation for removal effectiveness. Removal of pesticides, herbicides, tastes,

odors, and most colors and solvents require other purification (separation) mechanisms. Many units, even those with very low micron ratings, have little or no ability to remove anything other than particles.

According to federal regulations, all water-purification devices are defined as being either pesticide or device products. Pesticide products rely on chemically poisoning organisms (pests), while devices rely on physically removing them. It's easy to tell whether a product is categorized as a pesticide or a device. All products must carry an Environmental Protection Agency (EPA) establishment number. Pesticide products, however, must carry two EPA numbers, one for the manufacturing establishment and one for the pesticide being used. So, decide if you want to use a device or a pesticide for your water-purification needs, and be sure to check the label to choose the right type. In certain applications, it

Solar Still for Safe Water

No matter how fresh and clean water may appear to be in that mountain stream or creek, you can never be sure that it isn't contaminated with chemicals and bacteria that make it unsafe for drinking. It is common sense to always carry a container of water with your gear, especially in warm climates where dehydration is a danger. In a survival situation, a sportsman can get safe drinking water by building a solar still, which will usually provide at least a pint of water every 24 hours. Here's how to use the sun to get safe drinking water:

Step 1 • Dig a hole in the ground about 2 feet deep and 3 feet across.

Step 2 • Place a clean bucket or pan at the bottom of the hole.

Step 3 • Set a plastic sheet over the hole and hold it in place by piling stones or dirt around the edges.

Step 4 • Place a small stone in the center of the plastic sheet so that the water formed by condensation on the sheet's sides is funneled down into the catch container.

The sun causes condensation to form on the sides of the plastic sheet. As the water collects at the bottom of the sheet, it drips into the bucket. As an extra precaution, boil the water for 10 minutes or add a commercial water-treatment tablet.

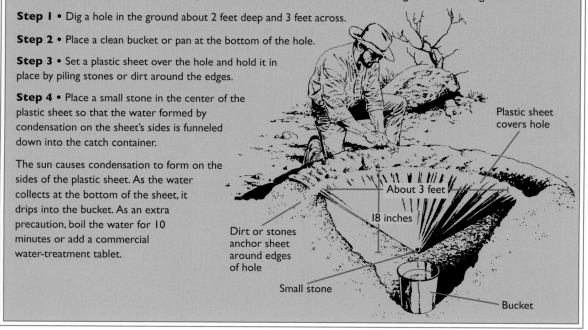

Plastic sheet covers hole

About 3 feet

18 inches

Dirt or stones anchor sheet around edges of hole

Small stone

Bucket

may be desirable to use a pesticide to purify water, but complete removal of the pesticide is very desirable after enough kill time is allowed. It is important to note that iodine resins are not effective against cysts.

All products being marketed today that carry an EPA establishment number are deemed to meet all current, pertinent EPA and other federal regulations. Otherwise, they would not be permitted on the market.

Safe Water

When looking for water, springs, wells, and other underground sources generally provide the safest drinking water. Streams and rivers always require some filtration.

SUSTENANCE: WILD PLANTS FOR FOOD

After water, food is your most urgent need. In a survival situation, you should always be on the lookout for wild foods and live off the land whenever possible. Plants are a valuable food source. Although they may not provide a balanced diet, they will sustain you, even in arctic areas, where the heat-producing qualities of meat are normally essential. Many plant foods such as nuts and seeds will give you enough protein for normal efficiency. Roots, green vegetables, and plant foods containing natural sugar will provide calories and carbohydrates that will give your body energy.

■ Edibility of Plants

Being able to recognize wild edible plants is important in a survival situation. There are certain factors you should keep in mind when collecting edible plants:

- Cultivated plants and wild plants growing in or near cultivated plants may have been sprayed with pesticides, so thoroughly wash whatever plants you collect.

- The surface of any plant food that grows in or is washed in contaminated water is also contaminated. If you are going to eat the plant raw, wash it in water suitable for drinking.

- Some plants may have fungal toxins that are extremely poisonous. To lessen the chances that these toxins are present, collect fresh seeds, fruits, or leaves—not those that have fallen to the ground.

- Plants of the same species may differ in the amount of toxic or subtoxic compounds they contain because of different environmental and genetic factors. One example of this is the foliage of the common choke-berry. Some chokeberry plants have high concentrations of cyanide compounds, while others have low concentrations.

- Some people are more susceptible than others to gastric upsets from plants. If you are sensitive this way, avoid unknown wild plants. If you are extremely sensitive to poison ivy, avoid products from this family of plants, including drinks made from sumacs, mangos, and cashews.

- There are some edible wild plants, such as acorns and water lily rhizomes, that are bitter. These bitter substances (usually tannin compounds) make them unpalatable. Boiling in several changes of water will help remove these substances.

- There are many valuable wild plants that have high concentrations of oxalate compounds. Oxalates usually produce a sharp burning sensation in your mouth, and they are bad for the kidneys. Boiling usually destroys these oxalates.

- The only way to tell if a mushroom is edible is by proper determination. Even then, some species are questionable, so do not eat mushrooms unless you are sure they are edible.

There are many, many plants throughout the world. Tasting or swallowing even a small portion of some can cause severe discomfort, extreme internal disorders, or death. Therefore, if you have the slightest doubt as to the edibility of a plant, apply the Universal Edibility Test before eating any part of it.

Before testing a plant for edibility, make sure that there are a sufficient number of the plants to make testing worth your time and effort. You need more than 24 hours to apply the edibility test.

Keep in mind that eating large amounts of plant food on an empty stomach may cause diarrhea or cramps. Two good examples of familiar foods that cause this problem are green apples and fresh berries. Even if you have tested plant food and found it safe, eat it in moderation with other foods.

■ Universal Edibility Test

You can see from the steps and time involved in testing edibility just how important it is to be able to identify edible plants.

1. Test only one part of a potential food plant at a time.

2. Break the plant into its basic components—leaves, stem, roots, buds, and flowers.

3. Smell the food for strong or acrid odors. Keep in mind that smell alone does not indicate whether or not a plant is inedible.

4. Do not eat for eight hours before starting the test.

5. During the eight hours you are abstaining from eating, test for contact poisoning by placing a piece of the plant part you are testing on the inside of your elbow or wrist. Usually 15 minutes is enough time to allow for a reaction.

6. During the test period, take nothing by mouth except purified water and the plant part being tested.

7. Select a small portion of a single component and prepare it the way you plan to eat it.

8. Before putting the prepared part in your mouth, touch a small portion (a pinch) to the outer surface of your lip to test for burning or itching.

9 If after three minutes there is no reaction on your lip, place the plant part on your tongue, holding it there for 15 minutes.

10. If there is no reaction, thoroughly chew a pinch and hold it in your mouth for 15 minutes. Do not swallow.

11. If no burning, itching, numbing, stinging, or other irritation occurs during the 15 minutes, swallow the food.

12. Wait eight hours. If any ill effects occur during this period, induce vomiting and drink a lot of water.

13. If no ill effects occur, eat ½ cup of the same plant part prepared the same way. Wait another eight hours. If no ill effects occur, the plant part as prepared is safe for eating.

Caution: Make sure to test all parts of the plant for edibility, as some plants have both edible and inedible parts. Do not assume that a part that proved edible when cooked is also edible when raw. Test the part raw to ensure edibility before eating it raw. Do not eat unknown plants that:

- Have a milky sap or a sap that turns black when exposed to air.
- Are mushroom-like.
- Resemble onion or garlic.
- Resemble parsley, parsnip, or dill.
- Have carrot-like leaves, roots, or tubers.

Preparation of Plant Food

Although some plants or plant parts are edible raw, others must be cooked to be edible or palatable. Some methods of improving the taste of plant food are soaking, parboiling, cooking, or leaching. (Leaching is done by crushing food, placing it in some sort of strainer, and pouring boiling water through it.)

Leaves, Stems, and Buds: Boil until tender. Several changes of water help to eliminate the bitterness.

Roots and Tubers: Boil, bake, or roast. Boiling removes harmful substances such as oxalic-acid crystals.

Nuts: Leach or soak acorns in water to remove the bitterness. Although chestnuts are edible raw, they are tastier roasted or steamed.

Grains and Seeds: Parch to improve the taste, or grind into meal to use as a thickener with soups or stews or as flour to make bread.

Sap: If the sap contains sugar, dehydrate it by boiling until the water is gone.

Fruit: Bake or roast tough, heavy-skinned fruit. Boil juicy fruit.

Surviving on Wild Edibles

The 3 Foragers, a family from Connecticut, have become experts on identifying, hunting, and eating wild edible plants. Robert Gergulics is the professional photographer whose photos appear in this section. Karen Monger has produced a clear and concise text describing each wild edible, including several of her tested recipes for some of these plants. Robert and Karen, both excellent cooks and restaurant chefs early in their careers, began their exploration of wild edibles in 2004, traveling from California to New York. Robert is a mushroom expert. Gillian, their 10-year-old daughter, shares their interest in discovering which wild edible plants should be of special interest to sportsmen who hike, fish, or camp. The information in this section is an excellent sample of edible vegetation available in our woods and waters. It is also an excellent start toward learning to live off the land. For more information on the 3 Foragers, visit the3foragers.blogspot.com.

EDIBLE PLANTS

■ Wild and Crab Apples *(Malus* species*)*

DESCRIPTION: These small trees (6 to 15 feet tall) produce ripe fruits in autumn along old field margins and in previously inhabited areas. The trees are planted as ornamentals for the attractive, five-petaled flower produced in spring. The quality and appearance of wild

Wild and Crab Apples

> **Disclaimer:** Never eat anything without first consulting an expert. See also Wild Plants for Foods and Universal Edibility Test on the previous pages.

or crab apple fruit vary in size, color, and taste, but the seeds will be arranged in a star pattern when the fruit is sliced open horizontally, and a small crown is visible at the bottom of the fruit.

RANGE AND HABITAT: Wild and crab apples can be found throughout North America, either wild or as forgotten fruit trees of old farmsteads. Apple trees grow in full sun or partial shade at roadsides and along the edges of fields.

EDIBLE PARTS AND PREPARATION: Wild and crab apples may be eaten raw, but are often cooked like traditional cultivated apples into desserts or fermented into cider, and their high pectin content makes them a good thickener. Wild apples can also be dehydrated.

Asiatic Dayflower

■ Asiatic Dayflower
(Commelina communis)

DESCRIPTION: Asiatic dayflower is a weedy-looking plant with lance-shaped leaves and slightly hairy, juicy stems. The flowers have two blue upper petals and one white lower petal; each flower only stays open for one day.

RANGE AND HABITAT: Asiatic dayflower is an annual invasive weed that grows from the Midwest throughout eastern North America, and in Washington and Oregon. Best collected in the spring and into the late summer, it is common in parks and gardens and grows in disturbed areas.

EDIBLE PARTS AND PREPARATION: The leaves, stems, flowers, and seeds are edible raw, but can also be chopped and cooked as a mild green in casseroles, soups, and stir-fries.

■ Autumn Olives / Silverberry
(Elaeagnus umbellata)

Autumn Olives / Silverberry

DESCRIPTION: Autumn olives are invasive shrubs. The undersides of the lance-shaped leaves are distinctly silvery, and the red berries that ripen in late summer and persist through the fall are also speckled with silvery dots. The shrubs can grow from 3 to 16 feet tall. Autumn olive berries each contain one football-shaped, ridged seed.

RANGE AND HABITAT: Autumn olives are found throughout the Midwest, eastern North America, and in the Pacific Northwest along roadsides, in large groups in forgotten fields, and in sunny or partially shaded areas.

EDIBLE PARTS AND PREPARATION: The ripe berries can be eaten raw, cooked into a lycopene-rich sauce or jam, or dehydrated into fruit leather. The soft seed can be chewed and eaten for fiber or removed using a mesh strainer.

■ Northern Bayberries
(Morella pensylvanica)

DESCRIPTION: Northern bayberry is a deciduous shrub with leathery, alternate, lance-shaped leaves. When crushed, the leaves emit a spicy aroma. The shrubs grow 1 to 6 feet tall. Only the female shrubs produce waxy, grayish-blue berries attached in clusters directly to the woody branches.

RANGE AND HABITAT: Northern bayberry grows from the eastern provinces of Canada south into North Carolina, and east of Ohio. It is a salt-tolerant shrub and is often found along the East Coast, as well as along waterways, at field margins, and planted as attractive landscape foliage. It prefers full sun but will tolerate partial shade.

EDIBLE PARTS AND PREPARATION: Northern bayberry

leaves can be collected from spring through autumn by plucking them from the branches, and are used to flavor soups, stews, and cooked bean dishes in similar ways as commercially available bay leaves. The leaves should be removed from the soup as they are a bit too tough to eat. Bayberry leaves dry well for preservation. The berries from the female shrubs can be collected in large amounts and a fragrant, burnable wax can be extracted by gently simmering the berries in water; the wax will float to the surface of the water as it cools.

Northern Bayberries

■ Black Cherries / Rum Cherries
(Prunus serotina)

DESCRIPTION: Black cherries are common trees that can grow from 40 to 90 feet tall. When young, the bark of black cherry trees is gray and streaked with horizontal brown lenticels; as the tree grows and ages, the bark appears rough and broken into burnt chips. The leaves are glossy, green, and lance shaped, and there are fine

Black Cherries / Rum Cherries

Black Locust Flower Doughnuts

Makes about 24 doughnuts

1 to 2 cups cooking oil
1⅓ cups flour
1½ teaspoons baking powder
¼ teaspoon salt
1 egg
⅔ cup milk
2 cups fresh black locust flowers
Powdered sugar

Heat your oil to 375°F. Mix the flour with the baking powder and salt. Beat the egg and add it to the milk. Gently whisk the wet ingredients into the dry ingredients. Fold in the black locust flowers. Fry about 1 tablespoon of batter for each doughnut, about 30 seconds on each side. Dust with powdered sugar for serving.

hairs on the underside of the midrib. The cherries grow in elongated clusters on short stems and have a single, hard pit. When scratched, black cherry twigs have a bitter almond odor.

RANGE AND HABITAT: Black cherry is a native tree growing from eastern Canada south into Texas, throughout the Midwest, and in Washington State. It prefers full sun and can often be found along roadways and the edges of fields, and is a pioneer tree of open spaces.

EDIBLE PARTS AND PREPARATION: Black cherries are not sweet like cultivated cherries, but have an intense grapefruit-like taste. They should be picked when they have ripened fully to black, and it is easiest to just collect the entire cluster rather than picking individual cherries. The pit is large compared to the flesh of the cherry, but easily spit out or removed. Black cherries can be eaten raw, or used to make jams, pies, liqueur and soda flavorings, juice, and ice cream. The wood of the black cherry tree can be used to smoke meat.

■ Black Locust *(Robinia pseudoacacia)*

DESCRIPTION: Black locust trees have deeply furrowed, gray bark and can grow up to 70 feet tall. The leaves are compound with seven to 21 smooth, oval leaflets attached to the leaf stem, and there are two small spines that grow where the leaf attaches to the branch. The flowers appear in mid spring before the leaves, and are drooping clusters of pealike, white and light yellow, fragrant flowers. Flat, hairless, black seedpods are produced in late summer, each containing four to seven round seeds.

RANGE AND HABITAT: Black locust trees are native to the Southeast, but have spread and can be found in the entire United States. They can be found along waterways

Black Locust

and at the edges of fields, and are frequently planted to provide nectar for honeybees.

EDIBLE PARTS AND PREPARATION: The flowers are the main edible part of black locust trees. They can be eaten raw or added to batters and fried, mixed into hot oatmeal, baked in custard, or made into floral sugar syrup. The flowers have a sweet taste and delicate crunch. The seeds have disputed edibility and are very difficult to collect in large enough quantities; consumption of black locust seeds is not recommended. All other parts of the black locust tree are toxic to humans and livestock, including the bark, leaves, and roots. Black locust lumber is extremely hard and valued for furniture making and fence posts, as well as firewood.

■ Black Raspberry *(Rubus occidentalis)*

DESCRIPTION: Black raspberries grow on 3- to 5-foot-long, arching, thorny canes that have a whitish-blue powdery coating that is easily rubbed off. The leaves are compound with three to five leaflets, green on top and whitish on the undersides. The flowers of black raspberries have five petals and are white, growing in clusters of three to seven on a prickly stem. The berries ripen from green to deep purple or black; unripe red berries will not easily come off the stem. Black raspberries are hollow, leaving the white core on the stem when picked, and have one small seed inside each juicy globule, meaning many seeds per berry.

RANGE AND HABITAT: Black raspberries are native to North America and can be found west of Colorado throughout the eastern United States, but are absent in

Black Raspberry

Black Walnuts

Florida and Texas. Black raspberries prefer partial shade and often grow at the edges of lawns and woodlands, but will tolerate full sun.

EDIBLE PARTS AND PREPARATION: Black raspberries are one of the first sweet berries to ripen during the early summer. They taste sweet and intensely fruity, and can be eaten raw from the canes. Black raspberries can be used the same way commercially grown blackberries or raspberries are used: in jams, sauces, ice creams, wine, fruit leather, and many desserts. Black raspberries freeze well.

■ Black Walnuts *(Juglans nigra)*

DESCRIPTION: Black walnut trees can grow up to 100 feet tall and have deeply furrowed gray bark. The leaves of black walnut trees are compound, consisting of 11 to 23 lance-shaped, lightly toothed leaves growing from a green midrib. When crushed, the leaflets will emit a spicy odor. The walnuts are covered in a green, pebbly surfaced hull that should be removed when the nuts ripen and fall from the tree, revealing a dark, brownish-black, hard nutshell.

RANGE AND HABITAT: Black walnuts are native to North America and grow from Utah eastward throughout the United States, and north into the eastern provinces of Canada. Black walnut trees will grow in mixed forests, but prefer roadsides, forest edges, and field margins for greater sunlight and optimal growth.

EDIBLE PARTS AND PREPARATION: It is the nut meat of black walnuts that is prized for its strong and distinctive flavor. The fibrous, green outer hull of the nuts is removed by either smashing it with a mallet or running it over in the driveway with the car, and the hard shells are best scrubbed with a wire brush to remove any residual hull bits, a process that requires gloves to avoid staining your skin brown. The nuts are easiest to remove from the shell if allowed to age for two to three months; then they can be opened with a hammer or a special black walnut cracker. The nut meats can be used in traditional baked goods like cookies and cakes, eaten plain, or added to ice cream and fudge. The green hulls can be used to produce a yellowish-brown dye for textiles, and the wood from black walnut trees is used to craft attractive bowls, furniture, flooring, and gunstocks.

■ Blackberries *(Rubus* species)

DESCRIPTION: The term *blackberries* refers to many different species of edible berries that ripen to black, grow on thorny vines or canes, and are picked with their white core still inside the berry; they are not hollow. The leaves of blackberry canes or trailing vines are compound, with five to seven serrated leaflets that tend to be green on the upper surface and lighter green or white on the underside. The flowers of blackberry plants are white

Blackberries

with five petals and often grow in clusters on short, prickly stems. Not all of the berries will ripen at once, and blackberry patches can be visited multiple times for subsequent harvests. Each berry contains many seeds, one inside each juicy globule attached to the white core.

RANGE AND HABITAT: Blackberries grow in full sun or partial shade. They are often found in old fields, along the edges of roads and trails, in hedgerows, and at woodland edges. Blackberries are found in almost all temperate climates of North America, only absent in desert areas. The blackberries that grow on ground-trailing vines are commonly called dewberries, and other regional common names include boysenberry, brambleberry, marionberry, Yankee blackberry, Himalayan blackberry, and Allegheny blackberry. Blackberries will hybridize with other species of blackberries, and this accounts for the many different types.

EDIBLE PARTS AND PREPARATION: All blackberries are edible, but their flavor varies between varieties. The ripe berries are edible raw out of hand, and can be used in similar ways to cultivated blackberries. Ripe blackberries can be added to cereals, yogurt, and oatmeal, baked into pies, made into jam, fermented into wine, and used in sauces for wild game. Blackberries can be dehydrated whole, or made into fruit leather. Blackberry leaves can be collected and dried for making an herbal tea high in vitamin C.

■ Burdock *(Arctium lappa* and *Arctium minus)*

DESCRIPTION: Burdock is a biennial plant that produces only a large rosette of leaves in its first year, and a 2- to 9-foot-tall flower stalk in its second year before dying. The leaves of burdock are large and shaped like elongated hearts with ruffled edges, and are whitish and fuzzy on the undersides. The flower stalk bears many purplish, thistle-like flowers in the summer that will dry into the recognizable burrs that seem to get hooked everywhere on clothes and in pet fur.

RANGE AND HABITAT: Burdock is a nonnative plant originally from Europe. Common burdock *(Arctium minus)* is found in almost all of North America with the exception of Florida and the northern provinces of Canada, while greater burdock *(Arctium lappa)* grows from California to the New England states, absent from

Burdock

the South. Burdock prefers disturbed and cultivated soil, and is often found at field edges, roadsides, and the edges of gardens and croplands.

EDIBLE PARTS AND PREPARATION: The easiest way to spot a patch of burdock is to look for last year's dried flower stalks with their round burr heads still attached. The taproot of the first-year burdock plants are best dug in the spring and fall as a nutritious root vegetable. The taproots can grow to more than a foot long and are easier to dig from sandy or recently disturbed soil. The roots should be cooked in soups, boiled and mashed, or roasted like any root vegetable to prevent flatulence due to the root's high complex carbohydrate content. In early summer, the flower stalk of the second-year burdock plant yields an even better-tasting vegetable. Cut the flower stalk at its base when it is 1 to 2 feet tall, remove the leaves and flower stems, and then peel the stringy skin off until you reach the tender, light green core. Steam or boil the peeled flower stalks until tender, and serve with butter and a squeeze of lemon juice. Burdock roots and flower stalks can be made into pickles.

■ Cattails
(*Typha angustifolia* and *Typha latifolia*)

DESCRIPTION: Cattails are perennial plants that have green, narrow, swordlike leaves growing from the underground or underwater rhizomes. In late spring, a flower spike is produced with the female flower parts growing on the lower part of the stalk and the male flower parts growing on the upper part. The upper, male flower will produce the pollen before it disintegrates, while the female flower will become the familiar-looking, brown "hot dog on a stick" in the autumn.

RANGE AND HABITAT: Broadleaf cattail (*Typha latifolia*) is native to North America and can be found throughout the entire United States and Canada. Narrow-leaf cattails (*Typha angustifolia*) are an introduced species that have a slightly smaller range; they are absent in the Deep South and northern provinces of Canada. Cattails grow in wetland areas, sometimes partially submerged, and some can tolerate brackish water in tidal zones. It is important to know the quality of the water source before collecting cattails for food: try to avoid roadside runoff ditches, proximity to agricultural runoff, and stagnant water.

EDIBLE PARTS AND PREPARATION: In the spring, the new shoots of cattails can be collected by cutting or pulling the shoot from the rhizome and then trimming the green parts from the tender, white, layered core. The shoot can be eaten raw, added to salads, or pickled. When cattails produce the flower spike in late spring, it will be enclosed in a single leaf sheath. Cut off the spike and peel off the sheath to find the immature, green flower spike. The upper, male portion of the flower can

Cattails

Cattail Flower Griddle Cakes

Makes about 12 (2-inch) cakes

1 tablespoon milk
2 large eggs
2 tablespoons flour
½ teaspoon baking powder
1 cup cattail flower spike pulp (male flower parts)
1 tablespoon minced sweet red pepper
½ teaspoon salt
Pinch of pepper
Sour cream and glasswort or chives, for garnish

Mix the milk, eggs, flour, and baking powder together with a whisk until no lumps remain. Stir in the cattail flower spike pulp, sweet red pepper, salt, and pepper. Cook the batter by the tablespoonful on a medium griddle, until browned on both sides. Allow the cakes to cool, and serve with a dollop of sour cream and glasswort or chives.

Chickweed

be pinched off the core of the spike and added to batters, or boiled while still attached to the core and eaten like corn on the cob. If allowed to mature, the male flower will produce pollen that can be collected, sifted, and added to smoothies and batters for a nutritional boost. Once the female flower matures, the dry, brown heads can be collected to use as fantastic tinder for fires. The underground or underwater rhizomes of cattails have two layers, and the harder, inner layer can be pounded and rinsed in water to extract a very small amount of starch that will sink to the bottom of a bowl of water to be used as a thickener. The yield of starch from the rhizomes is minimal and often not worth the effort.

■ Chickweed *(Stellaria media)*

DESCRIPTION: Chickweed is an annual, tender plant that is available in spring, drops seeds and dies back in the summer, and then reemerges in the fall for a second harvest. The green, pointy-tipped oval leaves grow in pairs along a stringy stem that bears hairs in a single line, like a miniature mohawk haircut, and that line of hairs switches position between each pair of leaves on the stalk. Inside the stalk, there is a tough, white inner core that can be observed by breaking the stem and gently pulling it apart. The flowers of chickweed are small, and have five deeply cleft white petals that appear as 10 petals. Chickweed produces many tiny, round, black seeds from each flower.

RANGE AND HABITAT: Chickweed is an introduced plant originally from Europe, but it has spread and become a naturalized mild pest throughout the entire continent of North America. It can be found in disturbed areas, fields, parks, and along the edges of gardens.

EDIBLE PARTS AND PREPARATION: All above-ground parts of chickweed are edible, including the leaves, stems, flowers, seed heads, and seeds. Chickweed gets a little stringy as it grows taller and may lie along the ground. The best parts to eat raw in salads or as a sandwich green are the top 3 to 4 inches of the stem and the leaves, along with the flowers; raw chickweed has a mild corn flavor. Chickweed can be added to soups and stir-fries as a green vegetable.

■ Dandelions *(Taraxacum officinale)*

DESCRIPTION: Dandelions are perennial plants whose leaves and flower stems grow from an unbranched, off-

Dandelions

white taproot. The leaves have sharp and irregularly toothed edges that point downward, and the underside of the midrib of the leaf is often sparsely hairy. Each hollow flower stalk will produce a single flower head composed of several yellow ray flowers clumped together to form what appears as one large flower. This flower head blooms for a day before turning into a seed head with fluffy parachutes that help it float on the wind and spread the seeds. The leaves and flower stems exude a milky white sap when cut.

RANGE AND HABITAT: Dandelions are originally from Eurasia, but have become naturalized throughout all of North America. They will grow in open fields, lawns, disturbed areas, and just about anywhere they can get full sun and enough moisture. Dandelions are one weed that most people love to hate, and are often a homeowner's biggest irritation in the lawn.

EDIBLE PARTS AND PREPARATION: In the spring before dandelions produce their flower stalk, the leaves are much more tender and mild and make an excellent green vegetable either raw in salads or cooked in any recipe. The leaves can be collected in great quantities and blanched and frozen for use later in the year. The entire rosette of leaves can be collected by using a knife and cutting down into the soil to cut it off just beneath the surface. As the season progresses and dandelions spend more time in the sun, their leaves become bitter. The flower heads can be collected and made into jellies or wine, once the yellow parts are separated from the green parts. The unopened flower heads can be collected in the morning and boiled and eaten as well. The taproot can be collected all year, but is less tough in the fall and spring. The taproot can be eaten as a root vegetable in soups, or chopped and roasted in an oven and then ground to make a coffee substitute.

■ Daylily *(Hemerocallis fulva)*

DESCRIPTION: Daylilies are perennial plants with curved, swordlike leaves that can grow from 1 to 3 feet long from a clump of underground tuberous roots. Flowers are produced on a tall, leafless spike that will hold 10 to 20 flower buds, each 1 to 3 inches long. The orange-and-yellow-veined flowers have six petallike parts called tepals that open for only one day (hence the name daylily), but not all the buds open at once.

RANGE AND HABITAT: Originally from Asia, daylilies have escaped cultivation from gardens and become a mild invasive pest in much of North America. Mostly absent from California and the Southwest, daylilies grow in most of the continental United States and eastern Canada. Daylilies grow along roadsides, field edges, and in disturbed areas, preferring partial shade.

EDIBLE PARTS AND PREPARATION: In the spring, daylilies produce compact shoots of the tender and small sword-shaped leaves that can be collected and eaten

Daylily Flower Bud

Daylily Shoot Tuber

Daylily Flower

Evening Primrose Flower and Root

raw in salads or cooked lightly and added to recipes. The starchy tubers can be dug in the early spring or again late in the fall when they are firm and large, then either scrubbed or peeled and cooked like small potatoes. The unopened flower buds make a good vegetable if collected and boiled for 5 to 7 minutes and added to casseroles. Once the flowers open, the orange tepals can be eaten raw in salads. As the flowers wither at the end of the day, they can still be collected and dried further, and used as a thickener for soups or stews.

■ Evening Primrose *(Oenothera biennis)*

DESCRIPTION: Evening primrose is a biennial plant whose flowers tend to open later in the evening rather than during midday or morning. In the plant's first year, it produces only smooth-edged, lance-shaped leaves with a noticeably lighter-colored midrib in a rosette, growing from a pale brown taproot that has a pink or reddish top. In the plant's second year of growth, a tall flower stalk grows that will have multiple yellow four-petaled flowers at the top. The flowers will mature into elongated, green seed capsules that eventually dry out and split into four sections filled with many irregularly shaped seeds.

RANGE AND HABITAT: Evening primrose is a native plant of North America, growing throughout most of the United States but absent in the Rockies south to Arizona. Evening primrose grows in fields, along roadsides, and in disturbed soils, and will tolerate sandy soils and full sun.

EDIBLE PARTS AND PREPARATION: In its first year of growth, when only the basal leaves are present, the taproot of evening primrose is a good edible boiled or roasted; once the plant starts producing the flower stalk in its second year, the taproot will become too fibrous and tough to eat. Add the roots to soups and stews like any root vegetable; it tastes similar to a peppery parsnip. The young leaves, flower buds, and green seedpods are also edible raw, but if large quantities of the seedpods are to be eaten, they should be lightly cooked first. All parts of evening primrose have a mild peppery taste that can be alleviated with brief cooking. The mature seeds can be collected and eaten in small amounts, or toasted and added to muffins or oatmeal.

■ Field Garlic *(Allium vineale)*

DESCRIPTION: Field garlic is a perennial species of wild, weedy onion. Its leaves are slender, sometimes slightly corrugated, hollow tubes from 8 to 18 inches long and grow from a small, layered bulb. Each bulb can produce a flower stem that is topped with a ball of tiny bubils and flowers that are purplish pink and have six petallike tepals. When cut or crushed, the long leaves and bulb emit a strong garlic aroma.

Field Garlic

RANGE AND HABITAT: Field garlic is an invasive plant introduced from Europe. It can be found along the West and East Coast of North America, throughout the South, and into the Midwest; it is absent from the Southwest and the Rockies. Field garlic grows in lawns, open fields, roadsides, and disturbed soils.

EDIBLE PARTS AND PREPARATION: When the long, hollow leaves first emerge in the spring, they are very tender and can be chopped finely and added like chives to any recipe. As the spring progresses, the leaves will toughen a bit, and the flower stalk will be even tougher. The tiny bubils growing on the flower stalk and the small flowers are edible and can be infused into vinegar. The bulb is also edible, although small and sometimes tedious to clean.

■ Garlic Mustard *(Alliaria petiolata)*

DESCRIPTION: Garlic mustard is a biennial plant in the mustard family. In its first year of growth, garlic mustard produces kidney-shaped leaves with scalloped edges and netlike veins on long stems that grow directly from a white taproot. In the early spring of the second year, garlic mustard produces a branched flower stalk that can grow up to 3 feet tall, with alternate, triangular, scalloped leaves and clusters of four-petaled, white flowers. The flowers mature into slender, green seedpods that dry out and bear many small, elongated black seeds.

RANGE AND HABITAT: Garlic mustard is an incredibly invasive plant originally from Europe. It grows in disturbed areas, in parks, yard and field margins, abandoned lots in urban areas, and in forests where partial sun is present. It grows throughout the East Coast, into the Midwest, and up into the Pacific Northwest. So far, it has not been widely reported in California, the Southwest, or along the Gulf Coast.

EDIBLE PARTS AND PREPARATION: All parts of garlic mustard are edible and have varying degrees of a mustardy bitterness and garlic flavor. The leaves can be cooked lightly and used as a green in any egg-based dish or casserole. The flower heads resemble broccoli before the flowers bloom, and can be eaten raw or stir-fried. The flowers can be added to salads, and the seeds can be collected before the dry seedpods split open, and a fiery, sinus-clearing mustard can be made. The taproot can be dug late in the fall from first-year plants and pulverized into a horseradish-like condiment with the addition of

Garlic Mustard Roulade

Serves 8 (one 12-inch roll)

1 pound garlic mustard greens
½ teaspoon ground nutmeg
½ teaspoon sea salt
1 teaspoon smoked paprika
2 teaspoons granulated garlic
½ teaspoon ground black pepper
4 egg yolks
4 egg whites
2 cups shredded mozzarella cheese

Heat oven to 425°F. In a large pot of boiling water, blanch the garlic mustard greens for 1 minute. Shock the greens in ice water to stop the cooking process, and squeeze as much water from them as possible. Add the cooked greens to a food processor. Add the nutmeg, sea salt, smoked paprika, granulated garlic, black pepper, and egg yolks. Pulse until the garlic mustard greens are finely chopped. In a mixer, whip the egg whites until stiff peaks form. With a spatula, fold one-third of the egg whites into the greens mixture, mixing until no more whites are seen. Then gently fold in the remaining egg whites, until the mixture is uniform. Spread the garlic mustard and egg mixture evenly on a 12-by-16-inch jelly roll pan lined with parchment paper, leaving an inch of exposed paper around the entire edge. Bake until the egg is set, about 12 to 15 minutes. Loosen the roulade from the parchment paper. Sprinkle the top with whatever you are using as a filling, or just mozzarella cheese. Starting with the wider side, roll the roulade up like a jelly roll, ending seam-side down. Bake an additional 10 minutes to melt the cheese and warm the filling.

Garlic Mustard

some vinegar. The leaves of garlic mustard can be collected in large quantities, steamed, and frozen for use all year.

Ginkgo *(Ginkgo biloba)*

DESCRIPTION: Ginkgo are large trees that grow up to 100 feet tall, with fan-shaped leaves that are sometimes bilobed. Ginkgo leaves turn a brilliant yellow in the fall. Ginkgo are dioecious, meaning there are male trees and female trees, and only the female trees produce the edible nut that has a hard shell and fleshy outer fruit. The outer flesh of the nut is soft and smells strongly of cheesy vomit as the seeds ripen and fall to the ground, and the flesh is a mild skin irritant. Once cracked open, the nut of the ginkgo is green.

RANGE AND HABITAT: Ginkgo trees are originally from China. Most trees found in North America have been planted in cities in the eastern and southern United

Ginkgo

States, as their growth is quite attractive, and ginkgo trees tolerate pollution and are resistant to insects. To avoid the smelly fruit that falls in the autumn, many cities are choosing to plant male trees only. The female trees can be found by following your nose to the rancid, rotting flesh of the seeds.

EDIBLE PARTS AND PREPARATION: The only edible part of the ginkgo tree is the mature nut, which is botanically a gametophyte. Collect the smelly fruits once they have fallen from the tree, wearing a pair of gloves to protect your hands. Try to remove most of the flesh in the field, as you don't want to bring that smell home. The nuts are mildly toxic when raw, so they need to be boiled or roasted before cracking open the thin shell and peeling away a papery brown skin. Ginkgo nuts are added to traditional Chinese foods like congee and Buddha's Delight, or can be eaten plain in moderate amounts.

Japanese Knotweed *(Polygonum cuspidatum,* syn. *Fallopia japonica)*

DESCRIPTION: Japanese knotweed is a perennial invasive plant that grows from an underground rhizome. When it first emerges in the spring, Japanese knotweed shoots have curled-up leaves, and hollow, jointed stalks that have a green- and red-mottled skin. The shovel-blade or heart-shaped leaves grow on hollow stems from each "node" on the stalk, which indicates where a cross wall is in the stem between the hollow chambers. Knotweed can grow up to 10 feet tall, and will bloom with attractive sprays of creamy white flowers late in the summer that mature into winged seeds. The hollow stalks will dry out in the winter and persist, making it easy to spot a stand of knotweed before it starts growing again in the spring.

RANGE AND HABITAT: Japanese knotweed is originally from Asia, but was planted in North America as an ornamental. It spreads by underground rhizomes and is very difficult to eradicate. Japanese knotweed grows in disturbed areas, roadsides, along rivers, and in urban areas, and will tolerate full sun to partial shade. Knotweed is currently invading the majority of the United States and Canada, and many states have made it illegal to sell or plant Japanese knotweed.

EDIBLE PARTS AND PREPARATION: Depending on how it is prepared, knotweed makes a good sweet or savory

Japanese Knotweed Muffins

Makes 8 muffins

1 cup sugar, divided
2 cups chopped Japanese knotweed stalks
¼ cup water
1 tablespoon lemon juice
1 egg
¼ cup oil
1 cup flour
½ teaspoon baking powder
¼ teaspoon baking soda
¼ teaspoon cinnamon

Preheat the oven to 325°F. Place baking papers in a muffin pan. In a saucepot, combine ½ cup sugar, knotweed stalks, water, and lemon juice. Cook over medium heat for 10 minutes, stirring often. Allow the stewed knotweed to cool. There should be about 1 cup of stewed knotweed. In a large bowl, whisk the egg with the oil, and stir in the stewed knotweed. Sift together the flour, ½ cup sugar, baking powder, baking soda, and cinnamon. Stir into the wet ingredients in the large bowl. Do not overmix. Fill the muffin papers about ¾ full. Bake for 24 to 28 minutes, until the top is set and springs back when touched. Cool and serve with butter or toasted.

Japanese Knotweed

or fruit juices, they can be stewed until soft and added to muffin or pancake batters. A pink jelly or green fruit leather can be made from large amounts of knotweed, and savory preparations include pickles, salt-brined vegetables, or soups. Mature stalks of knotweed tend to filter and collect water in their lowest chambers, and it can be collected and consumed by cutting into the stem just outside of the cross walls of a section. The dried stalks of last year's knotweed can be used as biodegradable straws.

■ Jewelweed / Touch-Me-Not
(*Impatiens capensis*)

DESCRIPTION: Jewelweed is an annual herbaceous plant with alternate, oval, lightly toothed leaves that grow along a succulent stem with prominent swollen nodes. Jewelweed can grow up to 5 feet tall, toughening

Jewelweed / Touch-Me-Not

vegetable when collected at its shoot stage—under 12 inches tall. If the knotweed becomes too tall, the stalk becomes very stringy and tough. The shoots can be sliced thinly and eaten raw in small amounts as a tart addition to salads and cold noodle dishes. With added sugar with age. When held underwater, the leaves appear to be covered with diamonds. The flowers of jewelweed can be orange (*Impatiens capensis*) or yellow (*Impatiens pallida*), with three petallike structures, and are shaped similar to a horn, with a spur at the end. The flowers mature into a seedpod that contains one to four brown-skinned seeds and explodes if brushed lightly, dispersing the seeds.

RANGE AND HABITAT: Jewelweed is a native plant of North America, and can be found throughout most of the United States and Canada, but is absent in the Southwest and Rockies as well as California. Jewelweed often grows in wetland areas, garden margins, ditches, and along creeks in partially shaded habitats.

EDIBLE PARTS AND PREPARATION: When the first leaves of jewelweed emerge in the spring, they are a nominal edible plant. Late in the summer, the seeds can be carefully (and tediously) collected and eaten, tasting similar to walnuts. Jewelweed has some anti-inflammatory properties that make it a useful relief to mosquito bites and an effective wash for poison ivy rashes. To use, crush the juicy stems of jewelweed (the lower, red portions are best) and rub the resulting thick mucilage onto a bite or areas where poison ivy has been encountered. Repeated applications may be necessary, but the "goo" is quite soothing for the skin.

■ Lamb's Quarters / Wild Spinach
(*Chenopodium album* and *Chenopodium berlandieri*)

DESCRIPTION: Lamb's quarters are annual herbaceous plants that have many common names, including goosefoot, fat hen, and wild spinach. The leaves are triangular or diamond shaped, alternately arranged, and have softly rounded teeth on their edges. The undersides of the leaves are coated with a white powder that easily rubs off, and the leaves have little smell when crushed or cut. Lamb's quarters can grow up to 8 feet tall. The flowers are small and green, growing in clusters that mature to many black and tiny seeds

RANGE AND HABITAT: Both varieties of lamb's quarters are found throughout the entire North American continent; *Chenopodium album* is a European import and *Chenopodium berlandieri* is native to North America. Lamb's quarters grow in abandoned lots, yard margins, in gardens, and in disturbed soil, and they prefer full sun.

Lamb's Quarters / Wild Spinach

EDIBLE PARTS AND PREPARATION: Lamb's quarters often grow in large stands from mid spring through late fall and the mild-tasting leaves can be eaten in similar ways to spinach. The stems can be tender and eaten when the plant is still young, but the leaves remain mild all season long. Add lamb's quarters leaves to soups, eggs, and casseroles, or steam them to freeze for later use. The seed heads can be collected once they start to dry out, and then dried further in a paper bag, and the chaff can be winnowed away. The seeds can be crushed in a mortar and added to baked goods or cooked oatmeal like a grain.

■ Milkweed (*Asclepis syriaca*)

DESCRIPTION: Common milkweed is a perennial herbaceous plant that can grow up to 6 feet tall, with opposite, oval-shaped leaves with pointed tips. The leaves are fuzzy on the underside and grow from a lightly fuzzy stalk that rarely branches. The pink-and-white flowers grow in pom-pom-shaped clusters on stems that originate where the leaves connect to the stem. Only a few of the flowers from each cluster will mature into warty, tear-drop-shaped pods about 1 to 3 inches long, which will split open when mature to release the flat, brown seeds attached to a silky plume that floats in the wind. All parts of milkweed will exude white, milky latex when cut or broken.

RANGE AND HABITAT: Common milkweed is native to North America and grows east of the Rockies. It is commonly found in fields, garden edges, and roadsides, growing in full sun.

Milkweed Pod and Chickpea Salad

Makes about 3 cups

SALAD:
2 cups small milkweed pods, about 1 or
    1½ inches long
1 (16-ounce) can chickpeas, drained
¼ red onion, sliced thinly
¼ cup crumbled feta cheese

DRESSING:
3 tablespoons red wine vinegar
1 tablespoon fresh basil, chopped
¼ teaspoon salt
¼ teaspoon pepper
½ teaspoon sugar
1 clove garlic, minced
2 tablespoons olive oil

Scrub the milkweed pods, and boil them for 5 minutes. Shock them in ice water. Slice the stem ends off the pods and slice them in half, removing the seeds and silk. Toss the milkweed pods with the chickpeas, onion, and feta cheese. To make the dressing, whisk the vinegar, basil, salt, pepper, sugar, and garlic together in a bowl. While whisking, drizzle in the olive oil slowly, making an emulsion. Toss the salad with the dressing, and allow it to refrigerate for at least an hour before serving.

EDIBLE PARTS AND PREPARATION: In the early spring, the shoots of milkweed that are under 8 to 10 inches tall with their leaves still unfurled can be collected, boiled for 5 minutes, and eaten as a vegetable in cooked dishes. It is important to observe the lightly fuzzy stalks at this stage to prevent confusion with other shoots. Later in the spring, the flower buds of milkweed look similar to small heads of broccoli, and can be collected, boiled, and eaten in salads, baked in quiche, or brined into a caper-like condiment. Once the flowers open, they can be col-

Milkweed Pod and Flower

lected and eaten raw in salads as a nominal edible. In the early autumn, the seedpods are still small and tender, 1 to 2 inches long. They can be boiled for 5 minutes and split open, and the insides can be removed and stuffed with cheese or meats, and then baked in a sauce or grilled. The cooked insides of the milkweed seedpod can be eaten as well, as long as the seeds are still white and soft. Once dried out completely at the end of autumn, the seedpods make excellent tinder for fire starting.

■ Mulberries *(Morus alba, Morus nigra, and Morus rubra)*

DESCRIPTION: Mulberries are berries that grow on medium-high trees up to 45 feet tall, with variably shaped, lobed, and toothed leaves that are alternately arranged on woody branches. Male and female flowers

Mulberries

are usually on separate trees, although they may occur on the same tree. The female flowers produce a berry that is a compound cluster of several drupes, similar in appearance to a blackberry. The color of the fruit varies between the varieties of white, black, and red mulberry trees, and the trees often interbreed and produce hybrids.

RANGE AND HABITAT: White mulberry trees (*Morus alba*) are native to Asia but have become a widespread, somewhat invasive pest throughout the continental United States. The black mulberry (*Morus nigra*) is another introduced tree from Asia, and only grows in Texas through the Mid-Atlantic states. Red mulberry trees (*Morus rubra*) are native to North America, growing east of the Rockies into the southern New England states. Due to the mess of dropped fruits and high pollen production, mulberries are considered pests in urban areas. Mulberries often grow wild in yards and at the edges of woods where the seeds are spread through bird droppings. They grow in full or partial sun in any temperate climate.

EDIBLE PARTS AND PREPARATION: In the spring, the newly unfurling leaves of mulberry trees are a good edible green, slightly mucilaginous but mild. The berries of the assorted species vary in color when ripe from white and pink to red, dark red, and deep black. As long as the berries are soft and juicy, they are ripe. Ripe berries can be eaten raw, juiced and made into ice cream or dessert sauces, or baked into pies and cobblers.

◼ Nettles
(*Urtica dioica* and *Urtica gracilis*)

DESCRIPTION: Nettles are perennial herbaceous plants that have built-in defense mechanisms; they can sting and you will know immediately when you stumble through a patch. The leaves of nettles are opposite, have deeply serrated edges, and are shaped like narrow, elongated hearts. The leaves are attached to a wiry stem that can be made into strong cordage. Nettle plants are either male or female; both plants produce hanging green or whitish-yellow flowers from the leaf stem axils, but only the female plants will produce tiny seeds. The leaves and main stem of nettles are covered with small stinging hairs that function similar to hypodermic needles, injecting you with a blend of histamines and other chemical compounds to produce a "sting" if you touch the plant.

Nettles

RANGE AND HABITAT: There are two prevalent nettles species in North America, both widespread. Our native stinging nettle is *Urtica gracilis*, and the introduced European stinging nettle is *Urtica dioica*. Both species of nettles are found in forests, near the edges of open fields, in disturbed soils, near rivers, and very often near human settlements.

EDIBLE PARTS AND PREPARATION: Surprisingly, nettles make a very nutritious green once the sting has been neutralized through cooking or drying. The leaves contain protein, iron, vitamin C, and provitamin A. Nettles can be collected while wearing gloves when they are about 6 to 12 inches tall. Once the nettles flower, they should not be collected for food since the leaves produce cystoliths that irritate the urinary tract. If cut repeatedly, new growth can still be collected for longer periods. The leaves of nettles can be steamed, boiled, sautéed, dried for teas, or added to soups and recipes in similar ways you would use spinach. Enterprising home brewers can make a nettle brew, a traditional favorite in the British Isles.

◼ Pineapple Weed
(*Matricaria discoidea*)

DESCRIPTION: Also commonly known as wild chamomile, pineapple weed is related to the plant from which you may make chamomile tea. Pineapple weed has alternate, finely divided leaves that appear almost feathery. The flower is a collection of yellow tubes that make up a cone-shaped flower head without any visible petals. The whole plant is less than 8 to 10 inches tall, and all parts smell strongly of pineapple when crushed.

Pineapple Weed

RANGE AND HABITAT: Pineapple weed is an introduced annual from northeast Asia that has become naturalized throughout North America, absent only from Florida, Georgia, and Alabama. It grows along roadsides, field edges, driveways, and disturbed soils. Pineapple weed seemingly prefers the worst soil: gravelly, sandy, and hard packed, a place where seemingly nothing else will grow.

EDIBLE PARTS AND PREPARATION: The flower cones of pineapple weed can be eaten raw in salads. The flower cones and the feathery foliage can be dried and made into a pineapple-scented hot tea for wintertime, or a chilled tea for a hot summer day. A tea made from pineapple weed has calming and sedative effects similar to commercial chamomile, and a wash or bath made with pineapple weed is soothing for dry skin.

■ Roses *(Rosa species)*

DESCRIPTION: Not just another pretty flower, many species of wild roses have edible flower petals and produce "hips" that are edible. In general, roses produce compound leaves with an odd number of leaflets that have toothed edges, and most wild rose species have prickles growing from the canes. Wild roses have fewer petals than their cultivated cousins, often white or pink. After a rose blooms and drops its petals, the base swells and ripens to a red or orange fruit called the hip. The hips of various wild rose species vary from less than ¼ inch to 1½ inches across, and the hips will persist into the winter long after the leaves have fallen from the canes.

RANGE AND HABITAT: Different species of wild roses can be found in all parts of North America. Along the Northeast into the Midwest and in Alaska, the invasive *Rosa rugosa* is the best rose to collect large hips and fragrant flower petals where it grows along the seashore and along inland water sources. The Wood's rose (*Rosa woodsii*) is common and abundant on the West Coast into Canada. The prickly rose (*Rosa acicularis*) is native to North America and abundant throughout the Great Plains and into all of Canada, growing along forest edges and in fields. The prairie rose (*Rosa arkansana*) is native and grows between the Rocky Mountains and Appalachian Mountains south into Texas in grasslands and forests. The pasture rose (*Rosa carolina*) is found east of the Great Plains in open woods, along rail lines, and open pastures. The tiny-hipped many-flowered rose (*Rosa multiflora*) is an invasive climbing shrubby

Rose Flowers and Rose Hips

rose that produces many small, white-petaled flowers and small hips, and is often referred to as a noxious weed where it grows throughout most of North America.

EDIBLE PARTS AND PREPARATION: The white or pink petals of wild roses are often very fragrant. They can be eaten raw in salads and used as garnishes for any meal, fermented in wines, or made into fragrant syrups. Collect the largest hips that can be found once they have ripened to orange or red, and cut them in half to scoop out the seeds and irritating hairs. The flesh of the hips can be eaten raw, tasting fruity and sweet like apricots, or the hips can be cooked into jams, sauces, and fruit leathers, added to vinegars, or dried to preserve and cook at a later time. The ripe hips of wild roses are incredibly high in vitamin C.

Sheep Sorrel

■ Sheep Sorrel *(Rumex acetosella)*

DESCRIPTION: Sheep sorrel is a small perennial weed. It grows in a rosette from underground spreading rhizome, and the leaves are arrowhead shaped with extended lower lobes. If you have a good imagination and turn the leaf upside down, it is shaped like a sheep's head. Most of the leaves are only 1 to 3 inches long. A flower stalk sprouting from the center of the rosette can grow up to 18 inches tall, bearing yellowish-green flowers on the male plants and reddish flowers on the female plants.

RANGE AND HABITAT: Sheep sorrel is native to Eurasia, but has become naturalized throughout all of North America. Sheep sorrel can grow in full sun or partial shade, and are some of the first plants to grow in disturbed soils, but also grow in lawns, along building foundations, along roadsides, in meadows, and in acidic soils.

EDIBLE PARTS AND PREPARATION: The leaves of sheep sorrel are tender and have a nice lemony tang. They can be eaten raw in salads, or cooked briefly and pureed into sauces for fish. Sheep sorrel will lose its bright green color when cooked, turning a dull camouflage green. Sheep sorrel gets its sour flavor from oxalic acid, and people prone to kidney stones should not eat very large amounts of foods containing oxalic acid, including cultivated spinach.

■ Sumac *(Rhus copallinum, Rhus glabra, and Rhus typhina)*

DESCRIPTION: Edible sumacs are perennial deciduous shrubs that grow up to 25 feet tall, with alternate,

---

Rose Petal Syrup

Makes about 4 cups

2¼ cups water
3 cups granulated sugar
2 cups packed rose petals, coarsely chopped
3 tablespoons ascorbic acid powder
    (found at vitamin shops)

Heat the water to boiling and add the sugar. Remove from the heat, and stir until the sugar dissolves. Allow the sugar syrup to cool to 80°F, and then stir in the chopped rose petals. Cover the pot and let the flowers steep in the syrup for 24 hours. Filter out the flowers and squeeze them well to extract all of the flavor. Filter the syrup through a fine mesh coffee filter. Remove 1 cup of the syrup, and warm it in a saucepan. Add the ascorbic acid, using a whisk to dissolve it. Add the warmed syrup back to the remainder, and mix it all well. Store in airtight, sterilized glass containers in a dark place for up to a year.

Staghorn Sumac   Smooth Sumac

and use the sour acids from the surface of the berries. Test the ripeness of the berries by licking a cluster. Collect the berry heads whole by breaking or cutting them off the sumac plants, and give them a shake to remove any bugs. Soak the berry clusters in room-temperature water to extract the acids and make a light pink, sour drink; strain through a coffee filter to remove any irritating hairs or other debris, and sweeten to taste and chill. Soaking additional clusters of the berries in the same water will yield a more concentrated sour liquid that can be frozen in ice cube trays. Use this sour concentrate as a lemon substitute in recipes. The berries of the smooth sumac can be ground to make a tart seasoning.

compound leaves comprised of 11 to 31 lightly toothed leaflets. Flower clusters are light green and grow from the highest point of each branch, maturing into a cluster of red to purplish-red hard berries that persist on the shrub through the winter. The foliage of sumacs often turns a brilliant scarlet in the autumn. Staghorn sumac (*Rhus typhina*) has berries that are covered with hairs and branches covered with fuzzy hairs as well, making it look like a stag's immature antlers. Smooth sumac (*Rhus glabra*) has smooth branches and leaf stems that are smooth and often light purple; the berries of smooth sumac are only lightly velvety and reddish orange when ripe. Winged sumac (*Rhus copallinum*) has compound leaves with additional small wings between each leaflet along the stem, and purplish, velvety berries.

RANGE AND HABITAT: All three of the described sumacs are native to North America, and the smooth sumac has the greatest range, present in the entire United States and lower provinces of Canada. Winged sumac has a more easterly range, growing east of the Rockies. Staghorn sumac grows from the Midwest into the Northeast. Sumacs grow in open spaces like fallow fields and along the edges of meadows and roadsides, and it is widely planted in landscapes for its attractive foliage.

EDIBLE PARTS AND PREPARATION: When the berries have ripened, they are covered with four acids: malic acid, gallic acid, ascorbic acid, and tannic acid. The berries themselves are hard, and you are looking to harvest

■ Sweet Cicely *(Ozmorhiza longistylus)*

DESCRIPTION: Sweet cicely is a perennial herbaceous plant also commonly called sweetroot. The leaves of sweet cicely are compound, made up of three to seven deeply toothed and lobed leaflets. The stalk of sweet cicely is fuzzy and purple, and the flower is an umbel of white, five-petaled flowers that mature into ½-inch- to

Sweet Cicely Leaves

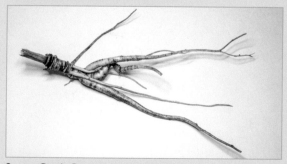

Sweet Cicely Root

1-inch-long, black, slender seeds that have two small prongs at the end. The root of sweet cicely is white and fragrant, smelling like black licorice

RANGE AND HABITAT: Sweet cicely is native to North America and found from Nova Scotia to Ontario, south to the Carolinas and Alabama, along the East Coast, and west into Colorado. Sweet cicely prefers rich soil and shady woods. Sweet cicely comes up and flowers in the spring, and the foliage dies back during the hot summer, only to resprout greens again in the autumn.

EDIBLE PARTS AND PREPARATION: The leaves of sweet cicely are only mildly aromatic, but are edible raw in salads. It is the sweet, licorice-flavored root that is collected to eat raw, or shredded and added to baked goods like cookies or cakes. The roots can be dried and used to make a boiled hot drink that is good for soothing upset stomachs.

Ramps
(Allium burdickii and *Allium tricoccum)*

DESCRIPTION: Ramps are the perennial wild version of leeks, with a bit of a garlic funkiness added to the onion mix. The leaves are elongated ovals pointed at both ends, have smooth edges, and have a slightly waxy feeling to them. The narrow-leaved ramp (*Allium burdickii*) has a white leaf stalk, while the more common ramp (*Allium tricoccum*) has a purplish-red leaf stalk. In late spring, the leaves die back as the bulb sends up a flower stalk that produces an umbel of white flowers that mature into circular black seeds. The underground bulb of ramps looks similar to a small onion, layered and with threadlike roots attached to the bottom. All parts of ramps emit a strong onion-garlic smell when crushed.

RANGE AND HABITAT: Both species of native, wild ramps occupy the same geographical area of North America from central Canada south into the higher elevations of Georgia, and along the East Coast. The Appalachians have the highest concentration of ramps growing under deciduous trees in rich forest soils, but ramps will also grow throughout the Northeast on rocky slopes and in floodplains.

EDIBLE PARTS AND PREPARATION: Almost all parts of ramps are edible with the exception of the mature seeds. The leaves can be collected sustainably in large

Ramps

quantities by collecting one of the two to four leaves that grow from each bulb, and adding them to soups, sauces, and grain salads. The green leaves can be made into a pungent pesto, or frozen successfully if chopped and packed tightly in a container. The flowers are a minimal edible, but add interest to a salad if eaten raw. The green, tender seeds can be eaten raw as a trail nibble, but become inedible once they harden. The bulbs are best collected in the autumn because the plant has returned all its energy to the bulbs to survive the winter. Locate a ramps patch in autumn by spotting the dried flower stalks that are now bearing seeds, and dig the bulbs, trying not to take more than 20 percent of a patch. The bulbs can be used in similar ways as onions—added to soups, roasted, or made into a savory jam that goes well with game meats.

Wineberry *(Rubus phoenicolasius)*

DESCRIPTION: Wineberries are perennial berries that resemble raspberries. They grow on arching canes covered in prickles and reddish bristles that are slightly sticky. The leaves are compound, comprised of three toothed leaflets that are papery and white on the underside. The flowers have white, five-petaled flowers and grow in clusters on prickly stems. Like a raspberry, wineberries are hollow once picked from the white receptacle and have one small seed inside each juicy globule, but appear shinier than a raspberry, and wineberries tend to be slightly sticky when collected.

RANGE AND HABITAT: Wineberries are originally from Asia, and are considered somewhat invasive where they

Wineberry

Beefsteak Polypore

grow throughout the Midwest into New England, south into Georgia. They prefer full sun but will tolerate partial shade. Wineberries are easily spread by birds, and their underground roots will create large thickets of canes, often at the edges of fields and yards, in lightly wooded areas, and along roadsides.

EDIBLE PARTS AND PREPARATION: Wineberries taste like a more tart and juicy raspberry. They can be collected in great quantities over several weeks because not all the berries in a cluster ripen at the same time. Wineberries are a bit delicate, so they need to be collected in large sturdy containers so they don't get crushed. Use ripe wineberries to make jams, jellies, or wines; juice them to make sorbets or desserts; or freeze them by laying them flat on a cookie sheet and freezing solid before storing in bags.

EDIBLE MUSHROOMS

■ Beefsteak Polypore
(*Fistulina hepatica*)

DESCRIPTION: The beefsteak polypore looks very similar to a raw slab of beef attached to a tree branch or trunk. The cap can be up to 12 inches wide, fan shaped, and the top is finely bumpy and reddish like liver. The underside is comprised of many tightly packed tubes, appearing as holes, that bruise reddish brown when handled. The flesh is streaked red and white like a steak, and oozes a red juice when squeezed. The spore color is pink to pinkish brown.

RANGE AND HABITAT: The beefsteak polypore is found throughout North America, but more often in the upper Midwest and Northeast, on dead or dying oak trees. It fruits from July through October.

EDIBLE PARTS AND PREPARATION: One of the very few mushrooms that can be consumed raw, the beefsteak polypore has a light lemony taste. To eat raw, slice very thin and sprinkle with salt to taste, or cut into thicker slices to pan fry.

■ Boletes
(*Boletus bicolor* and *Boletus edulis*)

NOTE: Boletes are mushrooms whose caps have pores on their underside rather than gills. A common misconception in North America is that all boletes are edible, but many are too bitter to eat, and some will produce

Boletes

gastrointestinal distress. Identifying boletes to species is difficult even for experienced mushroom hunters, so two common, safer-to-consume groups will be described.

DESCRIPTION: The two-colored bolete group includes the choice *Boletus bicolor*, and several others that look similar. The caps are 2 to 3 inches wide, convex, red, and smooth, with shallow, yellow pores on the underside that bruise blue when handled. The stem is red, often yellow near the top, bruising light blue when handled. The flesh is yellow, bruising blue when cut, but fading back to yellow, and any worm tunnels will be red. The porcini group includes the choice *Boletus edulis*, and several other firm mushrooms that look similar. The caps are 2 to 7 inches wide, convex, brown to orangish brown on top, and the pores appear white and "stuffed" or covered when young, but open up and mature to yellowish brown. The stem can be straight or bulbous, with a fine net of white reticulation near the top. The flesh is firm and creamy white, with little to no bruising when cut. Both have olive-green spores.

RANGE AND HABITAT: Both groups of boletes have wide distribution across North America but the species will be different according to regions. Boletes can fruit on the ground, associated with either hardwoods or conifers, and their season is June through October.

EDIBLE PARTS AND PREPARATION: The firm flesh of edible boletes makes them an excellent pan-frying mushroom, and their flavor is often buttery and nutty. They work well in sauces, tossed with pasta, and dried for storage (sliced thin). Discard any parts with obvious worm holes and be prepared to use your finds immediately; they do not keep very long unless dried.

▪ Black Trumpets *(Craterellus fallax)*

DESCRIPTION: Black trumpets are vase shaped, hollow in the center, and have very little wrinkling or are totally smooth on the outside. The flesh is thin, black to dark gray, and trumpets can grow singly or seemingly in clusters, up to 3 inches tall.

RANGE AND HABITAT: Black trumpets grow throughout North America on the ground, often in association with hardwoods and in moss. Black trumpets fruit in summer and fall. The spore color is white to creamy, sometimes light pink.

Black Trumpets

EDIBLE PARTS AND PREPARATION: Because of their thin flesh, black trumpets rarely have bugs, but always peek inside the vase for stowaway frogs or insects. Their flavor is slightly metallic, and they pair well with cream sauces, in creamy dips, with milder ingredients like potatoes and rice, and in soups. Black trumpets only need a brief sauté before use.

▪ Chaga *(Inonotus obliquus)*

DESCRIPTION: The outside of chaga has the appearance of a burned chunk of charcoal, black and covered with

Chaga

chunks and cracks, but once cut open, the inside is corky and golden. Chaga is a sterile fruit body that grows up to 18 inches wide, protruding from the trunk of the tree.

RANGE AND HABITAT: Chaga can be found in the northern forests of the Midwest, south to the higher elevations of the Appalachians, into New England, and throughout eastern Canada. While chaga can infect birch, elm, and alder, it is the chaga that grows on birch trees that contains the medicinal qualities that make it highly desirable.

EDIBLE PARTS AND PREPARATION: Use a hammer or even a rock to knock the chaga off a tree; don't dig into the tree or cut the chaga off. Fresh off the tree, chaga is

Chanterelles

not edible. It needs to be ground or cut into large chunks and lightly boiled for about 45 minutes to extract the medicinal properties, or ground and tinctured in alcohol to extract different properties that are not water soluble. The chaga grounds can be boiled several times, and the resulting liquid will be dark brown and taste similar to brewed black tea. Some people prefer to drink this decoction sweetened and chilled. Chaga is also known as the "tinder fungus" because it can catch and hold a spark easily, and burns slowly.

■ Chanterelles *(Cantharellus* species)

DESCRIPTION: Chanterelles have defined caps and stems, but no true gills. The undersides usually have folds, wrinkles that run down the stem, or are smooth. Chanterelles can vary in color from light yellow to bright yellow, pinkish yellow, golden, or golden brown, and one species is bright reddish orange. The spore color is most often yellow or pinkish yellow.

RANGE AND HABITAT: Chanterelles can be found throughout North America; they are a summer mushroom in the East, and a fall and winter mushroom in the West. Chanterelles grow on the ground singly, but sometimes in groups. They can be associated with both hardwoods and conifers, depending on the species.

EDIBLE PARTS AND PREPARATION: While chanterelles are often described as having a fruity, apricot-like odor, they vary in taste, smell, and texture among the species. Some chanterelles have thick, meaty stems and large frilly caps, while others are thinner fleshed. Chanterelles have a rich but subtle peppery flavor that works well with butter, cream, and game meats, and they have a

---

Chaga Tapioca Pudding

Makes about 3 cups

DECOCTION:
8 cups water
3 to 4 tablespoons ground chaga, with the black and golden parts mixed together

PUDDING:
1 cup brewed chaga decoction
4 tablespoons raw sugar or maple syrup
5 teaspoons quick-cooking tapioca

In a large pot, bring the water and ground chaga to a boil, and lower to a simmer. Cover the pot and simmer the chaga for 45 minutes. Allow the decoction to cool, and then strain out the ground chaga. Sweeten or chill to taste. To make the pudding, place the chaga decoction, sweetener, and tapioca in a medium saucepan and let it soak for 5 minutes. Slowly bring the mixture up to a rolling boil over medium heat, stirring often. Remove from the heat and chill; the tapioca will thicken as it cools. Cool overnight for a very firm tapioca.

satisfying mouthfeel and texture in cooked dishes. They can be cooked and frozen, but chanterelles should never be dried.

◼ Chicken Mushroom (*Laetiporus sulphureus* and *Laetiporus cincinnatus*)

NOTE: There are three other chicken species that may cause gastric upset in some people, and their appearance is very similar to the edible chicken mushroom, except the offending chickens grow on eucalyptus (*Laetiporus gilbertsonii*) or conifers (*Laetiporus huroniensis* and *Laetiporus conifericola*). Use caution when eating these chicken mushrooms and try to identify the host tree.

DESCRIPTION: Chicken mushrooms are polypores that grow in shelflike formations on dead or dying hardwood trees. The overlapping fronds can grow up to 12 inches wide. When young, the flesh of chicken mushrooms is firm but tender, bleaching to white with age and becoming chalky. Chicken mushrooms often fruit in great abundance.

RANGE AND HABITAT: The yellow chicken (*Laetiporus sulphureus*) is a heart-wood rotter found on the trunks of trees, and has a bright orange cap surface with

Yellow Chicken Mushroom

Thai Chicken and Coconut Soup

Serves 6

1 teaspoon oil
¼ cup diced shallots
1 clove garlic, minced
1 small chili pepper, chopped (seeds removed if you want it mild)
1-inch slice of ginger, peeled and grated
1½ cups cubed sulfur shelf mushroom
1 cup cubed russet potatoes
2 cups vegetable broth
1 teaspoon salt
1 cup coconut milk
¼ cup julienned lamb's quarters or baby spinach
1 tablespoon chopped cilantro
½ cup water (if needed)
Lime halves, for squeezing
Lime wedges, for garnish
Chopped cilantro and lamb's quarters, for garnish

Heat the oil over medium heat and add the shallots, cooking until translucent. Add the garlic, chili pepper, and ginger, and cook another minute. Add the cubed chicken mushroom, and cook until the liquids that come from the mushroom have evaporated, about 5 to 8 minutes, and the chicken mushroom starts to brown. Stir often. Add the cubed potato, vegetable broth, and salt, and cook for 6 to 8 minutes, until the potato is tender. Add the coconut milk, lamb's quarters, and cilantro. If the broth is too thick, add up to ½ cup of water. Remove the soup from the heat. Serve the soup with a squeeze of lime juice and lime wedges, along with some additional chopped cilantro and fresh lamb's quarters or baby spinach.

White Chicken Mushroom

Hedgehog Mushroom

bright yellow pores on the underside. The white chicken (*Laetiporus cincinnatus*) is a butt-wood rotter found at the base of trees with a pinkish-orange cap surface and white pores on the underside. Chicken mushrooms can be found throughout North America from May until November.

EDIBLE PARTS AND PREPARATION: As long as your knife cuts cleanly through the tender flesh, a chicken mushroom is young enough to eat; eating one past its prime is like eating sawdust. Many people agree that the texture of the chicken mushroom is similar to actual chicken, and use it in the same way: breaded and fried, skewered and grilled, baked into pot pies, ground into sausages, added to soups, and just sautéed and eaten plain. Chicken mushrooms retain their firm texture and will absorb flavors from sauces nicely. Sliced, they can be frozen raw or cooked, but do not dehydrate well unless the rehydrated pieces are only used to flavor a stock.

■ Hedgehog Mushroom (*Hydnum repandum* and *Hydnum umbilicatum*)

DESCRIPTION: Hedgehog mushrooms have pale, orange-brown caps that are 1 to 3 inches wide, and a stem that is white or the same color as the cap and slightly off-center. In place of gills, it has teeth or spines on the underside of the cap that run slightly down the stem. *Hydnum repandum* is a larger hedgehog mushroom, sometimes with caps up to 7 inches wide, while the smaller *Hydnum umbilicatum* has a bellybutton-like depression on the top of the cap. The spore color is white.

RANGE AND HABITAT: Hedgehog mushrooms can be found throughout North America, growing with hard-woods or conifers on the ground. They fruit individually, but often in great patches in the summer and fall months.

EDIBLE PARTS AND PREPARATION: Hedgehog mushrooms are sometimes called sweet tooth mushrooms because of their sometimes sweet or mild flavor. They are considered choice, and have a great texture when roasted or sautéed.

■ Hen of the Woods / Maitake (*Grifola frondosa*)

DESCRIPTION: Hens are polypore mushrooms, meaning they have small holes, or pores, on the white undersides of the caps. The caps, or fronds, are fan shaped, are ⅛ to ¼ inch thick, can be 1 to 3 inches wide, and range in color from tan to grayish brown. The solid white core branches out into the fronds, and the stems are short or not really present. Hens can grow very large, up to 3 feet wide and 20 or more pounds. Using your imagination, it looks like the backside of a hen that has her feathers all ruffled up. They are also called maitake, and are cultivated and prized as an edible and medicinal mushroom in Japan. The spore color is white.

RANGE AND HABITAT: Hens can be found east of the Rockies from Canada into Louisiana, throughout the Midwest, and along the East Coast. They fruit on dead or dying oak trees, on stumps, or on underground roots as soon as the cooler temperatures of autumn creep in, from August through November. Hens often return in the same place for many years, rotting the butt wood of trees, so you can return every year to try to find another hen.

EDIBLE PARTS AND PREPARATION: Hens are considered choice edibles because of their superior, meaty texture

Hen of the Woods Jerky

Serves 20 to 25

1 cup sweet apple cider
1 cup low-sodium soy sauce, or tamari
2 to 4 cloves garlic, chopped
½ teaspoon ground white pepper
½ teaspoon ground fennel
5 tablespoons maple syrup
1 tablespoon Sriracha chili-garlic sauce
1 large hen of the woods mushroom

Place the first seven ingredients in a blender, and puree for a minute. Pour the marinade in a glass or non-reactive shallow pan, preferably one with a cover. Clean the hen of the woods mushroom, making ⅛-inch-thick slices of the core and the larger fronds. All parts can be used, but they will dehydrate at different rates and shrink up quite small. Boil the mushroom for 10 minutes, and drain completely. Place the boiled hen pieces in the marinade while still hot, and refrigerate for 4 to 8 hours. Remove the pieces of hen from the marinade and drain the excess liquid off before arranging on dehydrator trays. If drying in the oven, use wire racks placed on a sheet pan. Arrange the marinated mushroom on the trays and dehydrate at 140°F for 6 to 12 hours, until dried and leathery. The time will vary based on the thickness and size of the pieces, so check it often. Store in an airtight jar or vacuum pack.

Hen of the Woods / Maitake

Hens freeze well cooked or raw, and dehydrate and reconstitute very well to make gravies and broths.

■ Lobster Mushroom
(*Hypomyces lactifluorum*)

DESCRIPTION: Lobster mushrooms are actually two mushrooms in one: one fungus (*Hypomyces lactifluorum*) is attacking and parasitizing another species, either a *Lactarius* or *Russula*. Colored a brilliant red orange similar to cooked lobster, the entire surface of the host mushroom becomes distorted and completely covered with a

Lobster Mushroom

and excellent flavor. They are often bug-free, but should be inspected for salamanders or other critters living between the fronds. The fronds can be cut off and sautéed, boiled, dehydrated, diced and cooked into duxelles, made into pot pies, or fried. Smaller hens can be marinated and roasted whole. The solid core can be sliced, marinated, and grilled like a steak, or sliced thinly and dehydrated into jerky.

pimply skin, and the gills from the host mushroom are covered and no longer visible. When sliced open, the interior flesh is white and solid. The spores are colorless.

RANGE AND HABITAT: Lobster mushrooms can be found throughout North America in hardwood and conifer forests. The host mushroom is often attacked before it emerges from the ground, so dirt, leaves, or conifer needles can be embedded in the red layer, making it difficult to clean. Lobster mushrooms fruit from July into October, at the same time as *Lactarius* and *Russula* mushroom species.

EDIBLE PARTS AND PREPARATION: Fresh lobster mushrooms can be sliced and sautéed with white wine, and some people claim they have a mild seafood aroma. As long as the flesh is white and solid, they are good to eat. They dry very well, and their flavor intensifies. Rehydrated and added to pastas, the brilliant color of lobster mushrooms makes beautiful and flavorful dishes.

■ Milky Mushrooms (*Lactarius corrugis, Lactarius hygrophoroides*, and *Lactarius volemus*)

DESCRIPTION: Milky mushrooms are characterized by the "latex" that bleeds from the flesh of the mushroom if cut. There are many species of milky mushrooms, and some have red, yellow, orange, pink, or even bright blue latex. The corrugated milky (*Lactarius corrugis*) has a cap that is 2 to 8 inches wide, is brownish red, appears coated with a velvety material, and becomes wrinkled and corrugated with age. It has pale tan gills that run slightly down the stem, which is the same dark color as the cap. The flesh of the corrugated milky stains brown

Voluminous Milky Mushroom

slowly when cut, and the gills produce copious amounts of white latex that stain the gills brown when exposed to air. The hygrophorus milky (*Lactarius hygrophoroides*) has a cap that is 1 to 4 inches wide, and is dull orange to reddish orange. It has whitish to cream-colored gills that are widely spaced and run slightly down the stem that is the same color as the cap. The flesh of the hygrophorus milky is firm and white, and the gills produce copious amounts of white latex that turns

Hygrophorus Milky Mushrooms

Morels

yellow after a long period of time. The voluminous milky (*Lactarius volemus*) has a cap that is 3 to 5 inches wide, is brownish orange with a darker zone in the center, and becomes flat at maturity. Its gills are creamy white, slightly forked at the outer edges, and packed tightly together, running slightly down the stem that is colored similarly to the cap. The voluminous milky has firm, white flesh that stains brown when cut, and copious white latex that stains everything it touches brown. The odor is mildly fishy. Milky mushrooms have white spores.

RANGE AND HABITAT: These milkies are summer and fall mushrooms. They are widely distributed in the eastern United States, associated with oaks, hardwoods, and sometimes conifers.

EDIBLE PARTS AND PREPARATION: Milky mushrooms have a firm, mild-tasting flesh that holds up well to cooking. The milky latex disappears once cooked, and the fishy smell of the voluminous milky disappears as well. Edible milkies can be salt brined or pickled, cooked into casseroles, or roasted. They make a great Hungarian-style mushroom paprikash.

■ Morels *(Morchella species)*

DESCRIPTION: True morels have caps that look like conical or elongated honeycombs and can grow 2 to 10 inches tall. The colors of the pits and ridges can be gray, greenish gray, tan, golden yellow, and light brown. The stem of true morels is lighter colored than the cap, attached fully to the bottom edge of the cap, and hollow. Half-free morels, also called peckerheads, have smaller bell-shaped caps that are partially attached to the hollow stem halfway up on the inside of the cap.

RANGE AND HABITAT: Morels are found throughout North America. They are found on the ground associated with hardwoods like ash, elm, or tulip trees, and conifers like spruce. They often fruit in newly burned forests on the West Coast and in the Pacific Northwest. Morels arrive in the spring, the first edible mushroom of the new year, eliciting much excitement and fervor in mushroom-hunting circles.

EDIBLE PARTS AND PREPARATION: All parts of morels are edible, but they absolutely must be cooked. Morels are often prepared with a cream sauce, cooked with butter, and they are great with chicken, fish, and mild cheeses.

Oyster Mushrooms

They pair well with other springtime foraged edibles like ramps and trout. Morels dry and reconstitute incredibly well.

■ Oyster Mushrooms *(Pleurotus ostreatus* and *Pleurotus pulmonarius)*

DESCRIPTION: Oyster mushrooms are wood rotters, with fan-shaped caps growing in overlapping bunches. The caps can be 1 to 12 inches wide, pure white (*Pleurotus pulmonarius*) or light tan to grayish brown on top (*Pleurotus ostreatus*), with whitish-ivory gills that run down the short stem. The flesh of the cap is fairly thick and substantial, and the odor is earthy and mushroomy. Oysters can be cultivated on logs, and some of the more exotically colored varieties with yellow or bluish-gray caps have escaped cultivation and can be encountered in the woods. The spore color is white to light lilac.

RANGE AND HABITAT: Oyster mushrooms can be found in all of North America, growing on dead or dying hardwood trees, most often maples and poplars. The white oysters are more common in the summer and the tan-capped varieties fruit in the cooler fall, winter, and spring months. The summer oysters tend to get buggy, while the cooler-weather oysters are often blissfully bug-free.

EDIBLE PARTS AND PREPARATION: Oyster mushrooms have a great mild flavor, and brown well when cooked over medium heat. Cultivated oysters are starting to show up on supermarket shelves. Oyster mushrooms are incredible if torn into shreds, lightly battered, and deep fried into fritters. They can be marinated and grilled, cooked and added to curries or soups, and sautéed with onions to fill pierogies.

◼ Puffballs
(*Calvatia* species and *Lycoperdon* species)

DESCRIPTION: Puffballs are called sac fungi, and they don't have gills or pore surfaces like other mushrooms, but their whole interior becomes a spore-filled mass upon maturity. The giant puffball (*Calvatia gigantea*) can be as big as a soccer ball, mostly round, and with a thin, white outer skin. Some species (*Calvatia cyathiformis*) have more of an upside-down pear shape, with a smaller base where it is attached to the ground, and with a light brown, cracked outer skin. Large puffballs can have greenish-yellow, blue, or reddish-orange spores depending on the species. Small puffballs (*Pyriforme* species) are smaller versions of the large puffballs, sometimes with spiky or granular ornamentation on the thin outer skin. Some are white and some are light brown, and their shape is either round or pear shaped. The spores of small puffballs are yellowish green.

RANGE AND HABITAT: Large puffballs grow on the ground, usually on lawns and in meadows, often in

Lycoperdon Puffballs

Calvatia Puffballs

large fairy rings. They can be found throughout North America from June through October. The smaller puffballs can grow on either the ground or on wood, depending on the species. They are widely distributed throughout North America, and can grow in large groups or singly, fruiting in the summer through the autumn months.

EDIBLE PARTS AND PREPARATION: Puffballs can be described as either bland or a choice edible—it is all in the preparation. The most important thing about collecting puffballs to eat is that the interior of the mushroom is completely white and solid when sliced in half; any hint of yellow, blue, or green spores, or a wet, squishy interior, are signs of old, inedible puffballs. Giant puffballs can be sliced about ¼ inch thick, breaded, and fried like eggplant parmesan, grilled and topped like pizza dough, fried and used as lasagna "noodles," and marinated and sautéed with various sauces. Small puffballs can be marinated, fried, sautéed, or chopped finely, browned, and made into meatless loaves. Puffballs have a very neutral flavor of their own, and will absorb any flavors they are cooked with. They are best eaten fresh, but prepared casseroles or baked dishes with puffballs can be frozen and reheated.

◼ Turkey Tail Mushrooms
(*Trametes versicolor*)

DESCRIPTION: Turkey tails are polypore fungi. The overlapping, shelflike caps are attached to wood, and have beautiful zones of color that can include cream, brown, gray, or tan, and more dramatic specimens have blue or orange bands of color. Sometimes there is a layer of green algae on the cap as well. The top of the cap is fuzzy

Turkey Tail Mushrooms

Winecaps

or finely haired, while the underside of fresh specimens is creamy white with tiny pores or holes. The caps are thin and flexible when fresh, becoming leathery with age. While there are several species of *Trametes*, most of the medicinal information is attributed to the true turkey tail. There are also lookalike species that can be confused with turkey tails; the most common is the False Turkey Tail (*Stereum ostrea*), which has a smooth underside.

RANGE AND HABITAT: Turkey tails are likely the most commonly seen fungi on dead wood in hardwood or mixed forests, rarely found on conifers. They are widely distributed throughout North America. They can be found all year, but the bug-free ones are easiest to find when they fruit in late autumn.

EDIBLE PARTS AND PREPARATION: The turkey tail is considered a medicinal mushroom. Most people use tinctures or teas to help with cancer treatments. Collect clean, fresh specimens with white pore surfaces, dry, and grind before filling tea bags. To tincture turkey tails, grind and add to 100-proof vodka and let it steep for two weeks before straining the mixture through a coffee filter to remove the solids. Consult with an experienced herbalist before adding medicinal turkey tails to any diet.

■ Winecaps *(Stropharia rugosoannulata)*

DESCRIPTION: Winecaps are large, sturdy mushrooms with a burgundy or reddish-brown cap that can be 2 to 6 inches wide, sometimes up to 12 inches wide in very large specimens, fading to tan in the sun. The gills are attached to the stem, and are grayish lilac, becoming purplish black with maturity. The stem is white, and there is a white, wrinkly ring near the top. In immature specimens, the gills are covered by a white membrane, which matures and becomes the fleshy ring on the stalk. The base of the stem often has white mycelial threads attached. The spore color is deep purplish brown.

RANGE AND HABITAT: Winecaps are widely distributed throughout North America. They grow on mulch, compost, or wood chips along trails, in gardens, and in landscaped areas. Winecaps fruit in the spring, and again in the cooler autumn months. Winecaps can be easily cultivated in your own mulch or wood chips by adding a slurry of chopped, mature winecap caps and bases to some chemical-free wood chips, covering with a layer of cardboard or more wood chips, and keeping it wet. Soon there will be mats of white mycelial threads throughout the wood-chip bed, and the mushrooms will fruit in cooler weather. Keep feeding the mycelium fresh wood chips to decompose, and a winecap garden can yield mushrooms for several years.

EDIBLE PARTS AND PREPARATION: Winecaps are a choice, large, firm mushroom to cook with. They tend to give off a lot of liquid when simply sautéing, so they work well cooked in soups or risottos, braised, stuffed, or roasted. Their flavor is rather strong and meaty, and they also make a wonderful hash with some diced potatoes, or cooked and added as a pizza topping.

POISONOUS MUSHROOMS

◼ Fly Agaric *(Amanita muscaria* var. *flavivolvata* and *Amanita muscaria* var. *guessowii)*

DESCRIPTION: The fly agaric is the fungi used most often when depicting a classic mushroom in art. The cap is convex and round, with white warts. The classic red cap is *Amanita muscaria* var. *flavivolvata*, while there is also a yellow-orange capped *Amanita muscaria* var. *guessowii*. Both have a ring around the upper part of the stem and concentric zones of shagginess at the top of the swollen base. The gills are white and not attached to the stem. The spore color is white.

RANGE AND HABITAT: The red fly agaric is found west of the Rockies from mid summer through the early winter on the ground, growing in association with pine, spruce, and birch trees. The yellow fly agaric is widely

Destroying Angel

distributed in the Midwest through New England, and south into the Appalachians. It grows with both hardwoods and conifers, growing on the ground and fruiting in summer and fall.

EDIBLE PARTS AND PREPARATION: Fly agarics are considered nonedible and mildly toxic. Symptoms of poisoning include delirium, raving, nausea, and excessive sweating.

◼ Destroying Angel *(Amanita bisporigera)*

DESCRIPTION: The destroying angel mushroom is a stark white fungus with a cap that is 2 to 5 inches wide, smooth, and flat when mature. The gills are white and not attached to the stem. A large ring is present near the top of the stem, and an egglike cup is at the base of the stem. The spore print is white.

Fly Agaric

Jack-O-Lantern

RANGE AND HABITAT: The destroying angel ranges from Texas north to Canada, and all along the East Coast of North America. It is associated with oaks and other hardwoods, and fruits in the summer months.

EDIBLE PARTS AND PREPARATION: The destroying angel lives up to its name, being one of the most poisonous mushrooms in North America. Symptoms of poisoning include vomiting, diarrhea, and cramps, followed by kidney or liver failure and death.

■ Jack-O-Lantern *(Omphalotus illudens* and *Omphalotus olivascens)*

DESCRIPTION: The jack-o-lantern mushroom is a bright orange mushroom that grows in clusters from dead trees and stumps. The caps are 3 to 8 inches wide with orange gills that are attached to and run down the solid, orange stem. The spores are white to pale yellow, and the gills of young specimens will give off a light green bioluminescence at night.

RANGE AND HABITAT: *Omphalotus illudens* is found widely distributed east of the Rockies. It is associated with hardwoods, and fruits in autumn. *Omphalotus olivascens* is found in eastern North America and in California, where it fruits from November through March.

EDIBLE PARTS AND PREPARATION: The jack-o-lantern mushroom is not edible. Symptoms of poisoning include severe cramps, vomiting, and diarrhea.

■ False Morels *(Gyromitra* species)

DESCRIPTION: False morels have convoluted caps that are brainlike in appearance and in varying shades of reddish brown to yellowish brown, with a lighter cream-colored stem. When sliced in half, false morels are not hollow, but have many chambers and wrinkles in the flesh.

RANGE AND HABITAT: False morels are spring fungi that can grow in association with hardwoods or conifers on the ground. Different species can be regional, and false morels can be found throughout North America.

EDIBLE PARTS AND PREPARATION: False morels contain gyromitrin, which is metabolized into monomethylhydrazine—rocket fuel—in the body when consumed. While some people claim false morels are edible once boiled, it is not recommended. Symptoms of poisoning include blood poisoning, diarrhea, headaches, and vomiting. The toxins build up in the body over time, causing jaundice, coma, or death.

False Morels

SUSTENANCE: ANIMALS AND INSECTS FOR FOOD

When you are lost in the wilderness and your chances for rescue do not look good, you may have to come to the realization that you will have to survive at all costs. This means you have to break all the rules to stay alive. First, and most important, you will have to fight fear and panic—your worst enemies in any survival situation. After several days without food, hunger will set in and you must start to hunt for food. Vegetation is the easiest solution and the previous special section on wild edibles will show you what plants to seek and how to eat them.

In certain areas, however, depending on weather conditions and different times of the year, edible plants might not be available. In this case, you may be forced to hunt wildlife for food. The following sections on animal tracks, traps, and snares will provide valuable advice on how and where to trap animals for food. This is not the time to be a fussy eater.

This section also includes information on the edibility of some species of animals, including insects and worms, and will give you a valuable insight to the amazing and wide variety of food sources in the woods and waters. It might be easier if you remind yourself that in various parts of the world, some of these animals and insects are considered delicacies.

■ Know Your Animal Tracks

It is hard to imagine a camper, hiker, or fisherman who would not be intrigued by scanning the ground carefully for animal tracks. Once I get off a paved road, I immediately start looking for tracks and signs of wildlife. It's a great learning experience. Tracks will tell you what animals, big and small, live in your area or may be visiting your campsite after dark. Identifying animal tracks adds a brand-new element to your camping and hiking trips.

The animal tracks shown here will help you identify big and small wildlife. The dimensions given will also be helpful, but regard them only as benchmarks. The track sizes here are for average adult animals. Obviously, smaller tracks are made by young animals and oversize tracks by exceptionally large ones.

Identifying tracks is largely a process of elimination. For example, if you find a single-file pad track, you can eliminate all hoofed animals and animals that leave a double or side-by-side track. Animals that leave a single-file track include wolves and lions. Also, if the track has claw prints, you can probably eliminate the mountain lion, which normally keeps its claws retracted. After you have narrowed tracks down to a couple of species, final identification should be easy.

When you've identified the species, you may also be able to determine its size by the depth of the track. If possible, compare the tracks to others of the same species over the same terrain. If one deer track is an inch deep and another of the same size is 2 inches deep, it follows that the deeper track belongs to a heavier deer or possibly a big buck.

Study animal tracks every time you're in the woods, and learn to identify the animals that left them. It will lend you insight into the wildlife around you.

A Lesson in Survival

Many years ago on a caribou hunt on Baffin Island in the Northwest Territories, I witnessed how our Inuit guides handled the harsh wilderness of the Far North. My first experience happened early on my hunt when Solomonie Jaw, my 31-year-old guide, shot at two ducks with a rusty open-sighted .22 rifle from a moving canoe. One duck fell. It was the most unbelievable shot I had ever seen. When we beached the canoe for lunch, Solomonie boiled the duck, feathers and all, in a pail. He then skinned it and ate it. I watched as I ate a salami sandwich.

A few days later, I killed a caribou. Solomonie, using only a sheath knife, cut up the entire caribou, leaving the hide on the quarters to keep the meat clean. That night, I fried my caribou's tenderloins in butter and pepper. Whether by choice or custom, I don't know, but our guides never ate with us. The next morning, I found out what Solomonie had had for dinner. There were two chewed-clean caribou ribs on his canoe seat. And all day Solomonie insisted that his dinner had been better than my tenderloins. He almost convinced me. There's no doubt that these Inuits could survive anywhere, on anything, and we would do well to pay attention to their methods.

IDENTIFYING ANIMAL TRACKS

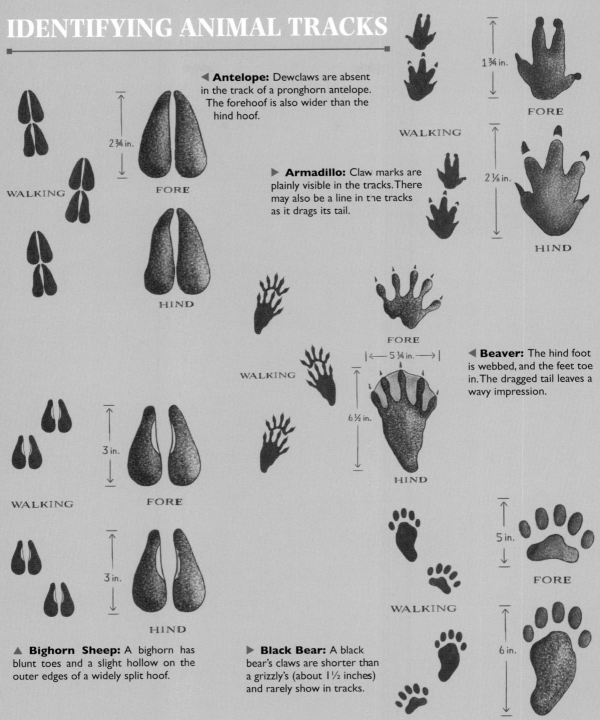

◀ **Antelope:** Dewclaws are absent in the track of a pronghorn antelope. The forehoof is also wider than the hind hoof.

▶ **Armadillo:** Claw marks are plainly visible in the tracks. There may also be a line in the tracks as it drags its tail.

◀ **Beaver:** The hind foot is webbed, and the feet toe in. The dragged tail leaves a wavy impression.

▲ **Bighorn Sheep:** A bighorn has blunt toes and a slight hollow on the outer edges of a widely split hoof.

▶ **Black Bear:** A black bear's claws are shorter than a grizzly's (about 1½ inches) and rarely show in tracks.

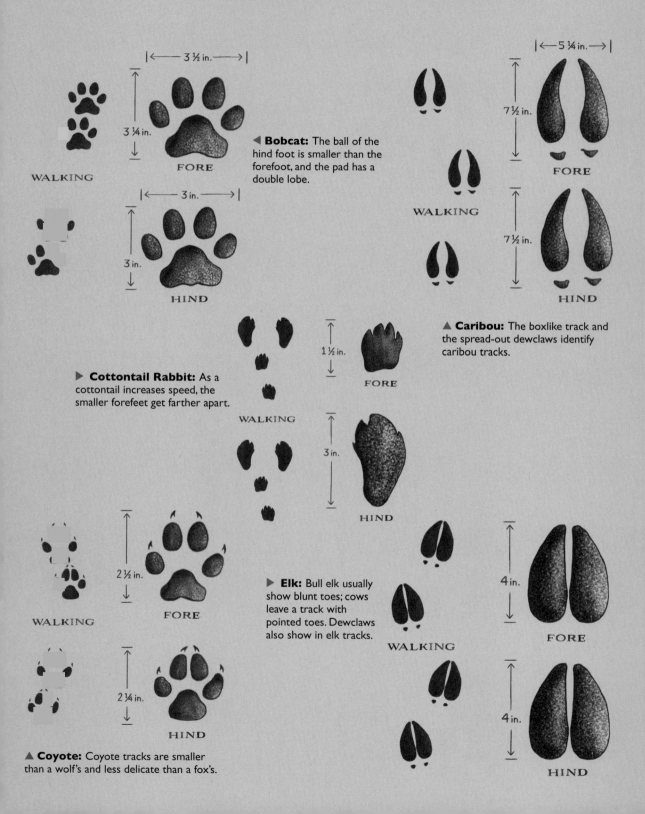

WALKING

3 ½ in.

3 ¼ in.

FORE

◄ **Bobcat:** The ball of the hind foot is smaller than the forefoot, and the pad has a double lobe.

3 in.

3 in.

HIND

5 ¼ in.

7 ½ in.

FORE

WALKING

7 ½ in.

HIND

▲ **Caribou:** The boxlike track and the spread-out dewclaws identify caribou tracks.

► **Cottontail Rabbit:** As a cottontail increases speed, the smaller forefeet get farther apart.

1 ½ in.

FORE

WALKING

3 in.

HIND

2 ½ in.

WALKING

FORE

► **Elk:** Bull elk usually show blunt toes; cows leave a track with pointed toes. Dewclaws also show in elk tracks.

WALKING

4 in.

FORE

2 ¼ in.

HIND

4 in.

HIND

▲ **Coyote:** Coyote tracks are smaller than a wolf's and less delicate than a fox's.

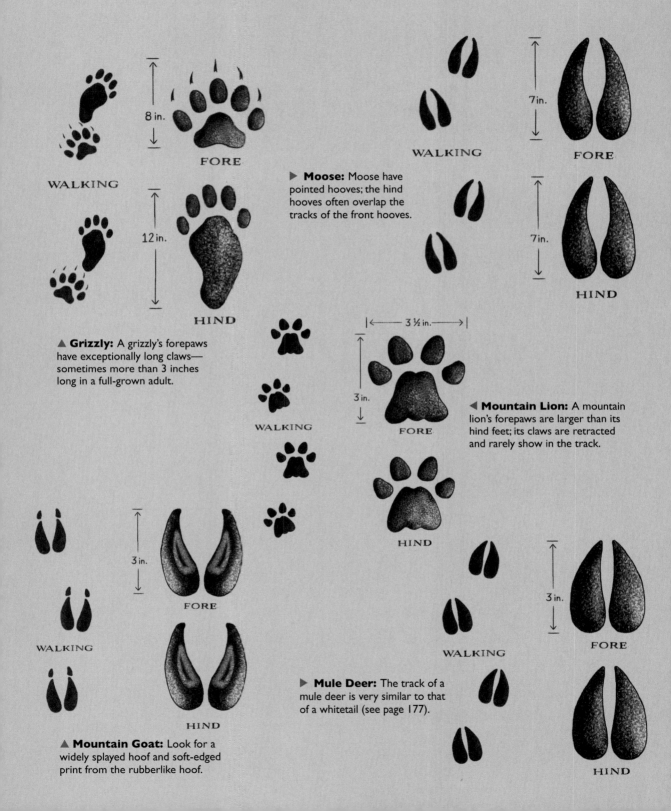

WALKING 8 in. FORE

WALKING 12 in. HIND

▲ **Grizzly:** A grizzly's forepaws have exceptionally long claws—sometimes more than 3 inches long in a full-grown adult.

▶ **Moose:** Moose have pointed hooves; the hind hooves often overlap the tracks of the front hooves.

WALKING 7 in. FORE

7 in. HIND

WALKING

3½ in.

3 in. FORE

HIND

◀ **Mountain Lion:** A mountain lion's forepaws are larger than its hind feet; its claws are retracted and rarely show in the track.

WALKING 3 in. FORE

HIND

▲ **Mountain Goat:** Look for a widely splayed hoof and soft-edged print from the rubberlike hoof.

▶ **Mule Deer:** The track of a mule deer is very similar to that of a whitetail (see page 177).

WALKING 3 in. FORE

HIND

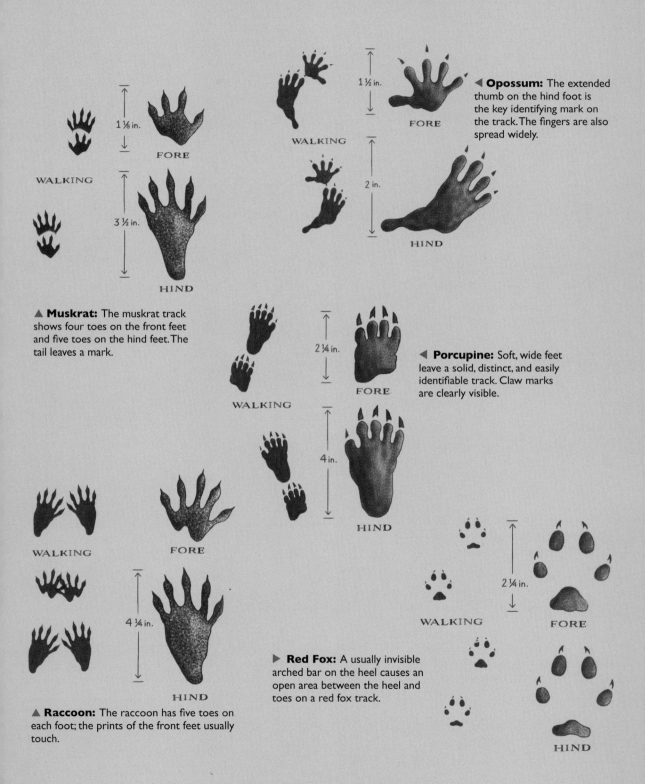

▶ **Opossum:** The extended thumb on the hind foot is the key identifying mark on the track. The fingers are also spread widely.

▲ **Muskrat:** The muskrat track shows four toes on the front feet and five toes on the hind feet. The tail leaves a mark.

◀ **Porcupine:** Soft, wide feet leave a solid, distinct, and easily identifiable track. Claw marks are clearly visible.

▶ **Red Fox:** A usually invisible arched bar on the heel causes an open area between the heel and toes on a red fox track.

▲ **Raccoon:** The raccoon has five toes on each foot; the prints of the front feet usually touch.

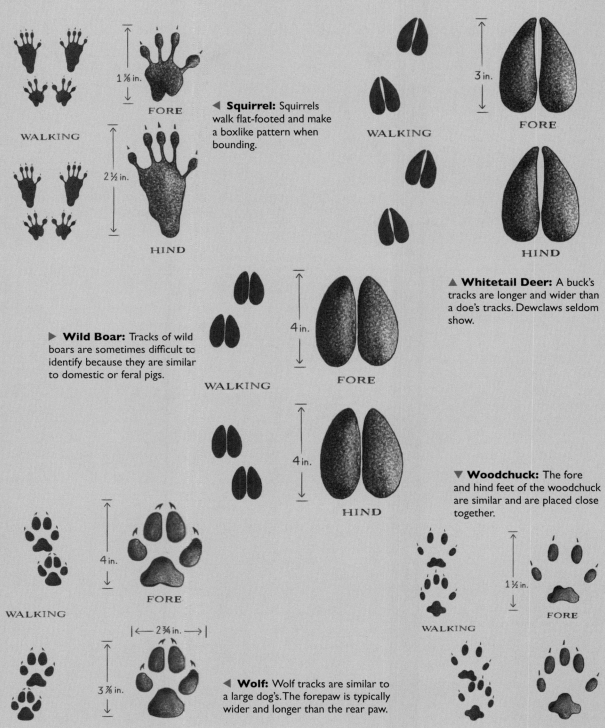

◄ Squirrel: Squirrels walk flat-footed and make a boxlike pattern when bounding.

FORE

WALKING

HIND

WALKING

3 in.

FORE

HIND

▲ Whitetail Deer: A buck's tracks are longer and wider than a doe's tracks. Dewclaws seldom show.

► Wild Boar: Tracks of wild boars are sometimes difficult to identify because they are similar to domestic or feral pigs.

4 in.

WALKING

FORE

4 in.

HIND

▼ Woodchuck: The fore and hind feet of the woodchuck are similar and are placed close together.

4 in.

WALKING

FORE

1 ½ in.

FORE

WALKING

2 ¾ in.

3 ⅜ in.

◄ Wolf: Wolf tracks are similar to a large dog's. The forepaw is typically wider and longer than the rear paw.

HIND

HIND

Setting Traps and Snares

It's not likely that you will ever have to trap animals for food to stay alive . . . but it can happen. It is not uncommon to hear stories of campers who were lost for one or two weeks. I came close many years ago when a bush plane couldn't reach us for nearly a week. When we couldn't catch fish, we hunted frogs and roasted the legs. But getting lost is not the only reason for knowing how to live off the land. Natural disasters, such as tornadoes and hurricanes, can also put you in a survival situation. Unless you know some of the basics, trapping animals can be very difficult and nearly impossible for most people.

The basic snare is a wire loop or snare set along visible game trails, streams, riverbanks, water holes, and similar places that you suspect are frequented by animals. Look for signs, such as tracks and droppings. The snare, typically made with 9-gauge wire, is anchored in the ground or to a tree. Snares and their nooses are most effective when sized for specific animals. The accompanying diagrams and chart show various sizes of snares for beavers and coons. For comparison, snare sizes are also included for coyotes, bobcats, and foxes, but these animals should not be considered primary targets in a survival situation.

Snare Placement

Snare locations may be the key to trapping your next meal. Look for any game trails that lead to water. Look for fresh droppings and tracks. The mouth of a den is an ideal place for a wire snare. Make sure the snare is secured to the ground. Check the snare often.

Squirrels and rabbits may be among the most easily trapped small game. The squirrel pole is probably the most effective of all squirrel traps. Look for squirrel nests in trees or squirrel signs on the ground. You can use an existing downed limb propped against a tree or cut your own and set it against a tree that has a nest

Suggested Snare Heights and Diameters

Critter Snare	Diameter (inches)	Snare Height from Ground (inches)
Fox	7	7
Coyote	9–10	9–10
Coon	7	6
Beaver	9–10	2–3
Bobcat	8	8

Here are recommendations for snare sizes for small-game animals. The illustrations show not only the diameters for specific species but also how high to secure the snares from the ground. As with all snares, placement is critical. Place snares at den openings, game trails, bases of trees with squirrel nests in upper limbs, and tunnels in thick hedgerows.

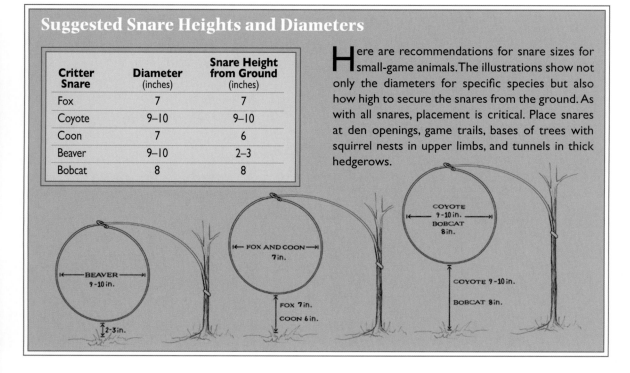

BEAVER 9–10 in. 2–3 in.

FOX AND COON 7 in. FOX 7 in. COON 6 in.

COYOTE 9–10 in. BOBCAT 8 in. COYOTE 9–10 in. BOBCAT 8 in.

Squirrel Pole

The squirrel pole is a very effective setup to snare squirrels and birds. Find an area where there are squirrel nests in the trees, and then prop an 8- to 12-foot pole against a tree that has a squirrel nest in the upper limbs. Make four or five wire snares and attach them to the log. Any squirrel climbing up the log will usually be caught in one of the snares.

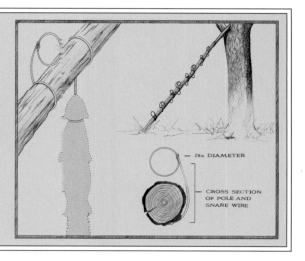

2¼ in. DIAMETER

CROSS SECTION
OF POLE AND
SNARE WIRE

or signs of squirrel traffic. Make a series of wire snares and anchor one end to the pole with the other end open along the pole or branch.

For rabbits, look for den openings in the ground. Hedgerows are good places to search for rabbit holes. Anchor the snare on an existing tree limb or drive in a stake. The open end of the snare is placed at the opening. The opening of the snare should be about 7 inches. If you can find a tunnel or funnel that looks well traveled, with droppings and tracks leading to water and food sources, you can also set up snares in these areas.

Simple deadfalls will work in any place where there are a lot of animals in the area. A deadfall with notched sticks or rocks is more complicated to build compared to snares and probably not as productive.

Deadfall

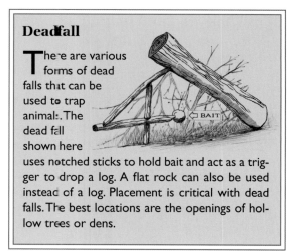

There are various forms of dead falls that can be used to trap animals. The dead fall shown here uses notched sticks to hold bait and act as a trigger to drop a log. A flat rock can also be used instead of a log. Placement is critical with dead falls. The best locations are the openings of hollow trees or dens.

Funneling

Look for animal trails in thick brush or hedgerows. They could lead to den openings. You can also narrow these paths to a den by stacking brush to form a funnel. Setting a snare along this path may well catch rabbits, woodchucks, or any other denning species.

■ Field Care of Game Birds

Many pheasants, grouse, chukars, and other game birds are ruined between the time of the kill and the time they reach the table. Some sportsmen will put a bird into a hot, rubber-lined game pocket, leaving it there to "cook" and perhaps spoil by the day's end.

Others may field dress a bird, let it hang a couple of days, and then try to pluck it. The usual result is that pieces of the skin are torn away and the bird is a big mess.

Here's some sound advice from more than a few shooting-preserve operators who have literally cleaned thousands of pheasants and other game birds. These experts agree on the right way to handle a bird in the field. Obviously, a pheasant should be field dressed soon after it is shot, particularly in warm weather. Field dressing is a simple operation. First, lay the bird on its back and pull the feathers off from below the breastbone to the anal opening, clearing the area for the first cut. Make the cut from the soft area below the breastbone down to the anal opening. Make this cut carefully so that no organs are cut or broken, which can taint the meat. First, cut the skin, and then cut through the meat. Reach in and take out the viscera, pulling down toward the anal opening. Now, remove the windpipe and crop.

During warm weather, pack the empty cavity with dry grass and then press the sides of the opening tightly together. The grass will absorb blood in the cavity and will keep insects from entering it. This is not necessary in cold weather, when you can leave the cavity open and let the meat cool, free of insects. You can expedite cooling in winter by placing some snow in the body cavity. Both dry grass and snow can also be used with equal effectiveness on furred small game, such as rabbits and squirrels.

Many sportsmen believe it is a crime to skin a bird, but some prefer to skin pheasants. One reason for skinning is because of the critical conditions necessary for effective plucking. You can easily pluck a bird immediately after it is shot and the body is warm. The feathers will pull out with little trouble, and the skin will not tear. But some sportsmen dislike stopping a hunt after each kill so that you can pluck a bird. Also, once a bird is plucked in the field, the bare skin is exposed to dirt and bacteria.

How to Skin a Bird

Nearly all wild birds are edible. How much food a bird will provide pretty much depends on its size. For illustration purposes, a pheasant is used in these drawings. Always field dress a bird immediately, removing all viscera. Skinning is the easiest and fastest way to prepare a bird for cooking. The followings steps would apply to skinning any bird.

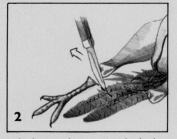

Step 1 • Begin by slitting the skin lengthwise. Next, peel the skin away from the breast, down to inside the legs and up to the neck. ■ **Step 2** • Work the skin over each thigh and leg. Now, bend each leg backward until the bone cracks. Cut off the legs at the joint.

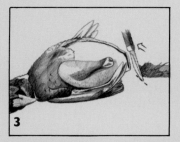

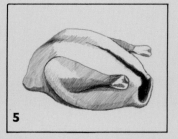

Step 3 • With the breast meat and both legs now freed from the skin, cut off the bird's tail at its base. ■ **Step 4** • Take each wing and bend backward at the first joint from the wing tip until it cracks. Cut off the tips. Then cut the head off. ■ **Step 5** • Peel the skin down toward the neck and then off the bird. Nothing should be left but tufts of feathers on the wing ends. Pluck them off.

Once the body has cooled, a pheasant cannot be dry plucked without being torn up. It must be dipped in hot water (180°F). If the water is cooler or warmer than 180°F, the skin will tear. Because of the difficulty in maintaining the correct water temperature, this method isn't recommended. If you plan to pluck pheasants, though, remember this temperature factor.

The best bet is to field dress the bird as soon as possible after it is shot and skin it when you get back to camp or home. If you prefer, you can hang your birds in a cool, dry place for a couple of days before skinning. This aging process has some merit for slightly tenderizing old cock birds, but you will generally be unable to detect any difference in taste between birds skinned at once and those skinned a few days later.

Skinning a bird is easy. Slit the skin lengthwise, keeping the cutting edge along the center of the breastbone. Now, peel the skin away from the breast, down to the legs, and up to the neck. Work the skin over each thigh and upper leg, stopping when you reach the leg joint. At this point, bend each leg backward until the joint cracks, and then cut off the leg. With the breast and both legs now free of skin, cut the tail off at its base.

Now, take each wing and bend it backward at the first joint until it cracks. Cut off the wing tips and the head. Finally, peel the skin down toward the neck and off the bird.

If you freeze your birds after skinning, make sure there are no air pockets in the package, since these air traps can cause freezer burn. When you plan to eat a bird, let it thaw slowly in the refrigerator. Don't rush it on the kitchen counter.

The absence of skin on your birds should not bother you, and it doesn't affect the table quality of the birds. Game birds are generally dry and must be basted frequently while cooking. Cover the birds with bacon strips. The bacon creates a "skin" for the birds, retaining body juices and adding moisture and taste.

■ Where to Hit Big Game

The most important factor in killing big game quickly and cleanly is bullet placement. Even a .375 Magnum won't knock down a small whitetail for keeps unless the deer is hit in a vital organ. Caliber means little if a sportsman doesn't put the bullet where it will be most effective. You'll minimize chances of losing wounded game if you take time to study the animals you hunt and learn the location of vital organs. The illustrations on the following pages show the anatomy of popular big game

and the aiming points that are important. The information should also benefit a bowhunter, whose arrow kills by hemorrhage. He should especially note the location of main arteries.

Though the most vital organ in any animal is the brain, you should rule out a brain shot 98 percent of the time. The brain is a small target and easy to miss. A brain shot is also a poor choice for a trophy hunter. A brain shot on a deer, for example, will shatter the base of the skull, making a head mount nearly impossible. Bears are scored by skull dimensions, and any head shot on a bruin will smash the skull and make scoring impossible. When is a brain shot justified? Only on dangerous game when it is charging. In North America, this means bears. Aim to hit 2 inches above the center of the eyes of a bear, and you should hit the brain.

Neck shots involve some risk of wounding antlered game because the spinal column in the neck is only about 2 inches in diameter. If you hit neck muscles and arteries but miss the spine, your deer may run a fair distance before dropping. A neck shot is a fair choice only at close range, where you can be reasonably sure of putting your bullet into the spinal column.

What is the best shot? Let's talk in terms of vital areas as opposed to vital organs. The forward one-third of a deer is a vital area since it houses the heart, lungs, several major arteries, spine, and shoulder. Any bullet hitting these areas will bring down a big-game animal.

The best shot, then, is at a vital organ in a vital area—specifically the heart. Though a heart shot frequently will not drop an animal in its tracks, it is always a fatal shot, and tracking a heart-shot animal is not difficult. One big advantage of aiming for the heart is that a miss will generally still hit some other vital organ. A shot at the heart, for example, will likely put the bullet into the lungs also. A hit in the lungs may knock a deer down through shock. If not, the animal will eventually die through hemorrhaging.

No animal can survive a bullet through the lungs, but it may sometimes travel a good distance. If you spot blood on brush a few feet off the ground and to the side of the tracks, blood is coming from the sides of the deer—a good indication of a lung hit. The deer will be bleeding freely, and tracking should not be difficult. Frothy blood is another sign of a lung hit.

Recognizing blood and hair signs can be useful. Bright-red blood generally means a heart or lung shot. A deer shot in the heart, however, may not start to bleed immediately, so follow the tracks until you can confirm a miss or hit. If you spot brown-yellow blood, particularly if there are bits of white hair in it, you can be reasonably sure that the deer is gutshot. This is unfortunate since a gutshot animal can travel a great distance before dying. If you've gutshot an animal, stick with the track. You'll get it eventually, but it won't be easy.

The track itself can be a tip-off to the location of a wound. A broken leg will show as drag marks in snow or mud. Blood in or right next to the tracks may mean a leg wound.

If your initial shot is high, missing both the heart and lungs, your bullet may still hit a vital spot. Such a shot may shatter the shoulder, breaking the animal down and rendering it helpless.

The only time you should intentionally aim for the shoulder is on dangerous game. A bear hunter, for example, wants to knock down and immobilize a bruin quickly, especially if it's charging. A shoulder shot will accomplish it (if a brain shot is considered too risky), and you can then put in a killing shot with little danger.

Once you know where the vital organs are, you must also know where to put your rifle sights in relation to the animal's position.

To hit the heart when an antlered animal is broadside, put your sights just above where the foreleg joins the body. Aim a bit high, so that if you miss the top

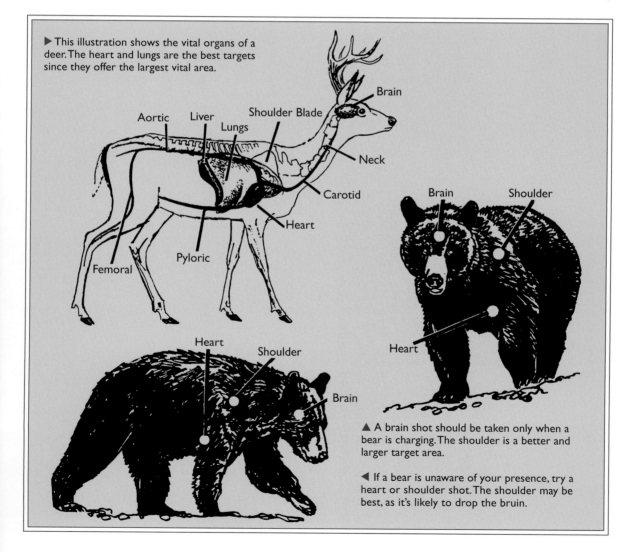

▶ This illustration shows the vital organs of a deer. The heart and lungs are the best targets since they offer the largest vital area.

Brain

Aortic   Liver   Shoulder Blade
          Lungs

Neck

Carotid

Heart

Femoral   Pyloric

Brain   Shoulder

Heart

Heart   Shoulder

Brain

▲ A brain shot should be taken only when a bear is charging. The shoulder is a better and larger target area.

◀ If a bear is unaware of your presence, try a heart or shoulder shot. The shoulder may be best, as it's likely to drop the bruin.

portion of the heart you will still hit the lungs. If a buck is facing you, put your sights just below dead center on its chest. If your shot is a good one, you'll hit the top of the heart as well as the lungs.

If you are in a tree stand and a buck walks under you, a somewhat different problem arises. Since less heart and lung area is available, the best aim is right between the shoulder blades for a hit in the heart and lungs. Remember that you are shooting from above and various angles must be taken into account.

Quartering animals present some problems. Sportsmen frequently assume that a quartering animal presents the same target as a broadside, but on a deer quartering away, your points of aim should be farther back.

◀ If a buck walks under your tree stand, aim between the shoulder blades to put your bullet into the heart and lungs.

Neck

Lungs

Heart

Spine

▶ For vital organs on a frontal shot, try aiming for the upper part of the heart so the bullet will also hit the lungs.

◀ When an animal is quartering away, aim farther back; drive the bullet at an angle.

Neck

Lungs

Heart

Neck

Lungs

Heart

Neck

Lungs

Heart

▶ Game quartering toward you presents a similar situation. Note the aiming points shown here.

Field Dressing Your Deer

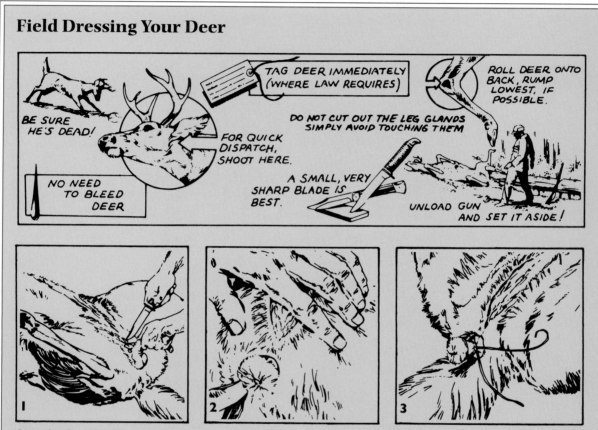

Step 1 • Remove the penis and scrotum with shallow cuts. Do not pierce the body cavity. ■ **Step 2** • With the tip of the knife, cut completely around the rectum to free it from the rest of the skin. ■ **Step 3** • Pull the rectum outside of the body and tie it off to prevent feces from reaching the meat.

Step 4 • Open the abdomen from the rear to the sternum (where the last ribs join). Hold the intestines down with your fingers and the back of your hand so that you do not cut or pierce the intestinal tract or paunch. ■ **Step 5** • Cut the bladder out very carefully. Try not to spill urine.

Step 6 • Pull the rectum inside the cavity and cut the tissue holding it in place. ▪ **Step 7 •** With the deer lying on one side, cut all tissues that hold the intestines in place all the way down to the animal's spine. ▪ **Step 8 •** The next step is to rotate the deer over so that you can free the intestines from the other side.

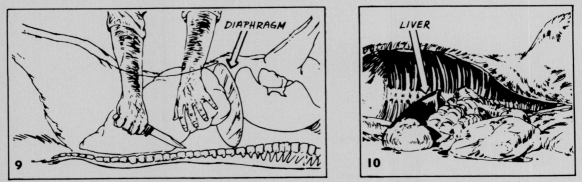

Step 9 • Repeat step 7; little cutting is needed. Then, sever the gullet in front of the stomach. Do not spill the contents. If you do, wipe clean. ▪ **Step 10 •** The contents of the abdomen come out in one big mass. Retrieve the liver and cool it quickly in open air or water.

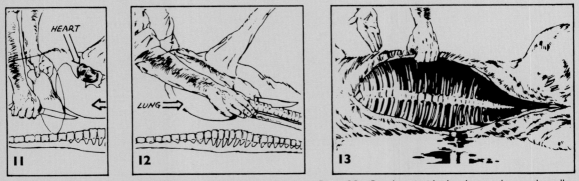

Step 11 • Cut out the diaphragm (wall from abdomen to chest). ▪ **Step 12 •** Reach up inside the chest and sever the gullet and windpipe. Pull them out with the lungs and heart. ▪ **Step 13 •** Wipe dry. If it's hot, it's better to split the breast, open the neck, and cut out the rest of the windpipe and gullet to avoid spoilage. If, however, the head is to be mounted, "cape out" (skin) the neck first.

Skinning Your Deer

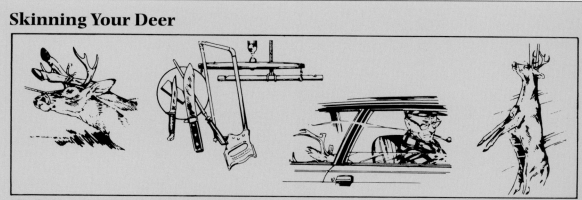

After field dressing, tie the forefeet over the neck. Drag out with rope around the antlers and half hitch around the upper jaw. Never subject the carcass to heat. Don't use the car heater; keep the windows open. Hang the deer in a cool place (41°F to 45°F) for a week with the hide still on to tenderize the meat and enhance the flavor before skinning. The methods shown here result in rawhide suitable for tanning. For a head-and-shoulders mount, see step 13.

Step 1 • With the point of the knife, cut the hide from the abdominal cut to just below both joints. Don't touch the leg glands. ▪ **Step 2** • Skin out both thighs. Try not to cut meat or the inner side of the skin. ▪ **Step 3** • With the deer still lying on the floor, skin out the thighs to the top of the legs. ▪ **Step 4** • Saw off the lower legs just below the joints. Use a meat-cutting saw or crosscut wood saw.

Step 5 • Hang the deer with a gambrel or stick in each leg between the bone and tendon. ▪ **Step 6** • If it wasn't done during field dressing, cut the H-bone of the pelvis with your saw. ▪ **Step 7** • Continue skinning. Leave the tail on the hide by tunneling under it between the hide and back. ▪ **Step 8** • Hide in this area usually comes off quite easily. Pull on the hide and then cut.

Step 9 • Sever the tail near the body inside the hide. This avoids cutting the hair, which you'd have to pick off the meat. ▪
Step 10 • Use a knife to separate the hide from the thin muscles near the abdominal lengthwise incision. ▪ Step 11 • Hoist the deer higher. Pull with one hand and "fist" the hide. ▪ Step 12 • Saw off the forelegs. Split the breast and neck and cut out the gullet.

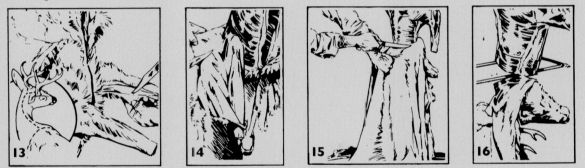

Step 13 • Slit the skin of the forelegs to the breast cut. (If you want the deer head mounted by a taxidermist, the inset shows cuts for caping out the neck. Unless you are skilled enough for meticulous skinning of eyes, ears, and nose, cut off the head. Refrigerate or freeze if there is a delay in delivery to the taxidermist. ▪ Step 14 • Skin out the legs and neck. The neck is the hardest area to skin. ▪ Step 15 • Pull the hide down and then use a knife. Continue to the base of the skull. ▪ Step 16 • Saw off the head. Again, doing it this way avoids cutting the hair.

Step 17 • Remove dirt and debris. Cut out and discard the bloodshot meat around the bullet holes. Pick off all deer hair, which otherwise lends a bad taste to the meat when cooked. ▪ Step 18 • The hide still has the head and tail attached. Cut the head off. Wipe the inside of the hide dry with a cloth. ▪ Step 19 • Sprinkle borax or salt on the inside of the hide. Fold lengthwise, hair out, roll it up, and tie. Send the hide to a taxidermist or tanner at once or store in refrigerator or freezer until you can do so.

Butchering Your Deer

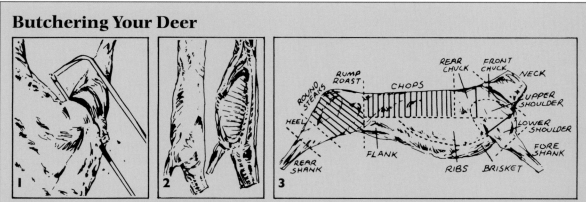

Step 1 • Cut the spine in half lengthwise. The cut can be corrected if it wanders. ■ **Step 2 •** With a meat-cutting saw or fine carpenter's saw, cut the carcass into two sides. Start where the tail was severed. ■ **Step 3 •** Dotted lines show the major cuts. Solid lines indicate secondary cuts that divide roasts into two or separate steaks and chops. This illustration shows the right-hand side. After cutting the whole side, repeat cuts on the left side.

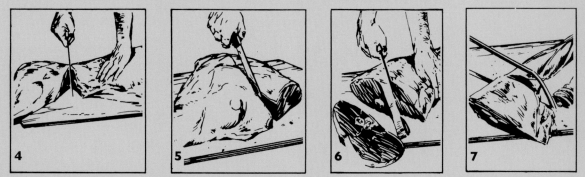

Step 4 • Divide the haunch from the loin. With all cuts, use a knife first. If you hit bone, use a saw to complete the cut. A cleaver is handy but not essential. ■ **Step 5 •** Cut the rump roast off the haunch. Make a neat, straight cut because it determines the angle of cuts for round steaks. ■ **Step 6 •** Cut thin or thick round steaks as you prefer, but keep the cuts parallel. ■ **Step 7 •** Down toward the joint, the meat is tough. There, take off a chunk called the heel, usually used for stew.

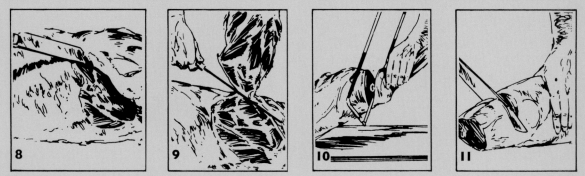

Step 8 • Now for the front part: cut the entire shoulder and foreleg off the side where the shoulder joins the body. The knife blade is horizontal. ■ **Step 9 •** There is no ball-and-socket joint, so this cut is easy. ■ **Step 10 •** Separate the shoulder from the shank at the joint or close to it. You need the saw for this cut. The shank is used as chop meat. ■ **Step 11 •** The shoulder is usually divided into two separate pieces for pot roasts or stew meat.

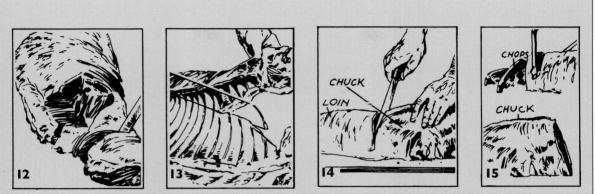

Step 12 • Cut off the neck. The neck is tough like the shank or shoulder and is best used as chop or stew meat. ▪ **Step 13** • Saw the ribs off. This long, angled cut is made where the thin meat between the ribs thickens toward the spine. ▪ **Step 14** • Separate the chuck (under the meat cutter's left hand) from the loin. The loin is cut into chops; chuck is usually cut into two roasts. ▪ **Step 15** • Cut the loin into chops, as thick as you like. They resemble lamp chops. These cuts are started with the knife and completed with the saw.

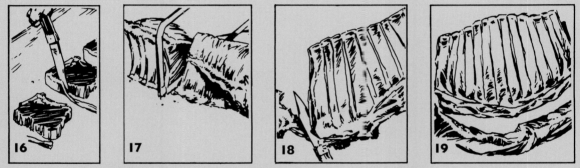

Step 16 • Trim the thick fat off the chops. Heavy fat should be trimmed off all cuts. It has an unpleasant flavor. ▪ **Step 17** • Cut the chuck into two equal portions. It's too big to cook whole (usually as a pot roast) unless you have a big family. ▪ **Step 18** • This long cut starts parallel to the first rib and outside it and then circles around the tips of the ribs. ▪ **Step 19** • The cut is completed. It separates the brisket and flank from the ribs. Brisket and flank go into chop meat.

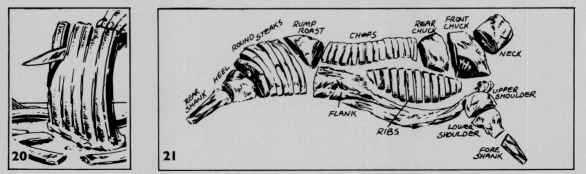

Step 20 • Separate the ribs. The knife slides along the bone to one side so all the meat between the two ribs stays attached to a single rib. ▪ **Step 21** • Here are all the cuts from the right side, properly trimmed. If you do mangle a piece, remember that you can always bone it out and grind it up for chop meat or mince meat or chop it up into chunks for stew.

Boning Your Deer

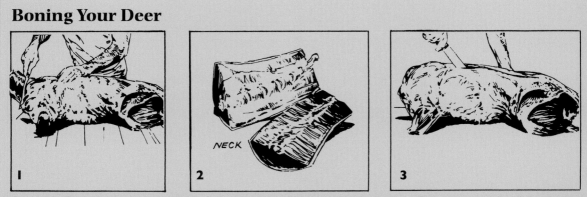

Step 1 • To begin the boning process, be sure to cut off the meatless lower legs. Then, cut the neck off the skinned carcass. ■ **Step 2** • Split the neck and unroll the meat from the neck bone. A small knife will help. Neck meat makes good stew and roasts. ■ **Step 3** • The next cut, to remove the backstrap, should be made from in front of the pelvic bone to the shoulder. Cut along the spine, 2 inches deep.

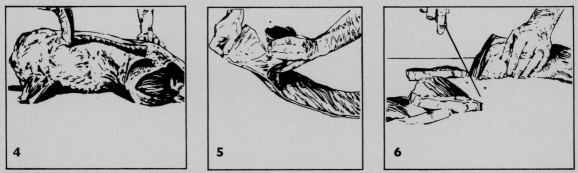

Step 4 • To extract the backstrap, cut along the side of the ribs over the point where the ribs curve down to join the backbone. Loosen with fore and aft cross cuts. ■ **Step 5** • Repeat the procedure to extract the second fillet. Pull and rip the layer of fat and tissue from the fillet. ■ **Step 6** • Many claim that this is the finest meat on the deer. Cut the trimmed loin into steaks about ¾ to 1 inch thick.

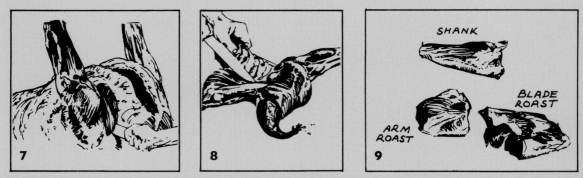

Step 7 • Remove the shoulders by working your knife through the tissue between the leg and ribs. ■ **Step 8** • Bone the shoulder for use as stew meat or rolled for roast, or simply cut into three pieces. ■ **Step 9** • Remove the shoulder roast from the leg by severing at the upper joint. Separate the arm roast from the shank with a saw. The shank makes excellent venison soup.

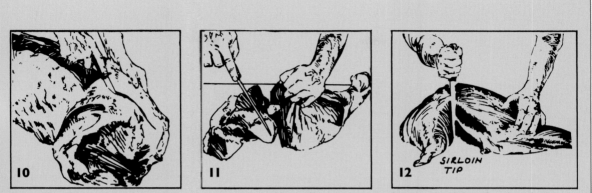

Step 10 • To detach the ham, start your cut near the tail bone. Slice the tissue and tendons, and then detach with a saw or by twisting the ball joint. ▪ **Step 11** • The rump roast is at the top part of the ham. To remove it, make your cut as vertical as possible, leaving enough meat for a meal. ▪ **Step 12** • Lay the hind leg on the table and remove the sirloin tip by using the leg bone to guide the knife. Start at the kneecap and work up.

Step 13 • Once the sirloin tip has been removed, trim the scrap and tissue. This piece, resembling a football, makes a great roast or can be cut into steaks. ▪ **Step 14** • In removing bone from the remaining piece (round), cut tissue separating the shank from the round and bone. ▪ **Step 15** • Shave and cut the meat loose from the leg bone. This will take maneuvering around the joints, but keep cutting.

Step 16 • Here's what the finished product should look like. Now, separate the round into its individual muscle pieces, each encased in tissue. ▪ **Step 17** • Divide by cutting the connective membrane. Avoid cutting into the meat. Trim the scrap for grinding or stew. ▪ **Step 18** • Chunks of trimmed round can be sliced thin for use as steaks and made on the barbecue or cooked whole as roasts.

Surviving on Wild Game

In a survival situation, you should be prepared to hunt, trap, or snare wild animals, including game birds and waterfowl. Some of the species listed here are easily caught and some may be difficult to hunt in a survival situation. Nearly all animals and birds are edible. Some species taste better than others, but all will make your survival possible.

Here are some of the species that may well keep you alive in the woods. I've included brief descriptions about their range, identification, size, food, and edibility. Generally, the smaller species are easier to catch and cook. Smaller species are also more plentiful. The more you know about these species and their range and eating habits, the easier it will be to find them. Your life may depend on it.

These enlightening profiles of game animals are not solely intended for those who may find themselves in a survival situation. The insights into the edibility factors of wild animals should be of interest to all sportsmen who venture into our woods and waters.

SMALL-GAME ANIMALS

■ Cottontail Rabbit *(Sylvilagus)*

RANGE: Combined, the four species of the cottontail, which include the Eastern cottontail (*Sylvilagus floridanus*), mountain cottontail (*S. nuttali*), desert cottontail

Cottontail Rabbit

(*S. auduboni*), and New England cottontail (*S. transitionalis*), inhabit much of the United States, except for some sections of the Far West.

IDENTIFICATION: The body pigment is basically brown with the possibility of a reddish or buff cast. Guard hairs with black tips are scattered throughout, but the belly, chin, and undersides of the legs are white. The underside of the tail is also white, resembling a cotton ball when the rabbit is scampering around—hence its name. The majority of cottontails have a white spot on the forehead between the eyes. The whiskers, though long, are light and relatively inconspicuous. The ears, 2½ to 3 inches long, are bare on the inside but lightly furred on the outside.

SIZE: The cottontail is from 14 to 19 inches long and stands from 6 to 7 inches at the shoulder. Females tend to be a bit larger than males. Weights vary from 2½ to 3½ pounds, the latter being the top weight ever recorded.

FOOD: The diet of the cottontail consists of crabgrass, bluegrass, and other grasses; all kinds of fruits and berries; such cultivated crops as clover, alfalfa, lettuce, beans, wheat, soybeans, and cabbage; weeds such as yarrow and goldenrod; sheep sorrel; wild cherry; and wild shrubs. Sumac is a favorite food in winter.

EDIBILITY: The meat, lightly colored and finely textured, is delicious. Rabbits are easily skinned and cooked over an open fire.

■ Jackrabbit *(Lepus)*

RANGE: The whitetail jackrabbit (*Lepus townsendii*) inhabits the sagebrush regions and grasslands from northern New Mexico north to southern Alberta, and from Lake Michigan west to the Sierras. The blacktail jackrabbit (*Lepus californicus*) lives in the deserts and open grasslands of the western United States from mid-Arkansas to the Pacific coast, north to southeastern Washington in the west and mid-South Dakota in the east.

IDENTIFICATION: The whitetail jackrabbit's tail is white on both top and bottom. Its conspicuous ears measure

Jackrabbit

5 to 6 inches in length. In summer, the coat is a light grayish brown over the sides and back, but the belly is lighter. The ear tips are black. When winter arrives, the coat is completely white or, on occasion, buff white. The blacktail's rump is black, as is the top of its tail. Its ears are longer than the whitetail's by an inch or so. The underside of the tail is white, as is the belly. The ears are white outside, brown inside, and black-tipped. Though the whitetail sheds twice annually, the color change is relatively insignificant.

SIZE: A typical whitetail jackrabbit measures between 22 and 26 inches long and weighs from 6 to 10 pounds. The average blacktail jackrabbit is 18 to 24 inches long and weighs between 4 and 7½ pounds. The heaviest jackrabbit on record was a whitetail that tipped the scales at 13 pounds.

FOOD: Though jackrabbits eat practically all kinds of vegetation in their diets, shrubs, weedy plants, and grasses make up the bulk of it. Main food items include spiderling, snakeweed, mesquite, grama grass, rabbitbrush, sagebrush, greasewood, filaree, prickly pears, eriogonum, and saltbrush.

EDIBILITY: Jackrabbits are not high on the edibility list. Younger jackrabbits are more palatable than older jackrabbits. Check the liver on jackrabbits when you skin one. If it has white spots, it would be risky eating it.

■ Gray Squirrel *(Sciurus carolinensis)*

RANGE: The eastern gray squirrel (*Sciurus carolinensis*) is located in hardwood forests from eastern Texas and eastern Saskatchewan to the Atlantic coast, and from the Gulf of Mexico to southern Canada. The Arizona gray squirrel (*Sciurus arizonensis*) inhabits pine and oak forests in southeastern and central Arizona. The western gray squirrel (*Sciurus griseus*) is also found in oak and pine forests, but in the region from southern California north to Washington.

IDENTIFICATION: The gray squirrel's coloring is salt-and-pepper gray. The body's underfur is solid gray with guard hairs that go from gray at the base to buff brown to black, and finish off in a white tip. The small hairs of the face, muzzle, and ears are a yellow tan, while those under the throat, its underparts, and the insides of its legs are a rich white.

SIZE: A large adult measures between 17 and 20 inches depending upon its range, the tail taking up approximately 8 to 8½ inches of that length. Males and females tend to weigh the same—slightly more than 1 pound. The heaviest gray squirrel recorded weighed 1½ pounds.

FOOD: Nuts are a staple in the squirrel's diet and are cached for later use. The squirrel also feeds on buds, berries, tree blossoms, fruits, fungi, and field corn, as well as eggs and baby birds.

EDIBILITY: The quality and flavor of gray squirrel meat

Gray Squirrel

Raccoon

FOOD: Wild raccoons eat snakes, eggs, baby birds, baby mice, baby rabbits, mussels, fish, frogs, grapes, berries, apples, and acorns. Crayfish are a delicacy to the raccoon, and both sweet corn and field corn are very important in the diet.

EDIBILITY: Hunters have long considered raccoon meat a delicacy. In a survival situation, raccoons generally make easy targets. Look for them in trees at night.

■ Woodchuck/Groundhog (*Marmota monax*)

RANGE: About 500 million woodchucks are said to inhabit North America, ranging from eastern Alaska to Labrador, south in the central and eastern United States to Arkansas and Alabama, and to northern Idaho in the western United States.

IDENTIFICATION: The round, barrel-like body is supported by short but powerful legs. Brown is the basic body color, but shades of red to nearly black are fairly common. The guard hairs are silver-tipped, giving the animal a grizzled look. The ears are short and round, and the black eyes stick out above its flattened skull.

is excellent. Squirrels are regularly consumed by small-game hunters. Squirrels may also be among the easiest small game to be caught in snares. These factors also apply to fox squirrels.

■ Raccoon (*Procyon lotor*)

RANGE: The raccoon inhabits nearly all of the United States, parts of Mexico, and also extreme southern Canada, northward along the border between Saskatchewan and Alberta.

IDENTIFICATION: Though this species varies in size and color depending on its location, two conspicuous features distinguish it—the black mask across the eyes and the ringed tail. The latter is usually 10 inches long. The dense underfur is brownish red. Guard hairs are tipped with white, but come in shades of black, red, yellow, and gray. The white face and ears offer sharp contrast to the black nose and mask. The soles of the feet are jet black, the tops light.

SIZE: An average male measures 34 inches in length and stands from 9 to 12 inches high at the shoulder. A typical adult weighs from 12 to 16 pounds, but some males exceed 25 pounds. The heaviest coon ever recorded tipped the scales at 62 pounds, 6 ounces, and measured 55 inches from tail tip to nose tip.

Woodchuck/Groundhog

SIZE: A large male measures up to 26 inches in length (5 or 6 inches of which is its tail), often stands 6 to 7 inches high at the shoulder, and averages 10 pounds in weight. Females tend to be a bit smaller. The heaviest recorded chuck weighed 15¾ pounds.

FOOD: Woodchucks are 99 percent vegetarian, feeding on soybeans, corn, alfalfa, beans, peas, clover, and lettuce among the cultivated crops. Bark, twigs, and buds of low-growing bushes like sumac and wild cherry are also part of the diet. Fruits and berries of all types are frequently consumed.

EDIBILITY: Woodchuck meat, particularly that of young woodchucks, makes very good eating. This does not apply to prairie dogs, which have an "earthy" flavor. Both woodchucks and prairie dogs can be easily dispatched with a .22 rimfire survival firearm. Look for them at dawn and dusk.

◼ Opossum *(Didelphis marsupialis)*

RANGE: The opossum is found in woods and agricultural regions from Ontario west to eastern Colorado and east to Florida. Many inhabit the Pacific coast stretch from Canada through California.

IDENTIFICATION: This species is the only marsupial (pouched animal) in North America, housing its somewhat underdeveloped young in a pouch where they are nourished through the mother's nipples until they can seek out their own food. The animal's ears are black, though often white-rimmed, as are the eyes, legs, and feet. The face and toes are white, while the nose is pink. Because of the silver-tipped guard hairs, the opossum's fur appears salt-and-pepper gray, but the underfur is cotton white. A whitish-yellow stain is apparent on the throat due to a gland secretion. The lengthy, whitish tail tends to be practically bare of hair.

SIZE: A typical opossum may measure up to 3 feet in length, 12 to 15 inches of which is the animal's tail. Though this marsupial generally weighs 5 or 6 pounds, one recorded male weighed 14 pounds.

FOOD: Persimmons are one of the opossum's favorite treats, but its diet ranges from mice, ground-nesting birds, moles, shrews, and rabbits to dead and crippled game to fruits and green vegetation. Earthworms, grains, reptiles, and amphibians round out the menu.

EDIBILITY: The opossum is certainly not an attractive animal, but it is generally accepted that opossum meat is tasty, just not as palatable as rabbits and squirrels. Opossums should be cooked well done.

Opossum

UPLAND GAME BIRDS

◼ Ruffed Grouse *(Bonasa umbellus)*

RANGE: Locales for this bird include the Yukon and Porcupine River Valleys of Alaska and the Yukon. In addition, it is found throughout Canada and the U.S. Pacific Northwest, northern Rocky Mountain states, and the Mid-Atlantic region.

IDENTIFICATION: The ruffed grouse has a large, square, reddish-brown or gray tail with thin, dark barring,

Ruffed Grouse

followed by narrow, light barring, followed by a broader black band, and terminating in a light band. A ruff composed of blackish feathers appears on both sides of the bird's neck. The upper parts range in color from gray to brown, mottled with darker colors. The undersides tend to be lighter, on occasion buffy, and are barred with black and dark brown. The head is crested, and a small, bare, red patch appears above each eye. The West Coast members of this species are reddish, while those of the Rocky Mountains are grayish. Eastern ruffed grouse are brownish. Females and young are duller in color, with less prominent ruffs.

SIZE: An adult ruffed grouse is usually 16 to 19 inches in length.

FOOD: About 90 percent of the diet consists of leaves, buds, fruits, seeds, and nuts. The remaining 10 percent is made up of insects.

■ Sage Grouse
(Centrocercus urophasianus)

RANGE: This species is found in parts of the western United States and minute sections of southeastern Alberta and southwestern Saskatchewan.

IDENTIFICATION: This game bird is the only grouse that has a black belly. Its tail feathers are long and pointed, its throat black with a tiny white necklace. The white breast features prominent feathers, and the remainder of the plumage is mottled or barred with white, black, dark brown, and light brown. Yellow is the color of the small, bare-skinned patch above the eye. The hen is mottled and

barred in black, brown, and white over most of its body, but, as in the male, the belly is black, flanked by white.

SIZE: The sage grouse is the largest of all grouse, measuring 22 to 30 inches in length. The average female is 22 inches, the average male 28 inches.

FOOD: This grouse's diet consists of tender, succulent vegetation and some insects. Adults eat the leaves of the sage, but their gizzards and stomachs are not constructed to accept harsh foods.

■ Chukar Partridge
(Alectoris chukar)

RANGE: The semiarid mountain regions of the western United States, specifically parts of Washington, Idaho,

Chukar Partridge

Nevada, Wyoming, Colorado, and California, are this bird's haunts.

IDENTIFICATION: The chukar partridge has a short tail that is brownish gray above. The wings are the same color. Two black lines begin at the forehead, run through the eyes, and then turn downward, forming a V on the upper breast that fully encloses the yellow throat and cheeks. The lower breast is gray; the rest of the underside (the dark-barred flanks inclusive) is yellowish. Red or pink is the color of the legs, bill, and feet. Immature birds are usually duller in color.

SIZE: This game bird, on average, measures 13 inches in length.

FOOD: Fruits, seeds, and leaves comprise 60 percent of the diet, the rest being insects and spiders.

Ring-Necked Pheasant
(Phasianus colchicus)

RANGE: The ring-necked pheasant ranges from southern Canada down through Baja California and northern Mexico, and can be found in parts of Texas, Oklahoma, Kansas, Missouri, Illinois, Indiana, Ohio, and Maryland.

IDENTIFICATION: The cock is more colorful than the hen. It has a head and neck that are a dark metallic green. A bright-red patch of bare skin is conspicuous around the eye and on the cheek. The lengthy feathers above the eye form a double crest. The plumage of the underparts, upper back, and shoulders is a rich, bronzy reddish brown with dark-brown, black, and white mark-

ings. The feathers of the rump and up the lower back are grayish green; the flank feathers are a light golden brown with dark-brown streaks. The slender, pointed feathers of the tail are dull bronze barred with dark brown, and cover more than half the length of the body. The legs and feet are gray; the bill is yellowish. The hen is brownish and much paler below, marked with darker brown and black above. Darker brown and whitish bars streak the long yellow-brown tail.

SIZE: This game bird measures between 21 and 36 inches in length, depending upon its sex. The cock tends to be about 10 inches longer than the hen.

FOOD: About 25 percent of the diet consists of insects, the remainder being shoots, nuts, and fruits.

FLIGHT SPEED: The ring-necked pheasant flies at speeds between 35 and 40 miles per hour.

Bobwhite Quail
(Colinus virginianus)

RANGE: This species is sparse out West, located only in parts of southern British Columbia, Washington, Oregon,

Ring-Necked Pheasant

Bobwhite Quail

Wild Turkey

IDENTIFICATION: The wild version of the turkey is slimmer and has longer legs than the domestic variety. Its wattles, neck, and head are reddish, grading to a blue. The attractive plumage is an iridescent bronze with black bars; the tail tips are buff. The male has a long hank, consisting of hairlike feathers hanging from its breast; the hen usually lacks this "beard." The wings are round and short; the feet and legs are large and strong. The large, sturdy bill appears to be hooked.

SIZE: This game bird measures from 36 to 48 inches long, with the hen usually averaging some 10 inches shorter than the cock. The average weight of these gobblers is between 15 and 20 pounds.

FOOD: Twigs, fruits, seeds, and nuts make up 85 percent of the wild turkey's menu; insects make up the rest.

FLIGHT SPEED: Though this species cannot fly long distances, it can attain speeds of 30 to 35 miles per hour when it does take flight.

■ Mourning Dove
(*Zenaidura macroura*)

RANGE: This species breeds throughout North America and southern Canada, and winters from the Great Lakes south to Panama.

IDENTIFICATION: The mourning dove has a smallish black spot behind and below its dark eyes. The tail is wedge-shaped and slender, the feathers being white-tipped except for the longer central ones. The plumage is buff brown with a metallic purplish sheen at the side of the neck. The wings are gray with a purple tinge to

Idaho, Arizona, and Mexico. But moving eastward, this bird is far more abundant and is found from southeast Wyoming, eastern Colorado, and eastern New Mexico all the way to the Atlantic, save for the New England states.

IDENTIFICATION: The bobwhite quail is a chicken-like bird with strong, lengthy legs, a stout bill, and a short, dark, strong tail. Its color tends to vary depending upon its range, but in general the bird is brownish, barred with white and lighter below. Above, it has brown marked with darker brown; frequently, these dark-brown areas have random whitish spots. The dark-brown head is slightly crested, featuring white eye stripes. Many—but not all—members of the species have a white throat as well. The female tends to be dull yellow or buff in color.

SIZE: Measuring 8½ to 10½ inches in length, this game bird is smaller than the average quail.

FOOD: About 85 percent of the bobwhite's diet consists of all types of plant life; the remainder is primarily insects.

FLIGHT SPEED: Over short distances, the bobwhite's flight is strong and rapid, often reaching speeds of 40 to 45 miles per hour.

■ Wild Turkey (*Meleagris gallopavo*)

RANGE: The wild turkey has six subspecies: the eastern (most of the eastern United States), the Florida (basically Florida), the Merriam (mostly western United States), the Mexican (central Mexico), the Rio Grande (southwestern United States), and the Gould (northwestern Mexico).

Mourning Dove

them, though the flight feathers are somewhat darker. Occasionally, the back will be sparsely covered with very dark brown spots.

SIZE: The mourning dove averages between 11 and 13 inches in length.

FOOD: This bird's menu consists almost entirely of seeds, mainly from weeds. Minute amounts of other vegetable matter are also eaten.

FLIGHT SPEED: The mourning dove has been clocked between 60 and 65 miles per hour.

■ American Woodcock
(Philohela minor)

RANGE: In warmer weather, this bird is found from southeastern Manitoba down through the eastern tip of Texas, and throughout the entire eastern United States. In winter, it is concentrated in the southeastern United States, spreading a bit farther into Texas, Oklahoma, Arkansas, Alabama, Georgia, and Florida.

IDENTIFICATION: The American woodcock has a straight bill that is twice the size of its head. Its neck is rather

American Woodcock

short, as is its tail. Above, the coloring is a variegated pattern of black, gray, and brown; below, it is rufous. There is a trio of wide, black bands separated both from one another and from the gray forehead by thin, rufous bands. The legs, feet, and bill are a dark-flesh color.

SIZE: This species measures 10 to 12 inches in length.

FOOD: Earthworms make up the bulk of the diet, but occa seeds, berries, and insect larvae are significant components of the diet.

WATERFOWL

■ Common Canada Goose
(Branta canadensis)

RANGE: The breeding range is from northern Canada down to central California. There are a couple of colonies south of this line. In the winter, the species travels down to the southern United States and even into northeastern Mexico.

IDENTIFICATION: The body is brownish, while the head, tail, neck, feet, and bill are black. Several white patches are apparent on the cheeks. The throat and underrump are also white.

SIZE: This species varies widely in size, measuring from 22 to 40 inches in length.

> **A Note on Edibility:** All ducks and geese are edible, but some are better than others. Sea ducks, feeding on saltwater vegetation, tend to be tough. For identification purposes, here are the more common species found in North America.

FOOD: The common Canada goose feasts on aquatic vegetation, grains, and grass.

Common Canada Goose

Black Duck

■ Black Duck *(Anas rubripes)*

RANGE: The breeding range includes central Canada east to northern Labrador and Newfoundland, and down to the Great Lakes region and eastern North Carolina. In winter, the bird ranges from the southern edge of the breeding area to the Gulf Coast and southern Florida. Its distribution is rather spotty.

IDENTIFICATION: Both sexes appear similar, having very dark brown bodies with paler cheeks and throats. The black-bordered speculum is purple. The yellowish-to-greenish bill has a black knob at its tip. The legs are red or dusky. The underparts appear nearly black when the duck is in flight.

SIZE: The typical black duck measures from 21 to 26 inches in length.

FOOD: Three-quarters of the black duck's diet is vegetable matter, mainly grasses and aquatic plants. The remainder consists of animal matter—specifically crustaceans, insects, mollusks, and small fish.

■ Green-Winged Teal *(Anas carolinensis)*

RANGE: This bird's breeding area is enclosed in a triangular region of North America from west-central Alaska and northwestern Mackenzie, British Columbia, south to lower California and east to Newfoundland. Winters are spent in southern British Columbia and throughout most of the United States.

IDENTIFICATION: Both the male and female feature bright, glossy-green speculums. The male's head is a bright, reddish brown with a wide, bright-green band

beginning around the eyes and continuing to the back of the head. The buffy breast is spotted with black. The feathers below the tail are buffy and edged with black. The belly is white; the remainder of the plumage is grayish. The female is grayish brown, though lighter below. Her feet and bill are grayish.

SIZE: This teal measures 12 to 16 inches in length.

FOOD: Plants (chiefly the aquatic type, but including grasses) comprise 80 percent of the green-winged teal's diet. Insects, mollusks, and maggots dining on rotting fish are also consumed.

■ Wood Duck *(Aix spousa)*

RANGE: Breeding ranges stretch from central British Columbia to central California, and are also located in such disparate areas as the Great Lakes, New England, Northeast Canada, the Gulf Coast, and Cuba. Winters are spent in the United States, and as far south as mid-Mexico.

IDENTIFICATION: This species is considered one of the most beautiful of all native American ducks. It has a big crest and a chunky body. The drake's head is a mix of iridescent green and blackish purple. On each side of the head there is a pair of thin white lines—one curving over the eye from the bill to the terminal point of the crest, and the other running parallel to it, but beginning behind the eye. The throat is white, with one finger stretching to just beneath the eyes and the other to the back of the head. Red, black, and white colorings comprise the variegated bill. The neck and breast are

Wood Duck

Mallard

a bright, reddish brown. The back is of a dark iridescence, and the flanks are a creamy buff with black-and-white vertical lines separating them from the breast. The upperparts are whitish. The female of the species has a grayish head that features a whitish ring around the eye. Her throat is white and her back is a moderate brown gray. The breast and flanks are brownish.

SIZE: The wood duck is 17 to 21 inches long.

FOOD: Mainly a vegetarian, this species dines on shrubs and tree seeds, grasses, and aquatic plants. Some insects and tiny spiders are also consumed.

■ Mallard *(Anas platyrhynchos)*

RANGE: This surface-feeding species is located throughout a major portion of the temperate Northern Hemisphere (save for northeastern Canada).

IDENTIFICATION: The adult male features a metallic-green head and neck that are separated from its bright-chestnut breast by a thin, white ring. The underparts are a light gray, the upperparts a dark gray. The tail is both black and white, with conspicuously curled feathers on top. The dark wings have a band of rich iridescent blue; the band is edged on each side first by a thin, black band and then a thin, white band. These bands, called speculums, are partly visible when the bird is at rest. The female also has a speculum, but it is predominantly dark or mottled brown and bordered by white. She has a tiny dark cap and an eye stripe, and lacks the curled tail feathers of the male. The male's bill is yellow, the female's orange. Orange feet are common to both sexes.

SIZE: The mallard ranges from 16 to 27 inches in length.

FOOD: Aquatic vegetables, acorns, berries, sedges, grains, and grasses are consumed, as well as small amounts of mollusks and insects.

BIG-GAME ANIMALS

■ Whitetail Deer *(Odocoileus virginianus)*

RANGE: The whitetail deer inhabits a vast section of North America, from southern Canada down through the southern border of the United States. Only a few dry regions of western North America are devoid of whitetails.

IDENTIFICATION: In spring, the whitetail sports a bright, brownish-red coat made up of thin hair. With the coming of winter, a new coat grows, with long, kinky hair varying in color from brownish gray to blue. The nose is pure black with two white bands behind it. The face is brown and the eyes are circled with white. The darkest part of the body is the middle of the back. Though gradually lighter on other parts of the body, the coloring turns abruptly white at the stomach. The antlers consist of two main beams that grow outward, backward, and then sweep forward.

A Note on Edibility: All big-game animals are edible and can certainly be hunted in a survival situation, though small animals and birds are obviously easier targets. Shooting an animal as big as a moose doesn't make any sense if you expect to be rescued in a matter of days. Handling an animal as big as a moose also presents a host of other problems. To a lesser degree, these facts also apply to deer, antelope, elk, and caribou. The information here is offered as a guide to big-game species in the event that you find yourself in a truly dire survival situation.

SIZE: A typical whitetail is slightly taller than 3 feet at the shoulder, measures 5 to 6 feet in length, and weighs about 150 pounds. The largest whitetail ever recorded, however, weighed 425 pounds.

Whitetail Deer

The world-record whitetail deer, according to the Boone and Crockett Club ratings, scored 213⅝ points. Taken by Milo Hanson on November 3, 1993, in Saskatchewan, the rack's inside spread was 27⅜ inches.

FOOD: Most types of vegetation are included in the whitetail's diet, which changes with both the season and the area of the country inhabited. Favorites on the menu are white cedar, white acorns, witchhazel, pine, red maple, apples, dogwood, oak, sweetfern, sumac, wintergreen, bearberry, Oregon grape, hemlock, willow, greenbriar, snowberry, and arborvitae. Among the cultivated crops it seeks out are soybeans, trefoil, rye, alfalfa, corn, rape, cabbage, clover, and lespedeza.

EDIBILITY: Whitetail and mule deer venison rates high on the edibility list. Its low-fat red meat is truly delicious, especially the tenderloins, which are easily removed for a quick survival food without butchering the entire deer. The backstraps, which are cut away from both sides of the backbone from the outside of the carcass, produce venison filet mignon. There are no cuts of a deer that can be considered bad tasting, including venison liver and heart.

■ Mule Deer *(Odocoileus hemionus)*

RANGE: The overall area encompassed by the mule deer extends from southeastern Alaska to Mexico, and east to west Texas, Minnesota, and the Hudson Bay. Those muleys inhabiting the coastal area from Alaska to mid-California are properly termed blacktail deer.

IDENTIFICATION: The mule deer's basic coloring in summer is a brownish red, changing to a brownish gray in winter. The nose and the band around the muzzle are black; the face and a section around the eyes are white. The deer's throat has two white patches separated by a dark bar, its belly and the inside of its legs are whitish, and its hoofs are jet black. The tail is round and white, but becomes black about 2 inches from the tip. The ears often reach 11 inches in total length. A buck's antlers, very large and heavy, divide into two main beams. Each beam forks into two tines.

Though closely related to the mule deer, the blacktail does have some distinctions. The ears measure 6½ inches and are narrower, and the tail is dark on top with a white underside. But like the muley, the blacktail's coloring is brownish red in summer and brownish gray in winter.

SIZE: This species stands about 3½ feet high at the shoulder, measures close to 6½ feet in length, and averages between 175 and 200 pounds in weight. The blacktail is slightly smaller on average. One mule deer that was recorded weighed 480 pounds.

The world-record mule deer, according to the Boone and Crockett Club records, was killed in Dolores County, Colorado, in 1972 by Doug Burris Jr. Scoring 226⅝ points, the rack's right main beam, sporting 6 points, measured 30⅛ inches; its left beam, sporting 5 points, measured 28⅝ inches. The rack's inside spread was 30⅞ inches.

FOOD: In summer, grasses play an important role in the mule deer's diet: ricegrass, needlegrass, grama grass, wheatgrass, bluegrass, fescue grass, and bromegrass. In winter, when grasses are scarce, browse takes over: mountain mahogany, cliffrose, sagebrush, poplar, bitterbrush, jack pine, sunflower, cedar, oak, snowberry,

Mule Deer

bearberry, fir, and serviceberry. Although the deer eats almost any vegetation, it prefers fungus, nuts, cactus fruits, acorns, wildflowers, ferns, and berries.

Rating high on the blacktail's menu are wild oats, manzanita, ceanothus, chamise, buckthorn, buttercup, bromegrass, and fescue grass. Cactus fruit, nuts, wildflowers, fungus, berries, and acorns are also preferred foods.

EDIBILITY: See Whitetail Deer.

■ Elk *(Cervus canadensis)*

RANGE: The bulk of the elk population is in the Rocky Mountains, ranging from British Columbia to New Mexico and Arizona. Herds are also found in some midwestern and eastern states. Alberta, Saskatchewan, and Manitoba also have fair-size elk populations.

IDENTIFICATION: The elk's normal winter coat is brownish gray with long chestnut-brown hair on its head and neck. Its legs are dark and its belly nearly black. The rump patch and short tail are yellowish white. Cow elk are lighter than bulls. In summer, the elk's coat turns a reddish color.

SIZE: Bull elk range in weight from 600 pounds to as much as 1,000 pounds. Cows are smaller, averaging about 600 pounds. A good-size bull may stand 5 feet tall at the shoulder and measure 10 feet in length. Antlers of a prime bull grow up to 5 feet above its head, with each antler sporting from 5 to 7 points and measuring 60 inches or more along the beam.

The world-record head, taken in 1968 in White Mountains, Arizona, had a Boone and Crockett Club score of 442⅜ points. Both beams measured 56⅞ inches long. The right beam had 6 points, the left 7 points. The inside spread measured 47⅛ inches.

FOOD: The diet consists mainly of grasses and browse. Some of the prime foods are pinegrass, bluegrass, blue bunchgrass, sweet vernal grass, and wheatgrass. Elk eat nearly all the conifers, aspen, and willows. Their diet may also include alder, maple, blackberry, and serviceberry.

EDIBILITY: Elk meat, particularly from a young cow and young bulls, is excellent. It is very low in fat content, and I have found elk meat tastier than either whitetail or mule deer.

Elk

■ Moose *(Alces alces)*

RANGE: The Alaska-Yukon moose is found in the Alaska and Yukon Peninsulas; the Canada moose is found in every Canadian province and in sections of northern Minnesota, Wisconsin, and Maine; the Wyoming, or Shiras, moose inhabits the area from the Rocky Mountain region of northern Colorado and Utah north to the border between Canada and the United States.

Moose

IDENTIFICATION: The moose is a large, antlered, ungraceful-looking creature. The primary color is black, though shades of dark brown and russet have been spotted. The nostrils, circles around the eyes, inner parts of the ear, and lower portions of the legs are whitish gray. The hindquarters are much more tapered than the forequarters, and together they hold the moose's belly approximately 40 inches from the ground. The immense antlers weigh around 90 pounds and often reach 6 feet in length. The tail is 3 inches long and stub-like. The ears are large, and the long face finishes up in a wide, downturned muzzle.

SIZE: A typical large bull is from 6½ to 7½ feet tall at the shoulder, measures 8½ to 10½ feet in length, and weighs between 1,300 and 1,400 pounds. Several recorded bulls have weighed as much as 1,800 pounds.

The world-record Alaska-Yukon moose scored 261⅝ points in the Boone and Crockett Club competition. Killed by John A. Crouse in Fortymile River, Alaska, in 1994, the trophy's greatest spread measured 65⅛ inches.

The world-record Canada moose, according to the Boone and Crockett Club rating system, scored 242 points. Killed by Michael E. Laub in 1980 near Grayling River, British Columbia, the trophy had a right palm measuring 44⅝ inches with 15 points and a left palm measuring 45 inches with 16 points. The greatest spread was 63 inches.

The world-record Wyoming moose, killed by John M. Oakley in Green River Lake, Wyoming, in 1952, scored 205⅝ points in the Boone and Crockett Club competition. Its greatest spread was 53 inches; its right palm was 38⅝ inches and its left palm was 38⅝ inches. Both palms sported 15 points.

FOOD: Favorite foods are dwarf willow, white birch, aspen, and balsam fir in forested sections. In summer, the moose seeks shelter from the heat and insects at lakes, where it dines on eelgrass, sedges, pondweeds, and water lilies. Red osier, alder, honeysuckle, chokecherry, striped maple, spiraea, snowberry, dwarf birch, currant, elder, cranberry, mountain ash, and cottonwood are also preferred items.

EDIBILITY: Moose is very close to beef in taste and in some cases considered better than beef. It's very lean and, surprisingly, is less gamey than deer.

■ Pronghorn Antelope
(*Antilocapra americana*)

RANGE: The pronghorn is located in the region from southern Saskatchewan south through the western United States to the Mexican plains.

IDENTIFICATION: The pronghorn is similar to a small deer in body structure and coloring. Both the males and females have similar markings—two black horns (both of which are longer than the ears) and a bright tannish-red hue on the upper body and the outside of the legs. The inside of the legs and underparts are a strong white, as is the rump patch. The necks of both sexes are streaked by two thick, brown bands. The buck, however, has a wide, black band that extends from the nose to just below the eyes.

SIZE: A full-grown male may reach 3½ feet in height at the shoulder, and 5 feet in length, with an average weight of between 100 and 140 pounds. Does usually peak at 80 pounds. There is a tie for the world-record pronghorn. The first was taken in Coconino County, Arizona, in 2000 by Dylan M. Woods and scored 95 points in the Boone and Crockett Club competition. The right horn measured 19⅜ inches, the left 18⅝ inches, and the inside spread was 11⅞ inches. The second—which also scored 95 points—was taken in Mohave County, Arizona, in 2002 by David Meyer. The right and left horns both measured 17⅞ inches and the inside spread was 10⅛ inches.

Pronghorn Antelope

FOOD: The diet consists chiefly of vegetable substances, such as saltbrush, onion, western juniper, sagebrush, and bitterbrush.

EDIBILITY: Antelope may be in a class by itself. Prairie sage may be a factor affecting the taste. Antelope must be field dressed quickly and cooled, but antelope meat is still very edible and tasty. It's just different from other big game. Antelope also makes excellent chili.

■ Collared Peccary *(Tayassu tajacu)*

RANGE: The peccary, or javelina, resides in arid, brushy regions and scrub oak forests along the border between the United States and Mexico, extending from eastern Texas west to Arizona.

IDENTIFICATION: The collared peccary resembles a pig in that it has a lengthy snout with a tough disc at its tip, along with a very short neck, short but stout legs, and a somewhat arched back. Also, its ears are small, erect, and pointed. Though the eyelids have long lashes, the eyes themselves are small. The body is covered with 2-inch-long, bristly, salt-and-pepper gray hair. A thin, white band begins under the animal's throat and joins on its back. About 8 inches above its short tail, on the center of its back, is a gaping musk gland.

SIZE: A typical member of this species is 2½ feet in length, measures 22 inches high at the shoulder, and averages between 40 and 65 pounds in weight.

FOOD: Prickly pears—fruit and spines—are the peccary's favorite food. It also eats roots, tubers, acorns, nuts, fruits, and berries. Being omnivorous, the species also dines on insects and the young and eggs of ground-nesting birds, amphibians, and reptiles. Snake meat is a special treat.

EDIBILITY: Unless you're stuck with an old boar hog, you will find that both peccary on a Texas ranch or wild sows in a Florida swamp will taste great. The meat, of course, is pork and, unless it's mistreated, will always taste good.

■ European Wild Hog *(Sus scrofa)*

RANGE: This species is far from numerous in the United States. To find European wild hogs, hunters must go to the areas of initial releases (e.g., Tennessee's Great Smoky Mountains and North Carolina's Hooper's Bald).

IDENTIFICATION: Thin and muscular (unlike its domesticated relative), the wild hog can have tusks measuring up to 9 inches in length. Its snout is long and saucer-like, its eyes rather small, and its always-erect ears about 5 inches long. The wild hog is usually pure black, but, on occasion, its bristly guard hairs may be white. Its long legs give it nearly the swiftness of a deer.

SIZE: A typical adult measures 30 inches in height at the shoulder and is 4 to 5 feet long. In North America, a big hog may weigh from 300 to 350 pounds. Some European wild hogs, however, have been recorded at close to 600 pounds.

FOOD: During the warmer months, wild hogs feed on roots, tubers, fruits, berries, and grasses. Their menu also ranges from fawns to nuts, including rabbits, mice, frogs, beechnuts, and even rattlesnakes (the wild hog appears to be immune to its poison).

EDIBILITY: See Collared Peccary.

Collared Peccary

European Wild Hog

■ Worms and Insects

Many years ago, one of my readers sent me a tin of earthworm cookies. I stared at them for a few days, and then decided it was time to sample them. I ate one worm cookie, then another. While no match for a chocolate chip cookie, the worm cookies tasted pretty good. It was simply mind over matter. Being a hunter, I have fed my family lots of fish and game. They loved the pheasant cutlets and elk steaks with artichoke hearts; they did, however, draw the line with moose nose. I'm very comfortable knowing that my family could live on wild game in a survival situation. They have a good start. But there are other foods in the wild that will also keep you alive.

WORMS: Don't turn up your nose at this quick and easy source of protein. Worms are about 95 percent protein. You can find earthworms and nightcrawlers in damp soil and in most vegetation after a rain. If you're accustomed to digging up worms for the opening day of trout season, you will know where to look. After you collect a bunch of worms, put them in clean water for five minutes or so to clean them up. You can either eat them raw or boil them for about five minutes. You can also bake them over an open fire. They probably won't taste like worm cookies, but worms may well keep you alive when nothing else is available.

INSECTS: Insects are probably the easiest source of food in the woods. Most are 75 to 80 percent protein. As distasteful as it sounds, bugs rank high as a survival food. The first thing to remember is to avoid all insects that are hairy and bite or sting . . . and this means spiders, centipedes, scorpions, caterpillars, and bees. Also to be avoided are insects that typically carry disease, such as flies, ticks, and mosquitoes.

Edible insects include ants, crickets, beetles, grasshoppers, slugs, and grubs. They are easy to find under rotting wood, logs, and rocks and stones. You can eat most insects raw, but always break off the heads and legs first. The legs of some insects may have barbs, which may make swallowing difficult. You can also mix them with edible vegetation. If eating them raw is distasteful, you can also fry, boil, or roast them.

SUSTENANCE: FISH AND SHELLFISH

If you are near fresh or salt water, you can find a host of edible fish and shellfish. Almost all fish are edible, with the exception of a few saltwater species that may contain some poison, such as blowfish, cowfish, puffer fish, and porcupine fish.

In freshwater streams and shorelines, you will find crayfish, shrimp, frogs, and snails. Look for crayfish at night along gravel banks. A flashlight will pick up the eyes of crayfish. They will always swim backward, so try netting crayfish from the rear. Frogs are easy targets along stream banks. Looking for them at night with a flashlight makes frog hunting even easier. The eyes will glow in the dark and frogs will freeze in the beam long enough for you to catch them with a net or, if you're fast enough, your hands or a club. Roasted or fried frog legs may be the only survival food that also ranks as a delicacy.

All freshwater fish are edible. You can catch them with hook and line, nets, or simply try to stun them with a rock. Saltwater rivers, bays, and tidal flats will yield clams, mussels, eels, crabs, lobsters, shrimp, and snails. All can be eaten raw, steamed, or roasted. (For information on how to catch fish, see the next two sections on natural freshwater and saltwater baits.)

All reptiles and lizards are edible, even venomous snakes. Snakes are also easy to find. Look for them early in the morning or late in the afternoon. If you are absolutely certain a snake is nonvenomous, you can catch it with a stick and your hand. (See page 283 for more information on venomous snakes.) Cut the head off at least three inches back and skin it. In a real emergency, you can eat snake meat raw, or you can boil, fry, or roast it.

■ Natural Freshwater Baits

Live bait is the real thing! Even the most avid purist would concede that live bait, when properly presented, is one of the deadliest of all lures. Many times, however, live bait is incorrectly rammed onto a hook. When this happens, the bait does not act naturally, may die quickly, and will likely turn away lunkers that grew big by learning how to recognize food that doesn't look right. Live bait will only appear natural if placed on the hook correctly, and this depends on how you plan to fish it. You wouldn't, for example, hook a minnow behind the dorsal fin if you plan on trolling. Minnows just don't swim backward. Let's take a look at the popular baits and learn how to hook them.

Even though garden worms and night crawlers will take most species of fish, they must still be presented differently. A worm washed into a stream, for example, would drift with the current, so it should be fished that way. Hook it once through the collar or girdle with both ends free to drift naturally, fish it with no line drag, and let the current do the work. The worm should look strung out, bouncing along quickly through riffles and slowly through pools.

Using worms for panfish requires a different tack. Generally, the panfish angler is still-fishing, so natural presentation is less important. A single worm should be used and threaded about three times on the hook. If you're bothered by nibblers, use only a piece of worm and thread it on the hook, covering the point and barb completely.

Night crawlers are effective on bass, and many fishermen still-fish for bass with the big worms the same way they would for panfish. Actually, bass prefer a moving bait and anglers would catch more big bass if they cast and retrieved night crawlers slowly along the bottom. Hook the worm by running the point of the hook into its head, bringing the point and barb out an inch below the head. Rigged this way and retrieved slowly, a night crawler will appear to be crawling on the bottom.

Next on the list of most common live baits are minnows, from 1-inchers for panfish to 8-inchers for big fish. There are two ways of hooking a live minnow, and how an angler intends to fish determines which one to use.

When trolling or fishing from a drifting boat, run the hook upward and through both lips of the minnow. The lip-hooked bait will move through the water on an even keel and look natural.

If you're still-fishing from an anchored boat or shoreline, hook the minnow just behind the dorsal fin. Be careful not to run the hook too deep or it will hit the spine and kill the bait. Hooked just behind the fin,

Natural Freshwater Baits

Natural Baits	Species of Fish
Minnows	Largemouth and smallmouth bass, trout, pickerel, pike, walleyes, perch, crappies, rock bass
Earthworms	Trout, white bass, rock bass, perch, crappies, catfish, sunfish, whitefish
Night crawlers	Largemouth and smallmouth bass, trout, pickerel, pike, walleyes, muskies, catfish, sturgeon
Crickets	Trout, crappies, perch, rock bass, sunfish
Grubs	Trout, crappies, perch, rock bass, sunfish
Caterpillars	Trout, largemouth and smallmouth bass, crappies, perch, rock bass, sunfish
Crayfish	Smallmouth bass, walleyes, trout, catfish
Hellgrammites	Trout, largemouth and smallmouth bass, walleyes, catfish, rock bass
Nymphs (mayfly, caddis fly, stone fly, and others)	Trout, landlocked salmon, perch, crappies, sunfish
Grasshoppers	Trout, largemouth and smallmouth bass, perch, crappies
Newts and salamanders	Largemouth and smallmouth bass, trout, pickerel, rock bass, walleyes, catfish
Frogs	Largemouth and smallmouth bass, pickerel, pike, muskies, walleyes
Wasp larvae	Perch, crappies, sunfish, rock bass
Suckers	Pike, muskies, smallmouth and largemouth bass
Mice	Largemouth and smallmouth bass, pike, muskies
Freshwater shrimp (scud)	Trout, smallmouth and largemouth bass, perch, crappies, rock bass, sunfish
Dragonflies	Largemouth and smallmouth bass, crappies, white bass, rock bass
Darters	Trout, largemouth and smallmouth bass, walleyes, pickerel, crappies, rock bass
Sculpins	Largemouth and smallmouth bass, walleyes, pickerel, rock bass
Salmon eggs	Trout, salmon
Cut bait (perch belly, etc.)	Pickerel, pike, muskies, largemouth and smallmouth bass, walleyes
Doughballs	Carp, catfish

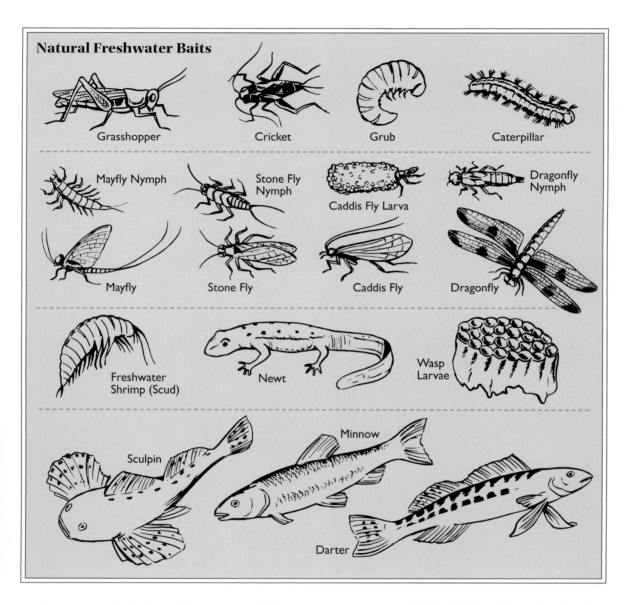

Natural Freshwater Baits

Grasshopper   Cricket   Grub   Caterpillar

Mayfly Nymph   Stone Fly Nymph   Caddis Fly Larva   Dragonfly Nymph

Mayfly   Stone Fly   Caddis Fly   Dragonfly

Freshwater Shrimp (Scud)   Newt   Wasp Larvae

Sculpin   Minnow   Darter

a minnow can swim freely and for a surprisingly long time. There is no hook weight near its head or tail to throw off its balance.

Frogs rank as another excellent bait. Stick with the small frogs, however, such as leopard and green frogs. An old sock makes a fine frog carrier, and frogs are easy to find along any shoreline or riverbank during the summer. There is only one good way to hook a live frog and that is under the jaw and up through both lips. Cast it out and let the frog swim freely, or use a twitch-and-

pause retrieve. A lip-hooked frog will stay alive for a long time. A frog can also be hooked through one of its hind legs. A hook through a frog's leg, however, will destroy some leg muscles, limiting its natural movement.

The crayfish, often called crawfish, is another top bait for bass and trout. The problem is that crayfish are often difficult to find. The best way to hunt them is at night in shallow water that has a rocky or gravel bottom. A crayfish's eyes will glow reddish in the beam of a flashlight. The light seems to freeze them and they can be

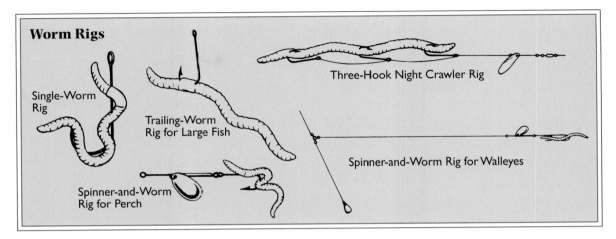

Worm Rigs

Single-Worm Rig

Trailing-Worm Rig for Large Fish

Three-Hook Night Crawler Rig

Spinner-and-Worm Rig for Perch

Spinner-and-Worm Rig for Walleyes

easily picked up. The best way to hook a crayfish is to run the hook up, through, and out the top of its tail. Cast into rocky shorelines or streams, they'll catch big trout, bass, and walleyes.

Salamanders or newts also take bass, trout, and similar species. Finding salamanders isn't hard. They like small springs and streams. They're active at night and easily spotted with a flashlight. Salamanders are fragile and must be hooked carefully. Use a fine-wire hook and run it through the lips or the tail. Salamanders produce best when drifted along stream and river bottoms.

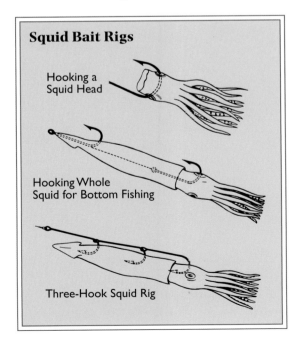

Squid Bait Rigs

Hooking a Squid Head

Hooking Whole Squid for Bottom Fishing

Three-Hook Squid Rig

The most popular live baits have been covered here, but there are still others worth mentioning. The hellgrammite, for example, ranks high with bass and trout. Water insects, hellgrammites average 1 to 2 inches long and can be caught in most streams by simply turning over rocks and holding a net just downstream from the rock. The hellgrammite has a hard collar just behind the head and this is where the hook should be inserted.

The nymph, an underwater stage of the aquatic fly, is still another top bait, particularly for trout. Nymphs differ in the way they behave. Some crawl on rocks, others climb shoreline growths, and still others float downstream. They will all eventually hatch into flies, but it is during this nymphal period that they can be effectively used as bait. There are two ways to put nymphs on a hook. They can be completely threaded—running the hook from the rear, through the body, and up to the head—or they can be simply hooked once just behind the head.

Grasshoppers also work well, and finding them is no problem. Most grassy fields are loaded with 'hoppers. Using a butterfly net, you should be able to fill a box quickly. It's easier to catch them at dawn and dusk. During midday, they are most active and will spook easily. There are several varieties of grasshoppers and nearly all of them take fish. It's best to use a fine-wire hook, running it down and through, behind the head.

■ Natural Saltwater Baits

Natural baits are no less important in salt water than they are in fresh water. That fact is well known to anyone who has seen a school of bluefish slash viciously

Natural Saltwater Baits

Species of Fish	Natural Baits and Lures	Recommended Methods	Hooks
Albacore	Feather lures	Trolling	7/0
Amberjack	Strip baits, feathers, spoons, plugs	Trolling, casting	6/0 to 9/0
Barracuda	Baitfish, plugs, feathers, spoons	Trolling, casting	1/0 to 8/0
Bass, channel	Mullet, mossbunker, crabs, clams, spoons, plugs	Casting, still-fishing, trolling	6/0 to 10/0
Bass, sea	Squid, clams, sea worms, crabs, killie	Drifting, still-fishing	1/0 to 5/0
Bass, striped	Sea worms, clams, eels, metal squids, plugs, jigs, live mackerel	Casting, trolling, drifting, still-fishing	2/0 to 8/0
Billfish (sailfish, marlin, swordfish)	Balao, mackerel, squid, bonito, strip baits, feathered jigs	Trolling	4/0 to 12/0
Bluefish	Rigged eel, cut bait, butterfish, plugs, spoons, feathers	Trolling, casting, drifting, still-fishing	3/0 to 8/0
Bonefish	Cut bait (mainly sardines and conch), flies, plugs, spoons	Casting, drifting, still-fishing	1/0 to 4/0
Bonito	Feather lures, spoons	Trolling	4/0 to 6/0
Codfish	Clams, crabs, cut bait	Still-fishing, drifting	7/0 to 9/0
Dolphin	Baitfish, feather lures, spoons, plugs, streamer flies	Trolling, casting	2/0 to 6/0
Eel	Killie, clams, crabs, sea worms, spearing	Still-fishing, drifting, casting	6 to 1/0
Flounder, summer	Squid, spearing, sea worms, clams, killie, smelt	Drifting, casting, still-fishing	4/0 to 6/0
Flounder, winter	Sea worms, mussels, clams	Still-fishing	6 to 12 (long shank)
Grouper	Squid, mullet, sardines, balao, shrimp, crabs, plugs	Still-fishing, casting	4/0 to 12/0
Haddock	Clams, conch, crabs, cut bait	Still-fishing	1/0 to 4/0
Hake	Clams, conch, crabs, cut bait	Still-fishing	2/0 to 6/0
Halibut	Squid, crabs, sea worms, killie, shrimp	Still-fishing	3/0 to 10/0
Jack Crevalle	Baitfish, cut bait, feathers, metal squid, spoons, plugs	Trolling, still-fishing, casting, drifting	1/0 to 5/0
Mackerel	Baitfish, tube lures, jigs, spinners, streamer flies	Trolling, still-fishing, casting, drifting	3 to 6
Perch, white	Sea worms, shrimp, spearing, flies, spoons	Still-fishing, casting	2 to 6
Pollack	Squid strip, clams, feather lures	Still-fishing, trolling	6/0 to 9/0
Pompano	Sand bugs, jigs, plugs, flies	Trolling, casting, drifting, still-fishing	1 to 4
Porgy	Clams, squid, sea worms, crabs, mussel, shrimp	Still-fishing	4 to 1/0
Rockfish, Pacific	Herring, sardine, mussels, squid, clams, shrimp	Still-fishing, drifting	1/0 to 8/0
Snapper, mangrove	Cut bait, shrimp	Trolling, still-fishing, drifting	1/0 to 6/0
Snapper, red	Shrimp, mullet, crabs	Trolling, still-fishing, drifting	6/0 to 10/0
Snapper, yellowtail	Shrimp, mullet, crabs	Trolling, still-fishing	4 to 1/0
Snook	Crabs, shrimp, baitfish, plugs, spoons, spinners, feathers	Casting, drifting, still-fishing	2/0 to 4/0
Sole	Clams, sea worms	Still-fishing	4 to 6
Spot	Crabs, shrimp, baitfish, sea worms	Still-fishing	8 to 10
Tarpon	Cut bait, baitfish, plugs, spoons, feathers	Trolling, casting, drifting, still-fishing	4/0 to 10/0
Tautog (blackfish)	Clams, sea worms, crabs, shrimp	Still-fishing	6 to 2/0
Tomcod	Clams, mussels, shrimp	Still-fishing	6 to 1/0
Tuna, bluefin	Mackerel, flying fish, bonito, squid, dolphin, herring, cut bait, feathered jigs	Trolling	6/0 to 14/0
Wahoo	Baitfish, feathered jigs, spoons, plugs	Trolling, casting	4/0 to 8/0
Weakfish	Shrimp, squid, sea worms	Still-fishing, casting, drifting, trolling	1 to 4/0
Whiting, northern	Sea worms, clams	Still-fishing, drifting, casting	4 to 1/0
Yellowtail	Herring, sardine, smelt, spoons, metal squids, feather lures	Trolling, casting, still-fishing	4/0 to 6/0

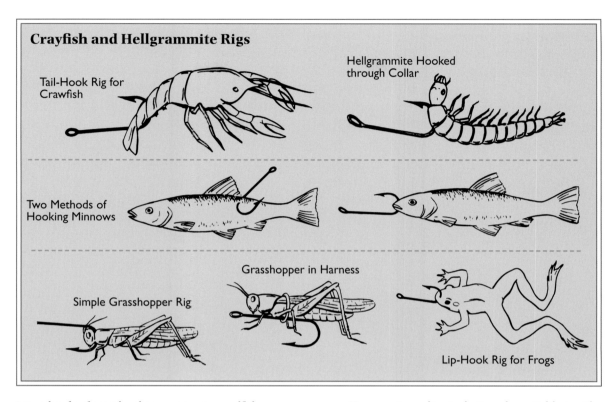

Crayfish and Hellgrammite Rigs

Tail-Hook Rig for Crawfish

Hellgrammite Hooked through Collar

Two Methods of Hooking Minnows

Simple Grasshopper Rig

Grasshopper in Harness

Lip-Hook Rig for Frogs

into a horde of mossbunkers or a tuna or sailfish ravaging a ballyhoo bait.

Which natural saltwater baits should you use and when? Those are questions that only time and experience can help you answer accurately. Generally, you will find that it pays to use any bait that is prevalent when and where you are fishing.

How you rig a saltwater bait can be a vital factor. The primary consideration in rigging most baits is to make them appear as lifelike as possible, whether they are to be trolled, cast out and retrieved, or bounced on the bottom.

The accompanying illustrations show proven ways to prepare and rig the most popular baits used in salt water.

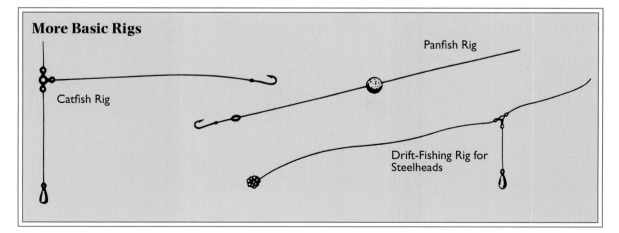

More Basic Rigs

Panfish Rig

Catfish Rig

Drift-Fishing Rig for Steelheads

How to Rig Saltwater Baits

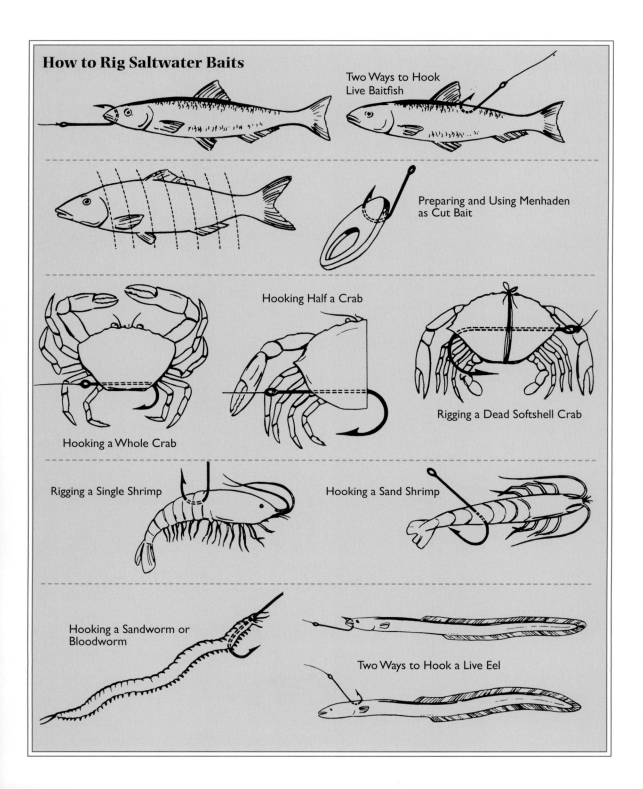

Two Ways to Hook Live Baitfish

Preparing and Using Menhaden as Cut Bait

Hooking Half a Crab

Rigging a Dead Softshell Crab

Hooking a Whole Crab

Rigging a Single Shrimp

Hooking a Sand Shrimp

Hooking a Sandworm or Bloodworm

Two Ways to Hook a Live Eel

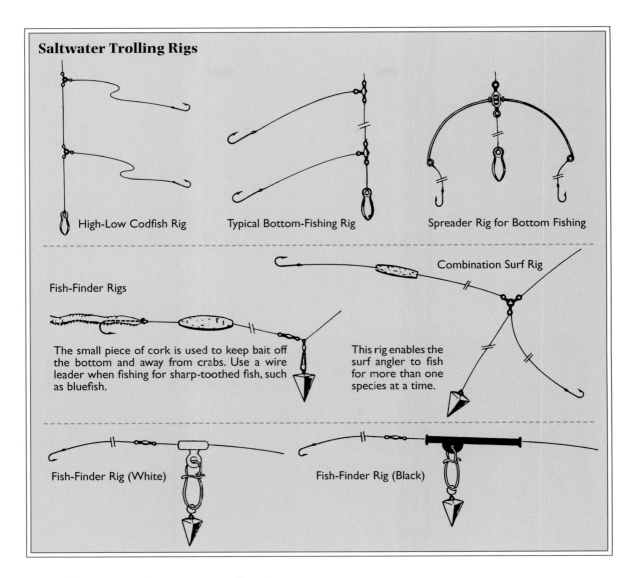

Saltwater Trolling Rigs

High-Low Codfish Rig

Typical Bottom-Fishing Rig

Spreader Rig for Bottom Fishing

Combination Surf Rig

Fish-Finder Rigs

The small piece of cork is used to keep bait off the bottom and away from crabs. Use a wire leader when fishing for sharp-toothed fish, such as bluefish.

This rig enables the surf angler to fish for more than one species at a time.

Fish-Finder Rig (White)

Fish-Finder Rig (Black)

■ Field Care and Dressing of Fish

If you bite into a poor-tasting bass or walleye fillet from a fish you caught, there's a good chance that the second-rate taste is your own fault. In all probability, the fish was not handled properly from the moment it came out of the water. Fish spoil rapidly unless they are kept alive or quickly killed and put on ice.

Here are the necessary steps involved in getting a fresh-caught fish from the water to your plate so that it will retain its original flavor. First, the decision to keep a fish dead or alive depends on conditions. For example,

if you're out on a lake and have no ice in your boat, you'll want to keep all fish alive until it's time to head back to camp. Under no circumstances should you toss fish into the bottom of the boat, let them lie there in the sun, and then gather them up at the end of the day. If you try that stunt, the fillets will reach your plate with the consistency of mush and a flavor to match. Instead, put your fish on a stringer as quickly as possible and put them back into the water, where they can begin to recover from the shock of being caught. Use the safety-pin type stringer and run the wire up

How to Field Dress a Fish

Step 1 • With the fish belly up, make a cut from the anal opening to the gills.

Step 2 • Make two cuts at the gills, one below and one above the gills where they form a V.

Step 3 • Next, stick a finger into the gullet as shown and begin to pull downward. The gills and entrails should come out easily.

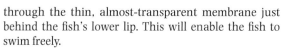

Step 4 • With the entrails out, run your thumbnail along the backbone to break and clean the blood sac. Wash the fish. Once is enough—the less water coming into direct contact with the meat, the firmer the flesh will be when you eat it.

through the thin, almost-transparent membrane just behind the fish's lower lip. This will enable the fish to swim freely.

Do not shove the stringer under the gill cover and out of the mouth. This damages the gills and kills fish fast. Also, avoid cord stringers, where all fish are bunched in a clump at the end of the cord. This is perhaps acceptable on short trips for small panfish, which are generally caught in big numbers and quickly cleaned, but if you're after bigger fish and want to keep them alive and fresh, use the safety-pin stringer. It does its job well.

If you're rowing or trolling slowly, you can probably keep the stringer in the water. If you have a big boat and motor, however, it's a good idea to take the stringer into the boat for those fast runs to other hot spots. If the run is fairly long, wet down the fish occasionally, but don't tow a fish in the water at high speed—you'll drown it.

If you're several miles from camp, use the following technique to get fish back alive. When returning to camp with a stringer of fish, stop your boat every half mile or so and ease the fish over the side. Let the fish swim around for five minutes or so before hauling them back into the boat and continuing the trip to camp. This way, you should have no trouble reaching camp with lively walleyes to be put in your shoreline live box. Keeping fish alive is especially important on extended trips to remote areas, where ice in sufficient quantities isn't generally available.

How to Fillet Pickerel and Other Bony Fish

Too many fish in the pickerel family are being wasted because anglers do not know how to cope with the Y-bones. Bone-free fillets of pickerel, pike, and muskellunge are delicious. Give it a try!

To bake the fish whole, first scale the fish; then follow steps 1 through 4, but leave the fillets attached to the skin. Then, skewer or sew the skin together to form a pocket for stuffing.

For pan frying or baking, there's no need to scale the fish, just wet the scales and work scaleside down on dry newspapers. Don't slip. Follow steps 1 through 4; then with a thin, flexible knife, press the blade flat against the skin and, with a sawing motion, slide the knife along, freeing fillets from the skin. Your efforts should result in four bone-free fillets ready for the frying pan or for dusting with prepared baking mix before placing them in the oven.

The narrow strips along each side of the back can be rolled up in pinwheel fashion and held together with a toothpick inserted horizontally. If you like this system, strip the flank flesh and make pinwheels of all of it. The pinwheels come out with a handle for easy eating or dipping in sauces.

Caution: Cuts shown in the accompanying illustrations are made only down to the tough skin, not through it.

Notes on the Y-Bone Cuts: Until you have dressed a few, run the tip of an index finger along the fish to locate the line of the butts of the Y-bones. Ease the knife through the flesh on these cuts, slightly twisting the blade away from the bones. The knife is pushed through, as opposed to regular cutting action. It will follow the bone line easily. If it catches a bone, back up, increase the angle, and continue. The Y-bone strip and backbone will rip out in single strips if pinched between the thumb and index finger next to the skin to lift the head end from the skin. Grasp the lifted portion and rip out toward the tail.

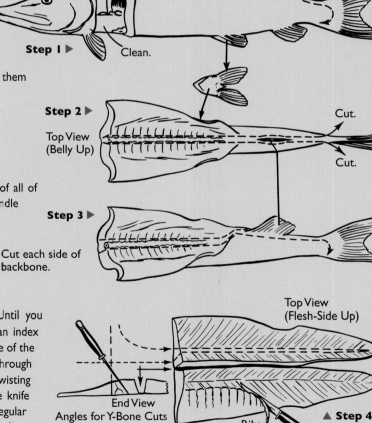

Cut off head.

Lift out dorsal fin.

Step 1 ▶

Clean.

Step 2 ▶

Top View (Belly Up)

Cut.

Cut.

Step 3 ▶

Cut each side of backbone.

Top View (Flesh-Side Up)

End View Angles for Y-Bone Cuts

Ribs

▲ **Step 4**

How to Fillet a Fish

Step 1 • Using a sharp knife, make two initial cuts, one behind the gill plate (as shown) and another at the base of the tail down to the backbone or spine. The cut at the base of the tail is optional. Some fishermen prefer to extend the final fillet cut through the tail.

Step 2 • Next, make a cut on one side of the dorsal fin lengthwise from the first two initial cuts, starting behind the head and cutting down to the base of the tail. As you extend the cut, carefully begin to separate the fillet from the backbone.

Step 3 • Your slice downward will begin to separate the fillet from the backbone. A good fillet knife should have a 7- or 8-inch blade with some flex. A stainless-steel blade may be easier to maintain and will not rust, but carbon-steel fillet knives are easier to sharpen and will take an edge faster.

Step 4 • As you continue to separate the fillet, make sure you avoid the stomach and organs. Note that on this fillet there are no broken organs, digestive juices, or blood to taint the fillet.

Step 5 • Now, carefully begin to cut the fillet free from the fish. Keeping the blade as flat as possible will avoid damaging the fillets.

Step 7 • This is how the fillet should look when cut from one side of the fish. Next, turn the fish over and remove the fillet from the other side of the fish exactly the same way. The next step (not shown here) is to remove the pinbones, which are in the forward third of the fillet. You can feel them easily with your fingers. Using needle-nose pliers, pull them out of the fillet. With a slight wiggle, they should slide out easily.

Step 6 • The final cut will free the clean fillet from the fish. If you prefer to skin your fillets, place them flesh side up, flat on the table. Work your knife blade between the skin and the meat, holding the skin down with your fingers. With a sawing motion, holding the blade flat and down against the skin, cut the meat free of the skin. The fillet and skin will separate easily.

Step 8 • This is the final product—two clean salmon fillets. With the exception of flatfish, this technique will work on all other species with similar body types, such as striped bass, grouper, largemouth bass, and walleyes.

How to Fillet a Flounder

Step 1 • Filleting a summer flounder or fluke is a simple process. An 8- to 10-inch fillet knife with a flexible blade works best. The same technique can also be used on winter flounder, a much smaller flatfish. First, lay the flounder on a large cutting board.

Step 2 • Next, cut around the head and down along the lateral line to the tail, and then across the tail as shown. Make sure the cuts are down to the backbone. Some fillet knives have a serrated tip, which makes it easier to start that initial cut through the skin and scales.

Step 3 • Using your fillet knife, begin to cut between the flesh and the rib bones, starting at the base of the head and working toward the tail. It's important to keep the knife blade as flat as possible against the bones.

Step 4 • Use long, smooth strokes to separate the fillet from the bones. Gently hold back the fillet as you make the cut to make sure the blade is against the bones.

On the subject of lengthy camping trips to remote areas where ice is not available, you can still keep fish alive for a week or more. Your best bet is to use a homemade collapsible fish box, which can be weighted with a rock in a foot of water onshore or floated in deep water. Either way, the fish will stay alive until the end of the trip. Keeping fish alive for lengthy periods in remote areas is impossible without such a box. Keeping fish on a stringer at dockside will not work for long periods. With some wood and wire mesh, a fish box is easy to build. This assumes, of course, that a fish has been unhooked and is placed in the fish box in good condition. If it has been deeply hooked and appears to be dying slowly, however, it's best to kill the fish immediately, gut it, and keep it on ice.

Killing a fish quickly is simple. Holding the fish upright, impale it between the eyes with the point of

Step 5 • Continue to use long, smooth strokes while cutting until the fillet is free from the body. Avoid using short strokes, which will make your fillet look like it has been chopped off.

Step 6 • The end result is a clean fillet. Each fillet will have a ribbon fin along the outside edge. Peel or cut it away from the fillet and save it for your next flounder trip. The ribbon fin makes an excellent bait.

Step 7 • The next step is to remove the skin. Hold the fillet skin down as shown, and, using a sawing motion with the blade flat against the skin, separate the skin from the fillet. You can use your finger to hold the fillet, but the tines of a fork may hold it more firmly to the cutting board.

Step 8 • Turn the flounder over, belly side up, and make the identical cuts to remove the fillets. Each flounder will produce four clean fillets ready for your favorite recipe.

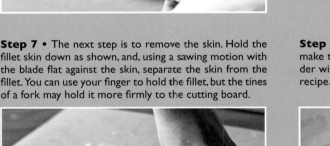

your knife or rap it on the head with a heavy stick. The important factor is killing it quickly, since the more slowly it dies, the more rapidly the flesh will deteriorate.

If you're a stream fisherman, it's wise to carry your catch in a canvas or wicker creel. The canvas creel works fine, so long as it is occasionally immersed in water. The traditional wicker creel will work just as well, but it should be lined with ferns, leaves, or wet newspaper.

If you're a surf fisherman, you can bury your catch in the damp sand. Just remember to mark the spot. A burlap sack occasionally doused in the surf also makes a practical fish bag. The important factor is to keep the fish cool and out of the sun.

Regardless of the various ways to keep fish cool, they should first be cleaned properly. With a bit of practice, the job can be done in less than a minute (see page 214).

Surviving on Fish

Atlantic Salmon

Any time you're near water, your chances of survival greatly increase. Most healthy adults can survive three weeks without food. However, even the healthiest adults can go no longer than three days without water before they may become delirious and lose vital body functions. There are several ways to make fresh water potable (see page 137).

A huge advantage in a survival situation near fresh or salt water is that it can provide a food source. Nearly all freshwater fish are edible and shorelines are also good places to look for amphibians. Some taste better than others, but in any kind of a survival situation, you may not have a choice. Many saltwater fish are edible, but there are a few exceptions. There are certain species that should be avoided and most are found in tropical waters and around coral reefs, where they feed on algae. The flesh of these reef fish can be toxic and transmit ciguatera poisoning.

The more you know about freshwater and saltwater species and their range and eating habits, the easier it will be to find them. These profiles of fish should be of interest to any camper or survivalist. Your life may depend on it.

FRESHWATER FISH

◼ Atlantic Salmon *(Salmo salar)*

DESCRIPTION: Atlantic salmon are anadromous fish, meaning that they are spawned in freshwater rivers and then migrate to the ocean to spend most of their lives before returning to fresh water to spawn themselves. When fresh from the sea, Atlantics are steel blue on top and silver on the sides and belly, and have dark spots on their sides. As their stay in fresh water lengthens, the colors become darker, with the sides taking on a pinkish hue as spawning time arrives. Very young salmon are called parrs. Parrs have distinctive dark vertical bars called parr markings. Unlike Pacific salmon, all of which die after spawning, about 15 percent of Atlantic salmon survive the spawning act and return to sea.

RANGE: The highly prized Atlantic salmon once ranged from Delaware north through Quebec and the Canadian Maritime provinces to Greenland, and in the western Atlantic Ocean to the British Isles and parts of Scandinavia. But today, because of "progress"—meaning dams, pollution, and urban and suburban sprawl—the range of the Atlantic salmon in the United States is restricted to a handful of rivers in Maine, though efforts are being made to restore this fine game fish to the Connecticut River and other northeastern rivers.

HABITAT: In fresh water, the Atlantic salmon must have clean, flowing, cold water. In upstream spawning areas, shallow water over a gravel bottom is a must so that the fish can create "redds," or spawning beds. When in the ocean, these salmon range over vast areas but tend to concentrate on feeding grounds, which are only recently being discovered.

SIZE: Mature Atlantic salmon weigh from 9 to 75 pounds, with the average being 12 pounds. Their size depends on how many years they have spent in the sea, where their growth is fast. Salmon that return to fresh water after only one or two years at sea are called grilse and weigh up to about 6 or 8 pounds.

FOOD: These fish feed on small baitfish and the like when in the ocean, but upon entering fresh water, they stop feeding almost completely. And yet they can be induced to strike an artificial lure, particularly dry and wet flies.

FISHING METHODS: Casting from shore or boats, mostly in tidal waters of rivers and river mouths during spawning migration

BAITS: Artificial lures (especially spoons) and dry, wet, and streamer flies

◼ Landlocked Salmon *(Salmo salar sebago)*

COMMON NAMES: Landlocked salmon, Sebago salmon, landlock, and ouananiche

Chinook Salmon

DESCRIPTION: The landlocked salmon is very similar in coloration and general appearance to the Atlantic salmon, of which the landlock is a subspecies. It is assumed that the subspecies descended from Atlantic salmon trapped in freshwater lakes thousands of years ago. As their name suggests, landlocks do not spawn in the sea. They either spawn in their home lakes or descend to outlet streams to spawn.

RANGE: Landlocks range over much of New England (they are most numerous in Maine), Quebec and other parts of eastern Canada, and north to Labrador. They have been introduced in New York and other eastern states and in South America.

HABITAT: The landlock survives best in deep, cold lakes that have a high oxygen content.

SIZE: Most landlocks average 2 to 3 pounds, but a 6-pounder is not unusual and an occasional 10-pounder is caught. The maximum weight is about 30 pounds.

FOOD: Landlocks feed mostly on small baitfish, particularly smelt.

FISHING METHODS: Casting and trolling

BAITS: Baitfish, smelt, artificial lures, and streamers

■ Chinook Salmon
(Oncorhynchus tshawytscha)

COMMON NAMES: Chinook salmon, king salmon, tyee salmon, and blackmouth (immature stage)

DESCRIPTION: The chinook, like all other Pacific salmon, is anadromous and seems to prefer the largest of Pacific coast rivers for spawning. Chinooks have a dark-blue back that shades to silver on the sides and white on the belly. Small, dark spots—barely noticeable in fish fresh from the sea—mark the upper part of the body.

RANGE: Chinook salmon range from southern California to northern Alaska, being more numerous in the northern part of that area. They often travel enormous distances upriver to spawn; in the Yukon River, for example, chinooks have been seen 2,000 miles from the sea.

HABITAT: Chinooks prefer large, clean, cold rivers, but often enter small tributary streams to spawn in shallow water over gravel bottoms.

SIZE: The chinook is the largest of the Pacific salmon, reaching weights of more than 100 pounds. Rarely, however, does a sportfisherman catch one of more than 60 pounds, and the average size is about 18 pounds.

FOOD: Chinook salmon eat ocean baitfish (herring, sardines, candlefish, and anchovies), freshwater baitfish, and fish roe.

FISHING METHODS: Casting and trolling

BAITS: Baitfish, egg sacks, spoons, spinners, and flies

■ Dog Salmon *(Oncorhynchus keta)*

COMMON NAMES: Dog salmon and chum salmon

DESCRIPTION: The dog salmon closely resembles the chinook salmon, but has black-edged fins and lacks the chinook's dark spots on the back, dorsal fin, and tail. During spawning, the male dog salmon often

Dog Salmon

Dog Salmon Spawning

exhibits red or green blotches on its sides. The dog salmon is rarely taken by sportfishermen.

RANGE: One of five species of Pacific salmon, the dog salmon is found from central California north to Alaska, but is far more numerous in Alaska than farther south. In their sea migrations, dog salmon travel as far as the Aleutians, Korea, and Japan.

HABITAT: Like all other salmon, the dog spawns in gravel in freshwater rivers, usually in the lower reaches of the parent streams, but occasionally far upstream.

SIZE: Dog salmon reach weights of 30 pounds or a bit more, but they average 6 to 18 pounds.

FOOD: The diet of dog salmon consists mainly of baitfish and crustaceans.

FISHING METHODS: Casting and trolling

BAITS: Baitfish, spoons, spinners, and flies, especially those in red

■ Sockeye Salmon
(Oncorhynchus nerka)

COMMON NAMES: Sockeye salmon, red salmon, and blueback salmon

DESCRIPTION: The sockeye is similar to the chinook, but it has a small number of gill rakers and tiny spots along its back. When spawning, sockeye males turn dark red, with the forward parts of their body being greenish. Females range in color from olive to light red. Sockeyes are more often caught by sportfishermen than dog salmon, and they will take artificial flies and are good fighters.

RANGE: Sockeyes are found from California to Japan, but few are encountered south of the Columbia River. A landlocked strain of the sockeye (see Kokanee Salmon), originally found from British Columbia south to Oregon and Idaho, is being stocked in freshwater lakes in various areas of the United States.

HABITAT: This species spawns over gravel in freshwater lakes, especially those fed by springs.

Sockeye Salmon

SIZE: Sockeyes reach a maximum weight of about 15 pounds, but the average weight is 4 to 9 pounds.

FOOD: Sockeyes feed mainly on crustaceans, but also eat small baitfish.

FISHING METHODS: Casting and trolling

BAITS: Crustaceans, baitfish, spoons, and streamer flies

■ Humpback Salmon
(Oncorhynchus gorbuscha)

COMMON NAMES: Humpback salmon and pink salmon

DESCRIPTION: Similar to other salmon but smaller, the humpback has small scales and its caudal fin (tail) has large, oval, black spots. At maturity, or at spawning time, the males develop a large, distinctive hump on their backs. The humpback is among the most commercially valuable of the Pacific salmon and is becoming more popular with sportfishermen.

Humpback Salmon

Humpback Salmon Spawning

RANGE: The humpback is found from California to Alaska and as far away as Korea and Japan.

HABITAT: This species spawns over gravel in freshwater rivers, usually near the sea.

SIZE: The smallest of the Pacific salmon, the humpback averages 3 to 6 pounds, attaining a maximum weight of about 10 pounds.

FOOD: Humpbacks subsist largely on a diet of crustaceans, baitfish, and squid.

FISHING METHODS: Casting and trolling

BAITS: Crustaceans, baitfish, spoons, spinners, and flies

■ Coho Salmon *(Oncorhynchus kisutch)*

COMMON NAMES: Coho salmon, silver, and hooknose

DESCRIPTION: The coho is generally silvery with a bluish back and has small, dark spots along the upper part of the sides and tail. When the spawning urge takes hold, the males assume a reddish coloration, but when they enter fresh water they become almost black. The coho is highly prized as a sport fish, striking artificials readily and leaping breathtakingly when hooked.

RANGE: The coho is found from California to Alaska and as far from the West Coast of the United States as Japan. It has also been transplanted with unprecedented success in all of the Great Lakes and in many landlocked reservoirs throughout the United States.

HABITAT: This fish spawns in gravel in freshwater rivers, either near the sea or far upstream.

SIZE: Cohos reach weights approaching 30 pounds, but they average 6 to 12 pounds.

Kokanee Salmon

Kokanee Salmon Spawning

FOOD: A coho's diet is mainly baitfish, squid, crustaceans, and crab larvae.

FISHING METHODS: Casting and trolling

BAITS: Baitfish, squid, crustaceans, spoons, and flies

■ Kokanee Salmon *(Oncorhynchus nerka kennerlyi)*

COMMON NAMES: Kokanee salmon, silver trout, blueback, little redfish, Kennerly's salmon, landlocked sockeye, redfish, and silversides

DESCRIPTION: The kokanee is a landlocked strain of the anadromous sockeye salmon. Biologically identical with the true sockeye (though much smaller), the kokanee is silvery on its sides and belly, but during spawning the males have reddish sides and the females have slate-gray sides. Kokanees resemble some trout, but differ from all trout in that they have more than 12 rays in the anal fin. The kokanee is the only Pacific salmon that matures in fresh water. It is much prized by fishermen.

RANGE: The kokanee's original range extended from Idaho and Oregon north to Alaska, but it has been introduced in recent years in lakes as far south as New Mexico and as far east as New England.

HABITAT: The kokanee spawns in gravel, both in lakes and in tributary streams, and ranges throughout lakes at other times.

Coho Salmon

Brook Trout

SIZE: Much smaller than the true sockeye salmon, the kokanee reaches a maximum weight of about 4 pounds. The average length varies greatly, depending upon water and food conditions. In some places they never exceed 10 inches, while in other places—California's Donner Lake, for example—their average length is more than 18 inches.

FOOD: Kokanees feed almost exclusively on tiny forage—minute crustaceans and other plankton.

FISHING METHODS: Casting and trolling

BAITS: Small crustaceans, artificial lures, and flies

■ Arctic Char *(Salvelinus alpinus)*

COMMON NAMES: Arctic char, Arctic trout, alpine trout, and Quebec red trout

DESCRIPTION: The Arctic char is a far-north salmonid whose colors vary greatly. Sea-run char are quite silvery as they enter freshwater rivers, but their freshwater colors soon predominate, turning the char into a stunning fish with sides ranging in color from pale to very bright orange and red. Char are usually spotted in red, pink, or cream, and have the white-edged fins of brook trout, but they lack the brook trout's vermiculations (wormlike markings) on the back. There are both anadromous and landlocked strains of Arctic char.

RANGE: Arctic char are found in northern Canada, Alaska, Iceland, Greenland, Scandinavia, England, Ireland, Scotland, Europe, and the Soviet Union.

HABITAT: As its range indicates, the char thrives in very cold, clean water, preferring fast, shallow river water near the mouths of tributary streams. Relatively little is known about the nomadic movements of anadromous char, but they apparently spend the summer near the mouths of rivers, where they feed heavily before moving inland.

SIZE: Arctic char reach weights of nearly 30 pounds, but the average weight is 2 to 8 pounds.

FOOD: Char feed on a species of smelt called capelin and on sand eels, various baitfish, some crustaceans, and occasionally on insects.

FISHING METHODS: Casting

BAITS: Small baitfish, crustaceans, spoons, spinners, and flies

■ Brook Trout *(Salvelinus fontinalis)*

COMMON NAMES: Brook trout, speckled trout, speck, and squaretail

DESCRIPTION: This best-loved American native fish is not a true trout but actually a member of the char family. It is a beautiful fish, having a dark back with distinctive vermiculations (wormlike markings), sides marked with yellow spots and with red spots encircled in blue, a light-colored belly (bright orange during spawning), and pink or red lower fins edged in white. Wherever they are found, brook trout willingly take the offerings of fly, bait, and lure fishermen alike, a fact that has contributed to their decrease in many areas, though pollution has done far more to decimate populations of native brookies.

RANGE: Originally native only to northeastern North America from Georgia to the Arctic, the brook trout is now found in suitable waters throughout the United States, Canada, South America, and Europe. Stocking maintains brook trout in many waters, but true native brookies are becoming rare.

HABITAT: Brook trout must have clean, cold water, seldom being found in water warmer than 65°F. They spawn both in lakes and in streams, preferring small, spring-fed brooks.

Arctic Char

Sunapee Trout

SIZE: Though the rod-and-reel record for brook trout is 14½ pounds, fish half that size are a rarity today. In fact, a 5-pounder is an exceptional brook trout, and fish of that size are seldom found anywhere but in Labrador, northern Quebec and Manitoba, and Argentina. Native brook trout caught in streams average about 6 to 12 inches in length.

FOOD: Brook trout eat worms, insects, crustaceans, and various kinds of baitfish.

FISHING METHODS: Casting, trolling, and streamers

BAITS: Baitfish, worms, insects, spoons, spinners, and flies

Sunapee Trout *(Salvelinus aureolus)*

COMMON NAMES: Sunapee trout and Sunapee golden

DESCRIPTION: This attractive fish—which may be a member of the char family or a distinct species of trout (there is some disagreement on the subject)—has a dark-bluish back that lacks the wormlike markings of the brook trout. Its sides have spots of pinkish white, yellow, or red, and the yellowish or orange fins are edged in white.

RANGE: Originating in New Hampshire, principally in Sunapee Lake, the Sunapee trout is exceedingly rare, being found only in Sunapee Lake and in a few lakes and ponds in northern New England. The introduction of lake trout in Sunapee and other lakes has had a deteriorating effect on populations of Sunapee trout.

HABITAT: Little is known about the wanderings of this attractive fish, but it is known that in Sunapee Lake these trout move into the shallows in spring and fall, while in summer they are found in the deepest parts of the lake—way down to 60 to 100 feet, where the water is quite cold.

SIZE: Many years ago, 10- and 12-pound Sunapees were

taken in the lake from which they derive their name, but today a fisherman is lucky to catch a 15-incher.

FOOD: Smelt makes up the majority of the Sunapee trout's diet.

FISHING METHODS: Casting

BAITS: Baitfish, smelt, spoons, spinners, and flies

Dolly Varden Trout *(Salvelinus malma)*

COMMON NAMES: Dolly Varden trout, Dolly, western char, bull trout, salmon trout, and red-spotted trout

DESCRIPTION: This member of the char family somewhat resembles the brook trout, but it lacks the brookie's wormlike back markings and is usually more slender. It has red and yellow side spots and the white-edged fins typical of all chars. In salt water, the Dolly is quite silvery. The Dolly, said to have been named after a Charles Dickens character, is not as popular in some parts of its range as other trout species, possibly because it is not as strong a fighter.

RANGE: Occurring from northern California to Alaska and as far from the United States as Japan, the Dolly is found in both fresh water and, in the northern part of its range, in salt water.

HABITAT: Dolly Vardens spawn in gravel in streams. At other times of the year, stream fish are likely to be found in places similar to those preferred by brook trout, such as under rocks, logs, and other debris and lying in deep holes. In lakes, they are likely to be found near the bottom near reefs and drop-offs. They are seldom found near the surface.

SIZE: Dolly Vardens reach weights of upward of 30

Dolly Varden Trout

pounds. The average size is 8 to 18 inches in some places (usually streams), and 3 to 6 pounds in other places (usually lakes).

FOOD: These fish are primarily bottom-feeders, though in streams they feed heavily on insects and may be taken on flies. Large fish feed heavily on baitfish, including the young of trout and salmon. It has been said that these trout will eat anything, which may be true considering that in some areas fishermen shoot ground squirrels, remove and skin the legs, and use the legs for Dolly Varden bait!

FISHING METHODS: Casting, trolling, and streamers

BAITS: Baitfish, spoons, spinners, and flies

■ Lake Trout *(Salvelinus namaycush)*

COMMON NAMES: Lake trout, togue, mackinaw, gray trout, salmon trout, forktail, and laker

DESCRIPTION: More somberly hued than most other trout, the laker is usually a fairly uniform gray or bluish gray, though in some areas it is a bronze green. It has irregular, pale spots over its head, back, and sides and also has the white-edged fins that mark it as a char.

RANGE: The lake trout is distributed throughout Canada and in the northern United States, principally in New England, and New York's Finger Lakes, the Great Lakes, and many large western lakes. Stockings have widened the laker's range considerably and have restored the species to portions of the Great Lakes, where an incursion of lamprey eels decimated the laker populations in the 1950s and early 1960s.

HABITAT: Lake trout are fish of deep, cold, clear lakes, though in the northern part of their range they are also found in large streams. Lakers prefer water temperatures of about 45°F and are rarely found where water rises

Lake Trout

Rainbow Trout

above 70°F. In the southern part of their range, they are usually found only in lakes that have an adequate oxygen supply in the deeper spots.

SIZE: The lake trout is the largest of the trout species, reaching weights of more than 100 pounds. Its average size often depends on the size, depth, and water quality of a given lake.

FOOD: Though the young feed on insects and crustaceans, adult lake trout eat primarily fish, such as smelt, small kokanee salmon, ciscoes, whitefish, and sculpin.

FISHING METHODS: Casting and trolling

BAITS: Baitfish, crustaceans, deep-running spoons, and plugs

■ Rainbow Trout *(Oncorhynchus mykiss)*

COMMON NAMES: Rainbow trout, steelhead, Kamloops rainbow, Kamloops trout, and redsides

DESCRIPTION: This native American trout takes three basic forms: the nonmigratory rainbow, which lives its entire life in streams or lakes; the steelhead, which is spawned in freshwater rivers, migrates to the sea, and returns to the rivers to spawn itself (large rainbows that live in the Great Lakes and elsewhere in the eastern United States are also called steelheads but are not true members of the steelhead clan); and the Kamloops rainbow, a large subspecies found mostly in interior British Columbia. Though the rainbow's colors vary greatly depending upon where it is found, the fish generally has an olive or lighter-green back shading to silvery or white on the lower sides and belly. There are numerous black spots on the upper body from head to tail and a distinctive red stripe along the middle of each side. Sea-run and lake-run rainbows are usually quite silver, with a faint or nonexistent red stripe and few spots. The rainbow is an extremely important sport fish and will take flies, lures, and bait willingly. It usually strikes hard and is noted for its wild leaps.

RANGE: The natural range of the rainbow trout is from northern Mexico to Alaska and the Aleutian Islands, but stocking programs have greatly widened that range so that it now includes most of Canada, all of the northern and central states of the United States, and some of the colder waters in such southern states as Georgia, Tennessee, Arkansas, and Texas.

HABITAT: The rainbow, like all trout, must have cold, clean water, though it does fairly well under marginal conditions. It is found in shallow lakes and deep lakes, in small streams and large ones. It may be found at the surface one day, and feeding on the bottom the next. The rainbow's universality is due partly to the fact that it can do well in a wide variety of environments.

SIZE: The average nonmigratory stream rainbow runs from 6 to 18 inches in length, though some much larger specimens are occasionally taken. Nonmigratory lake fish tend to run considerably larger—up to 50 pounds or more. An average migratory steelhead runs from 8 to 12 pounds, but this strain reaches 35 pounds or so.

FOOD: Rainbows feed heavily on insect life, but they also eat baitfish, crustaceans, worms, and the roe of salmon and trout. The diet of the Kamloops rainbow is mainly kokanee salmon.

FISHING METHODS: Casting and trolling

BAITS: Baitfish, worms, salmon eggs, spoons, spinners, and flies

■ Cutthroat Trout *(Salmo clarki)*

COMMON NAMES: Cutthroat trout, coastal trout, cut, native trout, mountain trout, Rocky Mountain trout,

Cutthroat Trout

black-spotted trout, harvest trout, Montana black-spotted trout, Tahoe cutthroat, and Yellowstone cutthroat

DESCRIPTION: Occurring in both nonmigratory and anadromous forms, the cutthroat trout gets its common name from the two slashes of crimson on the underside of its lower jaw. Its scientific name honors William Clark of the famed Lewis and Clark expedition. The cutthroat is often mistaken for the rainbow, but it lacks the rainbow's bright-red side stripe, and its entire body is usually covered with black spots, while the rainbow's spots are usually limited to the upper half of the body. The cutthroat usually has a greenish back, colorful gill plates, sides of yellow or pink, and a white belly. Coastal cutthroats are greenish blue with a silvery sheen on the sides and heavy black spots. The cutthroat is a fine sport fish, taking flies—particularly wet flies—readily and showing an inordinate liking for flashy spoons.

RANGE: The cutthroat is found from northern California north to Prince William Sound, Alaska, and inland throughout the western United States and Canada.

HABITAT: A fish of clean, cold water, the cutthroat frequents places like those preferred by the brook trout—undercut banks, deep holes, logs, and other debris. They prefer quiet water, generally, in streams. Unlike other trout that go to sea, anadromous cutthroats do not range widely in the ocean depths. Instead, they remain in bays at the mouths of their home streams or along the nearby ocean shores.

SIZE: Though cutthroats of up to 41 pounds have been caught by anglers, they seldom exceed 5 pounds and average 2 to 3 pounds. A fish weighing 4 pounds is considered large for a sea-run cutthroat.

FOOD: Young cutthroats feed mainly on insect life, while adults eat insects, baitfish, crayfish, and worms.

FISHING METHODS: Casting and trolling

BAITS: Insects, crayfish, worms, spoons, spinners, and flies

■ Golden Trout *(Salmo aquabonita)*

COMMON NAMES: Golden trout, Volcano trout, and Sierra trout

Golden Trout

DESCRIPTION: This rare jewel of the western high country is the most beautiful of all trout. The golden trout has an olive back and crimson gill covers and side stripes, while the remainder of the body ranges from orangish yellow to gold. The dorsal fin has orange tips, and the anal and ventral fins have white edges. Each side contains about 10 black parr markings. The coloring differs from lake to lake. The golden is a rarely caught but highly prized sport fish.

RANGE: Originally found only in the headwaters of California's Kern River, the golden is now present in high-mountain lakes in many western states, including California, Wyoming, Idaho, and Washington. Modern fish-breeding and stocking techniques have extended the range of the golden—or, rather, a golden-rainbow trout cross—to the eastern states, including West Virginia and New Jersey.

HABITAT: The true golden trout is found in small, high lakes and their tributary streams at elevations of 9,000 to 12,000 feet. The water in these lakes is extremely cold, and weed growth is minimal or nonexistent. Because of the golden's spartan habitat, it can be extremely moody and difficult to catch.

SIZE: Golden trout are not large, a 2-pounder being a very good one, though some lakes hold fair numbers of fish up to 5 pounds. The maximum size is 11 pounds.

FOOD: Golden trout feed almost exclusively on minute insects, including terrestrial insects, but also eat tiny crustaceans and are sometimes caught by bait fishermen using worms, salmon eggs, and grubs.

FISHING METHODS: Casting and trolling

BAITS: Insects, worms, salmon eggs, spinners, and flies

■ Brown Trout *(Salmo trutta)*

COMMON NAMES: Brown trout, German brown trout, and Loch Leven trout

DESCRIPTION: Introduced in North America in the 1880s, the brown trout is a top-notch dry-fly fish, and yet its daytime wariness and whimsy can drive fishermen to the nearest bar. The brown trout is generally brownish to olive brown, shading from dark brown on the back to dusky yellow or creamy white on the belly. The sides, back, and dorsal fin have prominent black or brown spots, usually surrounded by faint halos of gray or white. Some haloed red or orange spots are also present. Sea-run browns and those in large lakes are often silvery and resemble landlocked salmon.

RANGE: The brown is the native trout of Europe and is also found in New Zealand, parts of Asia, South America, and Africa. It is found in the United States from coast to coast and as far south as New Mexico, Arkansas, and Georgia.

HABITAT: The brown trout can tolerate warmer water and other marginal conditions better than other trout species can. It is found in both streams and lakes, preferring hiding and feeding spots similar to those of the brook trout. It often feeds on the bottom in deep holes, coming to the surface at night.

SIZE: Brown trout have been known to exceed 40 pounds, though one of more than 10 pounds is now considered exceptional. Most browns caught by sportfishermen weigh ½ to 1½ pounds.

FOOD: Brown trout feed on aquatic and terrestrial insects as well as worms, crayfish, baitfish, and fish roe. Large specimens will eat such tidbits as mice, frogs, and small birds.

FISHING METHODS: Casting and trolling

BAITS: Baitfish, insects, worms, salmon eggs, spoons, spinners, and flies

Brown Trout

■ Grayling *(Thymallus arcticus)*

COMMON NAMES: Grayling, Montana grayling, and Arctic grayling

DESCRIPTION: Closely related to trout and whitefish, the grayling's most distinctive feature is its high, wide dorsal fin, which is gray to purple and has rows of blue or lighter dots. Its back is dark blue to gray, and the sides range from gray to brown to silvery, depending upon where the fish lives. The forepart of the body usually has irregularly shaped dark spots. The grayling is a strikingly handsome fish and a fly fisherman's dream.

RANGE: The grayling is abundant in Alaska, throughout northern Canada from northern Saskatchewan westward, and northward through the Northwest Territories. It is less common in the United States, ranging in high areas of Montana, Wyoming, and Utah. Recently developed grayling-breeding procedures are extending the range of this fish into Idaho, California, Oregon, and other mountain states.

HABITAT: The grayling is found in both lakes and rivers, but is particularly at home in high and isolated timberline lakes. In lakes, schools of grayling often cruise near the shore. In rivers, the fish are likely to be found anywhere, but they usually favor one type of water in any given stream.

SIZE: The maximum weight of the grayling is 20 pounds or a bit heavier, but in most waters, even in the Arctic, a 2-pounder is a good fish. In U.S. waters, grayling seldom top 1½ pounds.

FOOD: The grayling's diet is made up almost entirely of nymphs and other insects and aquatic larvae. However, this northern fish will also readily eat worms and crustaceans.

FISHING METHODS: Casting

BAITS: Nymphs, insects, worms, and flies

■ Rocky Mountain Whitefish *(Prosopium williamsoni)*

COMMON NAMES: Rocky Mountain whitefish, mountain whitefish, and Montana whitefish

Grayling

DESCRIPTION: The Rocky Mountain whitefish resembles the lake whitefish, though its body is more cylindrical. Coloration shades from brown on the back to silver on the sides to white on the belly. The dorsal fin is large, but not nearly as large as that of the grayling. Where it competes with trout in a stream, the Rocky Mountain whitefish is considered a nuisance by many anglers, though it fights well and will take dry and wet flies, spinning lures, and bait.

RANGE: The Rocky Mountain whitefish is endemic to the western slope of the Rocky Mountains from northern California to southern British Columbia.

HABITAT: Found in cold, swift streams and in clear, deep lakes, these whitefish school up in deep pools after spawning in the fall, and feed mostly on the bottom. In spring, the fish move to the riffles in streams and the shallows in lakes.

SIZE: Rocky Mountain whitefish reach 5 pounds, but a 3-pounder is an exceptional one. The average length is 11 to 14 inches and the average weight is 1 pound.

FOOD: These fish feed almost entirely on such insects as caddis and midge larvae and stone fly nymphs. They also eat fish eggs, their own included.

FISHING METHODS: Casting and fly fishing (not an important game fish)

BAITS: Insects, nymphs, fish eggs, and flies

Rocky Mountain Whitefish

Lake Whitefish

■ Lake Whitefish
(Coregonus clupeaformis)

COMMON NAMES: Lake whitefish, common whitefish, Great Lakes whitefish, Labrador whitefish, and Otsego bass

DESCRIPTION: Similar in appearance—though only distantly related—to the Rocky Mountain whitefish, the lake whitefish has bronze or olive shading on the back, with the rest of the body being silvery white. It has rather large scales, a small head and mouth, and a blunt snout. Large specimens appear humpbacked. Lake whitefish, because they spend much of the year in very deep water, are not important sport fish.

RANGE: Lake whitefish are found from New England west through the Great Lakes area and throughout much of Canada.

HABITAT: These fish inhabit large, deep, cold, clear lakes and are usually found in water from 60 to 100 feet deep, though they will enter tributary streams in spring and fall. In the northern part of their range, however, lake whitefish are often found foraging in shallow water, and they will feed on the surface when mayflies are hatching.

SIZE: Lake whitefish reach weights of a bit more than 20 pounds, but their average size is less than 4 pounds.

FOOD: Lake whitefish feed primarily on small crustaceans and aquatic insects, but they will also eat baitfish.

FISHING METHODS: Casting (not an important game fish)

BAITS: Small baitfish, insects, and crustaceans

■ Cisco *(Coregonus artedii)*

COMMON NAMES: Cisco, herring, lake herring, common cisco, lake cisco, bluefin, Lake Erie cisco, tullibee, short-jaw chub, and grayback

DESCRIPTION: Though the cisco superficially resembles members of the herring family, it is not a herring but rather a member of the whitefish family. The cisco has a darker back (usually bluish or greenish) than the true whitefish. The body is silvery with large scales. There are more than 30 species and subspecies of ciscoes in the Great Lakes area alone, and all of them look and act alike. Ciscoes occasionally provide good sport fishing, particularly on dry flies, but they are more important commercially.

RANGE: The various strains of ciscoes occur from New England and New York west through the Great Lakes area and range widely through Canada. Their center of concentration seems to be the Great Lakes area.

HABITAT: Ciscoes prefer large, cold, clear lakes, usually those having considerable depth. Little is known of the wanderings of these fish; some species are found from the surface to several hundred feet down. They spawn in July and August over hard bottoms. In summer, ciscoes often come to the surface to feed on hatching insects, usually at sundown.

SIZE: The size of a cisco depends on its species. Some average only a few ounces in weight, while the largest attain a maximum weight of about 7 pounds. The average length is about 6 to 20 inches.

FOOD: Insect life—mainly bottom-dwelling types—is the blue-plate special of the cisco, though it sometimes feeds on surface insects and on minute crustaceans and worms as well.

FISHING METHODS: Fly fishing

BAITS: Insects, worms, and flies

■ American Shad *(Alosa sapidissima)*

DESCRIPTION: The American shad is an anadromous fish—meaning one that ascends coastal rivers to spawn but spends much of its life in salt water. A member of the herring family, the shad has a greenish back, with the remainder of the body being silvery. There are usually a few indistinct markings on the forebody. Shad

American Shad

put up a no-holds-barred battle on hook and line and are important sport and commercial fish, though pollution is putting a dent in their population in some areas.

RANGE: American shad were originally native only to the Atlantic, but they were introduced in the Pacific in the 1870s. On the Atlantic coast, they are found from Florida to the Gulf of St. Lawrence, while on the Pacific coast, they range from San Diego, California, to southern Alaska. They are also found in Scandinavia, France, Italy, Germany, Russia, and elsewhere.

HABITAT: American shad swarm up large, coastal rivers to spawn in the spring—from March to May, depending upon the location of the river. They are particularly susceptible to anglers below dams and in holes and slow runs just upstream of riffles, where they tend to rest before continuing upriver. They generally spawn in the main river.

SIZE: The average weight of an American shad is 3 to 5 pounds, while the maximum weight is 12 to 13 pounds. Egg-laden females are usually heavier than males.

FOOD: While in the ocean, American shad feed almost exclusively on plankton, so far as is known. After they enter fresh water on the spawning runs, these fish apparently do not feed at all. Curiously, however, they will strike at a small variety of artificial lures, including small, sparsely dressed wet flies and leadhead jigs tied on a gold hook and having a wisp of bucktail at the tail.

FISHING METHODS: Casting, jigs, and shad darts

BAITS: Artificial lures, small jigs, spinners, and spoons

■ Largemouth Bass
(*Micropterus salmoides*)

COMMON NAMES: Largemouth bass, bigmouth bass, black bass, green trout, Oswego bass, and green bass

DESCRIPTION: The largemouth bass is among the most important of this continent's freshwater game fish. In physical makeup it is a chunky fish, with coloration ranging from nearly black or dark green on the back, through varying shades of green or brownish green on the sides, to an off-white belly. The largemouth's most distinctive marking, however, is a horizontal, dark band running along its side from head to tail. In large, old bass particularly, the band may be almost invisible. There are two reliable ways to distinguish the largemouth from its close relative and look-alike, the smallmouth bass: the largemouth's upper jaw (maxillary) extends back behind the eye, while the smallmouth's does not; and the spiny part of the largemouth's dorsal fin is almost completely separated from the softer rear portion, while in the smallmouth the two fin sections are connected in one continuous fin.

RANGE: The largemouth is native to or stocked in every state in the Lower 48 and is found as far south as Mexico and as far north as southern Canada.

HABITAT: Largemouths are found in slow-moving streams large and small and in nonflowing waters ranging in size from little more than puddles to vast impoundments. They thrive best in shallow, weedy lakes and in river backwaters. They are warm-water fish, preferring water temperatures of 70°F to 75°F. Largemouths never venture too far from such areas as weed beds, logs, stumps, and other sunken debris, which provide both cover and food. They are usually found in water no deeper than 20 feet.

SIZE: Largemouth bass grow biggest in the southern United States, where they reach a maximum weight of a little more than 20 pounds and an 8- to 10-pounder is not a rarity. In the north, largemouths rarely exceed 10 pounds and a 3-pounder is considered a good catch.

FOOD: The largemouth's diet is as ubiquitous as the fish itself. These bass eat minnows and any other available

Largemouth Bass

baitfish, worms, crustaceans, a wide variety of insect life, frogs, mice, and ducklings.

FISHING METHODS: Casting and trolling

BAITS: All baitfish, worms, crustaceans, frogs, artificial lures, and flies

■ Smallmouth Bass
(Micropterus dolomieui)

COMMON NAMES: Smallmouth bass, black bass, and bronzeback

DESCRIPTION: A top game fish and a flashy fighter, the smallmouth bass is brownish, bronze, or greenish brown in coloration, with the back being darker and the belly being off-white. The sides are marked with dark, vertical bars, which may be indistinguishable in young fish. (For physical differences between the smallmouth bass and its look-alike relative, the largemouth bass, see Largemouth Bass.) The smallmouth is not as common as, and is a wilder fighter than, the largemouth.

RANGE: The smallmouth's original range was throughout New England, southern Canada, and the Great Lakes area, and in large rivers of Tennessee, Arkansas, and Oklahoma. However, stocking has greatly widened this range so that it now includes states in northern and moderate climates from coast to coast.

HABITAT: Unlike the largemouth bass, the smallmouth is a fish of cold, clear waters (preferring water temperatures no higher than 65°F or so). Large, deep lakes and sizable rivers are the smallmouth's domain, though it is often found in streams that look like good trout water—that is, those with numerous riffles flowing over gravel, boulders, or bedrock. In lakes, smallmouths are likely

Smallmouth Bass

to be found over gravel bars, between submerged weed beds in water 10 to 20 feet deep, along drop-offs near shale banks, on gravel points running out from shore, and near midlake reefs or shoals. In streams, they often hold at the head of a pool where the water fans out, and in pockets having moderate current and nearby cover.

SIZE: The maximum weight attained by smallmouth bass is about 12 pounds. In most waters, however, a 4- or 5-pounder is a very good fish, and the average weight is probably 1½ to 3 pounds.

FOOD: Smallmouths eat baitfish and crayfish mainly, though they also feed on hellgrammites and other insect life, worms, small frogs, and leeches.

FISHING METHODS: Casting and trolling

BAITS: All baitfish, worms, crustaceans, crayfish, frogs, artificial lures, and flies

■ Redeye Bass *(Micropterus coosae)*

COMMON NAMES: Redeye bass, Coosa bass, shoal bass, and Chipola bass

DESCRIPTION: Given full status as a distinct species around 1940, the redeye bass is a relative of the smallmouth. Though this fish is often difficult to positively identify, especially in adult form, the redeye young have dark, vertical bars that become indistinct with age and brick-red dorsal, anal, and caudal fins. This fin color and the red of its eyes are the redeye's most distinctive physical traits. The redeye is a good fighter and is good eating.

RANGE: An inhabitant of the southeastern states, the redeye bass is found mainly in Alabama, Georgia, and South Carolina. It is also found in the Chipola River system in Florida.

HABITAT: The redeye bass is mainly a stream fish, usually

Redeye Bass

inhabiting upland parts of drainage systems. It often feeds at the surface.

SIZE: The maximum weight of the redeye bass is 6 pounds, but, in Alabama at least, the average weight is about 12 ounces.

FOOD: A large portion of the redeye's diet is insects, but it also feeds on worms, crickets, and various baitfish.

FISHING METHODS: Casting and drift fishing

BAITS: Worms, crickets, small baitfish, spinners, spoons, and flies

Spotted Bass
(Micropterus punctulatus)

COMMON NAMES: Spotted bass, Kentucky bass, Kentucky spotted bass, and Alabama spotted bass

DESCRIPTION: The spotted bass, only recognized as a distinct species since 1927, is quite similar in appearance to the largemouth bass and has characteristics of both the largemouth and the smallmouth. The spotted bass is olive green on the back with many dark blotches, most of which are diamond shaped. A series of short blotches form a horizontal dark band along the sides that is somewhat more irregular than that of the largemouth. Spots below the lateral line distinguish the spotted bass from the largemouth, and that spotting, plus the lack of vertical side bars, distinguishes it from the smallmouth bass.

RANGE: The spotted bass is found in the Ohio-Mississippi drainage from Ohio south to the states bordering the Gulf of Mexico and western Florida, and west to Texas, Oklahoma, and Kansas.

HABITAT: In the northern part of its range, the spotted bass prefers large, deep pools in sluggish waters. Its preferred habitat in the southern part of its range is quite different, consisting of cool streams with gravel bottoms and clear spring-fed lakes. In lakes, spotted bass are sometimes found in water as deep as 100 feet.

SIZE: The maximum weight of spotted bass is 8 pounds, but few specimens top 4 or 5 pounds.

FOOD: Spotted bass, like most other members of the bass family, feed on various baitfish and insects, frogs, worms, crustaceans, grubs, and the like.

FISHING METHODS: Casting and drift fishing

BAITS: Baitfish, worms, frogs, artificial lures, and flies

Bluegill (Lepomis macrochirus)

COMMON NAMES: Bluegill, bluegill sunfish, bream, sun perch, blue perch, blue sunfish, copperbelly, red-breasted bream, copperhead bream, and blue bream

DESCRIPTION: Many fishermen cut their angling teeth on the bluegill, the most widely distributed and most popular of the large sunfish family. The color of the bluegill varies probably more than that of any other sunfish, ranging in basic body color from yellow or orange to dark blue. The shading goes from dark on the back to light on the forward part of the belly. The sides of a bluegill are usually marked by six to eight irregular, vertical bars of a dark color. A bluegill's prominent features are a broad, black gill flap, and long, pointed pectoral fins. Bluegills are excellent fighters, and if they grew to largemouth-bass size, they would break a lot of tackle.

RANGE: The bluegill's range just about blankets the entire 48 contiguous states.

Spotted Bass

Bluegill

HABITAT: The bluegill prefers habitat very much like that of the largemouth bass—that is, quiet, weedy waters, in both lakes and streams, where it can find both cover and food. In daytime, the smaller bluegills are usually close to shore in coves, under overhanging trees, and around docks. The larger ones are usually nearby but in deeper water, moving into the shallows early and late in the day.

SIZE: The maximum size of bluegills is about 4½ pounds in weight and 15 inches in length, but the average length is 4 to 8 inches.

FOOD: A bluegill's food consists chiefly of insect life and vegetation. Other items on the menu include worms, grubs, small baitfish, crustaceans, small frogs, grasshoppers, and the like.

FISHING METHODS: Casting, still-fishing, fly fishing

BAITS: Small baitfish, worms, insects, crickets, grasshoppers, and flies

Redear Sunfish
(Lepomis microlophus)

COMMON NAMES: Redear sunfish, redear, shellcracker, stumpknocker, yellow bream, and chinquapin

DESCRIPTION: A large and very popular sunfish in the South, the redear has a small mouth, large and pointed pectoral fins, and a black gill flap with a whitish border (the bluegill lacks the white gill-flap border). The body color is olive with darker olive spots, and the sides have five to 10 dusky vertical bars. The redear is distinguishable from the pumpkinseed—the member of the sunfish family it most closely resembles—by the lack of spots on the dorsal fin.

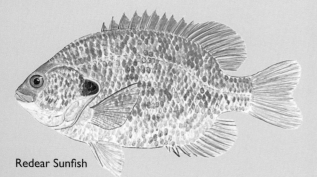

Redear Sunfish

RANGE: The redear sunfish ranges from southern Illinois and southern Indiana south to Florida and the other Gulf states and westward to Texas and New Mexico. Its heaviest concentration is in Florida.

HABITAT: The redear sunfish shows a definite liking for large, quiet waters, congregating around logs, stumps, and roots. It will, however, frequent open waters and seems to require less vegetation than other sunfish.

SIZE: The redear is more likely to run to a large size than most any other sunfish. The maximum weight seems to be 3 pounds, but 2-pounders are not uncommon.

FOOD: Redears depend mainly on snails for food, but will eat other mollusks, crustaceans, worms, and insects.

FISHING METHODS: Casting and still-fishing

BAITS: Small baitfish, worms, crickets, insects, artificial lures, and flies

White Crappie *(Pomoxis annularis)*

COMMON NAMES: White crappie, papermouth, bachelor perch, papermouth perch, strawberry bass, calico, calico bass, sago, and grass bass

DESCRIPTION: This popular freshwater panfish is a cousin to the true sunfish. In coloration, its back is olive green and its sides silvery olive with seven to nine dark vertical bands, while the sides of the very similar black crappie have irregular dark mottling. Another, more reliable way to tell the white crappie from the black is the number of spines in the dorsal fin: the white has six while the black has seven or eight. The white is more elongated in general shape, while the black, by comparison, has a high, rather arched back.

RANGE: The original range of the white crappie extended from Nebraska east to the Great Lakes, south through the Mississippi and Ohio River systems, and throughout most of the South as far north as North Carolina. Stocking has greatly extended that range, though the white crappie is still predominantly a southern species.

HABITAT: The white crappie can live under more turbid conditions than the black crappie—in fact, it prefers silty rivers and lakes to clear water and is common in southern impoundments and cypress bayous warm and weedy ponds, and slow streams. The ideal home for these schooling fish is a pile of sunken brush or a submerged treetop. In summer, crappies often seek such a spot in deep holes, moving into the shallows in the evening to feed.

SIZE: White crappies average 6 to 10 inches in length and less than a pound in weight. However, individuals of more than 5 pounds have been caught by sportfishermen, and 2- or 3-pounders are not rare.

FOOD: White crappies eat baitfish for the most part—gizzard shad is their blue-plate special in southern lakes—but also feed on worms, shrimp, plankton, snails, crayfish, and insects.

FISHING METHODS: Casting and still-fishing

BAITS: Small baitfish, worms, crayfish, insects, jigs, and flies

■ Black Crappie (*Pomoxis nigromaculatus*)

COMMON NAMES: Black crappie, calico bass, papermouth, and grass bass

DESCRIPTION: This near-identical twin of the white crappie is dark olive or black on the back. Its silvery sides and its dorsal, anal, and caudel fins contain dark and irregular blotches scattered in no special pattern. (For physical differences between the black and white crappie, see White Crappie.) Though it is a school fish like the white crappie, the black crappie does not seem to populate a lake or stream as thickly as the white.

RANGE: The black crappie, though predominantly a northern United States fish, is found from southern Manitoba to southern Quebec, and from Nebraska to the East Coast and south to Texas and Florida. However, stocking has widened this range to include such places as British Columbia and California.

HABITAT: The black crappie prefers rather cool, clear, weedy lakes and rivers, though it often shares the same waters as the white crappie. The black is a brush lover, tending to school up among submerged weed beds and the like. It occasionally feeds at the surface, particularly near nightfall.

SIZE: See White Crappie.

FOOD: See White Crappie.

FISHING METHODS: See White Crappie.

BAITS: See White Crappie.

■ White Bass (*Morone chrysops*)

COMMON NAMES: White bass, barfish, striped bass, and streak

DESCRIPTION: This freshwater member of the ocean-going sea-bass family has boomed in popularity among sportfishermen in recent years, thanks to its schooling habits, its eagerness to bite, tastiness of its flesh, and increase in its range. The white bass is a silvery fish tinged with yellow toward the belly. The sides have about 10 narrow, dark stripes, the body is moderately compressed, and the mouth is bass-like. The white bass may be distinguished from the look-alike yellow bass by its unbroken side stripes (those of the yellow bass are broken) and by its projecting lower jaw (the upper and lower jaws of the yellow are about even). The white bass is astonishingly prolific.

RANGE: White bass are found in the St. Lawrence River area and throughout the Mississippi and Missouri River systems, west into Texas, and in most of the other southern and southwestern states.

HABITAT: The white bass lives in large lakes and rivers, but it appears to prefer large lakes containing relatively clear water. The burgeoning number of large, deep reservoirs constructed recently in the South and Southwest are tailor-made for the white bass. These fish like large areas of deep water and need gravel or bottom rubble for

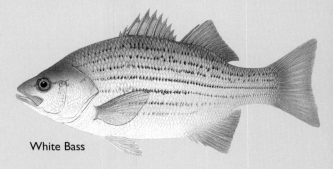

White Bass

spawning. Schools of whites can often be seen feeding voraciously on or near the surface, particularly in the evening.

SIZE: The maximum size of the white bass is about 6 pounds, but the average size is ½ to 2 pounds. A 3- or 4-pounder is an excellent specimen.

FOOD: Baitfish, particularly gizzard shad, form the main part of the white bass's diet, though it will also eat crustaceans, worms, and insect life.

FISHING METHODS: Casting and still-fishing

BAITS: Small baitfish, worms, insects, and artificial lures

■ Yellow Bass
(Morone mississippiensis)

COMMON NAMES: Yellow bass, barfish, brassy bass, stripe, striped bass, and streaker

DESCRIPTION: Quite similar in appearance to the white bass (for physical differences, see White Bass), the yellow bass has an olive-green back, silvery to golden-yellow sides with six or seven dark, horizontal, broken stripes, and a white belly. Like the white bass, the yellow bass is a member of the seabass family. It is a school fish, but its population levels tend to fluctuate drastically from year to year.

RANGE: The range of the yellow bass is quite restricted, being mainly the Mississippi River drainage from Minnesota to Louisiana and eastern Texas, plus the Tennessee River drainage, and Iowa. Even within its range, the yellow bass is found only in scattered lakes and streams.

HABITAT: One of the yellow bass's primary habitat requirements is wide, shallow, gravelly areas and rocky

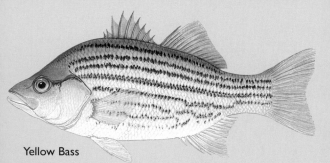

Yellow Bass

reefs. This fish prefers large lakes and large rivers, especially those with clear water. Yellow-bass schools tend to roam in deep water in daytime, coming into the shallows to feed late and very early.

SIZE: Most yellow bass caught by sportfishermen range from 8 to 11 inches, and from ¼ to ¾ pound. The maximum size is probably about 3 pounds.

FOOD: Yellow bass feed almost exclusively on baitfish, but occasionally take crustaceans and insects.

FISHING METHODS: Casting and still-fishing

BAITS: Small baitfish, worms, insects, jigs, and spinners

■ White Perch (Morone americanus)

COMMON NAMES: White perch, silver perch, and sea perch

DESCRIPTION: This fish is not a perch but rather a bass. And though it is often found in fresh water, it is not a freshwater bass. It is a member of the sea-bass family and superficially resembles one other member of that family—the saltwater striped bass—though it is much smaller. The white perch is greenish to blackish green on the back and silvery on the sides, particularly when living in salt water (freshwater individuals are usually darker). Young white perch have indistinct stripes on the sides, but adult fish lack them.

RANGE: In salt water, white perch range along the Atlantic coast from Nova Scotia to North Carolina. They are found inland as far as the Great Lakes and are especially abundant in New York State and New England.

HABITAT: In salt water, white perch are most likely to be found in brackish ponds and backwaters formed by coastal sandbars. Anadromous members of the clan run upriver to spawn. In inland lakes, these fish usually lie in deep water over a sand or gravel bottom during the day, sometimes at 50 feet or deeper, but often come into shoreside shallows in the evening and at night to feed. At those times, and on dark days, schools of white perch may be seen breaking the surface.

SIZE: White perch seem to run larger in salt and brackish water than in fresh water. The average size, generally,

White Perch

is 8 to 10 inches. As for the weight, 2-pounders are not rare, but white perch seldom exceed 4 pounds.

FOOD: In salt water, white perch forage on small fish, shrimp, squid, crabs, and the like. In fresh water, their diet includes larval and other insect forms, crustaceans, baitfish, and worms.

FISHING METHODS: Casting

BAITS: Small baitfish, crabs, shrimp, crustaceans, spoons, and spinners

■ Yellow Perch *(Perca flavescens)*

COMMON NAMES: Yellow perch, ringed perch, striped perch, coon perch, and jack perch

DESCRIPTION: The yellow perch, in no way related to the white perch, is an extremely popular freshwater panfish. Though its colors may vary, the back is generally olive, shading to golden yellow on the sides and white on the belly. Six to eight rather wide, dark, vertical bands run from the back to below the lateral line. Though the body is fairly elongated, the fish has a somewhat humpbacked appearance.

RANGE: The yellow perch is a ubiquitous species, being found in most areas of the United States. It is most com-

mon from southern Canada south through the Dakotas and Great Lakes states into Kansas and Missouri, and in the East from New England to the Carolinas. Stockings have also established it in such places as Montana and the Pacific slope.

HABITAT: The yellow perch is predominantly a fish of lakes large and small, though it is also found in rivers. It prefers cool, clean water with plenty of sandy or rocky-bottomed areas, though it does well in a wide variety of conditions. As a very general rule, the best perch lakes are large and have only moderate weed growth. These fish feed at various levels, and the fisherman must experiment until he finds them.

SIZE: The average yellow perch weighs a good deal less than a pound, though 2-pounders aren't uncommon. The maximum weight is about 4½ pounds.

FOOD: Yellow perch eat such tidbits as baitfish (including their own young), worms, large plankton, insects in various forms, crayfish, snails, and small frogs.

FISHING METHODS: Casting and trolling

BAITS: Small baitfish, worms, crayfish, insects, jigs, spinners, and flies

■ Walleye *(Stizostedion vitreum)*

COMMON NAMES: Walleye, walleyed pike, pike, jack, jackfish, pickerel, yellow pickerel, blue pickerel, dore, and pikeperch

DESCRIPTION: The walleye is not a pike or pickerel, as its nicknames might indicate, but rather the largest member of the perch family. Its most striking physical characteristic is its large, almost opaque eyes, which appear to be made of glass and which eerily reflect light. The walleye's colors range from dark olive or olive brown on the back to a lighter olive on the sides and white on the belly. Here's how to tell the walleye from its look-alike relative, the sauger: the lower fork of the walleye's tail has a milky-white tip, absent in the sauger; and the walleye's dorsal-fin foresection has irregular blotches or streaks, unlike the definite rows of spots found on the sauger's dorsal. The walleye isn't the best fighter among game fish, but it makes up for that shortcoming by providing delectable eating.

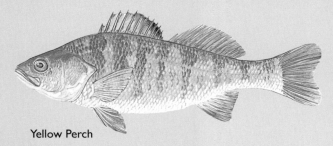

Yellow Perch

Walleye

RANGE: The walleye is found in most of Canada as far north as Great Slave Lake and Labrador. Its original U.S. range was pretty much limited to the northern states, but stocking has greatly widened this range to include all of the East and most of the Far West and southern states.

HABITAT: The walleye loves clear, deep, cold, and large waters, both lakes and rivers, and prefers a sand, gravel, or rock bottom. It is almost always found on or near the bottom, though during evening and night hours it may move into shallow water to feed. Once you find a walleye hole, you should catch fish there consistently, for walleyes are schooling fish and are unlikely to move their places of residence.

SIZE: The top weight of walleyes is about 25 pounds, but a 6- to 8-pounder is a brag fish. Most walleyes that end up on fishermen's stringers weigh 1 to 3 pounds.

FOOD: Walleyes feed primarily on small fish and crayfish. Strangely enough, though they don't often eat worms, night crawlers are a real walleye killer, especially when combined with a spinner.

FISHING METHODS: Casting and trolling

BAITS: Baitfish, worms, frogs, crayfish, spinners, and spoons

■ Sauger *(Stizostedion canadense)*

COMMON NAMES: Sauger, sand pike, gray pike, river pike, spotfin pike, and jack fish

DESCRIPTION: The sauger is very much like the walleye in all important respects, except that it is quite a bit smaller. It is olive or olive gray on its back and sides and has a white belly. Its large, glassy eyes are very much like those of the walleye. (For physical differences between the sauger and the walleye, see Walleye.)

Sauger

RANGE: The sauger's range is generally a blueprint of the walleye's. However, sauger are most common in the Great Lakes, other very large lakes in the northern United States and southern Canada, and in large rivers (and their tributaries), such as the Mississippi, Missouri, Ohio, and Tennessee.

HABITAT: In this category, too, the sauger is much like the walleye, though the sauger can tolerate siltier or murkier water than the walleye and tends to stick to deeper waters. A good place to look for sauger is in tailwaters below dams.

SIZE: The sauger's maximum weight is about 8 pounds. Its average size is 1 to 2 pounds.

FOOD: See Walleye.

FISHING METHODS: See Walleye.

BAITS: Baitfish, worms, frogs, crayfish, jigs, and spinners

■ White Sturgeon *(Acipenser transmontanus)*

DESCRIPTION: This huge, primitive throwback to geological history is one of 16 species of sturgeon in the world, seven of which occur in the United States. It is the largest fish found in this country's inland waters and the only member of the sturgeon family that is considered a game fish. The white sturgeon does not have scales but rather five rows of bony plates along its body. It has a large, underslung, sucking mouth, and its skeleton is cartilage rather than true bone. Sturgeon roe is better known as caviar. Though relatively few anglers fish for these behemoths, careful regulation of the fishery is necessary to prevent depletion of the populations of white sturgeon.

RANGE: The white sturgeon is found along the Pacific coast from Monterey, California, to Alaska. It is also

White Sturgeon

found inland in the largest of rivers, including the Columbia and Snake.

HABITAT: Some white sturgeon are entirely landlocked, but many spend much of their lives at sea and ascend large West Coast rivers to spawn. In large rivers, they lie on the bottom in deep holes.

SIZE: The largest white sturgeon reported taken pulled the scales down to 1,800 pounds. The average size is difficult to determine.

FOOD: In fresh water, the white sturgeon uses its vacuum-cleaner mouth to inhale crustaceans, mollusks, insect larvae, and all manner of other bottom-dwelling organisms. Bait used by sturgeon anglers includes night crawlers, lamprey eels, cut bait, and even dried river moss.

FISHING METHODS: This species is not typically sought by fishermen (check regulations).

BAITS: Worms, eels, and baitfish

■ Channel Catfish
(Ictalurus punctatus)

COMMON NAMES: Channel catfish and fiddler

DESCRIPTION: This sizable member of the large catfish family (which includes bullheads) is undoubtedly the

Channel Catfish

most streamlined, gamest, and most agile of the whole clan. In coloration, the channel cat is steely blue on top and shades to white on the belly, though young ones may be silvery even along the back. It is the only spotted catfish (it has dark speckles on the sides, though these spots may be missing in large specimens) with a deeply forked tail.

RANGE: The channel catfish occurs from the Saskatchewan River and entire Great Lakes area southward into Mexico. Stocking has transplanted this fish far west and east of its natural range.

HABITAT: Channel catfish are found in lakes, but they are more common in rivers, especially large ones. They are likely to be found in faster, cleaner water than other catfish and seem to prefer a bottom composition of sand, gravel, or rock. Like all other catfish, they are bottom-feeders and are especially active at night.

SIZE: Channel cats are among the larger members of the catfish family, attaining weights up to 60 pounds. The average size is 1 to 5 pounds.

FOOD: The channel cat's varied menu includes just about anything it can get its jaws around—small fish, insects, crustaceans, worms, grubs, frogs, and many other aquatic food forms.

FISHING METHODS: Still-fishing and drift fishing in rivers

BAITS: Small fish, insects, worms, frogs, crustaceans, and stink baits

■ Blue Catfish *(Ictalurus furcatus)*

DESCRIPTION: The blue is the largest member of the catfish clan. It has a deeply forked tail, but lacks the spots of the channel catfish. In color, the blue catfish is pale blue on the back, a lighter silvery blue on the sides, and white on the belly. The most reliable way to tell the blue from other catfish is by the number of rays on its straight-edged anal fin (there are 30 to 36 rays).

RANGE: The blue catfish is found mainly in the Mississippi River system, but it occurs south into Mexico and has been introduced into rivers on the Atlantic coast.

Blue Catfish

HABITAT: The blue is a catfish of large rivers and is likely to be found below the dams creating large impoundments, especially in the southern United States. It prefers less-turbid waters than most other catfish and seems to do best over bottoms of rock, gravel, or sand. It feeds in rapids or fast chutes.

SIZE: This heavyweight grows to more than 100 pounds. The average size, however, is 2 to 15 pounds.

FOOD: The blue catfish feeds primarily on small fish and crayfish. A favorite bait in some areas is a whole golden shad.

FISHING METHODS: Bottom fishing and drift fishing

BAITS: Baitfish, worms, crustaceans, and stink baits

■ Brown Bullhead *(Ictalurus nebulosus)*

COMMON NAMES: Brown bullhead, horned pout, and speckled bullhead

DESCRIPTION: Probably the most popular of the catfish—at least, it's the most often caught—the brown bullhead is a rather slender catfish with typical catfish features: sharp dorsal spine and sensitive barbels (the "feelers" projecting from the mouth area). The brown bullhead's chin barbels are dark brown or black. The tail has almost no fork, and the anal fin has 22 or 23 rays.

Brown Bullhead

The back is yellowish brown to light chocolate brown and has vague dark mottling, the sides are lighter, and the belly is yellow to milky white.

RANGE: Brown bullheads occur from Maine and the Great Lakes south to Mexico and Florida, but stocking has greatly expanded this range.

HABITAT: Brown bullheads prefer relatively deep, weedy waters in lakes and slow-moving streams. They may be found over sand and gravel bottoms and also over mud. They are almost exclusively bottom-feeders.

SIZE: The brown bullhead seldom weighs more than 3 pounds, with its average length being 6 to 16 inches.

FOOD: Insect larvae and mollusks constitute the majority of the brown bullhead's menu, but it will eat almost anything, from worms, small fish, and frogs to plant material and even chicken livers (a favorite catfisherman's bait).

FISHING METHODS: Still-fishing and drift fishing

BAITS: Baitfish, worms, frogs, and stink baits

■ Black Bullhead *(Ictalurus melas)*

COMMON NAMES: Black bullhead and horned pout

DESCRIPTION: Quite similar in appearance to the brown bullhead, the black bullhead is black to yellow green on the back, yellowish or whitish on the sides, and bright yellow, yellow, or milky on the belly. Its chin barbels are dark or spotted, and its pectoral spines have no serrations. The body is chunky.

RANGE: The areas in which the black bullhead is most numerous are New York, west to the Dakotas, and south to Texas. However, the fish has been introduced into most other areas of the United States.

HABITAT: The black bullhead is a fish of muddy, sluggish, turbid streams and lakes. It seems to do well, in fact, in any kind of environment except cool, clear, deep water. It is a bottom-feeder.

SIZE: The largest black bullhead taken by sport fishing weighed 8 pounds, but this catfish seldom weighs more than 2 pounds.

Black Bullhead

FOOD: See Brown Bullhead.

FISHING METHODS: Bottom fishing and drift fishing

BAITS: Small baitfish, worms, crustaceans, and stink baits

Carp *(Cyprinus carpio)*

COMMON NAMES: Carp and common carp

DESCRIPTION: This big, coarse, much-maligned rough fish belongs to the minnow family and is related to the goldfish. In color, the carp is olive to light brown on the back, golden yellow on the sides, and yellowish white on the belly. At the base of each of its large scales is a dark spot. On each side of the upper jaw are a pair of fleshy barbels, and the dorsal fin has a serrated spine. Though the carp is cussed out by most sportfishermen and often poisoned out of lakes and streams, it is taken by rod and line, bow and arrow, spear, ice gig, and set line, and it can put up a whale of a battle.

RANGE: Introduced into the United States in 1876, the carp has found its way into just about every area in the nation. It is also widely distributed throughout Europe and Asia.

HABITAT: The carp can live almost anywhere and under almost any conditions—except cold, clear waters. It is almost always found on the bottom, except during spawning, when schools of carp are often seen slashing around on the surface.

SIZE: Carp reach a maximum size of about 60 pounds, but the average weight is 8 to 15 pounds.

FOOD: Carp are mainly vegetarians, feeding on aquatic plant life and plankton, though they also eat insects and are often caught by anglers on doughballs, cornmeal, and such.

FISHING METHODS: Bottom fishing

BAITS: Mostly doughball mixtures

Alligator Gar *(Lepisosteus spatula)*

DESCRIPTION: Exceeded in size in fresh water only by the western sturgeons, the alligator gar is the largest of the ancient gar family. It can be distinguished from its relatives by an examination of the teeth. Young alligator gars have two rows of large teeth on each side of the upper jaw; other gars have only a single row. The alligator gar has a long, cylindrical body that is olive green or brownish green along the back and lighter below. The sides and rear fins have mottling or large, dark spots. Gars are of minor importance as sport fish, though they wage a wild, no-holds-barred battle when taken on rod and line.

RANGE: The alligator gar is found mainly in the Mississippi and Ohio River systems as far north as Louisville, Kentucky, and St. Louis, Missouri, and as far south as northeastern Mexico.

HABITAT: Alligator gars prefer sluggish rivers, lakes, and backwaters over muddy, weedy bottoms. They often congregate in loose schools, usually near the surface, where they roll around.

SIZE: The largest reported alligator gar was 10 feet long and weighed 302 pounds. The average size, however, is undetermined.

FOOD: Various kinds of fish, notably the freshwater drum (or gaspergou), are the principal food of alligator gars, though anglers catch them on wire nooses baited with minnows and on bunches of floss-like material that tangle tenaciously in the gar's teeth.

FISHING METHODS: Bottom fishing and drift fishing

BAITS: Baitfish (though most fishermen catch this fish with any material that will tangle in the gar's teeth)

Longnose Gar *(Lepisosteus osseus)*

DESCRIPTION: The longnose gar is the most common and most widely distributed of the entire gar family.

Its name derives from its long, slender beak (nose). Other distinguishing characteristics are its overlapping diamond-shaped scales and the unusual position of its dorsal fin—far back near the tail and almost directly above the anal fin. The coloration is similar to that of the alligator gar.

RANGE: The longnose gar occurs from Quebec's St. Lawrence drainage west to the Great Lakes (excluding Lake Superior) and as far as Montana, south along the Mississippi River system, and down into Mexico.

HABITAT: The longnose lives in much the same habitat as the alligator gar, though it is more likely to be found swimming and feeding in flowing water—that is, where there is a moderate current.

SIZE: Smaller by far than the alligator gar, the longnose reaches a length of 4 to 5 feet.

FOOD: The longnose, like the alligator gar, feeds mostly on other fish, though it also eats plankton and insect larvae when young.

FISHING METHODS: Drift fishing

BAITS: See Alligator Gar.

■ Muskellunge *(Esox masquinongy)*

COMMON NAMES: Muskellunge, maskinonge (and a variety of other spellings), muskie, pike, blue pike, great pike, jack, spotted muskellunge, barred muskellunge, and tiger muskellunge

DESCRIPTION: Moody, voracious, and predaceous, the muskellunge, the largest member of the pike family, presents one of the greatest challenges of any freshwater fish. Its adherents probably catch fewer fish per hour than do those who fish for any other freshwater species, and yet muskie fishermen are legion—and growing in number. The muskellunge—whose name means "ugly fish" in Ojibway Indian dialect—is green to brown to gray in overall color, depending upon its geographical location. Side markings are usually vertical bars, though the fish may be blotched or spotted or lack any distinctive markings. The muskie has no scales on the lower part of its cheek and gill covers; other members of the pike family have scales in those areas. There

Muskellunge

are three subspecies of the muskellunge: the Great Lakes muskie, the Ohio (or Chautauqua) muskie, and the tiger (or northern) muskie.

RANGE: The Great Lakes muskie is generally a fish of the Great Lakes basin area. The Ohio (Chautauqua) muskie occurs in New York's Chautauqua Lake and through the Ohio River drainage. The tiger (northern) muskie is common in Wisconsin, Minnesota, and western Michigan. In overall distribution, the muskellunge is found as far north as the James Bay and Hudson Bay drainages in northern Canada, across the northern United States, from Wisconsin east to New York and Pennsylvania, and south into Tennessee, North Carolina, Georgia, and in much of the northern Mississippi drainage. Stocking and propagation methods are greatly widening the muskie's range.

HABITAT: Muskies live in rivers, streams, and lakes, usually only in clear waters, though they may inhabit discolored water in the southern part of their range. They prefer cold waters, but they can tolerate water as warm as 70°F to 75°F. Favorite hangouts for adult muskies are shoreline weed beds, particularly near deep water, and such items of cover as logs, stumps, and rocks. They are usually found in water shallower than 15 feet, though midsummer may find them as deep as 50 feet.

SIZE: Muskies can reach weights of more than 100 pounds. However, the biggest rod-caught specimen weighed just shy of 70 pounds, and the average is 10 to 20 pounds.

FOOD: Muskies feed mainly on fish, including their own young, as well as suckers, yellow perch, bass, and panfish. They also eat crayfish, snakes, muskrats, worms, frogs, ducklings, squirrels, and just about anything else they can sink their ample teeth into.

FISHING METHODS: Casting and trolling

BAITS: Baitfish, small bass, panfish, worms, frogs, ducklings, big spoons, and plugs

Chain Pickerel

■ Northern Pike *(Esox lucius)*

COMMON NAMES: Northern pike, pike, northern, snake, great northern, jackfish, and jack

DESCRIPTION: This baleful-looking predator of the weed bed is of great importance as a sport fish. In color, it is dark green on the back, shading to lighter green on the sides and whitish on the belly. Its distinctive side markings are bean-shaped light spots, and it has dark-spotted fins. The entire cheek is scaled, but only the upper half of the gill cover contains scales. The dorsal fin, as in all members of its family, is far to the rear of the body, almost directly above the anal fin.

RANGE: The pike is found in northern waters all around the globe. In North America, it occurs from Alaska east to Labrador, and south from the Dakotas and the St. Lawrence River to Nebraska and Pennsylvania. Stockings have extended this range to such states as Montana, Colorado, North Carolina, and Maryland.

HABITAT: Over its entire range, the pike's preferred living conditions are shallow, weedy lakes (large and small); shallow areas of large, deep lakes; and rivers of moderate current. In summer, pike are normally found in about 4 feet of water near cover; in fall, they are found along steep, stormy shores.

SIZE: In the best Canadian pike lakes, rod-caught pike average 5 to 25 pounds, but in most waters, a 10- to 15-pounder is a very good pike. The maximum weight is a little more than 50 pounds.

FOOD: Pike are almost entirely fish eaters, but they are as voracious and predacious as the muskie and will eat anything that won't eat them first.

FISHING METHODS: Casting and trolling

BAITS: Baitfish, small bass, perch, panfish, worms, frogs, spoons, spinners, plugs, and flies

■ Chain Pickerel *(Esox niger)*

COMMON NAMES: Chain pickerel, jack, and chainsides

DESCRIPTION: This attractive pike-like fish with chain-like markings is the largest of the true pickerels. Its body color ranges from green to bronze, darker on the back and lighter on the belly. Its distinctive dark, chain-like side markings and larger size make the chain pickerel hard to confuse with the other, less common pickerel (mud or grass pickerel and barred or redfin pickerel).

RANGE: The chain pickerel originally was found only east and south of the Alleghenies, but its range now extends from Maine to the Great Lakes in the north and from Texas to Florida in the south.

HABITAT: The pickerel is almost invariably a fish of the weeds. It lurks in or around weed beds and lily pads, waiting to pounce on unsuspecting morsels. It is usually found in water no deeper than 10 feet, although in hot weather it may retreat to depths of as much as 25 feet.

SIZE: Chain pickerel attain a maximum weight of about 10 pounds, but one of 4 pounds is bragging size. The average weight is 1 to 2½ pounds.

FOOD: Chain pickerel eat fish for the most part, although they will also readily dine on frogs, worms, crayfish, mice, and insects.

FISHING METHODS: Casting and trolling

BAITS: Baitfish, worms, frogs, crayfish, spoons, spinners, plugs, and flies

■ Redhorse Sucker *(Maxostoma macrolepidotum)*

COMMON NAMES: Redhorse sucker, redhorse, northern redhorse, redfin, redfin sucker, and bigscale sucker

Northern Pike

Splake

DESCRIPTION: Many anglers look at the entire sucker clan—of which the redhorse is probably the best known and most widely fished for—as pests or worse. And yet countless suckers are caught on hooks, netted, trapped, and speared every year, particularly in the spring, when their flesh is firm and most palatable. The redhorse, like all other suckers, has a large-lipped, tubelike, sucking mouth on the underside of its snout. Its overall color is silver, with the back somewhat darker. The mouth has no teeth, and the fins lack spines.

RANGE: The redhorse is found east of the Rocky Mountains from the midsouth of the United States north to central and eastern Canada.

HABITAT: Unlike some of its relatives, the redhorse prefers clean, clear waters and is at home in large and medium-size rivers, even swift-flowing ones, and in lakes. These fish seem to prefer sandy shallows in lakes, and deep holes in streams. As spawning runs begin in the spring, the redhorse congregates at the mouths of streams.

SIZE: The redhorse sucker's maximum weight is about 12 pounds. Most of the redhorses taken by anglers weigh 2 to 4 pounds.

FOOD: This bottom-feeding species eats various small fish, worms, frogs, crayfish, various insects (both aquatic and terrestrial), and insect larvae.

FISHING METHODS: This species is not typically sought by fishermen.

BAITS: Small baitfish, worms, insects, and fish eggs

◼ Splake
(*Salvelinus namaycush* x *S. fontinalis*)

DESCRIPTION: The splake is a trout hybrid created by crossing lake trout with brook trout. The name is a combination of *speckled* (brook) trout and *lake* trout. The first important crossing of these two trout species was done in British Columbia in 1946, and some of the new strain was stocked in lakes in Banff National Park in Alberta. The body shape of the splake is midway between that of the brook trout and lake trout—heavier than the laker, slimmer than the brookie. Like the true lake trout, the splake's spots are yellow, but its belly develops the deep orange or red of the true brook trout (see Brook Trout

and Lake Trout). Splake mature and grow faster than lake trout. Unlike many other hybrids, the splake is capable of reproducing.

RANGE: The splake's range is quite spotty, including a number of lakes in western Canada, at least one of the Great Lakes, and a few lakes in the northern United States. Stockings are slowly increasing this range.

HABITAT: See Lake Trout.

SIZE: The world-record splake, caught in Georgian Bay, Ontario, Canada, was 20 pounds, 11 ounces.

FOOD: See Lake Trout.

FISHING METHODS: See Lake Trout.

BAITS: Baitfish, smelt, insects, crustaceans, spoons, spinners, and plugs

◼ Tiger Trout
(*Salmo trutta* x *Salvelinus fontinalis*)

DESCRIPTION: This hybrid is a cross between the female brown trout and the male brook trout. The tiger's most prominent physical characteristic is the well-defined vermiculations (wormlike markings) on its back and sides. Its lower fins have the white edges of the true brook trout. The tiger is an avid surface-feeder and is considerably more aggressive than either of its parent species. Under hatchery conditions, only 35 percent of the tiger's offspring develop. The tiger occasionally occurs under natural conditions, but it does not reproduce.

RANGE: The tiger, being a hybrid, has no natural range, but stockings have introduced it into a few streams in the United States. At least one state, New Jersey, has stocked this trout in its waters on an experimental basis.

HABITAT: The tiger's habitat is undetermined, but it is probably similar to that of the brook trout.

SIZE: The world-record tiger trout, caught in Lake Michigan, Wisconsin, was 20 pounds, 13 ounces.

FOOD: The tiger's food is undetermined, but it is probably similar to that of the brook trout.

FISHING METHODS: Casting and drift fishing

BAITS: Spoons, spinners, and flies

■ Rock Bass *(Ambloplites rupestris)*

COMMON NAMES: Rock bass, goggle eye, redeye, rock sunfish, black perch, and goggle-eye perch

DESCRIPTION: The rock bass isn't a bass—it's one of the sunfishes. And though it isn't much of a fighter, it is fun to catch and is sometimes unbelievably willing to gobble any lure, bait, or fly it can get its jaws around. The basic color of the rock bass is dark olive to greenish bronze, with a lighter belly. The sides contain brownish or yellowish blotches, and a dark spot at the base of each scale produces broken horizontal streaks. The mouth is much larger than that of most other sunfishes, and the anal fin has six spines, while the anal fin of most other sunfishes has only three spines. There is a dark blotch on the gill flap.

RANGE: The rock bass occurs from southern Manitoba east to New England, and south to the Gulf states. Stockings have somewhat widened this range in recent years.

HABITAT: Rock bass prefer large, clear streams and lakes and are often found in the same waters as smallmouth bass. As their name suggests, the more rocks and stones on the bottom of the stream or lake, the better a fisherman's chances of finding rock bass. The species seems to prefer pools or protected waters to fast current or open waters.

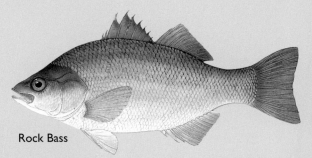

Rock Bass

SIZE: The top weight of the rock bass is a bit more than 2 pounds. Most of those caught by fishermen are 6 to 10 inches long and weigh about ½ pound.

FOOD: A voracious eater, the rock bass eats crawfish, minnows and other baitfish, worms, adult and larval insect life, and the like.

FISHING METHODS: Casting and drift fishing

BAITS: Small baitfish, worms, crayfish, spoons, spinners, and flies

■ Hickory Shad *(Alosa mediocris* or *Pomolobus mediocris)*

DESCRIPTION: The hickory shad—like its larger relative, the American shad—is a herring. In color, it is gray green above, with silvery sides and underparts. Behind the upper part of the gill cover is a horizontal row of dark spots, usually numbering about six. Spots on the upper rows of scales form faint horizontal lines. It has a shallow-notched upper jaw, and the lower jaw projects prominently. The hickory shad is not as important a food or sport fish as the American shad.

RANGE: The hickory shad is found along the Atlantic coast from the Bay of Fundy south to Florida.

HABITAT: An anadromous species (it lives in salt water but ascends freshwater rivers to spawn), the hickory shad's movements in the ocean are little known. But in the spring, it goes up the rivers—often the same rivers in which American shad spawn—though its runs usually precede those of the American shad.

SIZE: Though 5-pounders have been reported, the hickory shad seldom tops 2½ pounds in weight or 24 inches in length.

FOOD: The hickory shad feeds more on fish than does the American shad, and it is often caught by anglers using artificial flies and small spoons.

FISHING METHODS: Small jigs, shad darts, small spoons, spinners, and flies

BAITS: Artificial lures

■ Freshwater Drum
(*Aplodinotus grunniens*)

COMMON NAMES: Freshwater drum, sheepshead, gray bass, gaspergou, white perch, croaker, crocus, jewelhead, and grunter

DESCRIPTION: This species is the only freshwater member of the drum (croaker) family, which has about three dozen saltwater members. The freshwater drum has a blunt head, rounded tail, long dorsal fin, and a humped back. Colors are pearly gray on the back and upper sides, silver on the remainder of the sides, and milky white on the belly. A rather faint lateral line runs all the way into the tail. These fish make a weird "drumming" noise that, when they feed near the surface on calm evenings, seems to come from everywhere. It is caused by repeated contractions of an abdominal muscle against the swim bladder. Another oddity: the otoliths, or ear bones, of freshwater drum were used by Indians as wampum, as lucky pieces, and to prevent sicknesses.

RANGE: Freshwater drum are found from Guatemala north through eastern Mexico and the Gulf states to Manitoba, northern Ontario, Quebec, and the Lake Champlain area. East to west, they range from the Atlantic coast to the Missouri River drainage.

HABITAT: Found principally in large lakes and large, slow rivers, this species prefers modest depths (10 to 40 feet) and silty or muddy bottoms. It is a school fish, often congregating below large dams.

SIZE: Freshwater drum attain a maximum weight of about 60 pounds, but the average size is 1 to 5 pounds.

FOOD: Primarily a bottom-feeder, this species feeds almost entirely on mollusks—clams, mussels, and snails—which it "shells" with its large, strong teeth. Other foods include crawfish and some baitfish.

FISHING METHODS: Bottom fishing and drift fishing

BAITS: Clams, mussels, crawfish, snails, and baitfish

SALTWATER FISH

■ Bluefin Tuna (*Thunnus thynnus*)

COMMON NAMES: Bluefin tuna, bluefin, and horse mackerel

DESCRIPTION: The bluefin is the king of the tunas, all of which are members of the mackerel family. Bluefins—from those of school size (15 to 100 pounds) to giants of nearly half a ton—have incredible strength and tenacity, and they are highly sought by both commercial and sportfishermen. The bluefin has the blocky, robust body of a typical heavyweight. The head is rather small, and the snout is pointed. The bluefin has shorter pectoral fins than any of the American tunas. It has two dorsal fins—the forward one retractable and the rearward one fixed—and a sickle-shaped tail. In color, the bluefin is steel blue on its back and upper sides, shading to light gray or creamy white on its lower parts. In small bluefins, the lower sides have vertical white lines.

RANGE: Bluefin tuna are found throughout the world, mostly in temperate and subtropical waters. In the western Atlantic, they occur in abundance from the Bahamas north to the Labrador Current. In the Pacific, they seem to be less abundant, being found in greatest numbers in the general area of Catalina Island.

HABITAT: The bluefin is generally a fish of the open ocean, though school-size bluefins occasionally come quite close to shore. In summer, bluefins show up in large numbers from New Jersey to Nova Scotia, the smaller fish showing up first and closer to shore. Atlantic areas where bluefins tend to congregate and provide good fishing include the New York Bight, New Jersey, Block Island to Rhode Island, Cape Cod Bay, Wedgeport and St. Margaret's Bay in Nova Scotia, and Conception Bay in Newfoundland.

Bluefin Tuna

SIZE: For all practical fishing purposes, bluefins can be grouped into two size categories: school fish (those weighing 15 to 100 pounds) and adult fish (those weighing more than 100 pounds). The average schoolie weighs 30 to 50 pounds, while the giant bluefins attain maximum weights estimated to be 1,500 pounds or more. The rod-and-reel record is 1,496 pounds.

FOOD: Bluefin tuna feed on whatever is available, including a wide variety of fish (including herring, sand lance, hake, and even dolphin), as well as squid and crustaceans.

FISHING METHODS: Trolling, chumming, and chunking

BAITS: Whole fish, cut baits, rigged baitfish, and artificial lures

Yellowfin Tuna *(Thunnus albacares)*

COMMON NAMES: Yellowfin tuna and allison tuna

DESCRIPTION: Considerably smaller than the bluefin, the yellowfin tuna is a top sport and commercial fish, particularly in the Pacific. In color, the yellowfin is steel blue or nearly black on the back and upper sides, silvery white on the lower parts. Characteristics that distinguish it from the bluefin are its much longer pectoral fins and the generous amount of the color yellow in most of the fins. The yellowfin is difficult to distinguish from some of the other tunas, but in large specimens the second dorsal fin and anal fin are much longer than those of any other tuna. The side markings of the yellowfin include a sometimes indistinct golden-yellow horizontal streak and white spots and vertical stripes on the lower sides.

RANGE: Yellowfins are found worldwide in tropical and subtropical waters. They are most numerous in the Pacific, where they are found widely off the coast of southern California and Baja California. They also range from the Gulf of Mexico north to New Jersey.

HABITAT: Yellowfin tuna are more southerly in general range than bluefins. They are open-ocean fish, though there is some evidence that they do not make such long-range migrations as bluefins.

SIZE: Yellowfins are thought to reach a maximum size of some 500 pounds. However, the rod-and-reel record is 405 pounds, and the average size is less than 100 pounds.

FOOD: See Bluefin Tuna.

FISHING METHODS: See Bluefin Tuna.

BAITS: Whole fish, cut baits, rigged baitfish, squid, and artificial lures

Bigeye Tuna *(Thunnus obesus)*

COMMON NAMES: Bigeye tuna, Pacific bigeye tuna, and Atlantic bigeye tuna

DESCRIPTION: Its eyes are not abnormally large, so it's difficult to determine how the bigeye tuna got its name. Its coloration is similar to that of its big brother, the bluefin, though its pectoral fins are longer. It is often hard to distinguish the bigeye from some of the other tunas. Its dorsal and anal fins are never greatly elongated (as in the large yellowfins), and the finlets running along the back and belly from the dorsal and anal fins to the tail are yellow with black margins. Though Atlantic and Pacific bigeyes are the same species, the International Game Fish Association separates them for record-keeping purposes.

RANGE: Bigeye tuna range throughout the world in tropical and subtropical waters.

Yellowfin Tuna

Bigeye Tuna

Blackfin Tuna

HABITAT: Bigeyes are fish of the open oceans and deep water, as evidenced by the fact that many are caught by commercial longline fishermen.

SIZE: Bigeyes probably reach weights of 500 pounds and seem to grow somewhat bigger in the Pacific than in the Atlantic. The average size is about 100 pounds.

FOOD: See Bluefin Tuna.

FISHING METHODS: See Bluefin Tuna.

BAITS: Whole fish, cut baits, rigged baitfish, and artificial lures

◼ Blackfin Tuna *(Thunnus atlanticus)*

DESCRIPTION: Far more restricted in range than any of the other popular tunas, the blackfin is also one of the smallest members of the family. It is darker in color than the other tunas and has fewer gill rakers. The finlets behind the dorsal and anal fins are totally dark—not marked with yellow like most of the other tunas.

RANGE: Blackfin tuna are found only in the western Atlantic Ocean, ranging from Cape Cod south to Brazil.

HABITAT: Blackfins are open-ocean, deep-water fish, like almost all the other members of the tuna family.

SIZE: The blackfin's top weight is probably not much more than 40 pounds or so. Most average 10 to 15 pounds. The world-record, rod-caught blackfin—weighing 49 pounds, 6 ounces—is an exceptionally big tuna for this species.

FOOD: The blackfin's diet is about the same as that of the other tunas, except that its prey is smaller.

FISHING METHODS: Trolling, chumming, and jigging

BAITS: Cut baits, live pilchards, cigar minnows, rigged ballyhoo, and artificial lures

◼ Albacore *(Thunnus alalunga)*

COMMON NAMES: Albacore and longfin tuna

DESCRIPTION: The albacore is what you are likely to get when you buy a can of all-white-meat tuna. It is one of the tunas, and thus a member of the mackerel family. The albacore's most outstanding physical trait is its abnormally long pectoral (side) fins, which extend from behind the gills well past the second dorsal fin, ending about even with the third dorsal finlet. The coloring is an iridescent steel blue above, shading to silvery white on the belly. The fins are generally blue and bright yellow.

RANGE: Albacore are found in tropical, subtropical, and temperate waters in most parts of the world. In U.S. and adjacent waters, they are primarily a Pacific species, being plentiful from southern British Columbia to southern California and Baja. In the Atlantic, quite a few are caught off Florida, and they are occasionally found as far north as Massachusetts.

HABITAT: Albacore almost never come close to shore. They haunt deep, open waters and often feed near or on the surface. When on top, they can be seen smashing wildly into schools of frenzied baitfish.

SIZE: Albacore of up to 90 pounds have been taken in nets, and the record rod-caught fish was 88 pounds, 2 ounces. The average weight is 5 to 25 pounds.

FOOD: Albacore feed on a wide variety of fish, as well as squid and crustaceans.

FISHING METHODS: Trolling and chumming

BAITS: Whole or cut baits, squid, and artificial lures

Albacore

Oceanic Bonito

■ Oceanic Bonito *(Euthynnus pelamis or Katsuwonus pelamis)*

COMMON NAMES: Oceanic bonito, bonito, skipjack, skipjack tuna, oceanic skipjack, and striped tuna

DESCRIPTION: The oceanic bonito is the most important member of the bonito group (which also includes the common, or Atlantic, bonito and the striped bonito, among others) and is the only bonito classified as a game fish by the International Game Fish Association. The oceanic bonito is striking blue above and silvery below, with some shadings of yellow and red. It is unique in having four or more well-defined dark stripes running from the area of the pectoral fin to the tail along the lower part of the body.

RANGE: Oceanic bonito are found in tropical and subtropical waters throughout the world. In U.S. and adjacent waters, they are most common off the southern coasts.

HABITAT: All the bonitos are fish of offshore waters, though they come relatively close to shore if that is where their favorite food is. They are school fish and generally feed on or near the surface.

SIZE: The average weight of the oceanic bonito is probably 10 to 18 pounds. The maximum is about 40 pounds.

FOOD: All the bonitos feed on a wide variety of fish, plus squid and crustaceans.

FISHING METHODS: Trolling and chumming

BAITS: Cut baits, jigs, and artificial lures

■ Cobia *(Rachycentron canadum)*

COMMON NAMES: Cobia, crabeater, ling, coalfish, black salmon, lemonfish, black bonito, cabio, and cobio

DESCRIPTION: The cobia is something of a mystery. Little is known of its wanderings or life history, and the species has no close relatives. In color, the cobia is dark brown on the back and lighter brown on the sides and belly. A wide, black, lateral band extends from its snout to the base of its tail. Less distinct dark bands are found above and below the lateral. The first dorsal fin is actually a series of quite short, stiff, wide spines that look nothing at all like a standard dorsal.

RANGE: The cobia is found in many of the world's tropical and warm, temperate waters. It occurs in the western Atlantic from Massachusetts to Argentina, but its greatest abundance is from Chesapeake Bay southeast to Bermuda and in the Gulf of Mexico.

HABITAT: Young cobia are often caught in inlets and bays, but older fish seem to prefer shallower areas of the open sea. Cobias are almost invariably found around some kind of cover—over rocks, around pilings or bottom debris, and particularly under floating objects such as buoys, weeds, cruising rays, and flotsam.

SIZE: Cobia reach top weights of more than 100 pounds. The average size is 5 to 10 pounds in some areas, though in other areas, notably the Florida Keys and Gulf of Mexico waters, 25- to 50-pounders are not uncommon.

FOOD: Cobias feed largely on crabs, though they also eat shrimp and small fish of all kinds.

FISHING METHODS: Trolling and sight casting (typically found feeding under cruising rays)

BAITS: Live baits, especially grunts, cut baits, and jigs

■ Amberjack *(Seriola dumerili)*

COMMON NAMES: Amberjack, greater amberjack, and horse-eye bonito

DESCRIPTION: Amberjacks are related to pompanos and jacks, and more distantly to tunas and mackerels. The amberjack is a stocky, heavy-bodied fish with a deeply

Cobia

Amberjack

forked tail, the lobes of which are quite slender. Its body colors are bluish green or blue on the back, shading to silvery on the underparts. The fins have some yellow in them. A well-defined dark band runs upward from the snout to a point behind the eye. Mostly a solitary wanderer, the amberjack sometimes gathers in small groups in preferred feeding areas.

RANGE: Though occasionally found as far north as New England, the amberjack is primarily a fish of southern Atlantic waters from the Carolinas south to Florida and nearby islands. In the Pacific, it is abundant from southern Mexico southward.

HABITAT: Reefs are the favorite habitat of amberjacks, though these fish often cruise for food at moderate depths—approximately 20 to 40 feet.

SIZE: The average rod-caught amberjack probably weighs 12 to 20 pounds, though ambers of up to 50 pounds are far from rare. The maximum size is about 150 pounds.

FOOD: Amberjacks prey on many smaller fish, as well as on crabs, shrimp, and crustaceans.

FISHING METHODS: Bottom fishing

BAITS: Whole fish and cut baits

■ Jack Crevalle *(Caranx hippos)*

COMMON NAMES: Jack crevalle, jack, cavally, cavalla, common jack, horse crevalle, and toro

DESCRIPTION: Probably the best-known member of a very large family, the jack crevalle is considered a fine game fish by some anglers but a pest by others. The crevalle is short, husky, and slab sided. It is yellow green on the back and the upper sides, yellow and silvery on the lower areas. There is a dark mark on the rear edge of

the gill cover, and the breast is without scales except for a scaled patch just forward of the ventral fins.

RANGE: The jack crevalle is found from Uruguay to Nova Scotia in the western Atlantic, and from Peru to Baja California in the eastern Pacific. It is most numerous from Florida to Texas.

HABITAT: The crevalle seems to prefer shallow flats, though large, solitary specimens are often taken in deep offshore waters. It is a schooling species.

SIZE: Jack crevalles of more than 70 pounds have been caught, and 45-pounders are not uncommon in Florida waters. The average size is probably 2 to 8 pounds.

FOOD: Smaller fish are the main course of the jack crevalle, but shrimp and other invertebrates are also occasionally on the menu.

FISHING METHODS: Casting, live lining, chumming, and bottom fishing

BAITS: Live baits, cut baits, shrimp, and artificial lures

■ Bluefish *(Pomatomus saltatrix)*

COMMON NAMES: Bluefish, chopper, tailor, snapper, and jumbo

DESCRIPTION: Savage, cannibalistic, delicious, abundant, willing—all these adjectives fit the bluefish, the only member of the family *Pomatomidae*. In coloration, the bluefish is a rather dark blue on the back, shading through blue gray and gray silver to silvery on the belly. A fisherman getting his first look at a pack of blues attacking a horde of baitfish finds the sight hard to believe. The water boils white and then turns red and brown with the blood of the frenzied baitfish and the regurgitated stomach contents of the savage blues. Once

Jack Crevalle

Bluefish

hooked, the bluefish makes the angler fervently thankful that these fish don't reach the size of tuna, for blues are among the most powerful fighters in the sea.

RANGE: Blues are found in the western Atlantic from Massachusetts to Argentina, off the northwest coast of Africa, the Azores, Portugal, and Spain, and in the Mediterranean and Black Seas. They are also found in the eastern Indian Ocean, the Malay Peninsula, Australia, and New Zealand.

HABITAT: Though primarily a deep-water species, particularly the large ones, bluefish often come right into the surf and sometimes go quite a distance up brackish-water rivers. Blues are rather erratic wanderers, though their general migration routes are fairly constant. They usually travel in large schools. In winter, they are most numerous in Florida. As the waters warm, they head north to such bluefishing hotspots as the Carolinas, New Jersey, and New England. Tidal rips are top spots to look for blues.

SIZE: Bluefish average 2 to 5 pounds, though 15- to 20-pounders are not uncommon, and there was a 45-pounder taken off the coast of North Africa.

FOOD: Bluefish will eat anything they can handle—and some things they can't, as many fishermen who have been bitten by a just-boated blue will attest. Menhaden is a bluefish's blue-plate special, and other preferred foods are mullet, squid, and eels.

FISHING METHODS: Live lining, chumming, and trolling

BAITS: Cut baits, bunkers, mullet, eels, jigs, and spoons

■ Striped Bass *(Morone saxatilis)*

COMMON NAMES: Striped bass, striper, linesides, rock, rockfish, squidhound, and greenhead

DESCRIPTION: The striped bass is one of the most popular coastal game fish. It fights well, and it "eats well." It is not likely to be mistaken for any other game fish in its range, primarily because of its general shape, side stripes (there are seven or eight horizontal dark stripes on each side), and the separation between the front and rear dorsal fin. The coloration is dark green to almost black on the back, silver on the sides, and white on the underparts. The striper is anadromous, living in the sea but ascending rivers to spawn.

RANGE: On the Atlantic coast, the striped bass is found from the Gulf of St. Lawrence south to the St. Johns River in Florida and in the Gulf of Mexico from western Florida to Louisiana. Introduced on the Pacific coast in the 1880s, the striper is found there from the Columbia River south to Los Angeles, California. The center of the striper's range in the Atlantic is Massachusetts to South Carolina; in the Pacific, it is in the San Francisco Bay area. Efforts to establish the striped bass in fresh water have been successful in such spots as the Santee-Cooper impoundment in South Carolina, Kerr Reservoir in North Carolina, some stretches of the Colorado River, and elsewhere.

HABITAT: Striped bass are almost exclusively coastal fish, seldom ranging more than a few miles offshore. Among the striper's favorite haunts are tidal rips, reefs, rocky headlands, jetties, bays, inlets, channels, canals, and reedy flats in tidal marshes.

SIZE: Most striped bass caught by anglers probably fall between 3 and 15 pounds, but many fish of 40 to 60 pounds are caught each year, most of them by trollers in the Cape Cod to Delaware range. The rod-and-reel record is an 81-pound, 14-ounce fish caught in Long Island Sound, Connecticut, but there are reliable records of a 125-pounder having been caught off North Carolina in 1891.

FOOD: The striper is a voracious feeder that preys on a wide variety of fish and invertebrates. The list includes herring, mullet, menhaden, anchovies, flounder, shad,

Striped Bass

silver hake, eels, lobsters, crabs, shrimp, sea worms, squid, clams, and mussels.

FISHING METHODS: Casting, trolling, sight casting, and chumming

BAITS: Live and cut menhaden, eels, crabs, sandworms, bloodworms, and artificial lures

■ Snook *(Centropomus undecimalis)*

COMMON NAMES: Snook and robalo

DESCRIPTION: A fine fighter and excellent table fare, the snook is a much-sought prize of southern waters. In color, the snook is brown, green, or brownish gold on the dorsal surface (back), shading to greenish silver on the sides, and becoming lighter on the belly. Distinctive traits include a depressed upper jaw and a jutting lower jaw, a somewhat humped back, and, probably most distinctive of all, a prominent dark lateral line that usually extends to and into the tail. The snook strikes a fisherman's offering with a startling smash, but it is an unpredictable feeder.

RANGE: Snook are found throughout tropical waters on the Atlantic and Pacific coasts, though they have been known to stray as far north as Delaware. They are plentiful along the Florida coasts and along the Gulf Coast in the United States and Mexico.

HABITAT: Snook are shallow-water fish that frequent such spots as sandy shores, mangrove banks, tidal bayous, canals, flats, bays, bridges, and pilings, and sometimes go upstream into fresh water. In cold weather, they lie in deep holes.

SIZE: Snook probably average 2 to 5 pounds, but 10-pounders are not rare, and the top weight is more than 50 pounds.

Snook

Weakfish

FOOD: The voracious snook feeds on many varieties of fish, particularly mullet, but also eats crabs, shrimp, and crustaceans.

FISHING METHODS: Casting, live lining, and trolling

BAITS: Live shrimp, mullet, pinfish, crabs, artificial lures, and flies

■ Weakfish *(Cynoscion regalis)*

COMMON NAMES: Weakfish, common weakfish, gray weakfish, squeteague, yellowfin, and tiderunner

DESCRIPTION: The weakfish gets its name not from its fighting qualities, which are excellent, but rather from its quite delicate mouth, which is easily torn by a hook. This popular, streamlined game fish is olive, green, or green blue on the back and silver or white on the belly. The sides are quite colorful, having tinges of purple, lavender, blue, and green, with a golden sheen. The back and upper sides contain numerous spots of various dark colors. The lower edge of the tail is sometimes yellow, as are the ventral, pectoral, and anal fins. The weakfish is excellent table fare.

RANGE: The weakfish occurs along the Atlantic coast of the United States from Massachusetts south to the east coast of Florida. Populations of the fish center around the Chesapeake and Delaware Bays, New Jersey, and Long Island.

HABITAT: Basically a school fish (though large ones are often lone wolves), weakfish are a coastal species, being found in the surf and in inlets, bays, channels, and saltwater creeks. They prefer shallow areas with a sandy bottom. They feed mostly near the surface, but they may go deep if that is where the food is located.

SIZE: The average size of a weakfish seems to be declining. Today, most rod-caught fish are 1 to 4 pounds.

Black Drum

Those early fall "tiderunners" of past decades, fish of up to a dozen pounds, are seldom seen nowadays. The biggest rod-caught weakfish was 19½ pounds.

FOOD: Weakfish eat sea worms, shrimp, squid, sand lance, crabs, and such small fish as silversides, killies, and butterfish.

FISHING METHODS: Casting, chumming, and jigging

BAITS: Shrimp, spearing, mullet, clams, crabs, and killies

■ Spotted Weakfish
(*Cynoscion nebulosus*)

COMMON NAMES: Spotted weakfish, spotted sea trout, speckled trout, trout, and speck

DESCRIPTION: This species is a southern variety of the common weakfish (see Weakfish), which it resembles. As its name might suggest, its markings (many large, dark, round spots found on the sides and back and extending onto the dorsal fin and tail) are far more prominent than those of the common weakfish. In general, body coloration of the spotted weakfish is dark gray on the back and upper sides, shading to silver below. Like the common weakfish, the spotted variety has a projecting lower jaw and two large canine teeth at the tip of the upper jaw. It is a top food fish.

RANGE: The spotted weakfish occurs throughout the Gulf of Mexico, in Florida waters, and north to Virginia, though it is found as a stray as far north as New York. It is most abundant in the Gulf of Mexico and in Florida.

HABITAT: See Weakfish.

SIZE: The average size of a spotted weakfish is somewhat smaller than that of a common weakfish. Most rod-caught spotted weaks fall in the 1- to 3-pound range. The maximum size is about 15 pounds.

FOOD: In many areas, spotted weakfish feed almost exclusively on shrimp. They may also eat various smaller fish, particularly mullet, menhaden, and silversides, as well as crabs and sea worms.

FISHING METHODS: See Weakfish.

BAITS: Cut baits, shrimp, worms, clams, killies, and artificial lures

■ Black Drum *(Pogonias cromis)*

COMMON NAMES: Black drum, drum, and sea drum

DESCRIPTION: A member of the croaker family, the black drum is not as popular a game fish as the red drum. It is most easily distinguished from the red drum (channel bass) by the lack of a prominent dark spot near the base of the tail. The overall color of the black drum ranges from gray to almost silvery, usually with a coppery sheen. Young specimens usually have broad, vertical bands of a dark color. The body shape is short and deep, the back is arched, and the undersurface is somewhat flat. There are barbels on the chin.

RANGE: Black drums are an Atlantic species found from southern New England to Argentina, though they are rare north of New York. Centers of abundance include North Carolina, Florida, Louisiana, and Texas.

HABITAT: Usually found in schools, black drum prefer inshore sandy areas such as bays, lagoons, channels, and ocean surfs, and are also often found near wharves and bridges.

Spotted Weakfish

SIZE: The black drum is known to reach a maximum weight of nearly 150 pounds. However, the average size is 20 to 30 pounds.

FOOD: Black drum are bottom-feeders, preferring clams, mussels, crabs, shrimp, and other mollusks.

FISHING METHODS: Bottom fishing

BAITS: Clams, cut baits, and crabs

■ Spanish Mackerel
(*Scomberomorus maculatus*)

DESCRIPTION: This beautiful, streamlined fish—though of modest size as mackerels go—is a magnificent fighter, making sizzling runs and soaring leaps. Its body shape is rather compressed, and its colors range from iridescent steel blue or occasionally greenish on the dorsal surface to silvery blue below. The side markings are mustard or bronze spots, and are quite large. The dorsal fin is in two sections, and there are dorsal and anal finlets. Its side spots, lack of stripes, and absence of scales on the pectoral fins distinguish the Spanish mackerel from the king mackerel and the cero.

RANGE: Spanish mackerel occur from Cape Cod south to Brazil, but they are never numerous in the northern part of their range. They are most plentiful from the Carolinas into the Gulf of Mexico.

HABITAT: This warm-water species is usually found in open waters, cruising near the surface and slashing into schools of baitfish. They do, however, make occasional forays into the surf and into bays and channels in search of food sources.

SIZE: Spanish mackerel average 1½ to 4 pounds, but they can reach a maximum weight of about 20 pounds. A 10-pounder is a very good one.

FOOD: Spanish mackerel feed primarily on a wide variety of small baitfish and on shrimp. A favorite bait in some areas, particularly Florida waters, is a very small baitfish called a glass minnow.

FISHING METHODS: Casting, chumming, and jigging

BAITS: Live baits, cut baits, shrimp, and artificial lures

■ African Pompano (*Alectis crinitus*)

COMMON NAMES: African pompano, threadfish, Cuban jack, and flechudo

DESCRIPTION: The head profile in adult fish is slanted and almost vertical and the eyes are large. The body is flat with silver sides with an almost iridescent sheen. The forward rays of the dorsal and anal fins are long.

RANGE: The African pompano's range is from Brazil to Massachusetts. It is commonly caught in Florida waters.

HABITAT: Young African pompano like shallow reefs. As the young Africans mature and become adults, they seek deeper reefs and wrecks.

SIZE: Adults can grow to lengths of 3 feet, and weights of 30 to 35 pounds are common. They are tough fighters, especially on light tackle. The record fish in Florida weighed 50 pounds, 8 ounces.

FOOD: Not a true pompano, the African feeds on small baitfish and can be caught by chumming over reefs. Drifting or trolling a rigged bait is the most common technique.

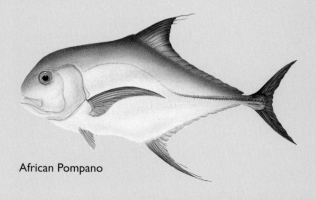

African Pompano

Spanish Mackerel

Pompano

FISHING METHODS: Bottom fishing, chumming, drifting, and trolling

BAITS: Whole fish, cut baits, live baits, and squid

■ Pompano (*Trachinotus carolinus*)

COMMON NAMES: Pompano, common pompano, and sunfish

DESCRIPTION: This high-strung, slab-sided character is the most abundant and most important member of the pompano family, which includes such fish as the much-prized permit. It has a small mouth, blunt head, and a relatively shallow body (its body depth decreases proportionally with growth). Dorsal-surface colors range from gray, silver, or blue to blue green, and the sides and underparts are silvery. The ventral surfaces are flecked with yellow. The dorsal fin is bluish, and most of the other fins are yellowish. The pompano is an epicurean's delight.

RANGE: The pompano is found from Brazil north to Massachusetts, and also in the West Indies and in Bermuda waters. It is particularly numerous in Florida and the Gulf of Mexico.

HABITAT: Pompano are inshore school fish, feeding on the bottom in shallow water in the surf, in channels and inlets and bays, and around bridges. They occasionally range well up into rivers with the tide.

SIZE: Pompano average about 2 pounds in weight, and the maximum size is thought to be about 8 pounds.

FOOD: Pompano feed mostly on bivalve mollusks and on small crustaceans, notably a small beetle-like crustacean called the sand flea.

FISHING METHODS: Bottom fishing, casting, and jigging

BAITS: Shrimp, sand bugs, cut fish, clams, jigs, and bucktails

■ Red Snapper (*Lutjanus blackfordi*)

DESCRIPTION: Most widely known for its eating qualities, the red snapper is among the best known of the more than 200 species of snappers found in the world's warm seas. The red snapper's color pattern (rose red overall, though paler red on the underparts, with red fins and eyes, and a black spot on each side), long pectoral fin, and more numerous anal-fin rays distinguish this species from other snappers.

RANGE: The red snapper occurs from the Middle Atlantic and Gulf Coast of the United States southward throughout the tropical American Atlantic.

HABITAT: The red snapper's preference for deep waters—it is sometimes found as deep as 100 fathoms and seems most prevalent at 20 to 60 fathoms—detracts from its importance as a sport fish. It usually is found a few feet above a hard bottom.

SIZE: Most red snappers caught commercially run from 5 to about 30 pounds. The maximum size seems to be about 35 pounds.

FOOD: Red snappers eat baitfish and various deep-water mollusks and crustaceans.

FISHING METHODS: Bottom fishing, drifting, and chumming

BAITS: Squid, cut baits, crabs, and live baits

Red Snapper

MEDICAL CARE

After sustenance, the second basic need is medical care. One need not be a doctor to be prepared to meet basic medical and health needs. While there are good outdoor first-aid kits available, make sure to take your circumstances into account and supplement any kit with items you will need. This means taking sufficient quantities of any prescribed medicines, bringing extra contact lenses or pairs of glasses, and taking additional supplies (bug spray, antivenin, seasickness medication, etc.) that are appropriate for the environment. (For medical treatment of any field emergencies and a detailed list of what a first-aid kit should contain, see next chapter on first aid.)

FIRE

It is often said that the presence of a fire means the survivor is going to make it. Although not an absolute truth, it certainly is the case that nothing can warm the soul, calm fear, and bring hope to a survivor more than a warm fire. In addition, fire is a resource that helps the survivor meet other needs—from purifying water to sterilizing bandages to day and night signaling. Fire is a versatile and often essential survival resource. Cold weather, wind, and moisture are three enemies of the survivor. A good fire can help fight and prevail against them all. Unfortunately, most survival kits offer only mediocre fire-making implements, and firecraft seldom is given the attention it deserves in survival guides.

It takes skill to build a warming fire in the pouring rain, and for a small investment of time, learning this skill can help save your life. First, use good judgment when selecting fire-making implements for a survival kit, and think about how the tools you are selecting might fail under various conditions. For example, most lighters work poorly in extremely cold temperatures, can blow out in the wind, and last only as long as the butane fuel source. Most waterproof matches are waterproof

Fibrous fire sticks, broken in half and inserted under loosely stacked wood, will start a campfire even if wet. You can also burn a single stick in a can for light and warmth. The magnesium fire starter is a good backup if your matches are damp or wet.

Fire Starters

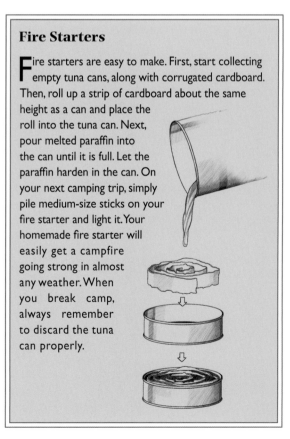

Fire starters are easy to make. First, start collecting empty tuna cans, along with corrugated cardboard. Then, roll up a strip of cardboard about the same height as a can and place the roll into the tuna can. Next, pour melted paraffin into the can until it is full. Let the paraffin harden in the can. On your next camping trip, simply pile medium-size sticks on your fire starter and light it. Your homemade fire starter will easily get a campfire going strong in almost any weather. When you break camp, always remember to discard the tuna can properly.

Building a campfire for warmth or cooking in bad weather will be a lot easier with a good supply of waterproof matches in a watertight case. This match case has added features of a compass, whistle, and fire-starter flint on the case.

only at the striking head and will stay lit for only four to five seconds.

In the hands of someone who has practiced with it, there is no better all-purpose fire-starting device than a large piece of flint and something to scrape it. Flints work effectively in the wind or rain and last a long time. Major outdoor retailers, such as REI, are excellent sources for flint-based fire-starter tools, as well as other survival gear.

Commercial fire starters or fuels, likewise, should be chosen with care to ensure that they will work in wet weather. For those wanting to save a few pennies, a good homemade tinder is a 100 percent cotton ball saturated with Vaseline. About 10 to 20 of these can be crammed into a waterproof match case or small plastic canister.

Good cutting tools can help immeasurably when you are preparing to make a fire. First, it makes sense to carry both a fixed-blade and a folding knife. A large, fixed-blade knife is great for cutting into the heart of dry wood. A smaller folding, locking-blade knife is good for preparing shavings and fire-starting materials. You should also always carry a good lightweight saw. Nothing works like a saw for quickly collecting dead, dry standing materials for fuel. The Ultimate Survival Saber-Cut pocket chain saw is flexible and comes packed in a floating case. Good fixed-blade saws include the Sven Saw and the Sawvivor.

SHELTER AND PERSONAL PROTECTION

Shelter starts at the human body and works its way to protection overhead. Insect repellent falls within this category because protection from the elements means all of them: insects, wind, sun, heat, rain, snow, snakebite, cold, and others. Clothing should be worn for the weather, workload, and activity, taking into account possible extremes and worst-case scenarios. Would these clothes be sufficient to spend the night in if you couldn't get back to camp or your vehicle? This is the question you should be asking yourself as you prepare to set out.

Personal survival protection items like space blankets, emergency tube shelters, and others lead far too many people down the road to false security. Most space blankets come with the statement that they reflect up to 90 percent of your body heat back to you. This might be true when used in perfect conditions, but these blankets can tear in the wind and are open at the end. The best of the lightweight shelters are the Mylar (or equivalent) film sleeping bags. This is because you can get inside of them and trap the heat while minimizing the loss of heat through convection. Heat transfer from the body in cold weather is done by evaporation, radiation, convection, conduction, and respiration. Up to 50 percent of all body heat can be lost through the head alone. The better reflective-type blankets are reinforced with polyethylene or polypropylene materials. These resist tearing and damage. Survival bags (oversize and double-strength garbage bags that go from head to toe) are widely available. This item in the survival kit makes an excellent emergency shelter to climb into, especially when used in conjunction with a Mylar space blanket sleeping bag. It is important to recognize, however, that these emergency shelters are not self-regulating and that they can become exceptionally hot and wet inside when moisture is not allowed to escape.

Sheltering not only affects the body directly, but it is important in meeting other survival needs as well. It is very difficult to build a fire in the pouring rain if you cannot keep the material you are preparing dry, including your hands.

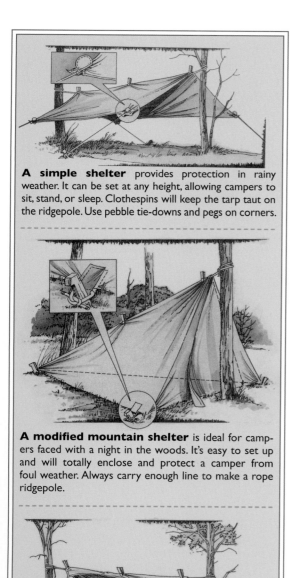

A simple shelter provides protection in rainy weather. It can be set at any height, allowing campers to sit, stand, or sleep. Clothespins will keep the tarp taut on the ridgepole. Use pebble tie-downs and pegs on corners.

A modified mountain shelter is ideal for campers faced with a night in the woods. It's easy to set up and will totally enclose and protect a camper from foul weather. Always carry enough line to make a rope ridgepole.

A lean-to is a quick and easy shelter for warm weather. If it gets chilly, a lean-to will reflect the warmth from a campfire built in front of it.

■ Emergency Tarp Shelters

Only your imagination limits the use of tarps. They can protect you from foul weather, keep your sleeping bag dry on wet ground, make an emergency stretcher, and a lot more. Tarps are most useful, however, when made into shelters or makeshift tents. The most practical tarp size is 12 by 8 feet. When setting up any of the shelters shown here, you will have to make strong tie-down points without puncturing the tarp. Place a small rock or pebble an inch or so from the edge, bunch the plastic tarp around it, and tie your line around the neck. You can also use duct tape. Make small loops of line, pass the duct tape through the loop, and tape it to both sides of the tarp.

RESCUE

The survivor can dramatically improve his chances of being rescued if he knows, and can use, some basic signaling skills. Being seen or heard is the key. No person should ever venture off into the woods, go anywhere in their car, boat, or plane, or engage in any other outdoor activity without a signal mirror and a whistle. You can't out-scream the best whistles, and even if you could, you could not sustain the effort.

The signal mirror is second only to the radio or telephone for communicating your need for help. Unfortunately, outside of the military, which uses signal mirrors religiously (including them in every survival kit), the general public has only limited knowledge of the value of a signal mirror. A targetable signal mirror—such as the official Air Force Star Flash, which enables the survivor to aim the signal flash—is the key.

Other widely available signaling devices include flashlights, strobe lights, and chemical lights. High-intensity, 12-hour chemical lights are a better choice in most instances than a flashlight, because they are lighter in weight and do not require batteries. A small string tied to the end of a chemical light and spun in a circle over your head makes an excellent night signal that can be seen from a great distance. Moreover, when considering items to place in your home disaster kit, take into account that the spark from the switch of a flashlight can trigger an explosion in a gas-filled room, while a chemical light poses no such danger. With signaling and rescue devices, the key is to be seen. Bigger, louder,

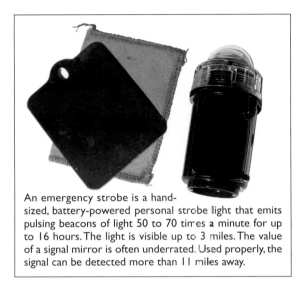

An emergency strobe is a hand-sized, battery-powered personal strobe light that emits pulsing beacons of light 50 to 70 times a minute for up to 16 hours. The light is visible up to 3 miles. The value of a signal mirror is often underrated. Used properly, the signal can be detected more than 11 miles away.

and more is better. A recognized international symbol of distress is a series of three signals. Three blasts of your whistle, three long honks of your car horn, three small fires (smoke or flame), or three shots from your rifle or shotgun are examples.

■ You're Lost . . . Now What?

You're lost in the woods! It can happen to anyone. I have a good friend who was suddenly stunned when he realized he was going to have to spend his first night in the woods alone. Darkness caught up with him while he was tracking a buck and he lost his way in the dark. It can happen easily when you're concentrating on tracks on the ground and not keeping your eyes on your surroundings. Fortunately, my friend didn't panic and his rain gear saved him from a wet, cold night in the woods.

Panic is your worst enemy when you realize you're lost. As scary as it might sound, your first night in the woods alone does not have to be a horrid experience. I have a very important rule when I'm camping or hiking and I never break it under any circumstances. When I leave camp, I always carry enough gear to keep warm and survive 72 hours, which is the longest most hikers stay lost or stranded. With most search-and-rescue techniques, lost hikers usually do not have to spend more than one night in the woods. First, remember the rule of threes: you can live three weeks without food, three days without water, three hours without protection in bad weather, and three minutes without air.

Never go hiking alone during winter, especially if you're out of shape. It's also important to tell your family or a friend where you are going and when you expect to return. If you are alone and become disabled or lost, this may be your only salvation.

Your survival kit should fit in a small daypack and you should focus on shelter, warmth, and food. A fully charged cell phone and a handheld GPS should be your first line of defense, but never count on batteries or phone towers to get you out of trouble. This means your pack should include rain gear, waterproof matches, space blanket, high-energy food, water, knife, map and compass, whistle, flashlight, and spare socks and gloves.

The purpose of the daypack is twofold: survival and peace of mind. Over the years, I've made some adjustments to my pack. For example, I carry two space blankets. They are no bigger than a deck of cards and one can make an emergency roof. I fill a plastic food bag with peanuts and raisins. It's a trail mix that will give you an energy jolt. I've added a box of juice, the kind you puncture with a straw. I also carry spare batteries and a bulb for my flashlight, a half-dozen Band-Aids for minor cuts and blisters, toilet tissue, and, if I'm hunting, enough spare ammunition to fire signal shots.

Nothing can warm the soul, calm fear, and bring hope to a survivor than a warm fire. Build a big and bright fire. In snow, you will have to start a fire on rocks or logs. A fire will do more than just keep you warm. It will give you light, dry clothes, a signal, hot food, and water from melted snow. Your pack should include a good supply of wood strike-anywhere matches or waterproof matches.

If you can't find waterproof matches, you can do the job yourself by dipping the whole batch in melted paraffin. I also carry a small candle for starting a fire. It burns a lot longer than any match. Carry several fire starters. Any kind will do, but I like the jelly in a tube. It's easy to use and a line of it on a log will set it ablaze. I urge any sportsman to practice starting a fire, especially in bad weather. Don't wait until your life depends on it. When you can get a warm fire going in the rain, you will feel more confident in an emergency.

I always feel more comfortable staying in the woods later in the day knowing that if I get "turned around" I can spend a night in the woods without fear or panic. You can customize your daypack to make yourself comfortable, but the basic gear listed here can get you through a night in the woods. You can build a shelter, start a campfire, snuggle up in a blanket, and have something to eat and drink. Who knows? You might even enjoy the new experience!

How to Signal for Help

Most fishermen, hikers, and campers never really get hopelessly lost, but if you ever find yourself in that unfortunate situation, you'd better learn how to use signals to help your rescuers locate you more quickly. This means sight and sound signals.

If you're a hunter, the standard three-shot signal is effective, but don't waste your ammunition during daylight hours when shots are commonplace. Wait until dark, when your friends may be searching for you and your three-shot signal will be more likely to attract attention . . . even if it's from a game warden. You should also be carrying a loud, piercing dog whistle. The sound will carry farther and last longer than your voice.

Build big fires! Your fire and smoke will signal help as well as keep you warm. Remember that the international distress signal is three fires about 50 feet apart in the shape of a triangle. Keep the fires smoky during the day and burning brightly at night. The most effective signal is black smoke because it can't be mistaken for a campfire. You can get black smoke by burning rubber or some synthetics. In an emergency, you can burn your gun's recoil pad, your rubber boot heels, or, if you have one, strips from an air mattress. If you can't make black smoke, you will have to settle for dense white smoke by piling leaves, grass, or moss on the fire.

If you're in an open area, learn the ground-to-air signals set by the International Civil Aviation Organization (ICAO). These signals are understood worldwide and every sportsman should know them. You can also tramp out SOS in snow, sand, or dirt. Another good daytime distress device is a signal mirror. There's no excuse for not carrying a 2-by-3-inch mirror in your shirt pocket. Search-and-rescue pilots claim they have spotted mirror flashes as far away as 25 miles.

The whole business of signaling simply means that you should do all in your power to let people know you're in trouble and exactly where you are. Remember to remove all distress signals as soon as you are located and rescued.

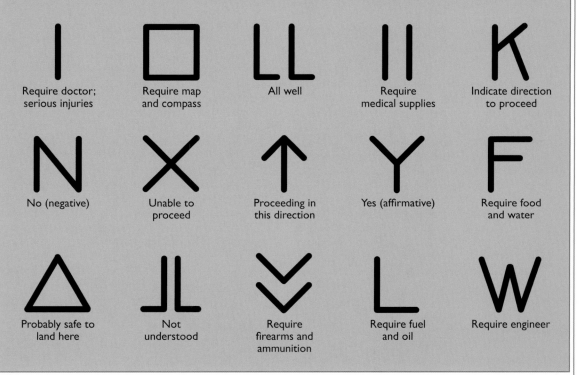

I	□	LL	II	K
Require doctor; serious injuries	Require map and compass	All well	Require medical supplies	Indicate direction to proceed
N	X	↑	Y	F
No (negative)	Unable to proceed	Proceeding in this direction	Yes (affirmative)	Require food and water
△	⊥⊥	⌄⌄	L	W
Probably safe to land here	Not understood	Require firearms and ammunition	Require fuel and oil	Require engineer

SURVIVING THE COLD

There is no way to beat the cold, but you can learn how to survive in it. High-tech manufacturing now offers clothing that is insulated, waterproof, and windproof, but even with all of these advantages, there will always be someone who will get into trouble. Hypothermia is the cold-weather killer, and it is caused by exposure to wind, rain, snow, or wet clothing. (For treatment of hypothermia, see next chapter on first aid.) Allow your body's core temperature to drop below the normal 98.6°F, and you will start to shiver and stamp your feet to keep warm. If these early signs are ignored, the next symptoms will be slurred speech, memory lapses, fumbling hands, and drowsiness. If not treated quickly, hypothermia can kill its victim when body temperature drops below 78°F, and this can happen within 90 minutes after shivering begins.

If you detect these symptoms in yourself or a friend, start treatment immediately. Get to shelter and warmth as soon as possible. If no shelter is available, build a fire. Get out of wet clothing and apply heat to the head, neck, chest, and groin. Use body heat from another person. Give the victim warm liquids, chocolate, or any food with a high sugar content. Never give a victim alcohol. It will impair judgment, dilate blood

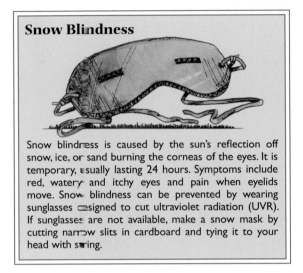

Snow Blindness

Snow blindness is caused by the sun's reflection off snow, ice, or sand burning the corneas of the eyes. It is temporary, usually lasting 24 hours. Symptoms include red, watery and itchy eyes and pain when eyelids move. Snow blindness can be prevented by wearing sunglasses designed to cut ultraviolet radiation (UVR). If sunglasses are not available, make a snow mask by cutting narrow slits in cardboard and tying it to your head with string.

vessels, and prevent shivering, which is the body's way of producing needed heat.

You can also survive the cold by staying in shape and getting a good night's sleep before going outdoors. Carry candy, mixed nuts, raisins, and any other high-

Cooling Power of Wind Expressed as Equivalent Chill Temperature

Wind Speed		Temperature (°F)																			
Calm	Calm	40	35	30	25	20	15	10	5	0	-5	-10	-15	-20	-25	-30	-35	-40	-45	-50	-55	-60
Knots	MPH	Equivalent Chill Temperature (°F)																			
3–6	5	35	30	25	20	15	10	5	0	-5	-10	-15	-20	-25	-30	-35	-40	-45	-50	-55	-65	-70
7–10	10	30	20	15	10	5	0	-10	-15	-20	-25	-35	-40	-45	-50	-60	-65	-70	-75	-80	-90	-95
11–15	15	25	15	10	0	-5	-10	-20	-25	-30	-40	-45	-50	-60	-65	-70	-80	-85	-90	-100	-105	-110
16–19	20	20	10	5	0	-10	-15	-25	-30	-35	-45	-50	-60	-65	-75	-80	-85	-95	-100	-110	-115	-120
20–23	25	15	10	0	-5	-15	-20	-30	-35	-45	-50	-60	-65	-75	-80	-90	-95	-105	-110	-120	-125	-135
24–28	30	10	5	0	-10	-20	-25	-30	-40	-50	-55	-65	-70	-80	-85	-95	-100	-110	-115	-125	-130	-140
29–32	35	10	5	-5	-10	-20	-30	-35	-40	-50	-60	-65	-75	-80	-90	-100	-105	-115	-120	-130	-135	-145
33–36	40	10	0	-5	-15	-20	-30	-35	-45	-55	-60	-70	-75	-85	-95	-100	-110	-115	-125	-130	-140	-150
		Little Danger				Increasing Danger (flesh may freeze within one minute)				Great Danger (flesh may freeze within 30 seconds)											
		Danger of Freezing Exposed Flesh for Properly Clothed Persons																			

Note: Winds above 40 miles per hour have few additional effects.

Shelters

▼ **If you're stuck in a snowstorm with huge drifts,** you can build a snow cave. Snow is effective insulation and will keep you warm in subzero temperatures. Make sure your snow cave is air-vented.

◄ **If you have a knife or small ax,** make the familiar lean-to. The big advantage is that you can build a fire in front of it. Pine boughs will break the wind.

► **A tree pit is the easiest snow shelter to build.** Find a tree and dig a hole in the snow next to it, then cover yourself with a piece of plastic or your space blanket draped over a small limb.

energy food. Stay as dry as possible and avoid overheating. Most important, dress properly. This means several layers of clothing and rain gear. And wear a wool hat with ear protection. An uncovered head can lose up to 50 percent of the body's heat.

■ Surviving a Snowstorm

If you're a winter sportsman, you should know how to survive a snowstorm. First, always travel with a daypack stocked with survival gear, such as a cell phone, handheld GPS, knife, compass, map, waterproof matches, whistle, space blanket, water, high-energy food, flashlight, spare socks, and gloves.

During the winter, never hunt alone. It's also important to tell a friend where you are hunting and when you expect to return.

If travel in a snowstorm is hazardous, find shelter and don't venture far from a trail. Next, build a fire. It will give you light, warmth, dry clothing, a signal, hot food, and even drinking water from melted snow.

If you're driving off-road, don't leave your vehicle. It will provide shelter. To keep warm, use seat covers and

carpeting. The stuffing from car seats makes good tinder for a fire. Unhook the carburetor hose and you will be able to drain enough gasoline to start a fire.

Snow Caves

Snow can provide excellent insulation against freezing temperatures. If you plan to build a fire inside your snow cave, however, it is critical that your snow shelter has an open-air vent. Unless your shelter is properly vented, an open flame will give off carbon monoxide. Carbon monoxide is a deadly toxic gas that is colorless, tasteless, and odorless.

You must also make sure that your fire doesn't start to melt your snow shelter. The floor of your snow cave should be at least 18 to 20 inches lower than the surface, where the temperatures will be warmer. Generally, unless you can see your breath, your snow cave may be too warm and may begin to melt.

SURVIVING THE HEAT

To survive in a hot area, you must know about and be prepared for the environmental conditions you will face. You must determine the equipment you will need, the tactics you will use, and how the environment will impact them and you.

■ Low Rainfall

Low rainfall is the most obvious environmental factor in a hot, arid area. Some desert areas receive less than 4 inches of rain annually, and this comes in brief torrents that quickly run off the ground surface. With the high desert-air temperatures, you cannot survive long without water. So, in a desert survival situation, you must first consider these questions: "How much water do I have?" and "Where are other sources of water?"

A key factor in arid-area survival is understanding the relationship between physical activity, air temperature, and water consumption. The body requires a certain amount of water for a certain level of activity at a certain temperature. For example, a man performing hard work in the sun at 110°F requires 5 gallons of water a day. Lack of the required amount of water causes a rapid decline in a person's ability to make decisions and to perform tasks efficiently.

Your body's normal temperature is 98.6°F. Your body gets rid of excess heat by sweating. The warmer your body becomes, whether caused by work, exercise, or air temperature, the more you sweat. The more you sweat, the more moisture you lose. Sweating is the principle cause of water loss. If a man stops sweating during periods of high air temperature and heavy work or exercise, he will have a heat stroke. This is an emergency that requires immediate medical attention.

Understanding how the air temperature and your physical activity affect your water requirements allows you to take measures to get the most from your water supply. These measures are:

- Find shade. Get out of the sun. Place something between you and the ground. Limit your movements.

- Conserve your sweat. Wear all your clothes, including a T-shirt. Roll the sleeves down, cover your head, and protect your neck with a scarf or similar item. This will protect your body from hot-blowing, sand-laden winds and the direct rays of the sun. Your clothing will absorb your sweat, keeping it against your skin so that you gain its full cooling effect. By staying in the shade quietly and fully clothed, not talking, keeping your mouth closed, and breathing through your nose, your water requirement for survival drops dramatically.

- If water is scarce, do not eat any food. Food requires water for digestion. Eating food will use water that you need for cooling.

Thirst is not a reliable guide for your need for water. A person who uses thirst as a guide will only drink two-thirds of his daily requirement. To prevent this "voluntary" dehydration, use this guide:

- At temperatures below 100°F, drink 1 pint of water every hour.

- At temperatures above 100°F, drink 1 quart of water every hour.

Drinking water at regular intervals helps your body to remain cool, decreasing sweating. Even when your water supply is low, sipping water constantly will keep your body cooler and reduce water loss through sweating. Conserve your sweat by reducing activity during the heat of the day. Do **not** ration your water. If you attempt to ration your water, you stand a good chance of becoming a heat casualty.

■ Intense Sunlight and Heat

Intense sunlight and heat are present in all arid areas. Air temperature can rise as high as 140°F during the day. Heat gain results from direct sunlight, hot, blowing winds, reflective heat (the sun's rays bouncing off the sand), and conductive heat from direct contact with the desert sand and rock. The temperature of desert sand and rock averages 30 to 40 degrees more than that of the air. For instance, when the air temperature is 110°F, the sand temperature may be 140°F.

Intense sunlight and heat increase the body's need for water. To conserve your body sweat and energy, you need a shelter to reduce your exposure to the heat of the day. Travel at night to minimize the use of water. You can survey the area at dawn, dusk, or by moonlight when there is little likelihood of a mirage.

Temperatures may get as high as 140°F during the day and as low as 50°F at night in arid areas. The drop

Protect Your Eyes

The sun is hard on eyes, especially if you spend a lot of time on the water in the summer. In fact, the effect of glare on the water can be 25 times brighter than if you stayed indoors. To protect your eyes, you need good sunglasses and the right type.

Sunglasses are one of those pieces of equipment that you shouldn't scrimp on. If you try to make do with a cheap pair, you're asking for eye strain, fatigue, and maybe a bad headache. For everyday use, most sunglasses should be able to absorb 60 percent or more of the sun's rays. If you're a hard-core fisherman or boater, look for sunglasses with darker lenses that absorb at least 80 percent of the sun's rays. Industry standards require that sunglasses designed for water sports absorb up to 95 percent of the sun's ultraviolet rays.

How can you tell if sunglasses are dark enough to provide the degree of protection that you need? Quality sunglasses will have tags indicating the degree of UV protection, but if the manufacturer does not disclose the rating on the tag, it might be difficult to determine. There is, however, a simple in-store test for lens darkness. Pick sunglasses off the rack, put them on, and look into a mirror. If the lenses are dark enough for general outdoor use, you will have some difficulty seeing your eyes in the reflection. This test doesn't work for photochromic lenses, which darken in reaction to the amount of light striking them.

Photochromic or all-weather sunglasses are good choices if you wear prescription glasses or if you want only one pair for both indoor and outdoor use. In cloudy weather, the lenses range from light to medium density and are usually amber or brown in color. In this state, negative blue filters screen out the scattered blue light that creates haze. The result is improved contrast and sharper details. When the sun breaks out, the lenses change to a deeper gray or brown for glare protection.

As for color, most vision experts agree that green, gray, or brown lenses work best to shield the eyes. Under extreme glare conditions, mirror lenses are most effective. If you're a fisherman, go with polarizing lenses, which are made by sandwiching polarizing film between two pieces of glass or plastic. This helps eliminate or greatly reduce reflections on the surface of the water. Taking it another step, choose sunglasses with side shields or mini lenses

that further block the sun's rays. It's also smart to attach a cord to the frame of the glasses so you don't lose them in the heat of a battle with a big fish or while you're running down the lake. If the earpieces aren't predrilled at the factory for such an attachment, it's easy enough to do it at home.

Regardless of the style of sunglasses you choose, it's important that they provide good protection against the sun's ultraviolet rays, which can be irritating and dangerous to vision. Ultraviolet rays can cause short- and long-term harmful effects, such as photokeratitis, cataracts, and various types of cancer.

Finally, if your sunglasses steam up in hot, humid weather or blotch in the rain, try rubbing the lenses with one of those new antifogging concoctions that are available at most sporting-goods stores. They're great for sunglasses.

in temperature at night occurs rapidly and will chill a person who lacks warm clothing and is unable to move around. The cool evenings and nights are the best times to work or travel. If you plan to rest at night, you will find a wool sweater, long underwear, and a wool stocking cap extremely helpful.

Sunburn results from overexposing your skin to the sun's rays. Keep your body completely clothed, including gloves on your hands and a scarf around your neck. Use sunscreen liberally on any exposed areas of skin. Sun poisoning equals nausea and dehydration. In addition, burns may become infected, causing more problems. Remember the following:

- There is as much danger of sunburn on cloudy days as on sunny days, especially at high altitudes.

- Most sunscreens do not give complete protection against excessive exposure.

- The glare on the sand causes eyestrain, and wind-blown, fine sand particles can irritate the eyes and cause inflammation. Wear goggles and use eye ointments to protect your eyes.

- The combination of wind, sand, or dust can cause your lips and other exposed skin to chap. Use lip balm and skin ointments to prevent or overcome this problem.

- Rest is essential in this environment. You need 20 minutes of rest for each hour in the heat and you need six hours of sleep each day.

■ Sparse Vegetation

Vegetation is sparse in arid areas. You will therefore have difficulty finding shade. Seek shade in dry washes or riverbeds with a thicker growth of vegetation. Use the shadows cast from brush, rocks, or outcroppings. The temperature in shaded areas will be 20 to 30 degrees cooler than the air temperature. Finally, cover objects that will reflect light from the sun.

Prior to moving, survey the area for sites that provide cover. A problem you will have is estimating distance. The emptiness of a desert terrain causes most people to underestimate distance by three: what appears to be 1 mile away is really 3 miles away.

DEALING WITH DANGEROUS WATER

When you are in a survival situation in any area except the desert, you are likely to encounter a water obstacle. It may be in the form of a river, stream, lake, bog, quicksand, quagmire, or muskeg. Whatever it is, you need to know how to cross it safely.

■ Rivers and Streams

A river or stream may be narrow or wide, shallow or deep, slow moving or fast moving. It may be snow-fed or ice-fed. Your first step is to find a place where the river is basically safe for crossing. Look for a high place from which you can get a good view of the river. If there is no high place, climb a tree. Check the river carefully for the following areas:

- A level stretch where the river breaks into a number of channels. Two or three narrow channels are usually easier to cross than a wide river.

- Obstacles on the opposite side of the river that might hinder your travel. Try to select the spot from which travel will be safest and easiest.

- A ledge of rocks that crosses the river. This often indicates dangerous rapids or canyons.

- A deep or rapid waterfall or a deep channel. Never attempt to ford a stream directly above or even close to such spots.

- Rocky places. Avoid such places; you can be seriously injured from falling on rocks. An occasional rock that breaks the current, however, may assist you.

- A shallow bank or sandbar. If possible, select a point upstream from a bank or sandbar so that the current will carry you to it if you lose your footing.

- A course across the river that leads downstream. This will help you cross the current at about a 45-degree angle.

How to Wade a River

Wading looks easy enough, but it can turn into a dangerous situation if you are swept off your feet in the swift current. The rules for safe wading are simple. First, never take a step in any direction unless your rear or anchor foot is firmly planted. Next, slide your lead foot forward until it is secure. When your lead foot is firmly planted, then slide your anchor foot ahead. Never try to wade by lifting your feet. The current will swing your leg out from under you and throw you off balance. Avoid wading big, wide stretches of river. It is safer to wade from pool to pool, taking advantage of slower current to rest.

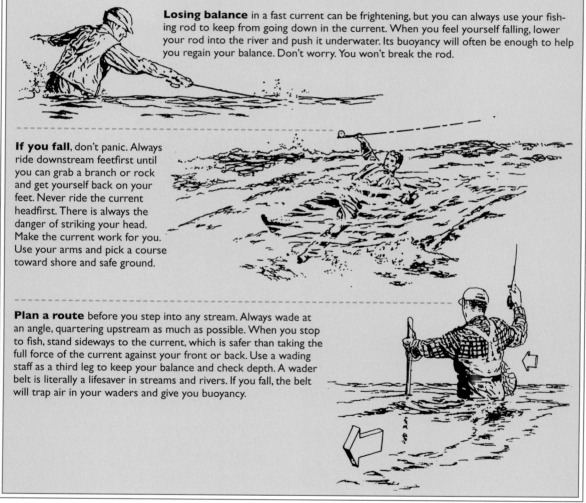

Losing balance in a fast current can be frightening, but you can always use your fishing rod to keep from going down in the current. When you feel yourself falling, lower your rod into the river and push it underwater. Its buoyancy will often be enough to help you regain your balance. Don't worry. You won't break the rod.

If you fall, don't panic. Always ride downstream feetfirst until you can grab a branch or rock and get yourself back on your feet. Never ride the current headfirst. There is always the danger of striking your head. Make the current work for you. Use your arms and pick a course toward shore and safe ground.

Plan a route before you step into any stream. Always wade at an angle, quartering upstream as much as possible. When you stop to fish, stand sideways to the current, which is safer than taking the full force of the current against your front or back. Use a wading staff as a third leg to keep your balance and check depth. A wader belt is literally a lifesaver in streams and rivers. If you fall, the belt will trap air in your waders and give you buoyancy.

■ Rapids

Crossing a deep, swift river or rapids is not as dangerous as it looks. If you are swimming across, swim with the current—never fight it—and try to keep your body horizontal to the water. This will reduce the danger of being pulled under.

In fast, shallow rapids, go on your back, feetfirst; fin your hands alongside your hips to add buoyancy and to fend off submerged rocks. Keep your feet up to avoid getting them bruised or caught by rocks.

In deep rapids, go on your belly, headfirst; angle toward the shore whenever you can. Breathe between wave troughs. Be careful of backwater eddies and converging currents, as they often contain dangerous swirls. Avoid bubbly water under falls; it has little buoyancy. If you are going to ford a swift, treacherous stream, remove your pants and underpants so that the water will have less grip on your legs. Keep your shoes on to protect your feet and ankles from rocks and to give you firmer footing.

Tie your pants and important items securely to the top of your pack. This way, if you have to release your pack, all your items will be together. It is easier to find one large pack than to find several small items.

Carry your pack well up on your shoulders so you can release it quickly if you are swept off your feet. Not being able to get a pack off quickly enough can drag even the strongest of swimmers under.

Find a strong pole about 5 inches in diameter and 7 to 8 feet long to help you ford the stream. Grasp the pole and plant it firmly on your upstream side to break the current. Plant your feet firmly with each step, and move the pole forward a little downstream from its previous position, but still upstream from you. With your next step, place your foot below the pole. Keep the pole well slanted so that the force of the current keeps the pole against your shoulder.

If there are other people with you, cross the stream together. Make sure that everyone has prepared their pack and clothing as described above. Have the heaviest person get on the downstream end of the pole and the lightest person on the upstream end. This way, the upstream person will break the current, and the people below can move with comparative ease in the eddy formed by the upstream person. If the upstream person is temporarily swept off his feet, the others can hold steady while he regains his footing.

As in all fording, cross the downstream current at a 45-degree angle. Currents too strong for one person to stand against can usually be crossed safely in this manner.

Do not be concerned about the weight of your pack, as the weight will help rather than hinder you in fording the stream. Just make sure you can release the pack quickly if necessary.

■ Surviving in Cold Water

Spring and fall are traditional times for trout fishing and waterfowl hunting, and this means greater chances of accidentally finding yourself in cold water. If you are suddenly the victim of a capsizing, you can survive a cold-water dunking if you follow a few survival rules.

Cold Water Survival

Solo Survival: H.E.L.P. (Heat Escape Lessening Posture) is the body position that will minimize heat loss if you are alone. If you are wearing waders, keep them on, and assume a sitting position. The trapped air in your waders will help keep you afloat. Cover your head and neck if possible.

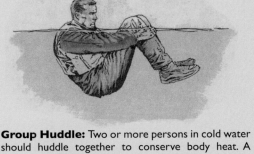

Group Huddle: Two or more persons in cold water should huddle together to conserve body heat. A small group in this position can extend survival time 50 percent longer than if they were swimming.

First, don't panic. Clothing will trap body heat, so don't remove your clothes. If you are wearing a life jacket, restrict your body movements and draw your knees up to your body, a position that will reduce heat loss.

Don't try to swim or tread water. That will just pump out warm water between your body and clothing. Instead, get into a protective posture and wait for rescue. See the accompanying illustrations for the body positions that will minimize heat loss and increase your chances of survival.

■ Ice Safety

Winter is the time of year when ice fishermen venture out onto frozen waters. Most will have fun, but a few will get into trouble because they don't know how to make sure that the ice is safe. The first rule is never take chances. There are two periods when accidents are likely to happen: early in the season when slush ice doesn't freeze uniformly and late in the season when ice melts at an uneven rate. It takes prolonged periods of freezing to make ice safe. Here are some rules to remember:

- Be cautious of heavy snowfalls while ice is forming. Snow acts as an insulator. The result is a layer of slush and snow on top of treacherous ice.

- Lakes that have a lot of springs will have weak spots of ice.

- Clear, solid river ice is 15 percent weaker than clear lake ice.

Ice Safety Guidelines

These guidelines—courtesy of the Minnesota Department of Natural Resources—are for new, clear, solid ice only. White ice or "snow ice" is only about half as strong as new, clear ice. When traveling on white ice, double the thickness guidelines below.

Ice Thickness	Maximum Safe Load
2 inches or less	Stay off the ice!
4 inches	Ice fishing or other activities on foot
5 inches	Snowmobile or ATV
8 to 12 inches	Car or small pickup truck
12 to 15 inches	Medium truck

- River ice is thinner midstream than near the banks.

- River mouths are dangerous because currents create pockets of unsafe ice.

- When walking with friends, stay 10 yards apart.

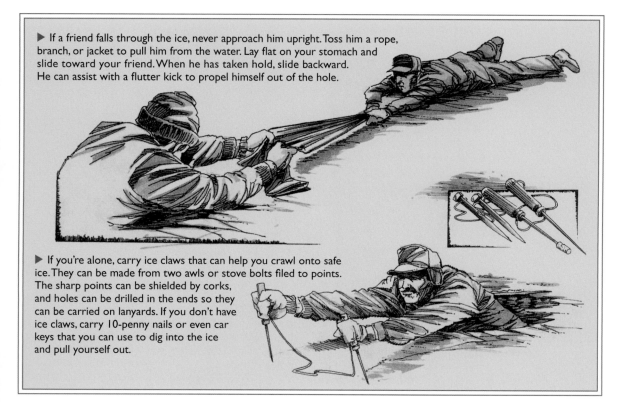

▶ If a friend falls through the ice, never approach him upright. Toss him a rope, branch, or jacket to pull him from the water. Lay flat on your stomach and slide toward your friend. When he has taken hold, slide backward. He can assist with a flutter kick to propel himself out of the hole.

▶ If you're alone, carry ice claws that can help you crawl onto safe ice. They can be made from two awls or stove bolts filed to points. The sharp points can be shielded by corks, and holes can be drilled in the ends so they can be carried on lanyards. If you don't have ice claws, carry 10-penny nails or even car keys that you can use to dig into the ice and pull yourself out.

PATHFINDING THE EASY WAY

There is nothing difficult about using a compass and map. If you're a sportsman, you need these tools to reach hot spots and to get in and out of the woods safely. Basic orienteering is quite easy to learn.

You should start with a topographic map, as it will contain a wealth of information. Topo maps have a scale of 1:24,000, which means that 1 inch on the map equals 24,000 inches (or 2,000 feet) in the field. It may be easier to visualize the area covered by such a map if the scale is translated as 2⅝ inches equals 1 mile.

The topo maps shown in the accompanying illustrations have a scale of 1:24,000. They show four important features: man-made structures, water, vegetation, and elevation. Though the maps later in this section are black and white, these four symbols usually have distinct colors. Man-made features include roads, trails, and buildings. All are in black except some major highways, which may be in red. Water features are printed in blue, and vegetation in green.

Elevation is represented by thin, brown contour lines. A contour line is an imaginary line on the ground along which every point is at the same height above sea level. Follow a brown line on the map, and you'll find a number—for example, 100. Everything on that line is

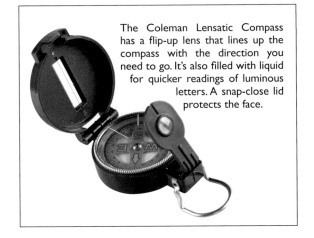

The Coleman Lensatic Compass has a flip-up lens that lines up the compass with the direction you need to go. It's also filled with liquid for quicker readings of luminous letters. A snap-close lid protects the face.

100 feet above sea level. If the line next to it reads 200, then you have a rise of 100 feet and a contour interval of 100 feet. (Generally, the contour interval is 20 feet.) This information is noted at the bottom of topographical maps. These maps are easy to get. Visit the U.S. Geological Survey website (www.usgs.gov/pubprod) to download free topographical maps.

Now let's talk about compasses. A compass contains a magnetized steel needle that points toward magnetic north. The end of this needle will be black or red, stamped with the letter N, or shaped like an arrow.

The force that attracts this magnetized needle is the earth's magnetism. The earth is similar to a tremendous magnet, with one pole in the north, the other in the south. Compass needles always point toward magnetic north when at rest. The magnetic North Pole is about 1,400 miles south of the true North Pole. That means you have two north directions to deal with—true north as it is shown on your map, and magnetic north as you find it with the compass.

Most compasses fall into one of two categories: conventional, which can be of watchcase, pin-on, or wristwatch design, or orienteering, which combines a compass, protractor, and ruler. The latter has a magnetic needle, a revolving compass housing, and a transparent base plate. Carry two compasses in the field: a pin-on model for quick reference and an orienteering compass for cross-country traveling when map work is involved.

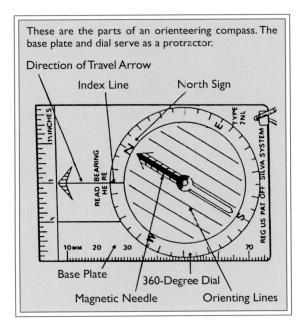

These are the parts of an orienteering compass. The base plate and dial serve as a protractor.

Direction of Travel Arrow
Index Line
North Sign
Base Plate
360-Degree Dial
Magnetic Needle
Orienting Lines

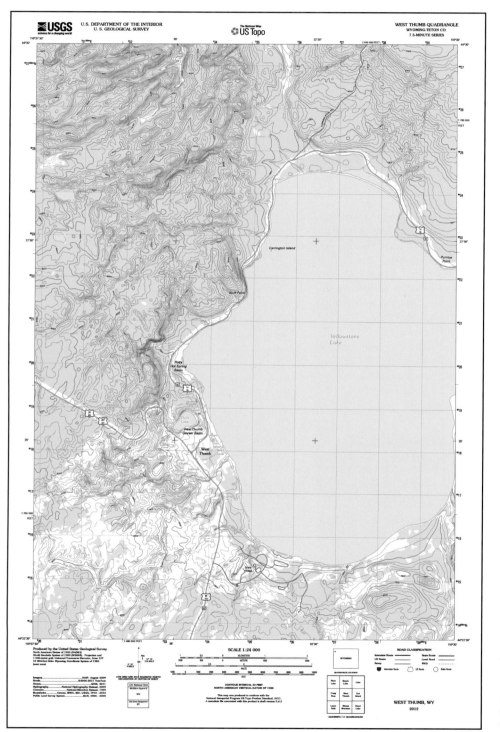

This topographical map is an example of the type you can download for free from the USGS website.

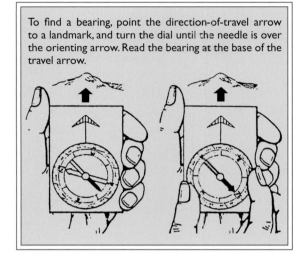

To find a bearing, point the direction-of-travel arrow to a landmark, and turn the dial until the needle is over the orienting arrow. Read the bearing at the base of the travel arrow.

Finding a Bearing

To find a bearing with an orienteering compass, face the distant point toward which you want to know the direction. Hold the orienteering compass level before you, at waist height, with the direction-of-travel arrowhead pointing straight ahead.

Orient your compass by twisting the housing (without moving the base plate) until the needle lies over the orienting arrow on the inside bottom of the compass housing, with its north part pointing to the letter N on the top of the housing. What you've done is made your compass show actual field directions.

Read the degrees of your desired direction—the bearing—on the outside rim of the compass housing at the spot where the direction line, as an index pointer, touches the housing. It's as easy as that with an orienteering compass.

Following a Bearing

Suppose you're standing in a field and have decided to travel cross-country to a distant hilltop. Set your orienteering compass for the direction of the hilltop by holding your compass in your hand with the direction-of-travel arrowhead pointing to your destination. Twist the compass housing until the north part of the compass needle points to the letter N on the housing rim. Proceed in the direction in which the direction-of-travel arrowhead points.

If you lose sight of the distant hilltop, hold the compass in front of you, orient it, and sight a nearby landmark in the direction in which the arrowhead points. Walk to that point, then take a similar reading to another landmark, and so on until you reach the destination.

You can forget about degrees and figures when you use an orienteering compass. Your compass is set. Just orient it and proceed.

■ Returning to Original Location

You have reached your destination and want to return home. How? Your orienteering compass is already set for your return journey.

When you went out, you held the compass with the direction-of-travel arrowhead at the front of the base plate pointing away from you toward your destination. The back of the base plate was in the opposite direction, pointing backward toward the spot from which you came. Make use of this fact.

Hold the compass level in your hand, but with the direction-of-travel arrow pointing toward you instead of away from you. Orient the compass by turning your body (don't touch the compass housing) until the north end of the compass needle points to the N on the compass housing. Locate a landmark, and head for home. Your compass is set—simply use it backward.

■ Using a Map and Compass Together

Let's take a look at how to use a compass and map together. The difference or angle between magnetic north and true north is called declination, and it varies according to your geographic location. The degree of declination is indicated on topo maps. Fortunately, magnetic north is also indicated on topo maps, and you can use it to avoid the whole problem of declination and adjusting map bearings.

Instead of compensating for declination, simply draw magnetic-north lines on your topo map. By using these lines instead of the true-north lines of the regular meridians, you make your map speak the same language as your compass. The settings you take on your compass using these lines do not require resetting to compensate for declination. The declination has already been addressed. To provide your map with magnetic-north lines, draw a line up through the map on an angle to one of the meridian lines corresponding to the degrees of declination given on the map. Then, draw other lines parallel to this line, 1 to 2 inches apart.

With your combined knowledge of map and compass, you can now travel from point to point: cabin to lake, camp to deer stand, and so on. It's done with three easy steps.

Step 1 • On the map, line up your compass with your route. Place the orienteering compass on the map with one long edge of its base plate touching both your starting point and your destination, and with the base plate's direction-of-travel arrow pointing in the direction you want to go. Disregard the compass needle.

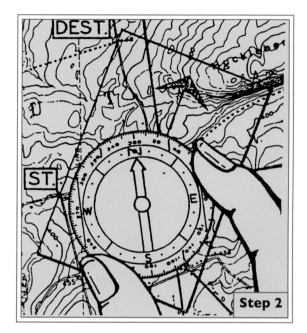

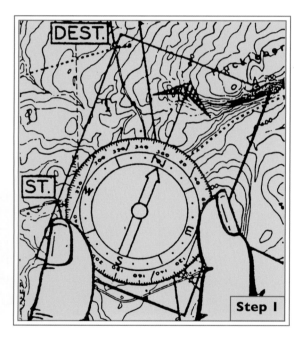

Step 3 • In the field, follow the direction set on the compass. Hold the compass in front of you, at waist height, with the direction-of-travel arrow pointing straight ahead. Turn yourself, while watching the compass needle, until the needle lies directly over the orienting arrow on the bottom of the compass housing, with the north end of the needle pointing to the letter N on the housing. The direction-of-travel arrow now points to your destination. Raise your head, pick a landmark, and walk to it. When you have reached it, again check the direction with your compass, on which you have been careful not to change the setting. Ahead is another landmark, and still another, until you reach your destination. When it's time to return to your starting

Step 2 • On the compass, set the housing to the direction of your route. Hold the plate firmly against the map. With your free hand, turn the compass housing until the orienting arrow on the bottom of the housing lies parallel to the nearest magnetic-north line drawn on your map, with the arrow pointing to the top. Disregard the compass needle. The compass is now set for the direction of your destination. By using the drawn-in magnetic-north line, you have compensated for any compass declination in the territory covered by your map.

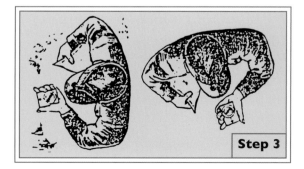

point, repeat Step 3, but keep the direction-of-travel arrow pointing toward you. Your compass is already set—simply use it backward to return home.

Applying what you've learned to camping situations is not difficult. If you can follow a bearing, you can easily travel across strange country to a remote lake that you've found on a topo map. You can head out in any direction from camp and be confident about finding camp again. When it's time to head back, simply let your compass lead you safely back to camp. With a little practice, you'll be able to travel in the woods with complete confidence.

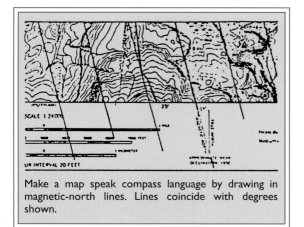

Make a map speak compass language by drawing in magnetic-north lines. Lines coincide with degrees shown.

■ Handheld Global Positioning System (GPS)

Learning to master a compass and map may sound easy, but it can be confusing to many sportsmen. If you fall into this group, select one of the many handheld GPS units available today. These units offer a range of sophisticated features that will easily track your travel in remote areas and guide you back to your camp at the end of the day. For example, the Garmin Montana 650 is a rugged navigator with a 4-inch touchscreen and a five-megapixel camera. The unit weighs only 10 ounces and is powered by a rechargeable lithium battery or three AA batteries, which will run the unit up to 22 hours. Handheld GPS models also serve double-duty in

The Garmin Oregon 450t, a waterproof GPS with touch-screen navigation, is preloaded with U.S. topographical maps. It will show shoreline detail, highways, roads, and hiking and snowmobile trails. This unit has a 3-inch color display and runs up to 16 hours on two AA batteries. It is a good option for those who have difficulty with compasses.

automobiles, boats, and ATVs. They are not expensive and will free you of worry about traveling off trails and possibly getting lost. Garmin, Magellan, and Lowrance are major manufacturers of handheld GPS units. If you venture far off the beaten path, it's also good advice to pair a GPS with a fully charged cell phone.

The Garmin Montana 600 GPS features a 4-inch sunlight-readable color touchscreen. This Wide Area Augmentation System (WAAS)-enabled GPS receiver with HotFix satellite prediction will wirelessly share routes, tracks, waypoints, and geocaches between compatible units.

FIRST AID
FOR CAMPERS AND SURVIVALISTS

FIRST AID
FOR CAMPERS AND SURVIVALISTS

EMERGENCY MEDICAL TREATMENT

Let's suppose that you and a companion are well out in the woods on a camping trip and one of the following mishaps occurs:

- Your friend is bitten by a snake that escapes before either of you can identify it. Can you tell from the bite itself whether or not the snake is a poisonous species? If it is, what should you do?

- Your companion suffers a severe fall and begins to act strangely. You fear that he may be going into shock. How do you tell for sure? How do you treat it?

- You've made an ambitious hike on snowshoes on a brilliantly sunny day after a heavy snowfall the night before. Your eyes begin to burn and smart, your forehead aches, and you can't seem to stand the glare from the glistening snow—all symptoms of snow blindness. What do you do?

- A toothache comes on suddenly and savagely. The nearest dentist is hours away by foot and car. Is there anything you can do to ease the pain?

Outdoor sports—as proved by studies made by American insurance companies—are among the safest of pastimes. But accidents do happen, and knowledge of first-aid procedures is especially important to outdoors enthusiasts, whose favorite haunts are seldom down the street from the doctor's office or within arm's reach of a telephone.

Most accidents or maladies suffered in the outdoors are minor. But if a serious injury should occur, these actions should be taken, in the order given:

1. Give urgently needed first aid immediately: stop severe bleeding, restore breathing, treat for poisoning, or treat for shock. Keep the victim lying down.

2. Examine the victim as carefully—and calmly—as you can, and try to determine the extent of his injuries.

3. Send someone for help if possible. If not, try signaling with a rifle (a widely recognized distress signal is three quick shots) or by building a smoky fire.

4. Take necessary first-aid steps for secondary injuries, making the patient as comfortable as possible and moving him only if absolutely necessary.

This chapter will give detailed step-by-step procedures for every first-aid situation the outdoors person is likely to encounter. It should be remembered, however, that these procedures, though vitally important, aren't the only form of first aid. The victim's mental distress also needs treatment. A reassuring word, a smile, your obvious willingness and ability to help—all will have an encouraging effect. The knowledgeable first-aider also knows what **not** to do and thereby avoids compounding the problem by making errors that could be serious.

The procedures and instructions that follow reflect recommendations of the American Red Cross, the American Medical Association, the U.S. Department of Agriculture, and, of course, respected physicians.

■ Bleeding

EXTERNAL BLEEDING: If a large blood vessel is severed, death from loss of blood can occur in three to five minutes, so it is vital to stop the bleeding at once. Always do so, if possible, by applying pressure directly over the wound.

Use a clean cloth—a handkerchief, an item of clothing, or whatever else is near at hand. Use your bare hand

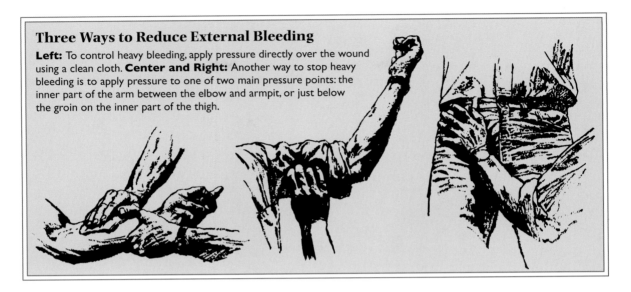

Three Ways to Reduce External Bleeding

Left: To control heavy bleeding, apply pressure directly over the wound using a clean cloth. **Center and Right:** Another way to stop heavy bleeding is to apply pressure to one of two main pressure points: the inner part of the arm between the elbow and armpit, or just below the groin on the inner part of the thigh.

if nothing else is available, and then, once the bleeding is under control, apply a cloth. Put on additional layers of cloth, and when the covering is substantial, bandage snugly with strips of cloth cut from a bedsheet, neckties, or similar materials. Don't remove the bandage. If it becomes saturated with blood, put on more layers of cloth, and perhaps tighten the dressing directly over the wound.

If you are sure that no bones are broken, try to raise the bleeding area higher than the rest of the body.

If extremely quick action is needed, or if the above method fails to stop the flow of blood, you may be able to diminish the flow by pressing your fingers or the heel of your hand at one of two pressure points. One of these is located on the inner half of the arm midway between the elbow and armpit; pressure applied here will reduce bleeding in the lower area of the arm. Pressure on the other point, located just below the groin on the front, inner half of the thigh, will reduce bleeding on the extremity below that point.

INTERNAL BLEEDING: Often caused by a severe fall or a violent blow, bleeding within the body can be difficult to diagnose, though it may be revealed by bleeding from the nose or mouth when no injury can be detected in those organs. Other symptoms may include restlessness, nausea, anxiety, a weak and rapid pulse, thirst, paleness, and general weakness.

The first treatment procedure is to use pillows, knapsacks, folded clothes, or something similar to raise the victim's head and shoulders if he is having diffi-culty breathing. Otherwise, place him flat on his back. Keep him as immobile as possible, and try to have him control the movements caused by vomiting. Turn his head to the side for vomiting.

Do not give the victim stimulants, even if the bleeding seems to stop.

If the victim loses consciousness, turn him on his side, with his head and chest lower than his hips.

Medical care is a must. Get the victim to a doctor or hospital as soon as possible.

NOSEBLEED: Nosebleeds often occur for no reason, while at other times they are caused by an injury. Most of them are more annoying than serious. It occasionally happens, though, that the bleeding is heavy and prolonged, and this can be dangerous.

The person should remain quiet, preferably in a sitting position with his head thrown back or lying down with his head and shoulders raised.

Pinch the victim's nostrils together, keeping the pressure on for five to 10 minutes. If the bleeding doesn't stop, pack gauze lightly into the bleeding nostril and then pinch. Sometimes the application of cold, wet towels to the face will help.

USE OF A TOURNIQUET: According to the American Red Cross, the use of a tourniquet to stop bleeding in an extremity is "justifiable only rarely." Because its use involves a high risk of losing a limb, a tourniquet should be applied only if the bleeding seems sure to cause death.

Applying a Tourniquet

Since a tourniquet can cause the loss of the affected limb, it should be applied only when no other means will reduce blood flow enough to prevent the victim from bleeding to death. **Left:** Wrap strong, wide cloth around the limb above the wound, and tie a simple overhand knot. **Center:** Place a short stick on the knot, tie another overhand knot over the stick, and twist the stick to stem bleeding. **Right:** Bind the stick with the ends of the tourniquet, but be sure to loosen it every 15 minutes.

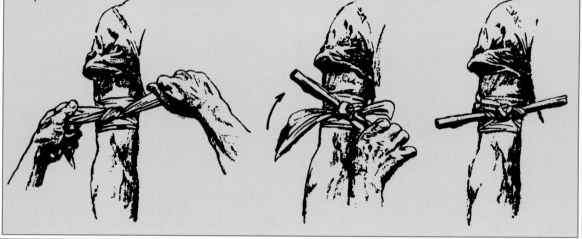

Use only a wide, strong piece of cloth—never a narrow strip of material such as rope or wire. Wrap the cloth around the upper part of the limb above the wound, and tie a simple overhand knot (half a square knot). Place a short stick on the knot, and tie another simple overhand knot (that is, complete the square knot) over the stick. Twist the stick just enough to stop the bleeding. Loosen the binding (untwist the stick) for a few seconds every 15 minutes.

Once the bleeding has been controlled, keep the victim quiet and warm. If he is conscious and can swallow easily, give him some water or maybe some weak tea—no alcoholic drinks. If he is not conscious, or if abdominal or other internal injuries are suspected, do not give him any fluid.

■ Artificial Respiration

Artificial respiration, now commonly called resuscitation, is the technique of causing air to flow into and out of the lungs of a person whose normal breathing has stopped. Causes of stoppage of normal breathing include inhalation of water, smoke, or gas, electric shock, choking, or drug overdose. In most instances, death will result within six minutes unless artificial respiration is administered.

The treatment may also be needed if breathing does not stop completely but becomes slow and shallow and the victim's lips, tongue, and fingernails turn blue. If you're in doubt, give artificial respiration—it is seldom harmful and can save a life.

Before beginning the artificial-respiration methods described below, check the victim's mouth and throat opening for obstructions; remove any foreign objects or loose dentures.

MOUTH TO MOUTH: Place the victim on his back. Put one hand under the victim's neck. At the same time, place the other hand on his forehead and tilt the head back.

Using the hand that was under the neck, pull the victim's chin up, thereby ensuring a free air passage. Take a deep breath, place your mouth over the victim's mouth, trying to make the seal as airtight as possible, and pinch the victim's nostrils closed. Blow into the victim's mouth until you see his chest rise.

Lift your head from the victim, and take another deep breath while his chest falls, causing him to exhale. Repeat the process. For the first few minutes, do so as

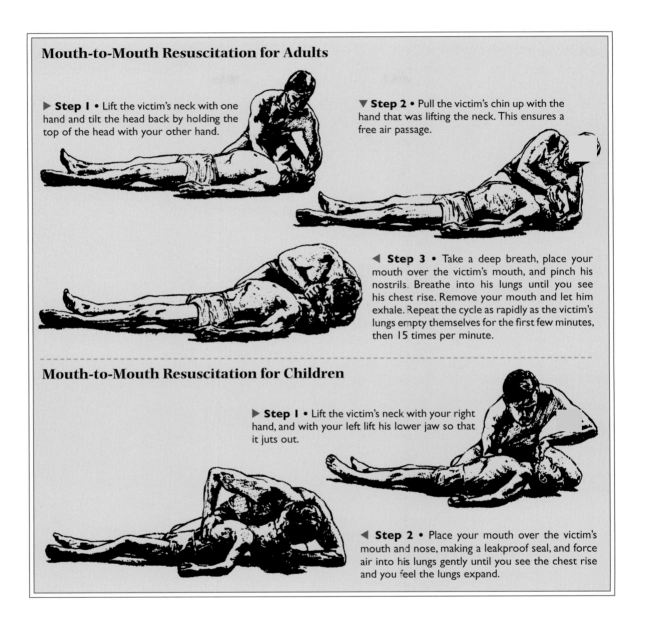

Mouth-to-Mouth Resuscitation for Adults

▶ **Step 1** • Lift the victim's neck with one hand and tilt the head back by holding the top of the head with your other hand.

▼ **Step 2** • Pull the victim's chin up with the hand that was lifting the neck. This ensures a free air passage.

◀ **Step 3** • Take a deep breath, place your mouth over the victim's mouth, and pinch his nostrils. Breathe into his lungs until you see his chest rise. Remove your mouth and let him exhale. Repeat the cycle as rapidly as the victim's lungs empty themselves for the first few minutes, then 15 times per minute.

Mouth-to-Mouth Resuscitation for Children

▶ **Step 1** • Lift the victim's neck with your right hand, and with your left lift his lower jaw so that it juts out.

◀ **Step 2** • Place your mouth over the victim's mouth and nose, making a leakproof seal, and force air into his lungs gently until you see the chest rise and you feel the lungs expand.

rapidly as the victim's lungs are emptied. After that, do it about 15 times per minute.

If the victim is an infant or small child, use the same procedure, but place your mouth over both the mouth and nose, and force air into his lungs gently.

CARDIOPULMONARY RESUSCITATION (CPR): If artificial respiration produces no response in an injured person, it may mean that his heart has stopped beating. You can

make a fairly certain diagnosis by checking his pulse at the wrist and holding your ear to the victim's chest. If you feel no pulse and hear no heartbeat, you will have to use external heart massage (CPR) in addition to artificial respiration.

Here are the warning signs of a heart attack:

- Pressure; feeling of "fullness"; squeezing or pain in the center of the chest lasting more than two minutes

Chest Compressions

For heart stoppage, employ extended chest compressions (CPR) using the weight of the upper part of your body.

- Pain radiating to shoulders, neck, jaw, arms, or back; tingling sensation down left arm
- Dizziness, weakness, sweating, or nausea; pale complexion and shortness of breath

If the victim's heart and breathing have stopped, begin CPR. The technique involves mouth-to-mouth resuscitation, which delivers air to the lungs, and chest compressions, which help circulate the blood.

CHEST COMPRESSIONS: Positioning yourself perpendicular to the victim, place the heel of one hand on the lower third of the victim's sternum (breastbone). Place your other hand on top of the first one. Press down firmly with both hands about 1½ to 2 inches and then lift both hands to let the chest expand. Repeat at a rate of 80 to 100 compressions per minute. The mouth-to-mouth breathing should continue at a rate of two steady lung inflations after every 15 chest compressions.

■ Choking

More than one person has died from choking on a fish bone, an inadvertently swallowed hard object, a piece of food that went down the "wrong pipe," and the like. Anything that lodges in the throat or air passages must be removed as soon as possible. Here's how to do it.

If the victim is conscious, give him four back blows between the shoulder blades. If the victim is lying down, roll him on his side, facing you with his chest against your knee. If the victim is sitting or standing, you should be behind and to one side of him. If the victim is an

Mouth-to-Mouth Resuscitation

Remember the ABCs: airway, breathing, and circulation, in that order.

Airway. If there are no head, neck, or back injuries, gently tilt the victim's head and raise the chin. This will lift the tongue and ensure a clear air passage. Check for breathing by placing your ear over the victim's mouth and feeling for any exhalation.

Breathing. If the person is not breathing, pinch his nose, take a deep breath, and place your mouth over his. Breathe into his lungs two times slowly—one and a half to two seconds each time. If the victim's chest does not rise, re-tilt the head and repeat the cycle at a rate of 15 times per minute, until the victim can breathe on his own.

Circulation. Check for a pulse. Keeping the victim's head tilted, place your index and middle fingers on the victim's Adam's apple, and then slide your fingers down to the next "ridge" on the neck. This is where you'll find the carotid artery. Press firmly to determine if there's a pulse. If there isn't, proceed with chest compressions.

infant, place him on your forearm, head down. Make sharp blows with the heel of your hand on the spine, directly between his shoulder blades.

If this doesn't remove the object, and the victim is standing or sitting, employ the Heimlich maneuver:

1. Stand behind the victim and wrap your arms around his waist.

2. Place the thumb side of your fist against the victim's upper abdomen, just below the rib cage.

3. Grasp your fist with your other hand and press into the victim's abdomen with two or three quick upward thrusts.

If the victim is in a lying position, do this:

1. Place him on his back and kneel close to his side.

2. Place your hands, one on top of the other, with the heel of the bottom hand in the middle of his abdomen, just below the rib cage.

3. Rock forward so that your shoulders are directly over the victim's abdomen and press toward the victim's diaphragm with a quick forward thrust.

4. Don't press to either side.

If the victim is unconscious, tilt his head back and attempt to give him artificial respiration. If this fails, give the victim four back blows in rapid succession. If the object has still not been forced out of the air passage, then stand behind the victim, put both of your fists into his abdomen, and give eight upward thrusts.

Finally, if none of these methods work, you should insert your index finger deep into the victim's throat, using a hooking action to try to dislodge the object.

FOR A SMALL CHILD: Put one arm around the youngster's waist from behind, and lift him up so that his head and upper torso are leaning toward the ground. With your free hand, give him several sharp taps between the shoulder blades. When the object has been dislodged, clear his throat with your fingers, and pull the tongue forward.

FOR AN INFANT: Hold him up by the ankles, head hanging straight down. Open his mouth, pull his tongue forward, and the object will likely fall out. If not, give him a tap or two on the back.

■ Shock

Medical (traumatic) shock is a depressed condition of many bodily functions and is usually caused by loss of blood following a serious injury (a burn, wound, fracture, exposure, and the like). However, some degree of shock can result from even minor injuries and from psychological shock.

Prolonged shock can result in death even if the injury causing it would not be fatal otherwise. In every health emergency, the possibility of shock should be considered. Signs of shock include the following: vacant, lackluster eyes and dilated pupils, shallow or irregular breathing, weak or seemingly absent pulse, skin that is pale and moist and cooler than it should be, nausea, perspiration, restlessness, thirst, and unconsciousness.

Symptoms usually develop gradually and may not be apparent at first. Even if a severely injured person exhibits none of the signs, shock is a real danger, and the following steps should be taken:

Choking: Back Blows

If the choking victim is conscious, give four back blows between the shoulder blades in hopes of dislodging the obstruction. If this doesn't work, employ the Heimlich maneuver.

Choking: Heimlich Maneuver

If the choking victim is standing and back slaps do not dislodge the obstruction, apply the Heimlich maneuver as shown here.

Lying Abdominal Thrust

If the choking victim is lying down, assume the position shown and perform the steps as described in the text.

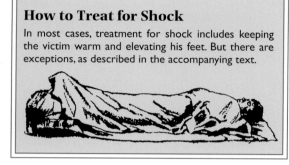

How to Treat for Shock

In most cases, treatment for shock includes keeping the victim warm and elevating his feet. But there are exceptions, as described in the accompanying text.

1. Keep the victim lying down, preferably with his head lower than the rest of his body. **Exception:** If there is difficulty in breathing, the head and chest should be elevated.

2. Raise his legs 8 to 12 inches. **Exception:** Do not raise the legs if there is a head injury, if breathing difficulty is thereby increased, or if the patient complains of pain during the raising process. If you are in doubt about the correct position, keep the victim lying flat.

3. Keep the victim warm. If the weather is cold or damp, cover him and put a blanket underneath as well. Do not overheat; keep him just warm enough to prevent shivering.

Fluids can have value in shock, but don't give the victim liquids unless medical help will be delayed at least an hour. If the victim is conscious and able to swallow, give him water that is neither hot nor cold—a few sips at first and then increasing the amount. If medical help will be considerably delayed, give the victim half-glass doses (at 15-minute intervals) of a solution made by adding 1 teaspoon of salt and ½ teaspoon of baking soda to 1 quart of water. Do not give any fluids if the victim is only partly conscious, if an abdominal injury is suspected, or if he is nauseated.

■ Oral Poisoning

If the victim has ingested poisonous material and is unconscious or otherwise unable to tell you what it was, you may be able to ascertain the source by the odor on his breath, discoloration on his lips or mouth, or a telltale container nearby.

Speed is vital in treating a victim of poisoning. You must take the following steps quickly, before the body has a chance to absorb much of the poison:

1. If you know the antidote (antidotes are printed on containers of almost all potentially dangerous materials) and if it is at hand, give it at once. If not, dilute the poison by giving the victim four or more glasses of milk or water.

2. Call a doctor or hospital if possible.

3. Induce vomiting by sticking your finger into the victim's throat or by making him drink a glass of warm water with 2 tablespoons of salt mixed in. **Exception:** Do not induce vomiting if the victim is unconscious, has pain or a burning sensation in the mouth or throat, or has swallowed a petroleum product (gasoline, kerosene, white gas, or the like) or any acid or alkali (caustic soda, an ammonia solution, or the like). When vomiting begins, position the victim facedown with his head lower than his hips to prevent the expelled material from getting into his lungs. If you can't identify the poison, save some of the vomitus for subsequent examination by a physician or hospital laboratory.

BITES AND POISONOUS PLANTS

■ Snakebites

It is doubtful whether any other first-aid situation is more feared and less understood than snakebites, and there is little agreement, even among leading authorities, about their treatment.

About 6,500 people are bitten by venomous snakes in the United States each year. Of those, only about 350 are hunters or fishermen. And the death rate is very low, an average of 15 persons annually in the entire country. Most of those bites occur south of an imaginary line drawn from North Carolina to Southern California. More than half occur in Texas, North Carolina, Florida, Georgia, Louisiana, and Arkansas.

There are four kinds of venomous snakes in the United States. Three are of the pit-viper variety: rattlesnakes, copperheads, and cottonmouth moccasins. The

North American Venomous Snakes

Cottonmouth • Eastern cottonmouths as well as Florida and western cottonmouths are frequently confused with non-venomous water snakes. Cottonmouths have dark blotches on an olive body and broad, flat heads.

Coral Snake • This snake is extremely venomous, but its small mouth prevents it from biting most parts of the body. It has red and black rings wider than the interspaced yellow rings. The habitat is open woods in the East and loose soil and rocks in the West.

Timber Rattler and Canebrake Rattler • In the South, there is a dark streak from the canebrake's eye to mouth, and dark chevrons and a rusty stripe along the midline. In the North, the timber rattler has a yellowish body and dark phase in parts of its range. The habitat for the canebrake is lowland brush and stream borders. The timber rattler prefers rocky wooded hills.

Eastern Diamondback • The body has dark diamonds with light borders along a tan or light-brown background. The diamonds gradually change to bands in the tail. The habitat is lowland thickets, palmettos, and flatwoods.

Copperhead • This snake has large, chestnut-brown cross bands on a pale pinkish or reddish-brown surface with a copper tinge on the head. The habitat in the North is wooded mountains and stone walls; in the South, it is lowland swamps and wooded suburbs.

Western Diamondback • This snake has light brown to black diamond-shaped blotches along a light gray, tan, and sometimes pink background. It also has black and white bands of about equal width around the tail. The habitat includes woods, rocky hills, deserts, and farmland.

fourth, the coral snake, is a member of the cobra family. The pit vipers are so named because they have a small, deep depression between the eyes and the nostrils. The coral snake has broad, red and black bands separated by narrow yellow bands, giving rise to the saying, "Red on yellow, kill a fellow."

The bite of a venomous snake—except for the coral snake, which chews rather than bites—is in the form of fang punctures of the skin. If you are bitten by a snake that leaves two U-shaped rows of tooth marks on your skin, relax—it is almost certainly a nonvenomous snake. The bite of a nonvenomous snake produces little pain or swelling.

Symptoms of a venomous snakebite include immediate pain, swelling and discoloration in the area of the wound, general weakness, nausea and vomiting, a weak and rapid pulse, dimming of vision, faintness, and eventually unconsciousness.

Most medical authorities now agree that the preferred treatment for a snakebite is antivenin administered as quickly as possible after the bite. If a snakebite victim is within a two-hour drive of a medical facility, get the person there as fast and calmly as possible. Keep the bite location immobile, even if you have to splint it. Also keep the bitten body part below the level of the heart. A snakebite victim may walk up to a half hour before symptoms start. If the distance is longer to transportation, the victim should be carried. If you are alone, you should still be able to walk for several hours even after symptoms start.

Most bites, however, occur in the field, often many miles from a road, so the victim cannot always get antivenin quickly enough. Survival in such cases depends upon the first-aid steps taken by the victim and his companions. And here is where the disagreement among medical authorities is most prevalent.

Proper treatment for a snakebite continues to confuse sportsmen, but the most reliable medical opinions today agree that the old treatments did more damage than good. There are still snakebite kits on the market, and they may make you feel better if you have one in your first-aid kit, but the best advice is don't use it. The use of a scalpel to make incisions is no longer recommended and may cause further injury. Suction devices used without incisions are also of questionable value. Some tests indicate that such suction devices may only remove about 1 to 2 percent of the venom.

Here's the currently recommended treatment for a snakebite. Call 911 or get to a hospital where you can get antivenin as quickly as possible. Properly treated with antivenin, snakebites are rarely fatal. If you can't get to a hospital within 30 minutes, immobilize the bite and, if possible, keep it lower than the heart. Wrap a bandage 2 to 4 inches above the bite. The bandage should not cut off blood flow from a vein or artery. Make the bandage loose enough so that a finger can slip under it. Do not put ice on the bite. Avoid exertion and excitement. Sit down and try to calm yourself; panic could bring on shock. Do not eat or drink alcohol. Do not remove any dressings until you reach a hospital. If possible, kill the snake and take the head for identification later. Use caution: The head of a snake can still bite through reflex action up to one hour after it is killed. Get to a hospital or doctor as soon as possible with a minimum of exertion.

■ Coping with Bugs

The outdoors is a great place, but bugs can turn a pleasant day into a nightmare. You can fight back! There are five bugs that will give you the most trouble: mosquitoes, black flies, no-see-ums, deerflies, and ticks. Mosquitoes, the worst of the bunch, are most active at dawn and dusk. Mosquitoes are attracted to dark colors, so wear light-colored clothing. Black flies draw blood. Male black flies use blood for food, and females need blood to complete their breeding cycle. Common throughout Canada and the northern United States, black flies bite as soon as they land and zero in on the face, hairline, wrists, and ankles. The peak period is spring and early summer. Aside from using a repellent, you should wear a hat, tuck pants into socks, tape cuffs around ankles, and wear long sleeves. No-see-ums are so small you can't see them, but they hurt when they bite. You'll find no-see-ums along lakes, beaches, and marshes. The deerfly is another painful biter and will attack the face, legs, arms, and neck. Once again, wear light-colored clothing. The tick, because of the threat of Lyme disease, is the most dangerous of these pests. Wear light-colored clothing, tuck pants into socks, avoid wooded areas and high grass, and use a tick repellent. The most effective repellent against these bugs contains DEET.

■ Bee Stings

Stinging insects are seldom more than an annoyance, even if they hit the target on your hide. Some people, however, are highly allergic to the stings of certain insects. If you or a member of your party has had a

How to Battle the Bugs

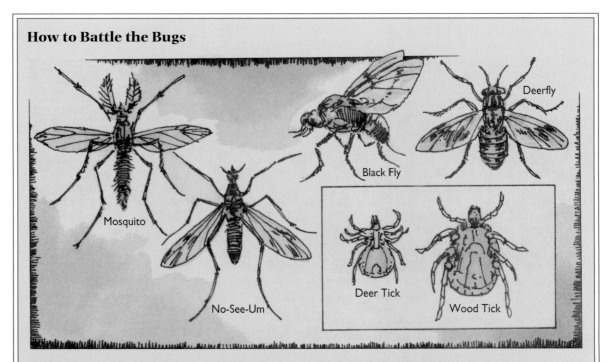

Mosquito

No-See-Um

Black Fly

Deerfly

Deer Tick

Wood Tick

Mosquitoes home in on warmth, carbon dioxide, and the odor of human skin. Your best weapon is a repellent on your skin that will set up a barrier to confuse the mosquito's sensors.

Black flies are inactive at night but a problem during the day. You will rarely feel the bite. The first thing you may notice is the blood. If you get bitten and begin to itch, coat bites with alcohol or witch hazel.

Deerflies are found anywhere in the northern woods, and both sexes can inflict painful bites. Use a headnet and tape cuffs, but be aware that deerflies can also bite through clothing.

No-see-ums are troublesome because it is difficult to protect yourself from them. They can fit through headnets, screens, clothing—almost anything. A repellent helps, but the only sure cure is a stiff wind.

Deer ticks pose a Lyme disease threat. They are half the size of the common wood tick and are orangish brown with a black spot near the head. Symptoms of Lyme disease include a red, ring-shaped rash, fever, chills, headache, stiff joints, and fatigue. Learn how to identify ticks and remove them from your body with tweezers. Don't burn, twist, or crush a tick on your body.

severe reaction to a bee sting in the past and is stung, take the following steps:

1. Use a tight, constricting band above the sting if it is on the arm or leg. Loosen the band for a few seconds every 15 minutes.

2. Apply an icepack or cold cloths to the sting area.

3. Get the victim to a doctor as soon as possible.

For the average bee-sting victim, these procedures will suffice:

1. Make a paste of baking soda and cold cream (if it is available), and apply it to the sting area.

2. Apply cold cloths to help ease the pain.

3. If there is itching, use calamine lotion.

■ Chigger and Tick Bites

The irritation produced by chiggers, which are the larval stage of a mite, results from fluid the tiny insects

The Threat of Lyme Disease

A deer tick is a speck of a bug, but unnoticed on your body its bite can infect you with spirochete bacteria, which produces the crippling effects of Lyme disease. Deer ticks are found on a wide variety of wild and domestic animals, but about 75 percent of deer ticks live on whitetail deer. This means that campers, hikers, and fishermen in deer country have a greater risk of contracting Lyme disease than most other sportsmen.

Anyone venturing into the woods along streams and lakes should tuck in the bottoms of their pant legs. If you prefer to wear your pants outside your boots, so that your pants shed rain outside your boots rather than inside, use masking tape to close off your cuffs. Before you go into the woods, spray yourself with a good tick repellent. There are several on the market that will do the job well, especially if they contain the ingredient DEET.

After a day in the woods, check your body for ticks. The bite of a deer tick is painless, so you may never know you've been bitten unless you look for a tick or signs of a bite. Look wherever you have hair. Check your scalp, and the back of your neck and head. Two favorite spots of ticks are your armpits and groin. It's important to check everywhere.

If you find a tick, don't panic. With tweezers, grab the tick as close to the skin as possible and pull outward slowly and steadily with firm force. Don't twist or jerk the tick out, which may break off parts of the tick in your skin. Squeezing it is also risky because you may release bacteria into your body.

It takes at least several hours for a deer tick to release its bacteria into your bloodstream, so it's critical to remove the tick as quickly as possible. When the tick is out, wash and disinfect the bite area thoroughly. If you see any signs of redness or a rash, call a doctor immediately.

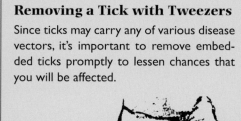

Removing a Tick with Tweezers

Since ticks may carry any of various disease vectors, it's important to remove embedded ticks promptly to lessen chances that you will be affected.

inject. Chiggers do not burrow under the skin, as is often suggested.

Since chiggers do not usually attach themselves to the skin until an hour or more after they reach the body, bathing promptly after exposure using a brush and soapy water may eliminate them. Once the bites have been inflicted, the application of ice water may help.

The itching and discomfort can be relieved by applying calamine lotion or a paste made of baking soda and a little water.

Ticks—flat, usually brown, and about ¼ inch long—attach themselves to the skin by making a tiny puncture and feed by sucking blood. They can thereby transmit the germs of several diseases, including Rocky Mountain spotted fever and Lyme disease. A new strain, granulocytic ehrlichiosis, has flu-like symptoms nearly identical to Lyme disease. Protecting yourself from granulocytic ehrlichiosis is the same as with Lyme disease.

If you have been in a tick-infested area, be sure to examine your clothes and body for the insects, paying particular attention to hairy areas. Removing ticks promptly is insurance against the transmission of any germs they may be carrying, since that process seldom begins until six hours or so after the insect attaches itself and begins to feed.

Use tweezers to remove a tick, but don't yank—that may cause the tick's head or mouth parts to break off and remain in the flesh. Pull it gently, taking care not to crush the body, which may be full of germs. If it can't be pulled off gently, cover the entire tick with heavy oil, which closes off its breathing pores and may make it disengage itself.

■ Spider and Scorpion Bites

Scorpions are most common in the southwestern United States and are found in such spots as cool and damp buildings, debris, and under loose banks. Most species of scorpions in the United States are non-venomous; few of their stings are dangerous.

The biting spiders in the United States include the black widow, brown widow, and tarantula. The brown widow—its abdomen has a dull-orange hourglass marking against a brown body—is harmless in almost all cases. The tarantula is a large (up to 3 inches long, not including the legs) and hairy spider, but despite its fearsome appearance its bite is almost always harmless, though it may cause allergic reactions in sensitive people. The black widow—the female's body is about ½ inch long, shiny black, usually with a red hourglass marking on the underside of the abdomen—has a venomous bite, but its victims almost always recover.

The symptoms of these bites may include some swelling and redness, immediate pain that may become quite severe and spread throughout the body (especially with a black-widow bite), profuse sweating, nausea, and difficulty breathing and speaking.

First-aid procedures are as follows:

1. Keep the victim warm and calm, lying down.
2. Apply a wide, constricting band above the bite, loosening it every 15 minutes.

3. Apply wrapped-up ice or cold compresses to the area of the bite.
4. Get medical help as quickly as possible.

■ Poison Ivy, Poison Oak, and Poison Sumac

You cannot escape from poison ivy, poison oak, and poison sumac. There are virtually no areas in the United States in which at least one of these plants does not exist. Poison ivy is found throughout the country, with the possible exception of California and Nevada. Poison oak occurs in the southeastern states, and a western variety exists in the West Coast states. Poison sumac grows in most of the states in the eastern third of the country.

If you're lucky, you may be among the 50 percent of the population that is not sensitive to these poisonous plants. If you are not lucky, however, and you've already had a few run-ins with poison ivy, oak, or sumac, you better know how to identify these plants and learn where they grow. Poison ivy grows along streams, lakes, and on sunny hillsides. It can also grow as a shrub, a small tree, or a vine.

If you want to avoid poison ivy and poison oak, beware of low or vine-like three-leaved plants, which in fruit have creamy white berries. Poison sumac has ivory to grayish-white berries. Poison sumac likes wet ground, so you are less likely to come in contact with it if you keep your boots dry.

Urushiol is the sticky, colorless oil that comes from the leaves and stems of poison ivy that causes the irritation when it gets on your skin. Urushiol in poison ivy is nearly the same in poison oak and poison sumac. If you're sensitive to one, you're sensitive to all of them.

If you don't wash the poison sap off your skin quickly, you will develop a rash within a couple of days. The rash will eventually produce swollen patches with blisters that will break and ooze.

Healing will take about two weeks, no matter what you do, but here is some advice to ease the intense itching and promote healing. The best medicine against poison ivy is cortisone, if given within the first 24 hours. Oral prednisone will also help. If you are sensitive to poison ivy, take a supply of cortisone along on your trips.

Here are other remedies that will at least relieve some of the symptoms:

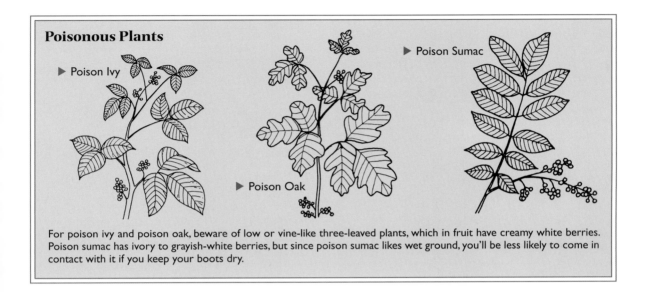

Poisonous Plants

▶ Poison Ivy

▶ Poison Sumac

▶ Poison Oak

For poison ivy and poison oak, beware of low or vine-like three-leaved plants, which in fruit have creamy white berries. Poison sumac has ivory to grayish-white berries, but since poison sumac likes wet ground, you'll be less likely to come in contact with it if you keep your boots dry.

1. Cool compresses with Burow's solution will ease itching and speed up the drying process. Apply them for 15 minutes three or four times a day.

2. Calamine lotion will also relieve the itching.

3. Oatmeal baths are helpful. Add a cup of Aveeno oatmeal to the tub and soak in it for 15 minutes two or three times a day.

4. Aloe vera will aid in skin healing. Apply the lotion twice a day.

5. Oral antihistamines will help eliminate the itching, but antihistamine lotions don't help. Don't use anesthetic sprays or lotions, which may actually sensitize the skin and irritate the rash.

6. If you're very sensitive to poison ivy, try Ivy Shield, an organic clay barrier that will give 95 percent protection to the skin.

7. If you come in contact with poison ivy, shower with soap and water immediately.

The best protection is learning how to identify these plants and avoid them. The shiny leaves grow in groups of three, so try to remember the saying, "Leaves of three, beware of me."

BURNS

■ Thermal Burns

Burns are classified according to degree. In first-degree burns, the skin is reddened. In second-degree burns, blisters develop. Third-degree burns result in destruction of tissue and the cells that form new skin. Another important factor in determining the seriousness of any burn is the extent of the affected area.

The following first-aid procedures have the primary objectives of treating shock (a major hazard that can quickly cause death in severely burned people), relieving pain, and preventing contamination.

Here is how to treat relatively minor first- and second-degree burns:

FIRST-DEGREE BURNS: Medical treatment is usually not required. To relieve pain, apply cold-water applications to the affected area or submerge the burned area in cold water. A dry dressing may be applied, if desired.

MINOR SECOND-DEGREE BURNS: Immerse the burned parts in cold water (not ice water) or apply freshly laundered cloths that have been wrung out in ice water until the pain subsides. Immediate cooling can reduce the burning effect of heat in the deeper layers of skin. Never add salt to ice water; it lowers the temperature and may produce further injury. Gently blot the area dry with sterile gauze, a clean cloth, a towel, or other household linen. Don't use absorbent cotton. Apply dry, sterile gauze or a clean cloth as a protective dressing. Don't break blisters or remove shreds of tissue, and don't use an antiseptic preparation, ointment, spray, or home remedy on a severe burn.

Because the degree of a burn is often difficult to determine at first, it pays—except with obviously minor burns—to seek medical help.

EXTENSIVE SECOND- AND THIRD-DEGREE BURNS: If a doctor or hospital is within easy reach, cover the burn with a sterile (or at least clean) dressing, treat for shock (see Shock section for procedures), and rush the victim to the doctor or a hospital. If the burn occurs in a remote area, take the following steps:

1. Remove all clothing from the burn area, cutting around any cloth that may adhere to the flesh and leaving it there (trying to remove it may worsen the wound).

2. Apply a sterile, dry dressing to the entire burn area. Do not treat a serious burn with any substance; that is, don't apply ointment, antiseptic, oil, or anything similar. Cover the dressing with at least six more layers of dressing (or clean, tightly woven cloth material). Try not to rupture blisters.

3. Bandage the dressings in place. Make the bandage snug enough to protect the burned area from possible contamination from the air, but not so tight as to cut off circulation.

4. Treat for shock if medical help will be delayed for more than an hour. Give the victim the shock solution: 1 teaspoon of salt and 1 teaspoon of baking soda mixed in 1 quart of water.

5. Arrange for medical help as quickly as possible, notifying authorities that plasma may be needed.

6. Don't try to change the dressing yourself. That is a job for a doctor.

■ Sunburn

Not everyone is aware of the genuine health hazard from the solar system. The National Cancer Institute estimates 600,000 malignancies a year are a direct result of careless exposure to the sun. Of that number, close to 7,000 people will die from malignant melanoma, the most deadly skin cancer.

The sun is the bad guy, causing at least 90 percent of all skin cancers. Fortunately, the sun warns its victims with early symptoms. Those symptoms include those fashionable tans you see around town.

The sun produces two different types of ultraviolet rays, both harmful to the skin. Beta rays (UVB) can cause skin cancer. Alpha rays (UVA) can cause both skin cancer and premature wrinkling of the skin. The easiest and most effective way of protecting yourself from these rays is through the use of a good sunscreen that is rated with an SPF (sun protection factor) of at least 15.

There are sunscreens with ratings of SPF 35 and higher, but in most cases, a rating of SPF 15 is all that is necessary for daily use. With an SPF 15, a person can stay in the sun 15 times longer than without any protection at all. Some doctors claim that regular use of an SPF 15 for the first 18 years of life may reduce the risk of skin cancer by 78 percent. For this reason, it's extremely important for parents to remember to keep small children out of direct sunlight, especially between 10:00 a.m. and 3:00 p.m., when the sun is the strongest and can do the most damage to the skin. Choose a waterproof SPF 15 sunscreen to screen ultraviolet rays. Apply it liberally an hour or two before you go out in the sun, and reapply it every two or three hours, especially after swimming and sweating. Some newer sunscreens are formulated to last all day, even after swimming.

Your skin type is also an important risk factor. If you're a Type I or II, which means fair skin, blond hair, and blue eyes, you will need more skin protection, and a doctor should check you for skin cancer at least once a year. At the other extreme is Type V or VI, which includes people of Middle Eastern and African descent, who will burn only after heavy exposure.

If you spend a lot of time in the sun, you should know about the types of skin cancers and how to detect them early. There are three kinds of skin cancers: basal cell carcinoma, squamous cell carcinoma, and malignant melanoma.

Basal cell carcinoma is the most common skin cancer (about 80 percent) and is seldom deadly. It usually appears on the neck, head, face, and hands. It may be as small as a pinpoint or as large as an inch. It may also crust and bleed.

Squamous-cell carcinoma is the second-most common and looks like a raised pink wart. If left untreated, it can spread to other parts of the body.

Malignant melanoma is the least common, but it is the most deadly skin cancer. It usually appears quickly on the upper back or legs. It can be brown, black, or multicolored. Malignant melanoma grows fast and spreads to other organs.

If you spend a lot of time in the sun, check your skin regularly. Look at the back of your hands and your face. Look for scaly, rough patches of skin. Are there any white spots or red nodules with scales? If you see anything that looks suspicious, see your doctor. Most of the time, skin cancers are easily and successfully removed.

■ Chemical Burns

Chemical burns—from acid, alkali, lime, petroleum products, cleansing agents, and the like—are unusual in the outdoors, but do happen occasionally.

For such burns on exposed skin, the first step is to immediately flush the area with water, thereby lessening the pain and probably reducing the extent of the skin damage. Thereafter, treat as you would a thermal burn.

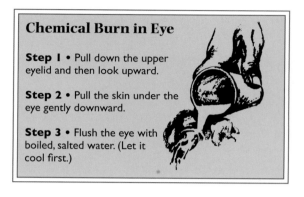

Chemical Burn in Eye

Step 1 • Pull down the upper eyelid and then look upward.

Step 2 • Pull the skin under the eye gently downward.

Step 3 • Flush the eye with boiled, salted water. (Let it cool first.)

If a noxious chemical gets into an eye, flush the eye with water at once. Do so by having the victim lie down with his head tilted slightly to one side. Pour the water in the corner of the eye nearest the nose so that it flows across the entire eye and out the other corner and does not enter the unaffected eye.

Cover the eye with a sterile compress, bandage it in place, and get the victim to medical help as fast as possible.

SURVIVING HEAT AND COLD

■ Sunstroke

Sunstroke is extremely dangerous. Aged people are the most susceptible. The usual symptoms are headache, dry skin, and rapid pulse. Dizziness and nausea may occur, and in severe cases the victim may lapse into unconsciousness. The body temperature soars, sometimes as high as 109°F.

Medical help, as soon as possible, is a must. Until it arrives, do the following:

1. Undress the victim and sponge the body freely with cool water, or apply cold cloths, the objective being to reduce body temperature to a tolerable level of 103°F or below. If you have no thermometer, check the victim's pulse; a pulse rate of 110 or below usually means a tolerable body temperature.

2. When the body temperature lowers to 103°F, stop the sponging or cool-cloth treatment for about 10 minutes. If the temperature again starts to rise, resume the sponging.

3. If the victim is conscious and can swallow, give

him as much as he can drink of a saltwater solution (1 teaspoon of salt to 1 quart of water).

4. Later, cover according to the victim's comfort.

■ Hypothermia

Hypothermia is one of the major causes of death among outdoorsmen, and it will strike anyone who is not prepared to handle extreme weather conditions. Hypothermia is caused by exposure to high winds, rain, snow, or wet clothing. A person's normal core (inner body) temperature is 98.6°F. When the body begins to lose heat, early stages of hypothermia will be apparent. The person will start to shiver and stamp his feet.

If these early signs of hypothermia are ignored, the next stage of symptoms will be uncontrollable spells of shivering, fumbling hands, and drowsiness. If not treated quickly, hypothermia will likely kill its victim when the body temperature drops below 78°F, and this can happen within 90 minutes after shivering begins. If you're outdoors and detect any of these symptoms

Dogs and Summer Heat

I was running some errands last summer when I saw a young boy pedaling his bike down the road with his Brittany spaniel in tow. The temperature was in the 90s, but that didn't slow the boy down. The dog, however, was having trouble keeping up. My heart went out to the dog and I hoped the boy reached his destination before his dog collapsed.

The summer heat is tough on all pets, but especially dogs. Though they can't tell you when they have had enough, they will give you some signals that something is wrong. Pay attention or you can kill your dog.

We humans are lucky. When it gets hot, we can take our shirts off and wipe our brows. Dogs are not so lucky. Dogs have to cool themselves by evaporation, and they do this by panting. When temperature and humidity rise, however, this evaporation process slows down and body temperature rises. When this happens, high body temperatures can harm the circulatory and respiratory systems, and the dog suffers. In some cases, high body temperatures can kill a dog.

Couple heat and humidity with hard exercise and a very definite danger of heat stress exists. Learn to recognize the signals that your dog may be in trouble.

First, not all dogs are created equal in how they handle the heat. Puppies, older dogs, overweight animals,

and pets that you just recently moved to a warmer climate are more susceptible to heat problems than young dogs in peak condition.

Next, don't be alarmed if your dog loses his appetite during the summer months. According to a major dog food company, dogs need about 7.5 percent fewer calories with each 10-degree rise in temperature.

When you walk or exercise your dog, constantly look for heat problems. Symptoms could vary, including heavy panting, dark red gums, a staring or anxious expression, a failure to respond to commands, high fever, excessive salivation, or vomiting.

If you recognize any of the signs, get the dog into the shade and cool him down. Flush the dog's mouth with cool, not cold, water. Don't allow him to drink too much. Wet the bare skin areas of his underbelly and flanks. As with the tongue, it's here that blood flows close to the surface for cooling before returning to the body core.

You can also carry a squirt-type plastic bottle. Squirt a small amount of water into your dog's mouth every 10 minutes or so. It will cool and calm him down.

Summer heat, however, doesn't mean you can't train or exercise your dog. How much of a workout can your dog handle? Short-haired breeds can cool down and run a lot longer than dogs with heavy coats. A heavy-coated dog, such as a setter, can run hard for about 30 minutes. The short-haired breeds can run for about an hour. Obviously, temperature and lots of other variables are involved. Use your judgment. If you suspect a heat problem, stop the training session immediately.

Traveling with a dog in summer also takes some special consideration. Even if it's cool outside, the temperature in a car can rise to a dangerous level quickly. If you must leave your dog in a car, park it in the shade and leave the windows slightly lowered. In summer weather, never leave your dog in a parked car for more than 30 minutes.

in yourself or a friend, start treatment immediately. First, get to shelter and warmth as soon as possible. If no shelter is available, build a fire. Get out of wet clothing and apply heat to the victim's head, neck, chest, and groin. Use chemical heat packs if you have them. If not, use body heat from another person. If you have a sleeping bag, the victim should be placed in it with another person.

As the victim begins to recover, give him warm liquids, chocolate, or any other high-sugar-content foods. Never give a hypothermia patient alcohol. It will only impair judgment, dilate blood vessels, and impair shivering (the body's way of producing heat).

If you're in a boat and capsize into cold water, don't take off your clothing; it will help trap heat. If you are wearing a life jacket, draw your knees up to your body, which will reduce heat loss. If there are several people in the water, huddle together so you can conserve heat. Survival in cold water depends on the water temperature. If the water temperature is 32.5°F, survival time may be under 15 minutes. If the water temperature is more than 80°F, survival time is indefinite.

Preventing hypothermia is a lot easier than treating it. First, stay in shape and get a good night's sleep before going outdoors. You should carry a survival kit with a change of clothing, waterproof matches, and candy, mixed nuts, raisins, or other high-energy snacks. Stay as dry as possible and avoid getting overheated. Wet clothing will lose 90 percent of its insulating qualities and will rob the body of heat.

Stop and rest often, and, most important, dress properly. This means wearing several layers of clothing to form an insulating barrier against the cold. Carry rain gear and use it when the first drops fall. Wear a wool hat with some kind of ear protection. Several manufacturers now make wool knit caps with a Gore-Tex lining, which will keep your head and ears dry in a downpour. It's a fact that an uncovered head can lose up to 50 percent of the body's heat.

■ Frostbite

Frostbite is the freezing of an area of the body, usually the nose, ears, cheeks, fingers, or toes.

Just before the actual onset of frostbite, the skin may appear slightly flushed. Then, as frostbite develops, the skin becomes white or grayish yellow. Blisters may develop later. In the early stages the victim may feel pain, which later subsides. The affected area feels intensely cold and numb, but the victim is often unaware of the problem until someone tells him or he notices the pale, glossy skin. First-aid treatment is as follows:

1. Enclose the frostbitten area with warm hands or warm cloth, using firm pressure. Do not rub with your hands or with snow. If the affected area is on the fingers or hands, have the victim put his hands into his armpits.

2. Cover the area with woolen cloth.

3. Get the victim indoors or into a warm shelter as soon as possible. Immerse the frostbitten area in warm—not hot—water. If that is not possible, wrap the area in warm blankets. Do not use hot-water bottles or heat lamps, and do not place the affected area near fire or a hot stove.

4. When the frostbitten part has been warmed, encourage the victim to move it.

5. Give the victim something warm to drink.

6. If the victim must travel, apply a sterile dressing that widely overlaps the affected area, and be sure enough clothing covers it to keep it warm.

7. Medical attention is usually necessary.

Hypothermia's Effects on the Body

When extreme cold causes the body to lose its interior heat, these symptoms occur as your temperature drops:

99 to 96 degrees • Shivering becomes intense; ability to perform simple tasks is slowed

95 to 91 degrees • Skin tone pales; shivering turns violent and speech is impaired

90 to 86 degrees • Muscular rigidity replaces shivering; thinking is dulled considerably

85 to 81 degrees • Victim becomes irrational and may drift into a stupor; pulse is slow

80 to 78 degrees • Unconsciousness occurs; reflexes cease to function

Below 78 degrees • Condition may be irreversible; death is likely at this point

■ Snow Blindness

The symptoms of this winter malady include a burning or smarting sensation in the eyes, pain in the eyes or in the forehead, and extreme sensitivity to light. First-aid steps include the following:

1. Get the victim into a shelter of some kind, or at least out of the sun.

2. Apply cold compresses to the eyes.

3. Apply mild eye drops to the eyes. Mineral oil is a suitable substitute.

4. Have the victim wear dark glasses.

■ Sun and Eyes

If you're a fisherman or a boater, you are probably already aware of the punishing effects of the sun's glare on your eyes. In fact, the effect of glare on the surface of the water can be 25 times brighter than the light level indoors. For most activities, sunglasses should be able to absorb about 60 percent of the sun's rays. For fishing or boating, however, sunglasses should be darker, absorbing at least 80 percent of the sun's rays. Bausch & Lomb suggests this simple in-store test for lens darkness: look in a mirror with the sunglasses on. If the lenses are dark enough, you will have some difficulty seeing your eyes. This test does not work for photochromic sunglasses because they

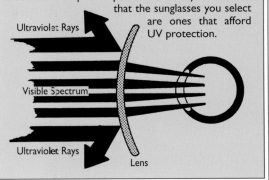

Effects of Sun Rays

Ultraviolet (UV) rays, hidden in the sun's rays, can be irritating and dangerous, causing both short- and long-term harmful effects on the eyes. Industry standards require that sunglasses designed for water sports should absorb up to 95 percent of UV rays. Make sure that the sunglasses you select are ones that afford UV protection.

Ultraviolet Rays

Visible Spectrum

Ultraviolet Rays

Lens

would be at their light stage indoors. If you are a fisherman, you should select sunglasses with polarizing lenses, which are usually made by sandwiching polarizing film between layers of dark glass or plastic. They eliminate reflections on the surface of the water and allow fishermen to see beneath the surface. Sunglasses come in a variety of lens colors, but most eye-care professionals recommend green, gray, or brown for outside activities.

DISLOCATIONS, SPRAINS, AND FRACTURES

■ Bone Dislocations

A dislocation results when the end of a bone is displaced from its normal position in the joint. The surrounding ligaments and other soft tissue always suffer some damage. The fingers, thumb, and shoulder are the areas most often affected.

Symptoms include severe pain, swelling, and loss of movement. Unless a dislodged bone is properly relocated and cared for, dislocations of the bone may occur repeatedly and eventually cause considerable disability.

Relocating a seriously dislodged bone should only be done by a doctor. The first-aider's primary concerns here are to prevent further injury and to see to the victim's comfort.

The dislocated part of the body should be kept as immobile as possible. Apply cold compresses, and get the victim to a doctor.

If an elbow or shoulder is dislocated, use a loose sling to keep the part immobile during transport. If the dislocation is in the hip, transport the victim on a wide board or on a stretcher that has been made rigid, and use blankets or clothing as a pad to support the leg of the affected side in whatever position the victim finds most comfortable.

If the dislocation is a finger and medical help is far away, you might try pulling—very cautiously—on the finger in an attempt to bring the bone back into place. If a gentle pull does not work, do not persist. And do not

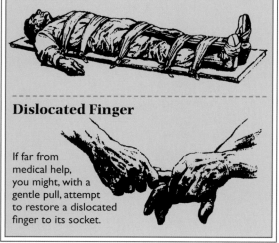

Dislocated Hip

Dislocated joints should be kept immobile and protected until the victim can be transported into the hands of a doctor.

Dislocated Finger

If far from medical help, you might, with a gentle pull, attempt to restore a dislocated finger to its socket.

try this on a dislocated thumb—the problem is more complicated at this joint, and further injury may result.

■ Bone Fractures

There are two kinds of bone fractures (breaks). In a simple fracture, the broken bone does not push through the skin. In an open fracture, the skin is broken and a wound extends from the skin to the fracture area.

It is often difficult to tell whether or not a bone has been broken. If the first-aider was not there when the injury occurred, he should ask the victim to tell him exactly what happened and then check the injured area for physical evidence.

Symptoms of a break include tenderness to the touch, difficulty or pain moving the injured part, swelling, skin discoloration, and deformity.

If you're not sure, treat the injury as a break. Never try to reset a broken bone yourself. Your basic objectives are to prevent further injury, treat for shock if necessary, and make the patient as comfortable as possible until medical help arrives.

With any break, handle the victim gently. Careless handling will increase the pain, and may also increase the severity of shock and cause jagged bone ends to damage muscle, nerves, blood vessels, and skin.

First-aid procedures for various kinds of breaks are listed below.

ARM OR LEG: If medical help will arrive shortly, don't move either the broken limb or the victim.

If there is bleeding, cut away as much clothing as necessary, place a sterile pad or a piece of clean cloth over the wound, and apply firm pressure. Bandage the pad in place.

If the patient must be moved, position the limb as naturally and comfortably as possible, and put on two splints. Boards, poles, metal rods, or any other firm objects—even a thick layer of newspaper folded to the proper shape and firmness—will do. Splints must be long enough to extend beyond the joints above and below the break. Use soft material as padding between the limb and the splints. Fasten the splints in place with bandage material (or handkerchiefs, cloth strips, etc.) in a minimum of three places: adjacent to the break, near the joint above the break, and near the joint below the break.

Check the splints every 15 minutes or so. If swelling of the limb has caused tightening of the bandaging so that circulation is cut off, loosen the bindings accordingly.

Apply cold packs to the fracture, and get the victim to medical help.

SKULL: Skull fracture symptoms include unconsciousness, mental confusion or dazedness, variation in size of eye pupils, and bleeding from the mouth, ears, or nose.

Keep the victim lying down. If his face has normal color or is flushed, prop up his head and shoulders. If his face is pale, try to position him so that his head is slightly lower than the rest of his body.

If there is an open scalp wound, apply a sterile gauze pad and bandage it in place.

If the victim must be moved, transport him in a prone position.

Never leave the victim alone, even during transport. If he begins to choke on blood, lower his head and turn it to one side so that the blood can drain from the mouth and throat.

NECK AND BACK: If the victim can't readily open or close his fingers or grip anything firmly, his neck may be broken. If finger movement seems normal but he can't move his feet or toes, his back may be broken. If he is unconscious and you suspect a spinal injury, treat as if the neck was fractured.

Fractures

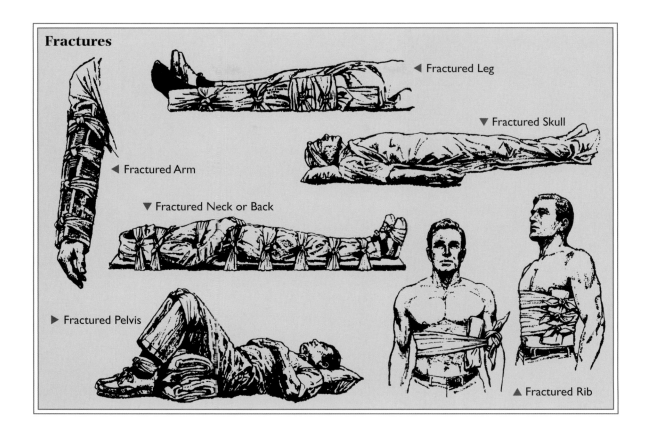

◀ Fractured Leg

▼ Fractured Skull

◀ Fractured Arm

▼ Fractured Neck or Back

▶ Fractured Pelvis

▲ Fractured Rib

Do not let the victim move his head. Cover him with blankets. Watch his breathing closely. If breathing stops, begin mouth-to-mouth resuscitation, but do not tilt the head back to open the airway. Use your fingers to gently grasp the jaw and lift it forward. If a second person is available, have him kneel behind the victim's head with one knee gently bracing each side of the victim's head for stabilization.

Medical help should be brought to the scene if at all possible. If a move is absolutely necessary, extreme caution is a must, for a slight twist or jerk can be fatal to the victim of a broken neck or spine. Pad the head at the sides to prevent movement. Tie the victim's hands across his chest, and tie his head and body rigidly to the stretcher, which should itself be rigid. Put a pad under the victim's neck.

PELVIS: The pelvis is a basin-shaped bone that connects the spine and legs. It also encloses or protects many important organs; therefore, a fracture of the pelvis is a serious injury that requires careful handling. Evidence of damage to organs or blood vessels includes difficulty urinating or blood in the urine.

Treat for shock, which may be severe.

Bandage the knees together, and then bandage the ankles together. Keep the victim lying down, either with the legs flat on the ground or with the knees flexed up and pads positioned under the knees, whichever position is most comfortable for the patient.

If the victim complains of pain when his lower extremities are moved, apply splints to the extremity. If the victim must be moved, transport him in a prone position on a rigid stretcher.

RIB: Symptoms include pain in the break area and shallow breathing (deep breathing causes pain). A broken rib sometimes punctures a lung, causing the victim to cough up frothy, bright-red blood.

If the broken rib has punctured the skin, it is important to guard against infection. Apply a dressing that is airtight. Keep the victim lying down and calm. If the skin is not punctured, apply one or more

Transporting the Seriously Injured

The first-aider's principal objectives in transporting a seriously injured person are to avoid disturbing the victim unnecessarily and to prevent injured body areas from twisting, bending, or shaking.

Transportation is a vital factor, and it requires proper planning by the first-aider and proper preparation of the victim. The rescuers must make every effort to remain calm and mentally alert.

In some situations, however—such as an auto accident, fire, and the like—there is not time for planning or preparation; the victim must be moved from the danger area, or he may suffer further injury.

If such a victim must be pulled to safety, the pull should be along the length of his body (that is, headfirst or feetfirst), not sideways. The danger of compounding the injury during pulling is reduced if a blanket or something similar can be placed beneath him so that he can "ride" the blanket.

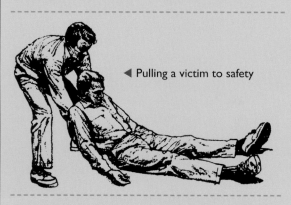

◄ Pulling a victim to safety

If a victim must be lifted to safety, the rescuers should try to protect all parts of his body from the tensions of lifting. The body should be supported at a minimum of three places along its length, not jack-knifed (lifted by head and feet only). Keep the body as straight as possible.

Once a victim is moved to safety, further transportation is inadvisable unless absolutely necessary. The first-aider should make every effort to get medical help to the scene. If the injury occurs deep in the backwoods, it may be possible to arrange for a doctor to come in via floatplane or helicopter.

If there is no way to get medical help to the scene and the victim must be carried to a cabin, farmhouse, or road, a stretcher of some sort is a must. A well-padded folding-type cot will serve adequately. If no cot is available, a serviceable stretcher can be made by inserting two sturdy poles inside a buttoned coat or a couple of buttoned heavy-duty shirts, or by wrapping a blanket around two poles as shown in the accompanying illustration.

The victim must be properly prepared for a long carry. In addition to being given the first-aid treatments called for by his particular injury, he may need a period of rest before the ordeal of transportation. Broken bones and other injured areas should be made as immobile as possible. Loosen any tight clothing, and in general make the victim as comfortable as you can.

Care is the watchword when loading a victim onto a stretcher. It is best if at least three persons take part in the loading. The victim should be lying on his back with his feet tied together, if feasible. Place the stretcher next to the victim.

The loaders should position themselves facing the victim's uninjured side,

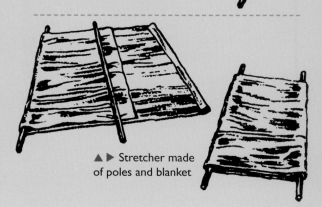

▶ Stretcher made of poles and buttoned coat

▲ ▶ Stretcher made of poles and blanket

one loader at the head, another at the midsection, the third at the feet. Each loader should kneel on the knee nearest the victim's feet. Arms are positioned under the victim as follows: loader at the head cradles the victim's head and shoulders with one arm and puts the other arm under the lower back; loader at the midsection supports the back and area just below the victim's buttocks; and the third loader's arms support the victim's thighs and calves.

One loader gives the command, "Lift," and all three together bring the victim up onto their knees, supporting him there without putting undue strain on the victim's body. One loader pulls the stretcher under the victim, and then all three, again on command, lower the victim down gently.

Provide enough blankets to keep the victim warm during the carry. Place padding wherever it's needed. (If the victim's injury is to the back of the head, he should be positioned on his side.) Tie the victim to the stretcher firmly enough to prevent him from slipping or rolling, but not so tightly as to interfere with blood circulation. Be sure that none of the bindings exert pressure on the injured area.

Ideally, there should be four stretcher-bearers, one at each end and one on each side. It's best to carry the victim so that he can see where he is going. In most cases, the head should be a bit lower than the rest of the body; however, the head should be elevated if there is a head injury or difficulty breathing.

Wooded trails can be treacherous, so stretcher-bearers should be especially alert for roots and other snags, rocks, slippery mud, and the like. If the carriers should lose their balance, the victim could incur further injury.

Bearers should watch the victim closely for signs of shock, discomfort, breathing difficulties, and other problems. Check the dressings periodically, and change or adjust them if necessary.

Loading a Victim onto a Stretcher

▲ **Step 1** • Loaders should be on the victim's uninjured side, all kneeling nearest the victim's feet.

▲ **Step 2** • At the command "Lift," loaders raise the victim gently to their knees.

▲ **Step 3** • Loader in command moves the stretcher under the victim and the victim is lowered to the stretcher.

▶ **Step 4** • The victim is covered and tied to the stretcher. If possible, there should be a bearer at each end and each side.

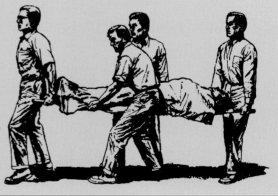

wide bandages around the chest, thereby restricting rib motion. One of the bandages should cross the area of the injury. The knot or knots should be on the side of the chest opposite the break. Put a folded cloth under the knots. If the bandages cause pain, remove them.

If the broken rib seems to be depressed—that is, pushed down into the chest cavity of the victim—do not apply bandages.

If the victim must be moved, transport him in a prone position.

NOSE: Most nose-break victims have a noticeable wound—or at least a bruise. There is usually some swelling and discoloration, and sometimes the shape of the nose is altered. Broken nose bones must be treated properly, or permanent deformity and breathing difficulties may result.

If there is bleeding, hold the lower end of the nose between your thumb and forefinger and press the sides of the nose against the septum (middle partition) for about five minutes. Avoid any side-to-side movement. Release pressure gradually. Apply cold cloths. Have the victim sit up, hold his head back, and breathe through his mouth.

If there is a wound, apply a sterile protective dressing and tape it in place, or bandage the dressing in place with strips of clean cloth tied around the head.

The nose-break victim should see a doctor as soon as possible.

JAW: In a fracture of the lower jaw, the upper and lower teeth often do not line up properly. There may be mild bleeding of the gum near the break, and jaw movement will cause pain. Speaking and swallowing are usually difficult. Lift the lower jaw gently so that the lower and upper teeth meet. Position the middle of a wide strip of clean cloth under the chin, and tie the ends on top of the head, thereby supporting the jaw.

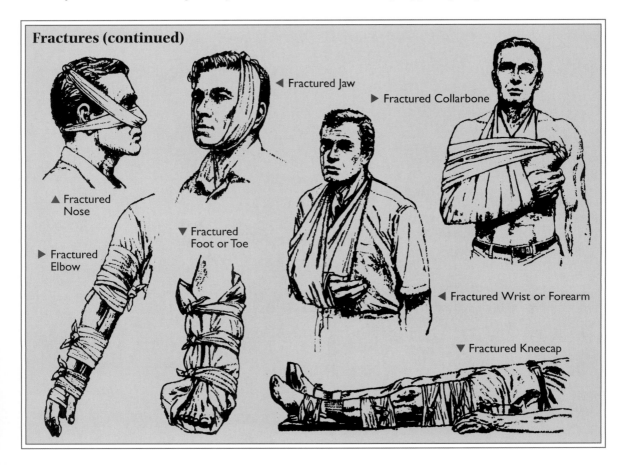

Fractures (continued)

◄ Fractured Jaw

► Fractured Collarbone

▲ Fractured Nose

▼ Fractured Foot or Toe

► Fractured Elbow

◄ Fractured Wrist or Forearm

▼ Fractured Kneecap

If the victim begins to vomit, remove the cloth bandage at once. Support the jaw with your hand. Replace the bandage when the vomiting stops.

COLLARBONE: A victim of this break will usually assume the following position: shoulder bent forward, elbow flexed, forearm across the chest and supported by the hand on the opposite side. There may be swelling, local tenderness, and possibly some deformity.

Use a sling—wide enough to extend from elbow to wrist—to support the arm on the injured side. Adjust the sling so that the hand is slightly above the level of the elbow.

Tie another bandage, not so wide, so that it encircles the arm on the injured side and the chest, snugging the arm against the side of the body. Don't tie the bandage so tight that it interferes with circulation.

Try to keep the victim's shoulders erect.

ELBOW: One symptom of this fracture is swelling above the elbow joint. Leave the arm in the position in which the victim holds it. Protect the joint from movement.

If the arm is held straight, put on a single splint that extends from fingertips to armpit. Position the splint on the palm side of the arm. Tie it on securely, but do not wrap any of the bindings around the elbow area.

If the arm is bent, put it in a sling, and use an around-the-chest bandage to bind the arm to the side of the body.

WRIST OR FOREARM: A break in one of the two bones in the forearm is quite common. The break is usually near the wrist. A break in one of the eight small wrist bones is sometimes thought to be only a sprain. With a break in either place, the fingers and thumb can be moved freely, though movement may cause some pain.

Put on a padded splint that extends from the victim's palm to elbow.

Put the arm in a sling arranged so that the fingers are about 4 inches higher than the elbow. The fingers should remain uncovered so that they can be watched for swelling or discoloration. If either of those signs occur, carefully loosen the splint or the sling, or both.

FINGER: Put a splint on the finger, immobilizing it. Support the hand with a sling. Don't treat this injury casually; get the victim to a doctor. Permanent deformity can result if proper treatment isn't given.

KNEECAP: Prompt and proper treatment of this injury is a must, because flexion of the knee can pull apart the pieces of a broken kneecap (patella).

Gently straighten the victim's leg.

Put on a splint on the underside of the leg. The splint should be inflexible, about 6 inches wide, and long enough to reach from the buttocks to just below the heel. Tie the splint in place firmly, but not so tight that circulation is impeded (check the ties every half hour or so). Do not make any of the ties over the kneecap itself.

Transport the victim in a prone position.

FOOT OR TOE: Remove the victim's shoe and sock quickly—swelling may be extremely rapid. Cut away the footwear if necessary.

Apply clean dressings padded with cotton, or tie a small pillow, folded blanket, or something similar around the foot and bottom of the leg.

Caution the victim against movement of the foot, ankle, or toes.

■ Sprains

Sprains are injuries to the soft tissues that surround joints. Ligaments, tendons, and blood vessels are stretched and sometimes torn. Ankles, fingers, wrists, and knees are the areas most often affected.

Symptoms include pain when the area is moved, swelling, and tenderness to the touch. Sometimes a large area of skin becomes discolored because small blood vessels are ruptured.

It is often difficult to tell whether the injury is a sprain or a fracture. If in doubt, treat as a fracture. Otherwise, take the following steps:

1. Elevate the injured joint using pillows or something similar. A sprained ankle should be raised about 12 inches higher than the torso. For a wrist or elbow sprain, put the arm into a sling.

2. Apply an ice pack or cold cloths to reduce swelling and pain. Continue the cold treatment for a half hour.

3. Always have a sprain X-rayed. There may indeed be a fracture or a bone chip.

If the victim of a sprained ankle is far from help and must walk, make the following preparations:

1. Untie the shoelaces to allow for swelling, but do not take off the shoe.

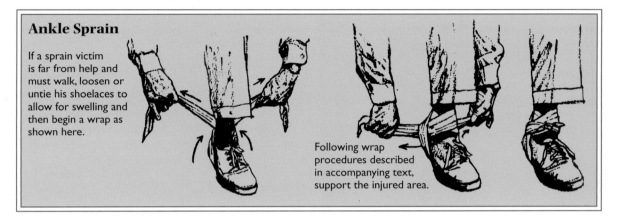

Ankle Sprain

If a sprain victim is far from help and must walk, loosen or untie his shoelaces to allow for swelling and then begin a wrap as shown here.

Following wrap procedures described in accompanying text, support the injured area.

2. Place the middle of a long bandage (a folded triangular bandage is best) under the shoe just forward of the heel.

3. Bring the ends of the bandage up and back, crossing them above (at the back of) the heel.

4. Bring the ends forward around the ankle, and cross them over the instep.

5. Bring the ends downward toward the heel, and slip each end beneath the wrap that comes up from each side of the heel.

6. Bring the ends of the bandage all the way around the ankle again, pull on the ends to produce the desired tension, and then tie a square knot in front.

OTHER INJURIES

■ Eye Injuries or Foreign Body in Eye

For first-aid purposes, eye injuries fall into three categories: injury to eyelids and soft tissue above the eye, injury to the surface of the eyeball, or injury that extends into the tissue beneath the eyeball surface.

In Category 1, treatment involves putting on a sterile dressing and bandaging it in place. If the injury is in the form of a bruise (the familiar "black eye"), the immediate application of cold cloths or an ice pack should halt any bleeding and prevent some swelling. Later, apply warm, wet towels to reduce discoloration.

Injuries in Category 2 usually occur when a foreign body lodges on the surface of the eyeball. To remove the object, pull the upper eyelid down over the lower one, and hold it there for a moment, instructing the victim to look upward. Tears will flow naturally and may wash out the object.

If that doesn't work, put two fingers of your hand on the skin just below the victim's lower eyelid, and force the skin gently downward, thereby exposing the inner area of the lower lid. Inspect the area closely, and if the object is visible, lift it out carefully, using a corner of a

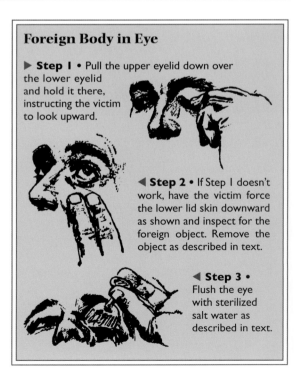

Foreign Body in Eye

▶ **Step I** • Pull the upper eyelid down over the lower eyelid and hold it there, instructing the victim to look upward.

◀ **Step 2** • If Step I doesn't work, have the victim force the lower lid skin downward as shown and inspect for the foreign object. Remove the object as described in text.

◀ **Step 3** • Flush the eye with sterilized salt water as described in text.

clean handkerchief or a small wad of sterile cotton that has been moistened with water and wrapped around the end of a toothpick.

If the foreign object can't be seen, it can sometimes be flushed out. Boil some water, add table salt (¼ teaspoon to an average glassful), and let the salt water cool to about body temperature. With the victim lying down, tilt his head toward the injured side, hold his eyelids open with your fingers, and pour the liquid into the inner corner of his eye so that it runs across the eyeball and drains on the opposite side.

Eye injuries in Category 3 are extremely serious. Never attempt to remove an object that has penetrated the eyeball, no matter how shallow. Apply a sterile compress or clean cloth, cover it with a loose bandage, and get the victim to a doctor at once.

■ Cuts, Abrasions, and Bruises

Minor mishaps frequently involve one of these three injuries. With abrasions (the rubbing or scraping off of skin) and small cuts, the emphasis should be on preventing infection.

Immediately clean the cut or abrasion and the surrounding area with soap and warm water. Don't breathe on the wound or let fingers or soiled cloth contact it.

If there is bleeding, put a sterile pad over the wound and hold it there firmly until the bleeding stops. Then apply an antiseptic, if available, and apply a fresh sterile pad, bandaging it in place loosely.

A bruise results when small blood vessels under the skin are broken, causing discoloration of the skin and swelling, which is often painful.

First aid may be unnecessary if the bruise is minor. If it is more severe, apply an ice pack or cold cloths to reduce the swelling and relieve the pain. Bruises on an extremity can be made less painful if the limb is elevated.

■ Puncture Wounds

A puncture wound results when a sharp object—knife, needle, branch end, or the like—penetrates the skin and the tissue underneath. The first-aider's primary objectives here, as with all other wounds, are to prevent infection and control bleeding.

Puncture wounds are often unusual in that they may be quite deep, but the bleeding, because of the small opening in the skin, may be relatively light. Generally, the lighter the bleeding the lesser the chance that germs embedded by the penetrating object will be washed out.

This means that the danger of infection is greater in puncture wounds than in other wounds. The danger of tetanus (lockjaw) infection is also greater in puncture wounds. First-aid procedures are as follows:

1. If the bleeding is limited, try to increase the flow by applying gentle pressure to the areas surrounding the wound. Do not squeeze hard or you may cause further tissue damage.

2. Do not probe inside the wound. If a large splinter or a piece of glass or metal protrudes from it, try to remove it, but do so with extreme caution. If the sliver cannot be withdrawn with very gentle pressure, leave it where it is, or you may cause further damage and severe bleeding.

3. Wash the wound with soap and water.

4. Apply a sterile pad, and bandage it in place.

5. Get the victim to a doctor for treatment, including a tetanus shot if necessary.

■ Gunshot Wounds

Tetanus is a special problem in gunshot wounds. First-aid steps are as follows:

1. Stop the bleeding (see the Bleeding section for more information).

2. Apply a sterile pad, and bandage it in place.

3. If there is a fracture or a suspected fracture, immobilize the part (see the Bone Fractures section for more information).

4. Treat for shock (see the Shock section for more information).

5. Get the victim to a doctor quickly. A tetanus shot may be needed.

■ Fishhook Removal

A doctor's care—and a tetanus shot, if needed—are recommended for anyone who has had a fishhook embedded past the barb in the flesh. In many cases, however, medical help is not within easy reach. The severity of the injury and the size of the hook determine what action the first-aider should take.

If the hook has penetrated only up as far as the barb or slightly past it—and if it is not in a critical spot such as the eye—you should be able to pull or jerk it out. Then clean the wound, and treat it as you would any other superficial wound (see Cuts, Abrasions, and Bruises section for more information).

If the hook has penetrated well past the barb and is not in a critical area, there are two recommended methods of removal:

1. Force the hook in the direction in which it became embedded so that the point and barb exit through the skin. Try to make the angle of exit as shallow as possible. This can be quite painful, so the victim should anchor the affected part as solidly as possible before beginning the process. Using wire cutters or a similar tool, cut the hook in two at a point on the shank just before the bend. Remove the two pieces.

2. Have the victim anchor the affected part solidly. Take a 12- to 18-inch piece of strong string (30-pound-test fishing line is ideal), and run one end around the

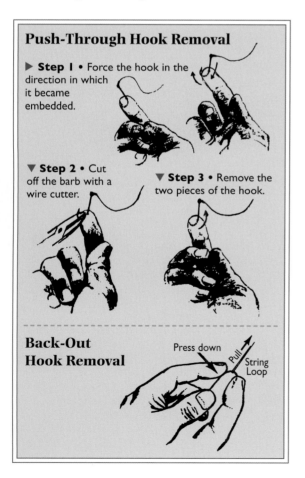

Push-Through Hook Removal

▶ **Step 1** • Force the hook in the direction in which it became embedded.

▼ **Step 2** • Cut off the barb with a wire cutter.

▼ **Step 3** • Remove the two pieces of the hook.

Back-Out Hook Removal

Press down
Pull
String Loop

bend of the hook as if you were threading a needle. Bring the two ends together, and tie them in a sturdy knot. With the thumb and forefinger, push down (toward the affected part) on the shank of the hook at the point where the bend begins. This disengages the barb from the tissue. Maintaining that pressure, grasp the line firmly at the knotted end, and give a strong yank. The finger pressure on the shank should reduce flesh damage to a minimum as the barb comes out the same way it went in. Do not use this method if the hook is large.

If bleeding is minimal after either of these procedures, squeeze the wound gently to encourage blood flow, which has a cleansing effect. Put on a sterile dressing, and get medical help.

If the hook is a large one and is deeply embedded, or if it is in a critical area, do not try to remove it. Cover the wound—hook and all—with a sterile dressing, and get the victim to a doctor.

▪ Boils

A boil—a round, reddened, and usually painful elevation in the skin—is mostly dead tissue and germ-laden pus. Actually, it is an attempt by the body to keep an infection localized.

Do not squeeze a boil, or you may spread the infection. If the boil is very painful or appears to be spreading, apply hot, wet compresses. These may reduce the pain and cause the boil to come to a head more quickly.

When the boil comes to a head and discharges its contents, do not touch the escaping pus. Soak it up thoroughly with a gauze pad or clean cloth, thereby preventing infection of the surrounding skin. Cover the boil with a sterile dressing.

▪ Blisters and Foot Care

There was a time when you were told, "Never take brand-new boots on a camping or hiking trip." That's no longer a hard-and-fast rule. Leather boots still require a break-in period, but composite boots that are synthetic do not require extensive breaking in. Opinions vary, but most sportsmen prefer 8-inch-high boots, while 6-inch boots are the favorite for hiking.

Besides boots, there are other ways to protect your feet in the field. You should always wear two pairs of socks. The first pair to go on your feet should be lightweight, preferably polypropylene to wick away perspiration.

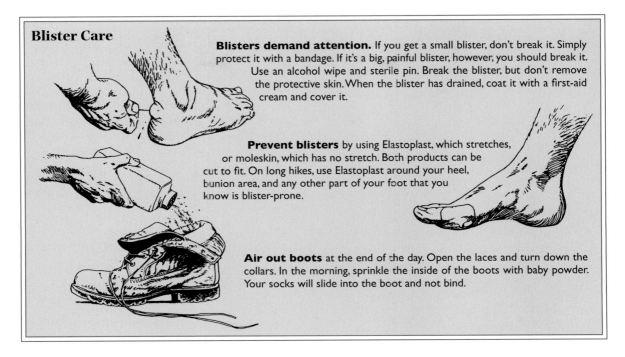

Blister Care

Blisters demand attention. If you get a small blister, don't break it. Simply protect it with a bandage. If it's a big, painful blister, however, you should break it. Use an alcohol wipe and sterile pin. Break the blister, but don't remove the protective skin. When the blister has drained, coat it with a first-aid cream and cover it.

Prevent blisters by using Elastoplast, which stretches, or moleskin, which has no stretch. Both products can be cut to fit. On long hikes, use Elastoplast around your heel, bunion area, and any other part of your foot that you know is blister-prone.

Air out boots at the end of the day. Open the laces and turn down the collars. In the morning, sprinkle the inside of the boots with baby powder. Your socks will slide into the boot and not bind.

The second should be heavyweight, to warm and cushion your feet. In addition to providing warmth, two pairs of socks rub against each other—not against your feet.

Finally, give your feet a break. On your next trip, occasionally take off your boots and socks and rest your feet on a log.

■ Infected Wounds

One of the primary objectives in any first-aid situation is the prevention of infection, but the first-aider is sometimes called on to treat a wound that has already become infected. Symptoms of infection include swelling, redness (including red streaks emanating out from the wound), throbbing pain, and a "hot" feeling in the infected area.

First-aid steps are as follows:

1. Keep the victim lying down and as comfortable and calm as possible.

2. Apply heat to the area with hot-water bottles, or put warm, moist towels or cloths over the wound dressing. Change the wet packs often enough to keep them warm and cover them with a dry towel wrapped in plastic, aluminum foil, or waxed paper to hold in the warmth and to protect bedclothing.

3. Continue applying the warm packs for 30 minutes. Then remove them and cover the wound with a sterile dressing for another 30 minutes. Apply warm packs again. Repeat the whole process until medical care can be obtained.

ILLNESS

■ Fever

A rise in body temperature is a signal that something is amiss internally. There are many causes of fever, infection being the most common. In fact, fever is one of the body's defense mechanisms against infection. But if the fever reaches 104°F or higher, it may become a danger in itself. Here's what to do:

1. Get the victim into bed, and take his temperature if possible.

2. Send for a doctor.

3. Sponge the victim's body with cool or lukewarm water, treating one part of the body at a time and keeping the other parts covered.

4. Apply an ice bag or cool cloths to his head.

5. If he is conscious and there is no evidence of abdominal injury, give him some cold water to drink.

■ Epilepsy

In a full-blown epileptic attack, the victim becomes pale, his eyes roll, and he falls down, usually with a hoarse cry. He may turn blue, bite his tongue, and froth at the mouth. His head, arms, and legs jerk violently, and he loses consciousness.

First-aid steps are as follows:

1. Do not try to restrain the victim's convulsions or thrashing; that phase of the attack will pass, usually within a few minutes.

2. Try to protect him against injury by moving away nearby objects.

3. To prevent him from biting his tongue, try to place an appropriate object (wad of cloth, piece of thick rubber, or piece of book cover) between the upper and lower teeth in one side of the mouth. Be sure that the object does not obstruct his breathing.

4. Do not give the victim stimulants.

5. When the attack subsides, let the patient rest without being disturbed.

■ Appendicitis

The principle symptom of appendicitis is pain in the lower right part of the abdomen and sometimes over the entire abdominal region. Nausea and vomiting may be present, as may a mild fever. Constipation often occurs and is sometimes thought to be the cause of the victim's discomfort. Do not give a laxative if appendicitis is suspected—it will increase the danger that the appendix will rupture.

1. Have the patient lie down, and keep him comfortable.

2. Do not give him any food or water.

3. An ice pack placed over the appendix area may relieve pain. Do not apply heat to the appendix area.

4. Get medical help as soon as possible.

■ Diarrhea

Diarrhea is a common malady among outdoorsmen. Its causes are often associated with change: during an extended camping trip, for example, the sportsman's eating and drinking habits are often much different than what they are at home. Attacks of diarrhea usually subside once the body adapts to those changes.

Paregoric is helpful in combating diarrhea, as are many of the products designed for that purpose and sold in drugstores. If you or your companions are particularly prone to attacks of diarrhea, see a doctor and ask him to prescribe a drug, preferably in tablet form, that will combat the problem during trips afield.

■ Earache

An earache is usually a sign of an infection, so the sufferer should seek medical attention as soon as feasible.

The following first-aid procedures should offer some relief:

1. Treat with either heat or cold. There is no way to predict which will work best, but try cold first, putting an icepack or cold compress over the ear. If that doesn't work, try a hot-water bottle or hot compress.

2. For further relief, put a few drops of warm mineral oil in the affected ear, if it is not ruptured.

3. Caution the sufferer against blowing his nose hard, which probably will increase the pain and may spread the infection.

■ Toothache

First-aid procedures are as follows:

1. Inspect the sufferer's mouth under the strongest light available.

2. If no cavity is visible, place an ice pack or cold compress against the jaw on the painful side. If that doesn't provide relief, try a hot-water bottle or hot compress.

3. If a cavity can be seen, use a piece of sterile cotton wrapped on the end of a toothpick to clean the cavity as thoroughly as possible.

4. Oil of cloves, if available, can give relief. Pack it gently into the cavity with a toothpick. Do not let the oil touch the tongue or the inside of the mouth—the stuff burns.

FIRST-AID KIT

Improvisation is an ability that most outdoorsmen seem to develop naturally. But an improvised dressing for a wound, for example, is a poor second-best for a prepackaged, sterile dressing. Any first-aider can function more effectively if he has the proper equipment. A first-aid kit—whether it is bought in a pharmacy or is put together by the individual—should meet the following requirements:

- Its contents should be complete enough for the purposes for which it will be used.
- The contents should be arranged so that any component desired can be located quickly and without removing the other components.
- Each component should be wrapped so that any unused portion can be repacked and thereby prevented from leaking or becoming soiled.
- How and where the kit will be used are the main factors to consider when assembling a first-aid kit. The two kits described below should fill the needs of most outdoor situations.

■ POCKET KIT

Suitable for one-day, overnight, or short-term backpacking trips in areas not far from medical help.

- 1-by-1-inch packaged sterile bandages (2)
- 2-by-2-inch packaged sterile bandages (2)
- 2-by-2-inch packaged sterile gauze pads (2)
- Roll of adhesive tape
- Band-Aids (10)
- Ammonia inhalant (1)
- Tube of antiseptic cream
- Small tin of aspirin (or 12 aspirins wrapped in foil)

■ ALL-PURPOSE OUTDOORS FIRST-AID KIT

Suitable for general outings.

- 4-inch Ace bandages (2)
- 2-inch Ace bandages (2)*
- 2-by-2-inch sterile gauze pads (1 package)*
- 5-by-9-inch combine dressing (3)
- Triangular bandage (1)
- Sterile eye pads (2)
- ½-inch adhesive tape (5 yards)
- Assorted Band-Aids (1 package)*
- Betadine liquid antiseptic
- Yellow mercuric oxide ointment (for eyes)*
- Bacitracin (ointment)

- Tylenol (aspirin substitute)
- Dramamine (for motion sickness)
- Sunscreen
- Insect repellent
- Single-edge razor blade
- Tweezers (flat tip)
- Small scissors
- Eye patch
- Needle
- Matches in waterproof container
- Needle-nose pliers with cutting edge
- First-aid manual

Add these items if going into a remote area for an extended period of time:

- Tylenol with codeine (painkiller)**
- Tetracycline (antibiotic)**
- Lomotil, 2.5 milligrams (for cramps, diarrhea)**
- Antihistamine tablets
- Phillips Milk of Magnesia (antacid, laxative)

* Items, in fewer quantities, are recommended for a small first-aid kit for day trips. ** Requires a prescription.

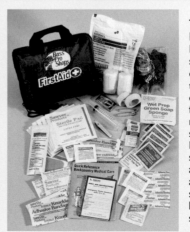

The Bass Pro Family First-Aid Kit is tailored specifically for outdoor activities and includes everything most families would need for a six-day trip. If you're not sure how to assemble a first-aid kit, a professionally packaged kit is a safe and sensible choice.

Index

■ ■ ■

Acknowledgments

The author would like to thank the following people, companies, organizations, and agencies for their permission, cooperation, and assistance in compiling information and photographs for this book:

Andy Anderson • Joe Arterburn, Cabela's • Fred Bekiarian • Serio Borders, Classic Vans • Tim Christie • Haley Clapp • James Daley, Orvis • Laura Davidson, Blogging Over Thyme • Bill Dermody, Savage Arms • Daniel D. Dye II, Florida Backyard Snakes • J. Wayne Fears • Tyson Fisher • Robert Gergulics, 3 Foragers • Ron Giudice, Blue Heron Communications • Tonya Giudice, Blue Heron Communications • William W. Hartley, Hartley Industries • Jeanne-Marie Hudson • Isaiah James, Windsor Nature Discovery • Ken Jorgensen, Ruger • Greg Lasiewski, Kawasaki • Chip Laughton, Days Afield Photography • Brian Lindley, Kamp-Rite • Mary Mardis, Bass Pro • Stephen Matt, G3 Boats • Mac McKeever, L.L. Bean • J. Richard McLaughlin • Katie Mitchell, Bass Pro • Karen Monger, 3 Foragers • Kellie Mowery, Cabela's • Chuck Newhauser, DutchOvenNet.com • Wes Owen, Garmin International • Cason Pilliod, Kalkomey • Len Rue Jr., Len Rue Enterprises • Dusan Smetana • Mitch Strobl, Kalkomey • Josh Ward, Blue Heron Communications • Jim Zumbo

Photography Credits

© Andy Anderson: pp. 12–13 and back cover (top row, middle).

Courtesy of Bass Pro: pp. 22 (top right), 23 (all except top right and bottom left), 33 (right), 34 (top and middle), 40 (bottom left and middle), 45, 46 (both), 53 (bottom left), 55, 57 (middle and right), 58 (bottom left and right), 60 (top), 79, 81 (top left and top right), 84, 102, 103 (all), 104, 111 (bottom), 116, 125, 134 (middle right and right), 137, 273 (top), and 305.

Courtesy of Cabela's: pp. 23 (bottom left) and 57 (left).

©TimChristiePhoto.com:pp. 192, 193 (both), 194 (top), 196 (both), 197 (both), 198 (top), 199 (bottom), 200 (bottom), 201, 202 (both), 203 (both), 204, and 205 (left).

Courtesy of Classic Vans, California: p. 29.

Courtesy of Coleman: pp. 106, 107, and 269.

© Laura Davidson/www.bloggingoverthyme.com: pp. 218–219 (all).

© Daniel D. Dye II: pp. 32 and 283 (all).

© Tyson Fisher: pp. 2–3 and back cover (top row, left).

Courtesy of G3 Boats: p. 78.

Courtesy of Garmin: p. 273 (bottom).

© Robert Gergulics: pp. 141–171 (all).

Courtesy of Harrington & Richardson: p. 135 (top).

© William W. Hartley: pp. 135 (bottom) and 136.

Courtesy of Kamp-Rite: p. 33 (left)

Courtesy of Kawasaki: p. 31 (both).

Courtesy of Chip Laughton/Days Afield Photography: p. 291.

Courtesy of L.L. Bean: pp. 22 (all except top right), 23 (top right), 34 (bottom), 36, 40 (top left and right), 42, 53 (all except bottom left), 56 (both), 57 (bottom), 58 (top left and right), 60 (bottom), and 81 (all except top left and top right).

© J. Richard McLaughlin: pp. 51 (all), 54 (all), 132, 134 (left and middle left), 256, 257, and 259.

Courtesy of Recreation Vehicle Industry Association: pp. 25 (both), 26, 27, and 28.

© Len Rue Enterprises, LLC: pp. 194 (bottom), 195, 198 (bottom), 199 (top), 200 (top), and 205 (right).

Courtesy of Ruger: p. 135 (second from bottom).

Courtesy of Savage: p. 135 (second from top).

© Shutterstock.com/eurobanks: pp. 274–275 and back cover (bottom row, right).

© Shutterstock.com/IldiPapp: front cover.

© Shutterstock.com/withGod: p. 264.

© Dusan Smetana: pp. 6–7, 11, 76–77, 100–101, 110, 111 (top), 130–131, 306–307, 319, and back cover (top row, right; bottom row, left and middle).

© Vin Sparano: pp. 123, 214 (all), 216–217 (all), and 320.

Courtesy of Woodsman's Pal: p. 48.

ILLUSTRATION CREDITS AND OTHER NOTES

Unless otherwise noted here, all black-and-white line art was picked up from the fourth edition of Vin Sparano's *Complete Outdoors Encyclopedia*.

© James Daley: pp. 14, 55 (both), 78, 102, 132, 136 (all), 173–177 (all), 178 (all), 179 (all), 180 (all), 256, and 276.

Courtesy of Kalkomey.com: pp. 29 (left and right), 30 (all), 88 (all), and 90 (all).

Courtesy of the United States Coast Guard: p. 97.

Courtesy of the United States Geological Survey: p. 270.

Courtesy of Windsor Nature Discovery: pp. 220–255 (all).

- Illustrations and information on snowmobiles, buoys, and personal flotation devices were provided courtesy of Kalkomey Enterprises (see page numbers listed above). For more information, visit the company's websites: www.snowmobile-ed.com and www.boat-ed.com.

- The member-driven Leave No Trace Center for Outdoor Ethics teaches people how to enjoy the outdoors responsibly. The copyrighted seven principles (p. 59) have been reprinted here with permission from the Leave No Trace Center for Outdoor Ethics. For more information, visit www.lnt.org.

- The information on dutch-oven cooking (p. 105) appears courtesy of Chuck Newhauser. For more information, visit dutchovennet.com. The dutch-oven venison recipe on the same page was taken from *Backcountry Cooking* by J. Wayne Fears and is used with permission.

- All recipes in the Campfire Cooking chapter (pp. 113–129) were taken from *The L.L. Bean Game and Fish Cookbook* and used with permission, except for p. 118

(Cooking a Cottontail), p. 122 (Grilled Rainbow Trout and Fast and Easy Walleye Shore Lunch), p. 124 (Quick and Easy Fried Panfish or Crappie), p. 126 (all), and p. 127 (Pan-Fried Tuna), which are all from Vin Sparano's personal collection. The Venison Heart recipe (p. 115) is from Jim Zumbo's book *Amazing Venison Recipes* and is used with permission.

• Photos, text, and recipes for wild edibles (pp. 141–171) were provided by the 3 Foragers (photographer Robert Gergulics, writer and chef Karen Monger, and their daughter Gillian). For more information, visit the3foragers.blogspot.com.

About the Author

Vin T. Sparano has been an outdoor editor and writer for more than 50 years. He earned his B.S. degree in journalism in 1960 from New York University. Sparano is editor emeritus of *Outdoor Life* magazine, having served as editor in chief from 1990 to 1995 and previously as executive editor for more than 10 years.

In addition to his long career with *Outdoor Life*, Sparano was a syndicated features writer for *USA Today* and Gannett newspapers. He has written and edited 20 books—including Universe's *Complete Outdoors Encyclopedia*, the full-color fifth edition of his classic encyclopedia originally published in 1976, and *Complete Guide to Fresh and Saltwater Fishing*—and has produced electronic software focusing on fishing techniques and hot spots through the use of navigational charts and satellite photos.

Sparano and his wife, Betty, live in Waretown, New Jersey, where he is a familiar sight fishing from his boat, *Betty Boop*. During the fall, his focus is on the great striped bass fishery off Barnegat Inlet. In the winter months, Sparano travels to Florida, where he fishes the famous Islamorada Flats for tarpon and bonefish, as well as the offshore waters for sailfish, tuna, and other bluewater game fish.

A certified NRA rifle, pistol, shotgun, and hunting safety instructor, Sparano has been a member of the Outdoor Writers Association of America, fulfilling a term on its board of directors, and is also a heritage member of the Professional Outdoor Media Association. Sparano was a recipient of a Lifetime Achievement Award from both the New York Metropolitan Outdoor Press Association and the Fisherman's Conservation Association.

In 1996, Sparano was awarded the United States Department of the Interior Conservation Award by Secretary of the Interior Bruce Babbitt for his extraordinary contributions to conservation and outdoor journalism. In 2013, he was enshrined in the Fresh Water Fishing Hall of Fame. In 2015, he won the POMA Pinnacle Award and Foreword Book of the Year Gold Award (Sports) for the fifth edition of *Complete Outdoors Encyclopedia*. Sparano is also listed in *Who's Who in America*.

■ ■ ■